Piaget Today

edited by
Bärbel Inhelder,
Denys de Caprona,
Angela Cornu-Wells

LAWRENCE ERLBAUM ASSOCIATES, PUBLISHERS
Hove and London (UK)   Hillsdale (USA)

Lawrence Erlbaum Associates Ltd., Publishers
27 Palmeira Mansions
Church Road
Hove
East Sussex, BN3 2FA
U.K.

British Library Cataloguing in Publication Data

Piaget today.
　1. Piaget, Jean　2. Developmental psychology
　I. Inhelder, Bärbel II. De Caprona, Denys
　III. Cornu-Wells, Angela
　155'.092'4　　BF713

ISBN 0-86377-047-9

Typeset by Tradespools Ltd., Frome
Printed and bound by A. Wheaton & Co. Ltd., Exeter

Contents

List of Contributors   vi

List of Discussants   vii

Acknowledgements   viii

Introduction
Bärbel Inhelder and Denys de Caprona   1

1. Structures and Functions
Guy Cellérier   15

2. Current Trends in Cognitive Development Research: Towards a New Synthesis
Harry Beilin   37

3. Piaget's Natural Logic
Marie-Jeanne Borel   65

4. Operatory Logic
Jean-Blaise Grize   77

5. Logical Reasoning, Development and Learning
Barry Richards   87

6. The Value of Logic and the Logic of Values
Seymour Papert   101

7. The Masculine Authority of the Cognitive
John M. Broughton   111

8. Sociology of Science and Sociogenesis of Knowledge
Rolando García   125

iii

9.   Theory Change in Childhood
Susan Carey   141

10.   Cognition in its Relationship to Total Development in the First Few Years of Life
Sybille K. Escalona   165

11.   Origins of Intentional Strategic Memory in the Child
Cesare Cornoldi   183

12.   Spatial Reasoning in Small-size and Large-size Environments: In Search of Early Prefigurations of Spatial Cognition in Small-size Environments
Gerhard Steiner   203

13.   Development as Construction: Nature and Psychological and Social Context of Genetic Constructions
Hans Aebli   217

14.   The Coordination of Values: Current Relevance of the Piagetian Concept of Philosophy
Reto Luzius Fetz   233

15.   Laws of Consciousness as Norms of Mental Development
Eduard Marbach   247

Closing Debate   263

List of Contributors

Aebli, Hans Abteilung pädagogische Psychologie, Universität Bern, Switzerland

Beilin, Harry, Developmental Psychology, The Graduate School and University Center of the City University of New York, New York, U.S.A.

Borel, Marie-Jeanne, Faculté des Lettres, Section de Philosophie, Université de Lausanne, Lausanne, Switzerland

Broughton, John M., Teachers College, Columbia University, New York, U.S.A.

de Caprona, Denys, Fondation Archives Jean Piaget, Université de Genève, Genève, Switzerland

Carey, Susan, Massachusetts Institute of Technology, Cambridge, Massachusetts, U.S.A.

Cellérier, Guy, Faculté de Psychologie et des Sciences de l'Education, Université de Genève, Genève, Switzerland

Cornoldi, Cesare, Dipartimento di Psicologia Generale, Università degli studi di Padova, Padova, Italy

Escalona, Sybille K., Rose Fitzgerald Kennedy Center for Research in Mental Retardation and Human Development, Albert Einstein College of Medicine, New York, U.S.A.

Fetz, Reto Luzius, Université de Fribourg, Fribourg, Switzerland

García, Rolando, Centro de Investigación y de Estudios Avanzados del Institúto Politecnico Nacional, Mexico City, Mexico

Grize, Jean-Blaise, Centre de Recherches Sémiologiques, Université de Neuchâtel, Neuchâtel, Switzerland

Inhelder, Bärbel, Fondation Archives Jean Piaget, Université de Genève, Genève, Switzerland

Marbach, Eduard, Philosophisches Institut, Universität Bern, Bern, Switzerland

Papert, Seymour, Massachusetts Institute of Technology, Cambridge, Massachusetts, U.S.A.

Richards, Barry, Centre for Cognitive Science, University of Edinburgh, Edinburgh, Scotland

Steiner, Gerhard, Institut für Psychologie, Universität Basel, Basel, Switzerland

List of Discussants

Ducret, Jean-Jacques, Faculté de Psychologie et des Sciences de l'Education, Université de Genève, Genève, Switzerland

Lawler, Robert, GTE Laboratories, Waltham, Maryland, U.S.A.

Maier, Robert, Instituut voor Ontwikkelingspsychologie, Rijksuniversiteit Utrecht, Utrecht, The Netherlands

Sinclair, Hermine, Faculté de Psychologie et des Sciences de l'Education, Université de Genève, Genève, Switzerland

Wermus, Henri, Faculté de Psychologie et des Sciences de l'Education, Université de Genève, Genève, Switzerland

Acknowledgements

Organising the Seventh Advanced Course of the "Fondation Archives Jean Piaget" and editing the proceedings involved more than three persons. Hermine Sinclair presided over the whole meeting in replacement of Bärbel Inhelder. Her total commitment helped fill the communication and language gaps and make the course a shared and successful event. Harry Beilin showed generous interest in the volume and its publication. The Scientific Committee of the Piaget Archives and collaborators M.-C. Rosat and A. Tryphon were instrumental in organising the course. M. Mounir, I. Schwarz and C. Zoells-Kessner kindly managed to be available for typing substantial parts of the manuscript, as did P. Steenken, the Archives' librarian, for editing the references. The whole enterprise of organising the course would have been impossible without financial support from the Swiss National Fund for Scientific Research, the Jean Piaget Foundation and the Faculty of Psychology and Education Sciences, University of Geneva.

We also thank the lecturers and participants in the course who shaped the views expressed in this book, as well as the editors at Lawrence Erlbaum Associates, whose welcome and understanding made the publication process a most enjoyable experience.

Bärbel Inhelder
Denys de Caprona
Angela Cornu-Wells

Introduction

Bärbel Inhelder and Denys de Caprona
University of Geneva

PIAGET IN THE LIGHT OF CURRENT RESEARCH

This volume contains the proceedings of the VIIth Advanced Course of the "Fondation Archives Jean Piaget", held at the University of Geneva from 22 to 27 September 1985. Although it coincided with the fifth anniversary of Jean Piaget's death, the course was meant to go beyond any formal homage, or perhaps to represent true homage paid by researchers who demonstrate how some major problems of Piagetian psychology and epistemology can be assessed in the light of current research. Indeed, "Piaget today" as a topic involved going back to Piaget's own writings and showing in what way a general theory of cognitive development or parts of the theory can define a number of relevant problems in several disciplines.

The status of Jean Piaget's works seems to require a double approach: Like a few other major scientific achievements in our century, they initiated new disciplines, such as genetic psychology and epistemology, where continuing research is taking place; but as the works of one man, they already belong to history. The lectures and discussions included in this volume reflect this peculiar status in that they help one to understand Piaget in the context of twentieth-century science and philosophy and to consider the present and future of the theory—i.e. the modifications that new problems bring. To this we must add that the interdisciplinary nature of Piagetian epistemology requires contributions from various branches of contemporary science, and therefore the reader will find here an assessment of Piagetian theory in terms of psychology, sociology, logic, cybernetics, egopsychology, philosophy and the history of science. Such an interdisciplinary approach is favoured by a number of problems (the role of modelling, the notions of development and of norms and values) that reflect some of the major concerns about Piaget today. They were proposed as a general, flexible framework for the course, within which each of the lecturers would make his or her own contribution.

The first of these problems revolves around the role attributed to logical modelling in Piaget's writings. This played a major part when Piaget elaborated his structural models of cognitive development. What he calls "formalisation" is an important tool in his theory of explanation, and it raises a number of epistemological and methodological questions. We shall see below that one of the major problems is to take into account the structural and functional types of analyses that coexist in Piaget's explanatory framework. A number of chapters in the book demonstrate that research is going on in this field, and they bring forth new considerations on the nature of operatory logic, on the relationships between natural logic and logic proper and on the logico-mathematical "idealisations" seemingly involved in Piaget's emphasis on formal thinking. Grize investigates the meaning of Piaget's formalising approach and the formal structure of the kind of models adopted to account for natural logic and its development. In order to prevent misunderstandings about the status of operatory logic, he indicates that Piaget's purpose was not to contribute to mathematical logic, but to provide an operatory analysis of intelligence—i.e. to elucidate the structures underlying formal thinking and marking the completion of cognitive development. Through a rich formal analysis of algebraic structures such as the INRC group and of the lattice structure, Grize makes a useful contribution to an evaluation and critique of the characteristics and explanatory value of the models used by Piaget.

Such a logical interpretation of natural thinking is, however, based on an epistemological purpose—hence a need to provide a new assessment of the relationship between logic and natural logic that are so central to Piaget's theory. Borel shows that the idea of a natural logic presupposes in Piaget the epistemological question of the relationship between the subjects' logical experience and the logicians' logic and of Piaget's use of the latter to represent the former. A notion that seems to us to be of utmost importance here (see also Cellérier's chapter) is that of "normative facts", a notion that validates, in Piaget's view, the structural analysis he proposes. A good understanding of this epistemological purpose accounts for the variety of the roles attributed to formalisation according to Piaget's stand as a rationalist philosopher or a naturalist psychologist.

Grize's and Borel's chapters provide us with a clearer picture of what is formalisation and of the epistemological issues involved. The problems associated with the notion of a natural logic are taken up by Papert, who brings up the question of relativity in logic and morals. Are we really certain that a hierarchical organisation ending up in formal thinking reflects the psychological reality? Through examples of non-formal mathematical proofs and with the help of recent works in developmental psychology by Gilligan and Turkle, Papert introduces the notion of psychological styles. Turkle's studies on the interactions of child and computer identify a *hard* cognitive style when the child has a deductive cognitive attitude and a *soft* style when he is negotiating with an object or with persons. The former is the only one to correspond to a logic of thinking, which is presently recognised as the only acceptable cognitive style in our culture. What is interesting here is that Papert deems that such distinctions can be applied to Piaget. Through an analysis of Piaget's relationships with the school of French mathematicians who called themselves Bourbaki, Papert shows that Piaget regarded the development of number as stemming from significant sub-systems that are appropriated and elaborated by the subject through a cognitive style of the *soft* type. The cybernetical inspiration of this chapter provides us with a richer functional understanding of the cognitive activities involved in the notion of a natural logic.

A good example of a formalising theoretical construction is then provided by Richards, who presents a model of the child's "reasoning" at the sensorimotor stage. This model is an effort at theorising the data provided by developmental psychology and an attempt to account for the fact that early forms of reasoning in the child obey not a classical bivalent logic, but a logic of relevance that would be the first in a series of protologics that are constructed in development. This kind of theoretical investigation about the early forms of logical thinking parallels Piaget and Garcia's 1987 study on the logic of meanings, where particular attention is paid to questions of relevance. While reading the chapter by Richards, whose model aims at formally representing the mechanisms responsible for the transition from one stage to the next and for the reinterpretation of one logic into the next, the reader may begin to feel that such theoretical constructions are required if one is to limit the variety of facts and interpretations in current developmental psychology.

These contributions on logic seem to expand the reflection on the role of modelling in two directions: Firstly, there is undoubtedly room for new formalisations, and both Grize's and Richard's chapters clearly illustrate the fruitfulness of such an approach. The role of such theoretical constructions is to provide explanatory means of reducing the theoretical fragmentation that seems to prevail in contemporary psychology by reasserting the usefulness of the formal tools of investigation. Secondly, there is a need to broaden our understanding of cognition by not reducing it to an interpretation in logical terms. This new perspective involves a revival of the old criticism of Piaget's overemphasis on logical thinking.

Was this emphasis so great that it led Piaget to go beyond all recognised forms of scientific methodology, as some scholars (Vonèche & Vidal, 1985) seem to believe? On more serious ground, this problem of the "idealisations" involved in Piaget's theory comes up as a major point in the Closing Debate. Let us note, however, that it comes up as a sub-problem within the wider problem of the possibility or impossibility of a unifying theory of cognitive development, of which Piaget's theory is an example. This might be an indication that a refutation of the idealisations involved in Piaget is not liable to an interpretation within the framework of the Popperian-style falsificationism that has often prevailed among Piaget's critics. Rather, the existence of idealisations indicates an interesting process occurring within general theory construction.

Indeed, one of the major problems debated during the course was that of the diversity and fragmentation of contemporary developmental psychology, and this was compared with the unifying synthesis that Piaget attempted. A series of contributions allow one to understand Piaget's works historically and to bring out some of the structures of explanation in the sciences of development. The problem here is to acknowledge the existing fragmentation and to try to put some order into it. When considering contemporary psychology of cognitive development, what is striking is that the divergences and affinities among the theories can be re-organised through the coupling of functionalism and structuralism. This is what H. Beilin does when he identifies these two components in current research in cognitive developmental psychology. Through a review of the various theories in contemporary American psychology, he shows that the renewal of functionalist hypotheses reiterates earlier periods in the history of psychology, but that functionalism and structuralism are not "incommensurable" paradigms (in Kuhn's terms), since, for example, some information processing theories are able to integrate in their models some elements of structural models. About Piaget's theory, Beilin elucidates the philosophical tradition to which it belongs and is able to assess it with respect to an adverse tradition. Whereas the opposition of rationalism and empiricism is constitutive of the very elaboration of Piaget's thinking, a new opposition between enlightenment and romanticism is thought of as being constitutive of neo-Piagetian research. The structuralist epistemology would belong to the former, and functionalism would be rooted in the latter. An analysis of the complexities and complementarities of this historical background allows Beilin to advocate a new synthesis of structuralism and functionalism that could be based partly on Piaget's research programme on equilibration.

J. Broughton's chapter is another way of assessing Piaget historically. It investigates the ideological components of scientific theories. According to Broughton, Piaget's theory reflects the instrumental conception of reason that the German philosophers of the Frankfurt School elucidated. Such a conception basically reduces knowledge to an adaptation, and it ends up in an objectification of knowledge and the subject of knowledge. In his view, this would be an obstacle to an emancipatory vision of knowledge. Although it shows some of the shortcomings of the new brands of historicism, this form of the ideological history of science is interesting in that it raises the problem of the cultural significance of the processes that rule the relationships between subjectivity and objectification in scientific thinking.

The problem of the social components in scientific activity is also tackled by García, who proposes a distinction between the sociogenesis and the psychogenesis of science. As a matter of fact, it is possible to study a sociogenesis that would be an important constituent of scientific knowledge in that each historical stage depends upon a *Weltanschauung* that influences the very content of science—i.e. the way concepts are elaborated. Such a sociogenesis does not come down to the socio-economical and political influences whose role is to give directionality to research. Thus, García develops the often misunderstood sociogenetic component inherent in Piagetian theory. His analysis of some developments in nineteenth-century science is a good example of how fruitful genetic epistemology can be in determining macro-genetic models of the growth of knowledge. Piaget and García's work in their book *Psychogenèse et histoire des sciences* (1983) is extended here to an analysis of the discovery of energy conservation. In opposition to an interpretation that Kuhn developed in a chapter of *The essential tension*, García demonstrates the benefits of an essentially epistemological reflection in terms of joint but distinct sociological, sociogenetic and psychogenetic analyses. In the present case, the industrial revolution in the United Kingdom, the scientific and technical problems linked to the French Revolution, and the emergence of *Naturphilosophie* in Germany define different sociogenetic conditions that contradict the hypothesis according to which several scientists simultaneously discovered the conservation principle. Instead, the epistemological analysis conducted here shows the extent to which the sociogenetic conditions of cognition—and therefore the types of questions—differed.

The chapters by Beilin, Broughton and García present major problems and perspectives in the sciences of cognitive development, and they permit a better understanding of the notion of development. The very nature of development is an important issue in contemporary psychology. This issue has been once again highlighted, for example, by the Piaget–Chomsky debate (Piatelli-Palmerini, 1980) or by the reassessment of the notion of developmental stages. The point here is to find again a somewhat lost unity in the description of the data in cognitive development. Some of the discussants in the Closing Debate try to lay the foundations for such a recovery of descriptive and/or explanatory unity, and some chapters in the volume also contribute to such a research programme. This problem of how to restore some form of descriptive unity in developmental psychology is tackled by Carey in a study of theory emergences in childhood. Closely linked to a reassessment of the notion of stage, such a study of the restructuring of knowledge leads to an identification of a limited number of domain-general intuitive theories indicating general constraints in cognitive development that would be paralleled in the history of science and would therefore give new relevance to the Piagetian notion of stage. As this has been the case ever since Piaget proposed the successive components of his theory, interdisciplinary research seems to provide a good angle to tackle these problems. Thus, Escalona is able to establish non-trivial links between egopsychoanalysis and Piagetian developmental psychology. Aebli shows how a view from educational sciences can help solve crucial problems in genetic psychology, such as where cognitive constructions take place. But disciplinary research is relevant as well, and the chapters on memory (Cornoldi) and spatial representation (Steiner) demonstrate that Piagetian concepts can be evolved through theoretical developments that have been occurring in these fields in recent years.

Escalona shows how advances in egopsychoanalytical research and theory permit some integration of cognitive development and the development of personality. In fact, they seem to be two different facets in a unitary process. Escalona describes two "nodal points" where cognition and the ego are both structured and depend upon one another. At the sensorimotor level, the mother's propensity to activate distant receptor systems favours the attention paid to inanimate environment and therefore sensorimotor intelligence. Similarly, it is hypothesised that mental activity when the semiotic function is being constituted depends upon delay capacity and impulse control, two prerequisites for semiotic function that belong to ego construction. Aebli takes up a problem that was not significantly investigated by Piaget. Development can be seen as a "structural puzzle" that integrates cognitive activities taking place in the experiment, at school and in everyday life. This view is supported by theoretical suggestions that aim at complementing Piaget's structural theory by a theory of the representation of cognitive structures and at incorporating the social and cultural factors of development.

The chapters by Steiner and Cornoldi illustrate the way the new experimental psychology and its theoretical framework can help develop Piagetian concepts and problems. In relation to spatial knowledge, Steiner investigates the continuity and/or discontinuity between spatial reasoning in large-scale and small-scale environments. A comprehensive analysis of the cognition of a familiar environment is followed by an investigation of the central processes that underlie spatial knowledge and skills in terms of the Piagetian interpretation of representational space and of new procedural models of spatial cognition. Cornoldi states the theoretical viewpoint that stems from his research on memory. After recalling that Piaget's studies on memory allow one to relate memory and intelligence and to investigate the variations of memory according to age, he gives a useful contribution to the study of the procedural aspects of memory through concepts such as intentional and strategic memories.

A third major problem was to give a better assessment of the notions of norms and values. This problem has seldom been studied in Geneva, but it is central in Piaget's epistemology. The notion of value gave Piaget the opportunity to develop important considerations about the relationships between science and philosophy. The whole debate is taken up by Fetz in the light of a dialogue that took place between Piaget and the French philosopher Ricoeur when *Insights and illusions of philosophy* first appeared in French. In Piaget's definition of philosophy as a "coordination of values", i.e. a rational stand as to the whole of reality, Fetz recognises a traditional definition of philosophy by its object and a modern definition which has a neo-Kantian origin and which links values to domains of reality and the corresponding acts. Piaget's problem was to determine whether philosophy was a form of knowledge or whether science only was knowledge. If philosophy is not limited to a simple commitment—which is sometimes Piaget's stand, especially in his controversy with existentialism—it becomes possible to look for the type of thinking or rationality involved in philosophical activity. Fetz endeavours to elucidate this type of activity with the help of Max Weber's description of the autonomisation cultural processes and of a study of the adolescent's representations of the world, for which an analysis in terms of Piaget's equilibration model is useful. The question of norms and values gives Marbach the opportunity to link phenomenological reflection to genetic psychology. In this view, the point is to account for psychological development as a development of mental states through a phenomenology of consciousness that envisions "laws of consciousness" both as norms for a subject and norms for the person who tries to understand cognitive development, a largely reflective viewpoint that proves fruitful here in the analysis of some aspects of the transition from sensorimotor activity to representation.

We hope that this presentation will open the way to a new appraisal and a renewal of the problems and concepts Piaget developed, in the interdisciplinary way that was dear to him and that is fairly well represented here. The question of norms and values shows that there can be a positive evolution in the relationships between science and philosophy and that reflective analyses can be beneficial to genetic epistemology. The problem of modelling demonstrates the usefulness of certain formalising approaches and the role they have in explanation. Concerning the notion of development, the descriptive and explanatory unity of psychology seems to be a major problem that we presently face, and the Closing Debate clearly raises the problem, thereby allowing a better understanding of Piaget's unifying approach. Such an approach is instantiated by Cellérier, who notices in his contribution that one major component of the theory—i.e. the equilibration model—was left by Piaget as an "open problem" which Cellérier proposes to take up in the general framework of a neo-Darwinian theory of schemes. A close and comprehensive development of Piaget's theory, Cellérier's chapter also shows how current developments in artificial intelligence (AI) can help in constructing a theoretical framework that would allow for an integration of the functionalist and structuralist approaches that are constitutive of Piaget's theory.

PIAGET'S DUALITY OF PERSPECTIVES

Indeed, we have mentioned above that, when reading Piaget with the purpose of finding out what is relevant for contemporary cognitive psychology, the duality of the structural and functional viewpoints we find in his writings is certainly of primary interest. Our own view here will be to try to show in what sense a functionalist interpretation of the construction of knowledge both complements Piaget's structural models and leads to new paths of investigation.

Now perhaps it will be useful to introduce this viewpoint by going back to some early works and books by Piaget in order to see the issues involved in this duality of perspectives. True enough, during some periods, and especially between 1941 and 1959, when he elaborated his logico-mathematical models of cognitive development, the structural interests prevailed. The functionalist approach, however, has played an important part as early as Piaget's first book in psychology *The Language and thought of the child* (1926), the major purpose of which actually was to answer the question: Why does the child speak? Claparède, in whose theory Piaget's functional approach is rooted, noticed in the preface to the book that "in Piaget, the functional question nourishes the structural question" (Piaget, 1926); that is, he saw both the functional nature of this study and the structural description of cognitive organisations that it implied. As a matter of fact, when Piaget set out to study the categories of knowledge, he used a type of analysis that amounted to a psychogenetic method. In order to do so, he needed some tools that characterised the concepts and invariants of scientific thinking at a given period of our century. Such are, for instance, the "groups of displacements", the peculiar importance of which had been pointed out by Poincaré in mathematics.

The scope of such a method can be best witnessed in Piaget's early and famous trilogy, *The child's construction of reality* (1954), *The origins of intelligence in children* (1952) and *Plays, dreams and imitation in childhood* (1951). When Piaget analyses in the first of these books the categories of space, time and causality at elementary levels, he goes back to the roots of knowledge through a very general kind of psychological analysis allowing a description of universals at the level of actions. These universals are the basis of thinking proper. Such a structural analysis entails the establishment of links between systems that had been studied separately hitherto: Space, time and causality were now regarded as interrelated systems based upon one another. This method was a tremendous incentive for detailed psychological analysis. It certainly brought new ways of thinking to psychology, even though we know now that hereditary structures are more complex and sooner operant and that inter-individual interactions appear earlier than Piaget thought at that time.

The child's construction of reality demonstrated the epistemological dimension that was to have such an important role throughout Piaget's writings. Piaget was actually looking for a relatively permanent universe that could be reached through a pure form of scientific research. This epistemological research was thought of as corresponding to the way the organism and the universe are constituted: At the outset, they are not revealed, in Piaget's view, as unorganised, but they obey regularities, frequencies and so on. Such a viewpoint permitted an epistemology that would correspond to the actual sciences and that in fact drew the attention of such prominent scientists as Einstein and Oppenheimer.

Although it bears on the same subjects at the same ages, *The origins of intelligence in children* (1952) is an altogether different book. Its explanatory concepts originated in biology, and the invariants Piaget was looking for were functional rather than structural. Actually, this book answered a new question: How does the child construct his own tools for understanding and discovering the world through a series of tasks that he himself is able to devise? Such is the case when the infant discovers the uses of a tool or when he finds ways of getting hold of an object that is either hidden or held back by some sort of obstacle. In that sense, this book clearly instantiated a functional viewpoint that was interpreted in terms of a growing equilibrium between assimilation and accommodation. Let us note, however, that at that time the child was not analysed as a subject looking for the uses of an object in a purely pragmatic way. Piaget's purpose was to study the coordinations of schemes, and they could not have been studied as true constructions without the help of a structural analysis and without asking the epistemological questions addressed in *The child's construction of reality*.

The functional aspect becomes obvious in the third volume of the trilogy, *Play, dreams and imitation in childhood* (1951), even though it has seldom been regarded from this standpoint. For example, play is viewed as a basically autotelic activity. Piaget did not see the development of play as a Häckelian repetition or as instantiating a pre-adaptation to adult games, but as a free functioning. The accommodative aspects have a minor role here, and play is a preliminary activity that prepares the free production of hypotheses in the adult. Dream activities are even characterised by a complete lack of accommodations. In this respect, let us notice that in his debate with Freud, Piaget interprets displacement, condensation and repression as mechanisms that do not obey the rules of intersubjective coordination and the constraints of communication. But his theory differed from psychoanalytic theory in that he did not study these various functions as contributing to the subject's internal equilibrium. Above all, Piaget opposed the idea that censorship would be the only mechanism ruling symbolic representations. Instead, he proposed to think in terms of disequilibrium between assimilation and accommodation that can also be witnessed in the cognitive unconscious (including the unconscious of scientists).

We have somewhat specified the early functional aspects of Piagetian theory. Before going further in this direction, we must take into account the major structuralist works that were carried out mainly in the 1940s and 1950s. In the studies on the development of number, space, time, quantity, logical thinking and so on, the problem was not so much to know whether structures actually exist in the subject. We think that the real issue revolved around the description of systems with internal rules that ensure a consistency of thinking and generate invariant concepts. Such concepts cannot be fully understood if their psychogenesis—i.e. the way they are constructed—is not analysed. Tools for an analysis had thus to be devised, and this is the reason why Piaget used Boolean algebra, the Klein groups and their weaker forms, the groupings.

The outcome of such a methodological approach to the problem of structures was that Piaget built up an architecture of knowledge with the developmental routes that are necessary for its constitution. To this we must add some specific contributions of Piaget's structural analysis in the 1970s. Actually, they amount to an identification of structures that are more general, more elementary and weaker than the structures described in the so-called classical part of the theory. Before being a theory, structuralism is a method that supports a constructivist epistemology. This epistemology demonstrates the most general aspects of knowledge, and it describes a hierarchy of structural organisations in order to reach the very processes of construction. Through the use of such a method, Piaget was induced to look for elementary structures on which the more complex operatory structures would be based. In that sense, the whole range of research carried out in the late 1960s and the 1970s at the International Center for Genetic Epistemology in Geneva can be understood as an effort at getting at the very psychological foundations of logical thinking and the operatory structures. Thus, mathematical functions are semi-reversible structures that precede the reversibility of concrete operations (Piaget, Grize, Szeminska & Vinh-Bang, 1977). Correspondences and morphisms are non-transformational operations that are both more general and weaker than transformational operatory structures (Piaget et al., unpublished). Moreover, Piaget's studies in meaning were intended to grasp a "natural logic" that would be closer to a logic of action than to the logic of the scientist (Piaget & García, 1987). In doing so, Piaget emphasised the study of the processes underlying natural logic. This process-oriented perspective is so important that it intervenes in the use of notions that were hitherto used in a more static way in the description of structural levels of development. For example, when he was studying dialectics and implication (Piaget et al., 1980), Piaget was actually looking for implicative processes, and he eventually regarded dialectics as the inferential aspect of equilibration—that is, a particularly important subprocess in the equilibration of cognitive structures. Especially in his later period, what interested him was not so much the formal links characterising structures once they are abstracted and liberated from their genetic conditions, but the way people think, the way they construct and use logical tools that will eventually evolve into structural compositions ensuring a certain permanency of knowledge. This viewpoint pervades the writings of this period, and it is even a clue to reading Piaget, whose seemingly less rigorous methods (Gréco, 1985) indicate flexibility and actually signal functional aspects in his own way of thinking.

During these years, a new functionalist trend appeared in Geneva independently of Piaget's own research programme. In the group of researchers working with one of us, attempts were made to break away radically from all forms of structural analysis and the abstract epistemic subject it intended to describe, in order to go back to observation and the individual's behaviour. This sharp shift in methods was a heuristically beneficial move. Whereas the former studies were intended to elucidate the epistemic subject—i.e. what is common to the cognitive structures at a given point in development—the new approach was meant to help in getting closer to a real subject, including his intentions, plans and means for controlling his actions. It also allowed us to realise that it was possible to reach mechanisms that would be more subtle than those that were demonstrated as macrogenetic transformations. This new research is now in the field of pragmatics, i.e. the subject's construction of cognitive tools that are adapted to specific situations. Even though Piaget's concern constantly was about praxis, he never studied pragmatics. The idea here is that discoveries take place in particular contexts. If epistemology is a study of what belongs to the subject and the object in the construction of

knowledge, then the study of pragmatics has an epistemological component, even though one is methodologically compelled to work on particular
contexts of elaboration.

This approach could bring a new understanding of psychological
functioning that would take into account the issues and outcomes of
Piaget's epistemology. Indeed, this concern about pragmatics goes back to
the study of formal thinking (Inhelder & Piaget, 1958) in which one of us
set out to study "experimental attitudes" (Inhelder, 1954) in the adolescent
while Piaget was constructing the formal tools for a structural description
of formal thinking. A first overall heuristical framework was provided in a
paper on the relationships between procedures and structures (Inhelder &
Piaget, 1980), which stressed the complementarities and differences of the
procedural and the structural analyses. On the one hand, procedures are
needed for structural organisations to function. On the other hand, any
problem-solving strategy makes use of structural knowledge that is either
available in the cognitive repertoire or discovered when solving the problem.
Procedures and structures are thus both distinct and complementary and
they correspond to the distinction between "knowing how" and "knowing
that". Both use transformations, but the realisation of transformations in
procedures is limited to specific goals. Procedures always have a teleonom-
ical and temporal dimension, whereas the structural knowledge relates and
composes transformations until atemporal systems are constructed. This
does not mean that there is no teleonomic dimension (in the present case,
it amounts to a purpose of general understanding) and no use of
procedures in the construction of structures. Once a structure is elaborated, however, it loses its teleonomic dimension and becomes atemporal.

We may say now that structural analysis enables us to be aware of the
upper and lower limits of the cognitive repertoire at a given point in
development—i.e. it gives the background according to which procedural
knowledge can be best studied. With regard to some current problems in
AI, the hierarchical dimension provided by the framework of genetic
epistemology allows one to go beyond a theoretical viewpoint that would
be reminiscent of certain forms of connectionism. Cellérier (Chapter 1, this
volume) clearly defines the issues involved in what he calls a distinction
between an "epistemological constructivism" and a "psychological constructivism". The former emphasises "structures and the acquisition of
knowledge", whereas the latter's emphasis is on "the function of knowledge in its application to problems". Such a complementarity between
epistemological and psychological constructivisms entails, however, some
differences in the methods adopted. The functional study of problem-
solving situations is based on open experimental situations in which the
invention and the transference of procedures can best be observed or
inferred if the outcomes of the subject's own actions are made available to
him. There is, in fact, a transition from the former method of investigation

in which the subject was left unaware of the outcomes of his actions to a new approach that allows for controls by the subject himself. In that view, the subject both organises his own plans and procedures and exerts control over his actions. This new method of investigation is especially useful if one is to study the relationships between action and representation. The problems the subject is presented with are concrete problems, and the observer's task is to infer from recorded behaviours the intentions that direct the way the subject understands the problem and his own procedures. As to the very nature of constructions, let us notice that once procedural knowledge is focused, more elementary constructions, at the level of actions, are likely to be met. Indeed, we have met some cases in which procedural activities seemed to end up in an equivalent of structural knowledge. For example, in an experiment conducted by Karmiloff-Smith (Karmiloff-Smith & Inhelder, 1975), we noticed that a procedural type of work on physical compensations (e.g. the equilibrium of unevenly weighted rods) occasionally produced a practical understanding of some aspects of gravity. In fact, it was only an equivalent in action of the physical law (what we called a theory-in-action), and in most cases procedures and procedural transferences lack the stability and permanency of structural knowledge.

This method allows one to investigate the relationships between procedures and the interpretative networks that underlie the subject's actions. The child himself does not necessarily have a conscious knowledge of them. They correspond to the most general schemes in the subject and to the regularities that are discovered in the object. The problem here is to study how the general schemes become specified in concrete situations. We are attempting, so to say, to understand how the structures function and the functions are structured. Of paramount importance here seem to be the attributions of meanings and the establishment of meaning implications in the very process by which general schemes intervene in the concrete situations and are accommodated to them. In the goals he sets as well as in the means he uses, the subject is constantly attributing meanings to the objects and tools, and such meanings therefore have a pivotal role in establishing specific or shared properties. Meanings and meaning implications seem to constitute the link between general schemes and procedures in that several types of shifts in meaning allow for a modification of strategies by ensuring a gradual adequation of the chosen or invented means to the goals.

Through specifically devised experimental situations, we attend thus to the construction of ad hoc models corresponding to the various problems. Such models belong to the study of pragmatics; in fact they are pragmatic models that are manifold but still display general functional similarities. We try to infer how such models are constructed in particular situations and how they are transferred to new situations. The important point here is that the study of applied knowledge shows how general knowledge is changed into a "knowing how"—that is, how schemes are accommodated to various contexts and their specific constraints. In this respect, the control of activities that aim at success in a given context is closely linked with the interpretative networks that the cognitive structures provide at each macrogenetic level. But the study of the specification of general schemes also allows us to understand how small modifications occurring in microgenesis prepare larger macrogenetic transformations, including transformations in the subject's epistemology, i.e. including the epistemic transformations that occur in a person's interpretation of reality. Our view is that of the functional dimensions of a psychological constructivism. Through a process-oriented psychological analysis, we hope to describe the complementary enacting of structural and procedural knowledge and to reach constructive mechanisms that would renew our understanding of psychological reality.

REFERENCES

Gréco, P. (1985). Réduction et construction. *Cahiers de la Fondation Archives Jean Piaget, 6;* and *Archives de Psychologie, 55,* 21–36.

Inhelder, B. (1954). Les attitudes expérimentales de l'enfant et de l'adolescent. *Bulletin de Psychologie, 7,* 272–282.

Inhelder, B., & Piaget, J. (1958). *The growth of logical thinking from childhood to adolescence.* New York: Basic Books. (First French ed., 1955.)

Inhelder, B., & Piaget, J. (1980). Procedures and structures. In Olson, D. R. (Ed.), *The social foundations of language and thought.* New York: Norton.

Karmiloff-Smith, A., & Inhelder, B. (1975). If you want to get ahead, get a theory. *Cognition, 3,* 195–212.

Piaget, J. (1926). *The language and thought of the child.* London: Kegan Paul. (First French ed., 1923.)

Piaget, J. (1951). *Play, dreams and imitation in childhood.* Melbourne, London, Toronto: Heinemann. (First French ed., 1945.)

Piaget, J. (1952). *The origins of intelligence in children.* New York: International Universities Press. (First French ed., 1936.)

Piaget, J. (1954). *The child's construction of reality.* New York: Basic Books. (First French ed., 1937.)

Piaget, J., Grize, J.-B., Szeminska, A., & Vinh-Bang (1977). *Epistemology and psychology of functions,* vol. 23: *Studies in Genetic Epistemology.* Dordrecht: Reidel. (First French ed., 1968.)

Piaget, J., Henriques, G. & Ascher, E. (1980). *Les formes élémentaires de la dialectique.* Paris: Gallimard.

Piaget, J., & García, R. (1983). *Psychogenèse et histoire des sciences.* Paris: Flammarion.

Piaget, J., & García, R. (1987). *Vers une logique des significations.* Genève: Murionde.

Piaget, J., Henriques, G., & Ascher, E. *Comparer et transformer des structures aux catègories.* (Unpublished.)

Piatelli-Palmarini, M. (Ed.) (1980). *Language and learning. The debate between Jean Piaget and Noam Chomsky.* Boston: Harvard University Press.

1

Structures and Functions

Guy Cellérier
University of Geneva

EPISTEMOLOGICAL AND PSYCHOLOGICAL CONSTRUCTIVISM

Traditionally, epistemology is a branch of philosophy. Piaget's central project was to make it an experimental science founded on biology. In this project, psychology is both a link between the structures of the organism and those studied by epistemology, and it permits the experimental study of the psychological realisation of epistemological structures in the mind. Thus, the problems that determine Piaget's research programme are epistemological ones, and he rightly insists on the fact that his work cannot be reduced to "a research in pure psychology". His genetic psychology appears as a "by-product" (to quote the terms of an award he received from the American Association of Psychology), because it belongs to the experimental part of the project—it is a means and not an end in itself.

This does not mean that psychology is a minor aspect of his project: one of his earliest hypotheses was that psychological states, such as feelings of normative or logical necessity, correspond to states of equilibrium between parts and whole in a structure. So from the very start, the elaboration of a psychological theory that explains how the "normative permanence" of epistemological structures may emerge from the empirical flow of mental states [devenir mental] was a central part of the project. Thus, the theory of the equilibration of parts of thought into structural wholes was a long-standing project. He returned to it on many occasions, the last one being in his book on *The equilibration of cognitive structures* (Piaget, 1985), which is part of a research project in which he returns to psychological problems and searches perhaps for a more closely psychological realisation of epistemological structures, such as a "logic of meaningful implications", for instance. His article on "Structures and procedures", written with Bärbel Inhelder (Inhelder & Piaget, 1980) is related to this research, as is Inhelder's own research project on "Strategies and Procedures". So genetic psychology may well be a by-product, but it is not a minor one, either in the results it produced, or in the importance and interest it had in Piaget's own mind.

If we now ask in which direction Piaget's constructivism is going or should go today, my answer is that we may well follow his own diagnosis, i.e. his own modest conclusion that the equilibration of cognitive structures is still "an open problem". This is the theme I will develop, by proposing some steps towards a more Darwinian theory of the equilibration of schemes. Much of what follows is the development of an earlier conference for the "Cours des Archives Jean Piaget" on genes and schemes (Cellérier, 1984), and I must again acknowledge my debt to Minsky and Papert's initial version of the society theory of mind and to Minsky's various intermediate and final versions of the same theory (Minsky, 1986) for the inspiration to pursue a functional theory of schemes.

There is a fundamental homology between the Darwinian theory of the evolution of genes (phylogenesis) and Piaget's theory of the equilibration of schemes (psychogenesis), because both address the same question: how can a system with limited knowledge and limited computational capacities evolve strategies for overcoming these limitations, i.e. how can it acquire more knowledge and more cost-efficient computational strategies to solve the external problems of its adaptation to an environment (a problem universe), and reflexively or self-referentially and recursively solve the internal problem of overcoming its epistemic and computational limitations, including those that its very evolution generates. The repeated solution of these two "majoration" problems produces a (psycho- or phylo-) genesis of the system.

The central question of phylogenesis is: how does a new equilibration of genes concur to the reproductive efficiency of the organism that carries it, and to the productivity of the genetic system that generates it. Both are locally evaluated but not distinguished by the differential reproduction of the organism. The same question must be asked of schemes: how does a new equilibration of schemes concur to the solution of the external adaptation problems of the cognitive system and to its future productivity.

I will suggest that schemes, like genes, compete for control of the activity and evolution of the system in which they cohabit and participate, and that differential reproduction of genes and Piaget's notion of acquisition (and therefore conservation) of schemes, structures, etc. are two realisations of the same function: the differential conservation of knowledge in a memory that reflects the relative (differential) success of these entities in solving the two majoration problems, i.e. in controlling the adaptive activity and evolution of the system. This means that knowledge appears, evolves genetic "descendants" in the system, and also disappears from it, and these continuous changes constitute the system's evolution.

We must thus focus, as Darwin did, on two complementary aspects of the mechanisms that produce this evolution: how new forms are generated to solve problems on the present dimensions of adaptation and how to pose and solve new problems that open new dimensions of adaptation. This part of the evolutionary mechanisms constitutes the generator of candidate solutions. In phylogenetic evolution, new forms are generated by a (random) combinatorial search on at least two levels: the first is on the basic level of the universal genetic code primitives (mutation); the second level, evolving from the first, is a combinatorial search on combinations of solutions that have been generated at the first level and "stored" in the genetic pool (Mendelian combination of chromosomes and post-Mendelian recombination of genes). We may distinguish two similar levels in psychogenetic evolution: that of "universal procedural primitives" that permit the construction of sensorimotor coordination, i.e. of schemes, and that of the combination or coordination of schemes. We shall endeavour to show that the cognitive system's generation strategy consists of evolving itself into an increasingly anti-chance generator, whose procedure is increasingly preguided by accumulated knowledge and methods and by higher-level combinations thereof.

The second part of the mechanism of evolution is of course selection, a deceptively simple concept (like variation, as we have just seen). For "majorative" evolutions to occur, it is not enough that new forms be constantly generated; they must be submitted to what we call differential conservation. This means they must be evaluated with respect to their double majorative value, and either "positively" or "negatively" reinforced" as a consequence of this evaluation. The effect of this reinforcement must be to make them more or less (or not at all) *accessible* for the generation of forms, or, in other words, to give them greater or lesser access to the *control* of *the activity of the generator*. Thus, selection assigns credit (and blame) to both new and old forms for their contribution to adaptation and adaptivity and this credit consists of differential (greater or smaller) access to the present and future control of the solution generator.

Thus, lowering the frequency of a gene, or "negatively reinforcing" or inhibiting a scheme, has the same effect: that of lowering their access to the control of the problem-solving activity of their respective systems. This is the reason why we may say that schemes, like genes, compete for control, and that control is the ultimate evaluative currency of majorative evolutionary systems.

Furthermore, the biological mechanisms of generation (variation) and selection constantly act on both new and old solutions. This means that there are no such things as "permanent memories" in a gene pool. An old "permanent" gene is constantly mutating (at a low frequency); this means that for its present form to be "permanent", it must be constantly positively selected from its mutant variants. But this, in turn, means that it must stay locally optimal in a variety of evolving gene pools, and that its permanence is a consequence of its being constantly tested and reinforced through the results of its activity.

The important consequence of the preceding remarks is that the accessibility structure of the genetic memory is thus made to reflect the adaptive value of its constituents, in that the priority of accessibility of a gene is a function of its priority of reproductivity value, and that this accessibility structure of memory is constantly updated and evolving with the evolution of the genetic system itself. Impermanent memories are thus intrinsic to evolving systems.

We suggest that the apparent self-erasing property of psychological memory (whether it was designed as, or is a side-effect of, neural storage that was exploited by the genes during the evolution of the brain) serves the same function for selection, albeit through very different mechanisms. We know very little about neurophysiological storage and retrieval, and therefore about whether schemes are forgotten because they are erased by random fluctuations in the hardware, or (improbably) specific garbage collection and overwriting or erasing procedures, or misfilings that occur during accessibility reorganisations, or simply owing to their relative inaccessibility, etc., or a mixture of these phenomena and others not imagined. However, a scheme that is not accessible in time to produce a solution to a problem is effectively forgotten at this functional level of description. The fact that the formation of a scheme needs repeated exercise, and that its conservation over the longer time spans of psychogenesis would seem to entail periodic reactivation, suggests that the exercise of the scheme serves internally to re-evaluate it periodically through its results, and to modify its accessibility level, thereby both updating its value and reorganising locally the accessibility structure of memory, i.e. the relative priorities of access of the schemes with which it competes or co-operates for control. It also suggests that the problem of collecting memory cells for re-use is not solved, but circumvented, by giving the cognitive system ample memory space, and instead of post-erasing obsolete schemes, being strongly pre-selective about what to store: candidate schemes have perhaps to run the gauntlet of medium-term memory and repeated spontaneous rehearsal, during which they must prove their efficiency at cooperating with the variety of existing "permanent" schemes that called on them, until they can take their place among them, by being "filed" in the knowledge net, in locations "associated" with the callers—we notice that here the classical "associations" become accessibility relations.

CLOSING THE EQUILIBRATION LOOP

This outlines some steps toward a variation and selection theory of the equilibration of schemes. The question arises, however, of why such a theory is necessary. The answer is, of course, that there is no spontaneous generation of information in any cognitive system. This means that any non-preformist theory of knowledge, that is, any theory that does not postulate complete and preadapted knowledge of its problem universe in the cognitive system, must incorporate feedback from the environment in the form of a fundamental trial-and-error loop. This loop is quite explicit in Piaget's definition of adaptation as an equilibrium between assimilation from which the trials originate, and accommodation that results from the errors. However, as his theoretical focus is epistemological, the main emphasis of his psychological theory is on the acquisition and the structure of knowledge and not on its application and its function. This results in a theory of equilibration where the emphasis is more on the generation of new forms, and less on their selection and differential conservation for their function.

The emphasis on structures and the acquisition of knowledge characterises what I shall call epistemological constructivism. The complementary emphasis on the function of knowledge in its application to problems defines what I propose to call psychological constructivism. The two perspectives are complementary; the latter's object is merely to develop and generalise the functional aspects of a theory of schemes that are already present in Piaget's genetic psychology. The reciprocal functional complementarity of acquisition and application of knowledge is already quite explicit in the interactionist thesis of genetic psychology, whereby it is only when previously acquired knowledge effectively interacts with a material or symbolic problem universe during its application to a problem that schemes are accommodated, and that new constructs result from empirical or reflexive abstraction, which, in turn, permit new potential applications and problem formations. Thus acquisition serves application, and vice versa.

What we propose is to close explicitly this majorative "generation and selection" loop at the top level of the equilibration theory of schemes, reflecting at this level the closure that already exists at the lower theoretical levels of the abstraction of concepts and the adaptation of schemes. Introducing the double feedback of external selection by adaptation to the external environment and internal selection by co-adaptation to the other components of the internal epistemic universe at the top level of equilibration induces precisely the kind of top-down "vection" (by local guidance with no preset target) on the construction of knowledge that Piaget has often postulated.

A central theoretical consequence is that the microgenesis of knowledge that may be observed during a problem-solving episode or a sequence of such application episodes becomes the basis of the macrogenetic evolution of knowledge over the longer time spans of psychogenesis. During an application episode a problem is assimilated to existing schemes, which must be accommodated and coordinated to produce a solution. As we suggested previously, this coordination becomes a protoscheme, a candidate for differential conservation and eventual accession to the psychogenetic repertoire of permanent acquisitions of the cognitive system. Thus microgenesis is both a *product* of macrogenesis, and a *producer* of potential macrogenetic acquisitions—and application episodes relate microgenesis to macrogenesis by constructing the future of psychogenesis from the coordination of its past with its present.

Thus the integrated accumulation of these micro-modifications, which are the object of psychological constructivism, result in the psychogenetic macro-evolution of knowledge that is the object of Piaget's structural analysis and epistemological constructivism. It must be noted here that in this perspective, large-scale behavioural restructurations need not result from large-scale reorganisations of knowledge, but may be the effect of a new coordination, or solution construction form (such as "inverse covariation of dimensions suggests compensation") embodied in a scheme with high-access priority that will thus be tried on many problems. This scheme will merely re-coordinate old knowledge in a different way, producing the fast microgenetic emergence of new notions in a variety of problem universes. These new notions (that combine previous ones) then become candidates for differential conservation. If they succeed, their slow cumulative effect will then result in the large-scale restructuration of knowledge we associate with a stage. Stage transitions may thus again be the effect of the integrated accumulation of micro-modifications.

In this quasi-Darwinian perspective, then, the question we must ask in psychology about structures and schemes, these "organs" of the mind, is the same as the one we must ask in biology about anatomical structures and their physiology. In biology the question is, what are they for, what is their function with respect to the differential reproduction of the organism? In psychology the question becomes, what is the function of structures and schemes, how do they contribute to the majoration of the cognitive system? This merely elaborates Piaget's thesis of the continuity between life and thought, in which intelligence continues and expands the adaptation of the organism, and where schemes are the organs or instruments of the organism's non-material, or functional (we would say informational), exchanges with the environment. It focuses, however, on the second less explicit aspect of adaptation, namely adaptivity. A new scheme must not only be adapted to the external environment, but must also be co-adaptable to the entities of the internal epistemic environment, i.e. to the other schemes with which it must cooperate to form new solutions that could not be attained without it, thus contributing to the adaptivity of the cognitive system.

STRUCTURAL AND FUNCTIONAL ANALYSIS

The central question of psychological constructivism is, as we have seen, that of the function of structures. For each particular acquisition it asks what is its function in the majoration of the products and of the productivity of the cognitive system.

The notion of function itself is not widely accepted in the tradition of science and thus needs to be somewhat elaborated and clarified. We will first relate it to the principal method of constructivism, which I will call structural analysis. The latter is a typically Piagetian synthesis of the methods of conceptual analysis that characterise philosophical episte-mology, with those of axiomatic decomposition that characterise formalisa-tion. Furthermore, these methods are transposed and applied to the intuitive notions of the child, and the resulting decomposition is given a temporal dimension, with the underlying hypothesis that what is properly decomposed by the analysis may be what is synthesised by psychogenesis. A typical example is, of course, the decomposition of natural number into its ordinal and cardinal aspects, and of these into their psychogenetic precursors, until the level of actions on concrete objects and collections is reached. Alternative decompositions suggested by epistemology lead to psychological experiments at each level, which may, in turn, suggest novel decompositions. The final analytic arborescence then serves as a hypo-thesis for a possible psychogenetic synthesis.

To relate this method to what I shall call functional analysis and synthesis, we should first note that structural analysis is based on an implicit functional decomposition that guides it, and without which it would simply not be possible. We could not, for instance, decompose a car into substructures such as "engine, transmission, suspension, brakes, steering" etc. (to quote the standard decomposition format of specialised magazines) if we did not have a (pre)conception of the function of these substructures. Notice in passing that the terms used in the format to label substructures are all functional ones—the function of brakes is braking, they are not called "disk and pad combinations".

At a more fundamental level of description, we could not even distinguish the molecules of a machine from those of its physical environment if we were not able to distinguish two chemically structurally isomorphic molecules on the basis of their different function, within the machine and outside it. The same is true of organisms, whose molecules are indistinguishable in vivo and in vitro, as the adage goes, since Claude Bernard at least.

The reason that functional analysis has no name in science or philosophy is presumably that it is a method that typically belongs to technology, where it is widely practiced and is called design. Engineers, for instance, distinguish up to sixteen levels of functional decomposition, from the top-level sub-functions of a car—steering, accelerating, braking—to the nuts' and bolts' and gears' level of primitive structural (and functional) components, from the ascending coordination of which emerges the variety of top-level functions we have progressively delegated to machines. Functional decomposition is widely used in biology, where organisms are decomposed into organs with different subfunctions (circulation etc.) down to the macromolecular level of enzymes with their specific catalytic functions. It is, however, frowned upon as redolent of teleology. We may note that the fact that organisms exploit and coordinate physical phenomena to produce higher-level rule-governed phenomena, whose rules such as self-replication are not laws of physics, does not make them ipso facto metachemical and metaphysical devices, and the concepts that describe these higher-level phenomena non-scientific ones, except perhaps for naïve reductionists.

Functional analysis has mostly been applied to material structures such as organisms and machines, though it was practised from the very beginning on the symbolic structures constituted by programs, and has recently received names such as top-down structured programming in this new branch of engineering.

Thus, if functional questions are central to psychological constructivism, then we must propose functional analysis as its basic method. In this perspective, our cognitive system must thus be apprehended as a symbol structure that is self-designed, bottom-up (we shall say evolved), from an initial primitive level of schemes and scheme-making machinery evolved by the genes, another symbolic machine.

This analytical method also has ancestors in psychology, such as the psychology of faculties, which endeavours to decompose the mind into the higher faculties, with specific functions—consciousness, will, etc.—and these in turn into sub-faculties (perception, memory, etc.). What it actually does is to thematise and organise into a hierarchy the concepts of our practical psychology, the ones we use to describe and communicate our "states of mind". However, the real difficulty with such a project is that, in minds as in machines and organisms, many structures cooperate for one function, one structure participates in many functions, and that symbolic or software machines are designed or evolved to be highly reconfigurable, with the consequence that their functional distribution varies over time according to needs. This only makes the problem harder, but not impossible in principle. What was impossible was the psychology of faculties' implicit goal of finding a unique fixed and hierarchical decomposition.

Let us now briefly return to number to illustrate our thesis and to introduce our next theme, that of functional synthesis, or emergence. We first ask, what is the functional basis for distinguishing the traditional structural ordinal and cardinal aspects of number? This question may be addressed by establishing the classes of problems that ordinality and cardinality are used to solve separately. It we have a successor scheme, defined over otherwise indistinguishable elements, that allows us to find or to compute the successor of any element, we can answer the question, "what is the next element", but only if we are *shown* its immediate predecessor or *given* an initial distinguished element. From then on we can answer the same question again and again, producing an ordered sequence. But we cannot answer the question, "what is the next of the next...". For this, we need to count the "nexts" in the sentence, or to construct a bijection between them and our "successor" moves. This is not too different from the problems we can and cannot solve with a limited knowledge of the alphabet: what is the fifth successor of k? It allows us to fumble our way through directories and dictionaries. We can also formulate the converse question, "what is the rank of c?" The answer should be, "it is the successor of the successor of a", but this concept (successor) is not defined. It is a well-known phenomenon in mathematics that questions may be formulated in the language of a system that cannot be answered within it: $5 + x = 3$ can be formulated in the natural numbers, but it cannot be answered because -2 is not a natural number.

The point is that functions induce new functions that open new possible adaptive dimensions—that is, new possible goals for the cognitive system—because problem *solution* schemes may be used as a problem *position* language to conceive and pose new problems. Thus the more knowledge it acquires as a consequence of the problems it faces in its adaptation to an environment, the more the vection of an equilibration system can become self-determined by the problems it invents and poses, and not by the one it meets. This threshold is reached as soon as the system is adapted enough to have some free time to "play", and it is artificially lowered for us and kept so by parental care and later by the high productivity arising from our social strategies of division of labour.

The solution schemes to the successor problem serve to pose the rank problem, "what is the rank of d?" To answer this, we need to introduce a new notion, that of a collection (it is new because successors are defined only on elements), and to collect d and all its predecessors into the collection *a b c d*. But this moves us into the problem universe of collections and bijection, where we can only answer questions about (cardinal) equality of collections: we can now say that *d* has the same rank as April, but not that *d* is before *g*, for instance. To do this we need to order the collections by inclusion: A + A' + B' + C' . . . When this order is complete, the classes A', B' etc. are one-element classes, and we now can establish a one-way correspondence from the elements *d* and *g* to the singleton classes D' and G' and answer within this second system that *d* is before *g* because D is included in G. This is half of Piaget's synthesis of class inclusion and serial order to form number. We could have started from classes and bijection to form and propagate problems in this knowledge net towards that of seriation and established the converse correspondence from singleton classes to series elements, to form the other half of the synthesis and a two-way correspondence. This suggests in passing that the problem formation and propagation must be two-way in psychogenesis: from cardinal to ordinal, and vice versa.

One more problem must be solved, however, to attain the full functionality of number. The synthesis of classes and series constitutes a net of schemes, that is, of non-thematised numerical know-how. We need entry and exit points into and from the net to selectively activate its components and to read the results of their activity—in other words, to control and exploit the activity of the net. For example, we need to be able to selectively activate (refer to) the D collection and the *d* element. This is what language allows us to do, by establishing reference links between the standard names "four" and "fourth" and the collection D and the element *d*, respectively. We may not know how many letters there are from *d* to *j*, but when by "counting" we associate *d* with four and *j* with ten, these names selectively activate the corresponding net components and we immediately produce the answer, and read it at the exit point "six", or we "see" it because we have memorised such common answers, between one and eighteen, by learning the addition table, thus forming the transitive closure of "plus one" between these limits and adding it as a labelled link in the net. Thus, progressively establishing these reference links and the corresponding structures consists of building the meaning of the otherwise meaningless and functionless words of numeral language. We may notice in passing that, in this perspective, language has the internal function of a communication and control language to and from the "mute" computational machinery of schemes.

From the perspective of psychological constructivism, schemes thus appear as problem solution methods together with a small knowledge base of assimilatory and predictive schemes (that incorporate fundamental facts and useful usual results of their problem universe) that have been selected for permanent status in the cognitive system. Structures are then special "regroupings", i.e. coordinations of schemes that have strongly improved the productivity or "psychogenerativity" of the cognitive system in that (like number, of course) they are highly plurifunctional: i.e. they are applicable to a wide range of different *external* problems, and they are co-adapted to cooperate with a wide range of other schemes in the *internal* epistemic universe. Thus the structural links that form the "normative permanence" of such concepts as number are originally functional links that have been selected out of the "mental flux" of microgenetic problem resolutions for differential conservation. Structure is, in a sense, captured function and activity, stored in the knowledge net for further application and evolution. Furthermore, the fact that we can move with ease from a structural to a functional analysis based on the problems that structures can resolve indicates that we must rely at least on two cross-connected classification or filing systems to organise the accessibility structure of our memories. Structural descriptions and classifications or generalisation hierarchies based upon them are economical in that they are highly invariant over function. A cube is a geometrical cube whatever it is used for: as a building block, a box, a room. Structures can thus be cross-indexed to the various functions they permit in the complementary functional classification, allowing access from the means and instruments to the multiple ends they may serve. Conversely, functions and functional classifications are invariant over the structures that realise them: seats are seats, whatever their mechanical structure—solid blocks, with legs, suspended, etc. This allows cross-access from the ends to their multiple means. These cross-connected hierarchies allow us to generate plans through a "top-down" functional analysis or decomposition of a problem, exploring alternative decomposition into sub-functions without being encumbered with the structural details of their realisations and coordinations. They also allow us to execute these plans "bottom-up", constantly supplied with alternative structural realisations of the subfunctions. In both cases our problem-solving unfolds in a knowledge-laden net already rich with preconstructed solutions of various sizes and levels.

STRUCTURAL AND FUNCTIONAL SYNTHESIS

Class inclusion and seriation define specific problem universes in which different classes of problems can be solved, such as the successor problem for qualitatively distinguishable elements (what is the next bigger stick in a seriation) and the inclusion problem for qualitatively distinguishable collections (are there more roses than flowers). Their coordination into number forms a new structure, of course, but from the functional perspective of psychological constructivism it also *forms new functions*: a new problem universe emerges with novel adaptive dimensions on which new goals can be defined, new problems (how many collections or elements are there between d and g) can be posed and solved. Thus a new whole is formed with emergent properties, i.e. properties that its isolated parts do (and did) not have. The "how many" problem can neither be posed nor solved in class inclusion or seriation.

Many theories have rightly insisted on the emergence of these new higher-level properties that are irreducible to those of their lower-level components (vitalism and holism in biology, spiritualism and Gestalt theory in psychology, "organic" solidarity theories in sociology and law, phenomenology in philosophy, etc.).

Piaget, contrasting structure and Gestalt, used to observe that emergence only appears to be a mysterious spontaneous generation of new properties because by focusing only on the properties of the parts and on those of the whole we forget the novel relationship between the parts that have been introduced to coordinate them into a whole.

What we would focus upon is again the fact that these new properties are not only structural but functional as well, and above all that they are the *reason* such coordinations of parts into wholes are selected or constructed. This is perhaps the most basic, functional thesis of a psychological constructivism. The function of the construction of any structure is to produce a construct with properties its parts did not have in isolation. If this is not the case, then the construction has failed and is pointless, and it is also so in the converse case, when the parts already have the emergent properties. If this were true for machines, then buying an isolated spare part, a steering-wheel perhaps, would supply us with the automotive functions of the whole. This is perhaps the central justification for introducing in constructivism the question, what is the function of a structure? We may note here that when a structure is formed, the simultaneous emergence of new functions is its psychological concomitant, with the feelings of rational necessity that then relate means to ends in the new problem universe. This functional means–end aspect of logical necessity is neatly expressed in Minsky's (1967) remark about computing machines, concerning the necessity of the proposition "$2 + 2 = 4$", that if a machine sometimes produced "$2 + 2 = 5$" we would conclude that the machine has malfunctioned. We could add: or that it has been badly designed or built. This remark also applies, of course, to the internal machinery of our numerical schemes. The subjective phenomenology of functional emergence must also be related to the *Aha Erlebnis* of the Gestaltists that accompanies the high-level coordination of subsolution into an "emergent" solution, when our ideas suddenly "click into place" to form a novel coherent (re)configuration—that is, a new idea. We will thus identify the phenomenon of emergence with the synthesis of a new function from components that did not have this function or, more generally, as we shall submit, from components that had other functions, and thus acquire new ones, as subfunctions of the new whole. It has been suggested that one of the main mechanisms of evolution is the change of function of a pre-existing organ. The evolution of lungs from the oesophagus of air-swallowing fish in stagnant water is a paradigmatic example. We shall argue that this generation strategy is the "inevitable consequence" of what we shall call the epistemic strategy in the autogenetic systems of phylogenesis, psychogenesis and sociogenesis.

Functional synthesis has recently been rediscovered (it was noticed by Darwin), but it has been re-elaborated and given a central theoretical status by François Jacob (1981). "Biological evolution", he writes, "is thus founded on a kind of molecular tinkering, on the constant reutilisation of the old to make the new". He then shows how this mechanism works within the biological hierarchy of functional levels, from macromolecules to the regulatory genes that reconfigure the same structural genes to generate the multitudinous variety of vertebrate forms.

As we have seen, functional synthesis is also central in the coordination of schemes, with previously different problem-solving functions to produce the structuration (or equilibration or synthesis or construction) of number. We suggest that these terms all capture different aspects in different theoretical contexts of functional synthesis.

But this strategy of using the old to construct the new is not confined to the coordination of schemes within the cognitive system. When it is externalised to the coordination of schemes belonging to different cognitive systems, it becomes the basic strategy of sociogenesis: division of labour, i.e. the subdivision of a task or problem between the schemes of cooperating psychogenetically specialised and functionally complementary cognitive systems. This cooperation requires the communication of goals so that the individual schemes may be coordinated by their subordination to a common goal, and the inter-subjective transmission of knowledge so that the individuals live in shared (inter-subjectively objective) realities, i.e. they perceive and act on the same shared problem universe. The function of language in filling both of these prerequisites is obvious. The recursive application of this ascending combination strategy is again a central mechanism of the evolution of the sociogenetic hierarchies of economic and legal order structures.

Finally, we may see the construction of tools and machines as an externalisation of our schemes by their progressive mechanisation, starting with the inclusion of instruments in their sensorimotor loops. The mechanisation of these loops themselves, and of their (re)coordinations by higher cognitive functions is the object of automation and artificial intelligence. The construction strategy is again apparent in the higher-level combinations of known machines and techniques to produce new ones.

The deep functional homologies between the recombination, coordination, cooperation and design construction strategies that act upon very different structures in these different autogenetic systems thus motivate and justify the frequent heuristic shifts between them that we need to make explicit and to elaborate our functional intuitions

CONSTRUCTIVISM AND CONSTRUCTIBILITY

Our initial formulation of equilibration was, how can a system with limited knowledge and limited computational capacities overcome these limitations? We now turn to these basic functional limitations and endeavour to show how, by bounding their constructibility, they constrain the forms that certain types of cognitive systems may evolve.

Any physically realised cognitive system is subject to the limitations of its physicality and finiteness: it has finite size, finite memory, finite computational power, etc. These constraints constitute its "resource limitations". Some less obvious epistemic constraints appear as preconditions of adaptation. No system can solve adaptation problems if it cannot generate actions that effectively change its problem universe and at least perceive these changes precisely and finally evaluate them as solutions or non-solutions. This means that its basic actions and perceptions must be pre-adapted to interact with the problem universe, and with each other. This is the central intuition of preformist and a priorist epistemologies: no system can self-organise from an epistemic and computational tabula rasa.

The first two of these preconditions were presumably in a sense vacuously satisfied at the origins of life by the common and (pre)initially coextensive carbon chemistry of pre-biotic systems and their environment (the Oparin-Haldane "primeval organic soup") in that stereochemical "recognition" and selective catalytic "action" were common to proto-organism and environment, thus allowing them to interact effectively in these chemical terms. The third evaluative condition, *differential* reproduction, automatically emerges from the interaction of explosively self-replicating and varying (mutating) systems competing for finite resources in matter and energy to fuel and feed their *individual* reproduction.

As we shall see, this partial pre-adaptation condition on self-organisation remains true even when higher levels of organisation are attained. It is expressed in such maxims as "to learn something we must already nearly know it" or "the complexity of the structures activated to solve a problem is much greater than that of the problem itself", or as Piaget once said, "If I had a completely new idea, I would not be able to understand it". A final constraint is that of real-time response: the system must respond slightly faster than the events of its environment. This means that the definition of "real time" depends on the physical time constant of the environment (rocks and coconuts and organisms fall faster in heavier gravity) and of the other organisms, both predator and prey.

The adaptive strategies of a cognitive system evolve within these constraints, which thus decisively determine this evolution. To consider an extreme case—the pure computational strategy—a system with unlimited computational power could presumably make arbitrarily precise observations on an arbitrary number of parameters and from a limited axiomatic knowledge of its universe, quasi-instantaneously compute solutions to its adaptation problems and indefinitely recompute them when faced with similar problems. Such a system could thus be intrinsically amnesic and live in an eternal present consisting of the local, the compressed past, present and future of its problem-driven computation episodes, forgetting both the results and the history of these episodes.

In contrast, the adaptive strategies we observe in the computationally limited systems that have evolved on the planet are memory- and therefore knowledge-based. We shall therefore call them epistemic strategies. They rely on the differential conservation or "memorisation" of solutions and solution methods, which sometimes allows them to avoid recomputation. Thus we may observe that learning is an adaptive strategy but not an inevitable one in principle, so that evolution as its consequence (as we observe it in psychogenesis or phylogenesis) is not inevitable either. Neither is it independent of the pure computational strategy, but related to it by the function of partially overcoming computational limitations.

We now turn to the psychological realisations of the epistemic strategy. Piaget subdivides the functional invariant of adaptation into two subfunctions: assimilation and accommodation. We observe that they realise the basic epistemic strategy in the cognitive system. Reproductive assimilation, by re-producing a solution, transforms its production method into what we would call a candidate scheme, thus preserving it temporarily in memory long enough for it to be tested for permanent status. The testing is effected by recognitive assimilation: we suggest that if the proto-scheme is rarely externally activated by recognition of its problem (or internally by schemes related to the satisfaction of other motivational dimensions), then its too infrequent differential re-production will not lead to its selection from other candidate schemes for permanent conservation. These two basic mechanisms already produce more than the conservation of solutions, which is the basic epistemic strategy; they also produce their differential conservation by selecting those solutions that would plausibly be recomputed (thus saving computation time) and rejecting those that would not (thus saving memory space). Thus, by imposing resource limitations on the pure memorisation strategy, we obtain a basic generate and select loop.

The generator part of the loop is what Piaget calls accommodation. Our remarks about the necessity of pre-adaptation at the primitive level of any problem-solving system suggest that there must be an initial layer of "universal primitive schemes" that allow for the composition of all necessary representation schemas and procedural schemes in a *restricted* problem universe. The schemas form the problem recognition parts of a scheme, the procedures its action parts. We further suggest that there are many distributed specialised basic problem-solving systems, and not a unique centralised one. This is related to the distribution of function observed over brain areas. Furthermore, contrary to our intuitive representation of the conscious or attention field as a kind of inner fovea or screen, the distribution of accommodation over many agencies suggests that the "conscious field" is not a "screen" but an active symbol system that can be driven and read by the different agencies in order to transmit problems and goals, to make selections amongst them according to motivational priorities and thus subordinate the different problem-solving sub-systems to common goals, and to communicate (sub)solutions. The conscious field with its imagery and inner language thus has the function of a common communication and control language for the coordination and cooperation, i.e. the division of labour between problem-solving sub-systems. Our central emphasis is, however, on the fact that the evolution of the epistemic strategy progressively constrains the generator to search less for elementary plausible moves and more within an organised knowledge net of previously constructed and selected schemes.

This is already the case with recognitive assimilation, as it constrains the generator to search first in the inner memory space of previously constructed schemes to "recognise" a known problem. If it fails, it must then attempt to construct a solution from primitive schemes and schemas. The latter, we must remember, are already elementary solutions to the problems of feature recognition and motor command coordination, constructed by the genetic system of the species. If again it fails, the problem cannot be solved with the limited resources available at this level of psychogenesis. These resources thus define the assimilatory power of the cognitive system at each level.

The recognition strategy only permits the re-application of past solutions. With generalising assimilation, this strategy is extended to new problems and becomes the first psychogenetic strategy *stricto sensu*, in that it is the first one to generate new solutions from old *acquired* solutions. First, we note again that it economises computation: instead of regenerating a complete solution, the whole computational power is concentrated on the sub-problem of modifying the small part of an old solution that must be accommodated to a similar but not identical problem. The gain may be very great: if we know nine out of the ten numbers of the combination of a safe, the size of the space we search is 10 instead of the original 10^{10}.

The generalisation strategy introduces some fundamental novelties that are characteristic of our thought and have deep roots in the epistemic memory strategies upon which it is based. Generalisation introduces heuristics and plausibility as a basis of thought, as there is no guarantee that a problem method may be generalised to an apparently similar problem. At a more profound level, cognition becomes intrinsically analogical and metaphorical as its constant apprehension of reality becomes that of assimilating the unknown to the known, i.e. apprehending the new as "a *kind* of the known with eventual *specific* differences". Diagnosing these specific differences allows accommodation to concentrate on them and thus regulates the metaphor. Thus there can exist no literal meanings in a cognitive system based on the epistemic strategy, but only more or less precisely regulated metaphorical ones, of which isomorphism is the extreme abstraction. Generalisation is based on recognition, and the latter on reproduction; this suggests that these strategies may have evolved from their precursors, psychogenetically or otherwise. At this fundamental level, we should note that a child who did not discover any of them would remain amnesic and thus never exploit the neurophysiological machinery on which they are based. The functional perspective thus suggests that they must have a strong hereditary basis.

If a new strategy opens new functional possibilities, it also generates new constraints: the greater the number of schemes acquired by the epistemic strategies, the longer it will take to search through them exhaustively. We suggest that the same strategy that produces this computational problem is re-applied internally to reduce it. The epistemic strategies accumulate knowledge about the external universe to reduce search in it. When they are reflexively applied to the internal epistemic universe they thus generate, they must accumulate knowledge about it (thus producing knowledge about knowledge, or meta-knowledge) to reduce search within the repertory of schemes that constitute this internal universe.

The similarities and differences between problems that are generated by the applications of generalising assimilation (this problem is a kind of known one, with the following specific differences) can thus be used to produce qualified accessibility links between the various specialisations and generalisations of the original scheme. This induces generalisation (accessibility) hierarchies between schemes, that are perhaps reflected as class inclusions between their problem universes. As was suggested earlier, these two generalisation hierarchies—the one based on functional descriptions, the other on structural ones—must be cross-linked by accessibility relations.

Thus an internal knowledge classification system evolves, founded on kind (genus) and specific differences. The various parallel generalisation hierarchies thus initially founded by reproductive assimilation then form psychogenetic filiations in which, from the functional perspective, inventions and discoveries made at different times, in different places and for different functions by the problem-solving systems can be captured by the growing knowledge net and classified—i.e. stored in an organised manner designed for their real-time access. Thus the problem of where to store a new acquisition is solved at the same time as that of how to retrieve it fast enough to produce a real-time response, by subordinating the solution of the first problem to that of the second. This imposes a design upon our cognitive system that evolves it into an automatic real-time solution-producing network. It also has the consequence that the classification system evolves with its contents, because its categories and reference indexes are produced by the evolution of its contents.

The last strategy we will examine is based on Piaget's reciprocal assimilation of schemes, and it corresponds to a particular psychogenetic version of the production of the new by combination of the old, characterised by Jacob (1981) as evolutionary tinkering. It is what might be called a quasi-recursive extension of the generalisation strategy, whose first phase, as we noted, contains a heuristic application of the recognition strategy.

When a new problem is encountered, it is first assimilated to a "familiar" scheme—i.e. a scheme that is high in the accessibility hierarchy. In relation to the present assimilatory power of the cognitive system, the novelty of the problem will or will not produce an obstacle to the (generalising) application of the scheme. This obstacle may be represented as a new (sub)problem, and in its turn be assimilated by a (sub)scheme, which may solve the problem, allowing the initial scheme to resume its application (until it meets an eventual obstacle), or it may recursively produce a new subproblem, etc. We called this "quasi-recursion" because there is, of course, no guarantee that the process will bottom out, i.e. that a level will be reached where a sub-scheme produces a solution. This again depends on the state of the knowledge net at the present level of expertise of the evolving cognitive system.

The effect of this strategy is to combine previous solutions that originally had different functions individually into a new solution with a new function, thus producing the functional emergence or synthesis that is central to constructivism. It again economises computational power in a new way, by concentrating the problem-solving only on the construction of the "reciprocal accommodation" interfaces between schemes that are necessary to combine them. Furthermore, it constrains the generator to look for high-level solutions first, producing a decomposition of the problem into high-level sub-problems. This again economises computation: if a total problem that entails one hundred basic operations can be decomposed into two solved sub-problems, then in the optimal case it can be solved in only one combination operation. The consequence is that the assimilatory power of the cognitive system grows in its evolution: the greater the number of high-level solutions it has acquired, the more problems it can solve in one step, which means that they have become non-problems: commonsense evidences.

We may note that limited resources impose a graduality on the acquisition of new knowledge that is related to stages. If in principle any notion may be, indeed must be, constructible from representational and procedural primitives at any time during evolution, it is in fact only attainable when it can be constructed in a limited number of operations by the composition of existing components. Thus, resource limitations impose a psychogenetic functional acquisition order on knowledge that is, in principle, independent of the structural complexity of the acquisition, but which depends on the combinability of its components. However, as the combination strategy produces and selects bigger components, this graduality may be masked, giving an illusion of saltationism. It is due to the fact that although the number of possible construction steps remains the same, the size of the components they assemble does not, and this is precisely the primal source of the power of the combination strategy of reciprocal assimilation. The psychological version of the combination strategy is half-way between the blind random combination of solutions that characterises evolution's "tinkering" and the perfectly knowledge-controlled combination that is the ideal of AI planning programs. The biological generator may randomly combine any gene with any other gene; these combinations are then found a function (if any) by selection. The combinations are determined neither by the nature of their components (the "means"), nor by that of the function to be filled (the "goal"). In contrast, the perfect artificial generator should plan in a space of pre-selected solutions, chosen for their pertinence to the goals and indexed for functional and structural co-accessibility, and use both this knowledge of the means and that of the goal to produce a solution. The planning phase with perfect knowledge should thus produce a plan that is faultlessly effective during the execution phase. The artificial planner thus starts with a function to be filled and finds a structure for it, while the biological generator does the converse.

The psychological generator of psychological constructivism is intermediate: it works in a space of unselected plausible knowledge; it thus meets unanticipated obstacles and interactions of solutions and has to replan, so planning and execution are recursively interwoven. With more skill (and thus more pre-selected and pre-adapted knowledge), it moves close to the ideal artificial planner: with less skill and knowledge, it moves closer to the blind biological generator. It is also in some sense intrinsically random, in that its constant problem-driven combinatorial activity inevitably produces unanticipated side-effects, some of which are found to be functional after the fact. Creative serendipity is thus the inevitable consequence of the intersection of independent telic sequences in the knowledge net that serves as an internal random generator in cognitive systems based on the epistemic strategy. When a new solution is thus generated by combining existing schemes in an association of specialists that cooperate to achieve a given task, this association becomes a candidate scheme upon which the reproduction and recognition strategies may act at this higher level to produce a new scheme (thus founding a new generalisation hierarchy precursor). A central consequence is that the "association links" between the component schemes are thus transformed into accessibility relations between schemes belonging to different existing filiations. Thus the knowledge net evolves from a state where it was composed of multiple independent filiations, whose elements were accessible from the outside by problems, to a state where these filiations are cross-linked by internal scheme-to-scheme accessibility relations.

One emergent effect of these progressive cross-connections is that when the same schemes originating from a variety of filiations repeatedly cooperate on a class of problems, their individual problem universes are integrated into a higher-level problem universe (such as that of geometry, for instance) and the schemes themselves are regrouped into stable agencies, some of which may, as we mentioned earlier, become structures. This provides the nucleus of a new accessibility classification of knowledge "by content". The emerging problem universes will ultimately be thematised to produce the various disciplines or branches of the classification of sciences, while their schemas and schemes will be thematised as the axioms and inference rules that result from the formalisation of a natural geometry, physics, arithmetic, etc. This classification process is of course much more general; the less formal domains of expertise are also regrouped into the sub-categories of arts, games, etc. We may again observe the role of language as an internal communication and control system: by making the classification system that is implicit in the evolving organisation of knowledge net explicit and evocable, it increases the real-time accessibility of pertinent knowledge. Much as it is faster to scan a list of titles than to read the corresponding texts, and to follow the references of a catalogue than to explore the web of cross-references from text to text, so the linguistic reference system allows an external access from scheme to scheme which would not have been possible in real time by following their accessibility relations within the knowledge net. Furthermore, the specialised combinatorial schemes that act on the objects of the linguistic universe may impose relations between schemes that are not related in the network. Thus if the generalisation hierarchies serve mainly to increase the adaptation of the cognitive system by increasing the accessibility of problems to schemes, the cross-connections that result from the combination strategy increase its inventiveness by making any scheme potentially accessible to any other scheme. The consequence is that inventions and discoveries accumulated in independent filiations may be combined in the same representational attention space and time to interact and produce the emergent properties of structural and functional synthesis. Cognitive systems are thus self-evolved for automatic "creativity", and the problem of creativity is not that of the generation of ideas, but of the control and exploitation of this spontaneous generation process to produce non-random "associations" of ideas. We all constantly produce new ideas, but few of them, alas, are good ideas: this is part of the cost of variation and selection systems.

ADAPTATION AND FUN AND GAMES
WITH THE SEMIOTIC FUNCTION

In our suggestion for a psychological constructivism, we have mainly developed Piaget's view of intelligence as a higher form of the adaptation of the organism to its environment. Arts, games, sports and the endless varieties of what Pascal calls "le divertissement" share with the more austere pure mathematics and fundamental research the property of being "goals" in themselves, with little adaptive motivation. They could be construed as cases of adaptation of the cognitive system to symbolic self-generated problem universes, but this does not answer the question of their biological adaptive value. To do this, we must first reframe Piaget's view: the cognitive system is a general-purpose problem-solving system evolved by the genetic system of the species, to which some of the problems of the adaptation of the organism's behaviour are delegated. Much of the ulterior adaptive power of this cognitive system accrues from the semiotic function, which allows the development of a new epistemic strategy based on the fast internal coordination of schemes, which makes it possible to predict and plan action and event sequences that have never been experienced before. But prediction and planning is a game of imagination or fiction: it contains the essence of the hypothetico-deductive. In its simplest form, it entails moving from present antecedents to imaginary future consequents—from this situation, what other situations can be anticipated or produced by action. We are one step away from the position and solution of self-generated imaginary problems. It has often been remarked that the cognitive system is a costly biological investment. So having it maintain and ameliorate its skills during its "free time" when the biological constraints of self-preservation are satisfied would be a good way of fully exploiting this instrument. One way to do this would be to have it simultaneously symbolically exercise and enhance its problem-solving skills, and at the same time exploit its knowledge of its environment by solving hypothetical adaptation problems. This would pre-adapt it to possible future situations by making it form new imaginary combinations of schemes. This may be the precursor of the "pre-adequation", as Piaget calls it, of some mathematical structures to reality. Pre-setting the evaluation function of the cognitive system so that it is "bored" when inactive, and so that it finds "functional pleasure" when exercising its skills, may be a way the genes discovered to make it more effective. But this means that by being able to freely pose its own imaginary problems, and thus to build its own self-generated symbolic problem universes, the cognitive system takes over control of its cognitive finalities, which may thus contradict those of the differential reproduction of the very genes that built it.

Finally, the cognitive system is a learning system; it must have some evaluation function of its majoration to guide this learning toward greater productivity. Some phenomenology that relates to this is that when a task is too difficult, no learning can occur, and this evaluation function may well be genetically pre-set to "anxiety" or "frustration", but when the task is too simple, no learning occurs either, and the evaluation is "boredom". So by systematically seeking amongst its various problem universes, symbolic or otherwise, those where its majoration is highest, the cognitive system takes control of its own evolution. It may thus specialise in some activity (from games to the "higher pursuits" of science), to the exclusion of all else. Thus the powers of the human cognitive system (sometimes described as admirable in essence, but deplorable in practice) that ultimately enabled it to adapt this environment to itself, rather than itself to the environment, may have originated from the over-utilitarian tricks of the genes that built it. It is typical of the paradoxes of functional logic that these very tricks may have allowed the cognitive system to escape the limitations of biological utility, and that this in return enabled it to master and use its environment, and finally to master the genes themselves.

REFERENCES

Cellérier, G. (1984). Of genes and schemes. *Human Development, 27,* 342–352.
Inhelder, B., & Piaget, J. (1980). Procedures and structures. In D. R. Olson (Ed.), *The social foundations of language and thought.* New York: W. W. Norton & Co.
Jacob, F. (1981). *Le jeu des possibles.* Paris: Fayard.
Minsky, M. (1967). *Computation, finite and infinite machines.* Englewood Cliffs, NJ: Prentice-Hall.
Minsky, M. (1986). *The society theory of mind.* New York: Simon and Schuster Books.
Piaget, J. (1972). *The principles of genetic epistemology.* London: Routledge & Kegan Paul. (First French ed., 1970.)
Piaget, J. (1985). *The equilibration of cognitive structures.* Chicago: The University of Chicago Press. (First French ed., 1975.)

2 Current Trends in Cognitive Development Research: Towards a New Synthesis

Harry Beilin
City University of New York

The current state of developmental psychology is such as surely to confuse a Kuhnian philosopher of psychology. Instead of a well-defined paradigm dominating the field since the ostensive displacement of influential structuralist theories like Piaget's and Chomsky's,[1] one sees a bewildering variety of development theories. There is social learning theory, schema theory, rule learning theory, skill theory, information processing theory, componential theory, activity theory, dialectical theory, neo-Piagetian theory, ecological theory, modularity views and much more. Gone are the days when the theoretical landscape was divisible into large areas defined simply by behaviourism, psychoanalytic theory, Gestalt theory and Piagetian theory. To some observers, theoretical discourse in developmental psychology has the sound of the Tower of Babel: many tongues and little communication among the speakers.

I see the situation differently. The diversity of theories is as described, but it shows only the surface features of the terrain, not its underlying unity. There is instead a meta-theoretical substructure that binds these diverse views together. Its character is defined by interest in the study of psychological functions, and its philosophical commitment is to functional explanation—in a word, to functionalism.

---

[1] I am not making a distinction between Chomsky's theory of generative grammar and structuralist theories in linguistics (such as those of Harris and Saussure). Only for the moment am I overlooking the functional aspects of Piaget's theory.

PHILOSOPHICAL FUNCTIONALISM

First, a word about the terms I employ. Although functionalism is used somewhat differently in psychology and philosophy, its meaning is more closely shared than with other disciplines (Block, 1980). In both philosophy and psychology, functionalisms are typified by a form of explanation based on common function. A second feature of functionalism is the assumption that mental states (with which current functionalisms are identified) are realised by a wide variety of physical systems. That is, establishing functional equivalence is not dependent on the identification of any particular physical system to which it is causally related. The difference of functionalist views from others is illustrated in explaining the nature of specific mental states. Functionalists grant, as would structuralists, that for a particular mental state or event, such as a particular pain, there is a single type of physical state that causes the pain. However, for all manner of pains, the functionalist asserts that what is common to them is functional; the physicalist says it is physical, and the behaviourist says it is behavioural.

In philosophical discourse, *functional explanation* "relies on a decomposition of a system into its component parts; it explains the working of a system in terms of the capacities of the parts and the way the parts are integrated into one another" (Block, 1980: 171). This view is particularly consonant with current practice in information processing analysis. It omits from consideration, however, reference to intentions or purpose—i.e. for what a part is designed or usually used. These differences are reflected in two very different philosophical positions. One position is primarily identified with the MIT computationalists, the other with West Coast (USA) cognitive scientists.

CURRENT FUNCTIONALISMS— COGNITIVE SCIENCE

The characterisation of mind represented by the group loosely identified with MIT cognitive science[2] holds that mind is both cognitive and computational—i.e. thinking is information processing. Thought is analysable into a set of component processes (inference, problem-solving, search, etc.). It is computational in that it involves symbol manipulation, and it relies on representation, which consists of a system of symbols with a syntax and formal rules of symbol manipulation. The semantics of the symbols connect thinking to the external world. In essence, thought has a language by which the symbols refer to objects and events in experience (Dennett, 1984).

---

[2] This group includes, among others, Fodor, Newell and Chomsky (Dennett, 1984).

The aim of the alternative view[3] is to explain "the intentionality of mental events in terms of systems of mental events of what in the end must be brain processes" (Dennett, 1984: 2). Not only does intentionality appear in the definition of mind, but the characterisation of mental events is not independent of the hardware that produces them. In the strongest version of this view there is no formal rule-governed computational level of description; thinking instead is holistic, emergent and organic (Dennett, 1984). At the heart of the controversy over the nature of mind among philosophical functionalists and cognitive scientists, then, is (1) the role of intentionality (as against causal–functional description), (2) the relation of mind to its physical realisation, and (3) the appropriate conception of thought as computational or holistic. The extremes of these positions are occupied by psychologists as well as by philosophers and linguists.[4] There is, however, a group of cognitive scientists who are dissatisfied with the extremes and seek a middle ground (Dennett and Boden are examples). Dennett's (1984) compromise proposal reflects developments by the so-called *new connectionists*. These models are based more on neural architecture and brain structure than on mind itself (i.e., they are closer to physicalism than functionalism). Their fundamental premise is that individual neurons (on which these models are based) do not transmit symbolic information but compute the values of threshold-like parameters that have no external-world semantic role (i.e. do not refer to things external). The system is thus computational, but not with respect of symbols located in a logically defined system. There are higher levels of description at which external-semantic (i.e. meaning-bearing) units are identified, but interactions at this level are statistical, emergent and holistic. The model for this approach is the influential work of Marr (1982) on vision, but it is applied instead to central systems (i.e. thought, problem-solving, planning). It is characterised as *rule-described* and is offered as an alternative to the *rule-governed* computational approach, i.e. rule-following behaviour described in the MIT version. (Fodor, 1983, also derives inspiration from Marr's work but uses it differently.)

Margaret Boden (1982), in her presentation at an earlier Piaget Archives course, offered a similar proposal for a *rapprochement* between what she referred to as the hermeneutic (continental) and objectivist (anglo-saxon) positions, in which the former stress the role of intentionality, the latter a positivist approach to objective fact and causal inference.

---

[3] These include Dawkins, Dreyfus, Searle, Taylor, Winograd, Hofstader and others (Dennett, 1984).

[4] Pylyshyn and Simon are typical of the computational group; Norman and Rumelhart of the other. Neisser was allied earlier to the former but under the influence of J. J. Gibson switched to the latter (Dennett, 1984).

Her theoretical move is to define representation as an intentional and hermeneutic concept (in contrast to MIT functionalists whose descriptions are designed to deny intentionality a place in their models). Boden also cites David Marr's computational model of vision, to emphasise that intensity gradients that are *computed* at lower levels of analysis are *interpreted* at higher levels of representation as lines, edges etc. She differs from Dennett in attempting to preserve symbol manipulation in her model. She accomplishes this by asserting that representation entails a process of interpretation that can only be described in the language of symbol manipulation. Boden's model for an empirical hermeneutics reflects the view shared with Dennett and others that the direction a theory of mind should take is to integrate computational models with more meaning-bearing elements, in order to account better for the structure and procedural complexities of thought. Parallel moves are evident in the proposals of a number of psychological functionalists.

PSYCHOLOGICAL FUNCTIONALISM

Psychological functionalism's concerns are seemingly broader than those of philosophical functionalism. They fit better into accounts of the origin of mind than of the nature of mind. The recent rejection by functionalists of structuralist accounts of the development of mind (like Piaget's and Chomsky's) are paradoxical in that these theories are based neither on particular material assumptions of mind (of brain or neural structure), nor are they dualist in any meaningful sense.

As with philosophical functionalism, psychological functionalism, reflected in most current developmental theories of mind, shows an emphasis—if not a complete reliance—on functional explanation. The significance of this development requires some spelling out and, as Piagetians can best appreciate, a historical view of the development of functionalism as a meta-theoretical tradition[5] (paradigm or world view) can best illuminate an understanding of its present form.

As much as Boden's (1982) middle ground in cognitive science defines an area between extremes, it does not capture some of the broader domains of inquiry in current cognitive developmental research, a portion of which is quite sceptical of the aims and claims of cognitive science.

---

[5] The view expressed considers functionalism to represent a set of theoretical assumptions and research strategies that bind a disparate group of theories into a common structure. It could be seen variously as a world-view (Pepper, 1942), a paradigm or disciplinary matrix (Kuhn, 1962), a research program (Lakatos, 1978) or a research tradition (Laudan, 1977). Laudan's assertion that the core elements of a tradition can undergo change (whereas in Lakatos's theory they do not) accords better with the historical and conceptual changes in functionalism.

Nevertheless, it is evident that the major influences on current theory in cognitive development have been shaped by functionalist thought. These influences are identified more with past psychological functionalisms than with current philosophical discourse. There have been three phases in the history of American psychological functionalism.[6]

Historical Roots of the New Functionalism

The beginnings of modern psychology are arbitrarily marked. The issues that Wundt and the early experimentalists addressed were not invented by them. What did mark a departure from earlier philosophical treatments was the experimental approach to issues of mind, not simply empirical attempts to understand human behaviour. The early experimentalists also created a new vocabulary to identify the directions in which their investigations were taking them. It was Titchener who used the term "functionalism" to identify a position that he opposed to his own structuralism. It was not a structuralism as we understand the term today, but a form of elementalism based on the analysis and inventory of the roots of consciousness, the starting point for which were the sensations, and the organisation of which was defined by laws of connection (association). Although some psychologists believed mind to be a process and not decomposable into sense data, it was William James who led the way in making explicit the nature of mind as process. Early functionalism reflected the confluence of a number of forces, most important of which was Darwin's evolutionary theory, which was taken up by G. Stanley Hall and James Mark Baldwin directly, and indirectly by others, including Dewey. Developmentalists linked Darwinism to the study of child psychology in the dictum that the mind grows and develops. Functionalists were concerned primarily with the conditions and nature of that development. Taking their models from biology, they called for the longitudinal study of human development. Thus evolutionary theory provided the impetus for the study of process and not just of the products of development and for the study of growth and structure in relation to function. On the Continent these ideas were given form by Claparède and Binet, among others. When functionalism began to coalesce as a movement in psychology, it did so around some well-delineated characteristics. (These were detailed in a classic paper by Angell in 1908.) The three principal tenets of the functionalist "movement" still inform current functionalist views, although not in quite the same ways (Beilin, 1983). First, in contrast to structuralist

---

[6] Although the emphasis in this presentation is on American psychology, I believe parallel developments can be discerned in Continental, British and other psychologies and would find parallels in other sciences, particularly the social sciences.

interest in the contents of mind, functionalist interest was in its operations, in the discovery of how mental processes work, what they accomplish and under what conditions they appear. The emphasis on mental functions arose because functionalists believed that only functions persist, whereas sensations and other contents in mind do not. Furthermore, just as common physiological functions might be carried out by different morphological structures, so the same mental function might be performed in different contexts. Early functionalism was also positioned within the ideology of the new experimentalism that took the form of a conjunction of cause and effect. From the start, functionalism was an S–R psychology, although to functionalists like Dewey and James mental entities were not isolated and unique. They were more like reflex circuits (for Dewey) and "circular reactions" (for Baldwin). Thus, early functionalism had the form of a cause–effect psychology of mental operations in context. Second, functionalism, despite its cause–effect experimentalism, placed considerable emphasis on the utility of mental processes with mental activity conceived as an adaptive feature of biological activity and organic evolution. Functionalism thus positioned the mind as a mediator between the environment and the needs of the organism. The emphasis on utility— that is, on mental activity and adaptation to environmental context—was a reflection of the influence, particularly in American psychology, of the pragmatism of Peirce, James, Dewey and Mead. It also occasioned the movement of psychologists out of the laboratory into applied settings: to the practical problems of measurement and testing, mental hygiene and school learning. Third, functionalism was concerned with the mind/body problem inherited from philosophy, but which for psychology had a direct application. The functionalist solution was to reject dualism (in which mind and body are of different orders, one not reducible to the other) by emphasising the interaction between the mental and the physical, as in psychosomatic medicine.

Early functionalism, despite considerable success in broadening the scope of psychological activity, did not survive the attack of one of its early adherents, John B. Watson and his behaviourism. The attack was in the form of a radical positivism, although the root of that positivism was in functionalism itself. What behaviourism primarily rejected was mentalism, the idea that the focus of psychology was the study of mental activity. Watson sought to expunge from the psychological lexicon all reference to consciousness, introspection, mental states, mind, imagery and the like. The only admissible data were the (objective) data of observed and measured behaviour and not subjective (introspectively noted) contents of mind. Behaviourism was as successful as it was, in no small part, because it appeared to enhance the effort to make psychology more like hard science (physics) and less like metaphysics. As behaviourist theories became more extended and complex, so did their problems. In the end, efforts were made to incorporate psychoanalytic theory into behaviourism (in the Hullian theories of Miller and Dollard), as well as Gestalt characteristics (in the molar behaviourism of Tolman) (see Gholson & Barker, 1985, for a description of these developments).

Functionalism nevertheless survived the behaviourism of this era, although in a diminished form, in the research of Woodworth and others in experimental psychology, and in the various applied psychologies. This *middle-era functionalism* was chastened in its confrontation with behaviourism, which had exposed a number of its fundamental features to view. (Hilgard, 1956, was one of the principal chroniclers of its program.) Hilgard, for one, emphasised the eclectic nature of functionalism with its tendency to borrow freely from other traditions. At the time, in the 1930s, 1940s and 1950s, it was tolerant of introspective methods (while behaviourism was not), as well as of objective observation and measurement and of case studies and mental tests, and it was willing to cross the boundary between pure and applied psychology. It accepted multiple origins for psychological activity and avoided universals (i.e. psychological "laws") that failed to take into account all relevant variables and contexts. The emphasis in functionalism on continuity of function led to the study of situational dimensions (principally to task variables) and to process differences. The emphasis on dimensionality and continuity resulted in the rejection of discontinuities and typologies, and in the disposition to reject stage-related theories (like Gesell's), which were enormously popular with the applied professions and the public.

There was a curious split among functionalists with respect to method. The preferred method of study was still experimental, but applied functionalists were more eclectic in their methods. American functionalism of the 1940s and 1950s on the surface appeared to be theoretically neutral, but its biases were still very much inclined toward associationism. Toward the end of this era many newer developments were encouraged by functionalism. To put it another way, a number of newer developments in psychological theory were based on assumptions that were clearly functionalist in nature. This was evident in the models of the newer mathematical psychology, in the functional analysis of Skinner (essentially dimensional analysis) and in the probablistic functionalism of Brunswick. But this functionalist era was coming to a close in the late 1940s and 1950s. It was the end not only of middle functionalism but behaviourism as well. The end came with the cognitive revolution. Although middle-functionalism was an unspectacular era, having been overshadowed in large measure by behaviourism, particularly by Hull–Spence theory and by gestaltism in the work of Werthheimer, Kofka, Kohler and Lewin, it was important in preserving a point of view and a type of analysis that emphasised functional activity, context, adaptation, process, experimentalism and catholicity of method. For the most part, what was lost or considerably diminished by behaviourism was the concern with mentalism, although Woodworth insisted on the importance of organismic variables, and Tolman's molar behaviourism incorporated notions of cognitive maps. Lewin's theory and Tolman's molar behaviourism in particular clearly anticipated the start of the new cognitive era.

The Cognitive Era

Two periods may be discerned in the advent of the cognitive revolution. In its formative period, the influence of gestalt psychology was primary in its emphasis on organisation in mind and nature, and in its rejection of the assumptions of positivism. Phenomenalist theories also played a role, as did Piaget's pre-1950s investigations.

In the era following World War II, the cognitive era began in earnest. In the 1950s, behaviourism was already in difficulty even within its own constituency, with Osgood and the Kendlers' introduction into Hull–Spence theory of (principally verbal) mediational processes. The significance of this is that it began to erode behaviourist abhorrence of mentalist concepts, although behaviour theory was still closely tied to the tenets of logical positivist forms of explanation. The post–World War II reports of Piaget's theories were an important source for change, particularly in developmental psychology. The newer ego-oriented Freudian theories of Rapaport, Hartmann and Erikson were also influential in changing attitudes toward cognitive processing and structure, as was Freudian theory itself. What really moved the field, however, was the emerging influence of information theory, cybernetic theory and most critically the growing computer revolution. Hypothesis testing theories of Bruner, Levine and others pushed behaviour theories even further into the background. These influences converged, so that by the time Miller, Galanter and Pribram's (1960) seminal work (*Plans and the structure of behavior*) appeared, the cognitive revolution was well under way. What was needed to give behaviourism the *coup de grace* was Chomsky's (1959) devastating attack on Skinner's *Verbal behavior*.

It is well to realise that two revolutions occurred during that era. The first, the advent of cognitivism, persists; the other, structuralism, does not. The principal contribution of cognitivism was the return of mental constructs to psychological theorising. It became not only acceptable, but desirable to include mentalism in all manner of theory, to the extent that cognition has become the keystone to the explanation of most psychological phenomena. Radical positivism, which accompanied behaviourism, was long dead, and it was not long before logical positivism was also swept away by "world-view" philosophical theories (like Kuhn's) that to some extent gave legitimacy to the revolutionary transition to cognitivism from methodological and conceptual behaviourism. The rise of cognitivism brought structuralism with it, in the form of Chomskyan linguistic theory, Piagetian theory, psychoanalytic theories, neo-Gestalt theories, and allied structuralist theories such as those of Levi-Strauss in anthropology and Parsons in sociology. Even some tried and true functionalists such as Bruner were for a time drawn to the structuralist assumptions of Piagetian and like theories, in the era when structuralism swept through intellectual circles in the sciences and humanities, spurred on by the spectacular success of the molecular biologists.

What structuralists achieved was a radical shift in the form of acceptable explanation for psychological phenomena. The introduction of mental constructs into psychological theory meant that there could be no forms of explanation based on direct observation and measurement. Mental entities could only be inferred from patterns of behaviour or from experimental manipulations in which input–output conditions allowed such inferences. It encouraged forms of experimentation other than those involving the specification of antecedent–consequent events that could be related by a covering law (i.e. logical positivist causal forms of explanation). The use of formal (i.e. logical and mathematical) models of explanation by structuralists was not unique, but there is little doubt that there was a greater disposition for structuralists to make use of them.

The progressive introduction and extension of the computer model in psychology gave impetus to modes of explanation different from the traditional causal models in experimental psychology. Information processing and artificial intelligence approaches that utilize simulation techniques and computer experiments have shifted the bases of making inferences about the nature of mind. The form of explanation is essentially functional, although, as will be seen, it is not entirely free of structuralist features.

The radical shift to functional explanation and a concomitant rejection of many features of structuralist theorising characterises the present era in cognitive development research, and in psychology generally. The character of the new era is best identified by a new functionalism, because in many respects it introduces important departures from earlier functionalisms, at the same time retaining significant features of earlier functionalisms.

The New Functionalism

Although information processing theories have been important in creating the present functionalist tradition, the diversity of views in the new functionalism suggests an equal diversity of origins. The theorists covered by the rather broad functionalist umbrella often have great difficulty in accommodating to one another's positions, which is illustrated in the case of the ecological psychologists, such as the Gibsons, who as self-styled functionalists (Gibson, 1982) stand in clear opposition to the goals and methods of computational psychologists, who are also functionalists.

What nevertheless binds this group together, first and foremost, is the commitment to functional explanation, and partial or complete rejection of structuralist forms of explanation. As pointed out earlier, functional explanation is ideally made with respect to common functions exercised among discrete individuals or species, or continuity of function among the same individuals in different contexts. To use biological analogy, if we were interested in judging whether animals "think" as humans do, the judgement could be made in two ways. It could be made for one on the basis of common physical structure across species, where it had been established in the first place that those structures were causally related to human cognitive function. This would be a structural analysis. By contrast, in functional analysis the judgement that both species think would be inferred if it were shown that both species engage in the same types of problem-solving, search, planning or related functions. Thus, if similar functions are carried out by otherwise dissimilar species or individuals, and again, if it could be shown that the functions in humans were critically related to human thought, then by a similar process of inference one could assume that the two species have the same capacities, despite differences in underlying physical structure. According to functionalists, because different physical (and cognitive) structures can yield the same functions, one's primary concern should be with function—particularly if functions are more critical than structures to species or individual adaptation. A second justification for functionalism is the challenge addressed to the ontological status of many inferred cognitive structures, i.e. to their psychological reality. Thirdly, there is the question of the necessity or even desirability of arguments of the type that reduce psychological phenomena to cognitive structure. In theory, such reductionism is not excluded from psychology; quite the contrary, it is demanded by non-dualist science. Rather, the argument goes, it is not at present scientifically possible, with existing facts and technology, to make such reductions reliably. For these and other reasons, functionalist methodology is said to offer the best basis for explanation in psychology, and most cognitive developmental research is now committed to this type of explanation, either explicitly or implicitly. As will be evident from later discussion, however, an increasing number of theorists are attempting to encompass both functional and structural forms of explanation in their theories, despite the claims of some Kuhnian-type arguments (e.g. Overton & Reese, 1973) that distinct world-views, which structuralist and functionalist meta-theories represent, are essentially incompatible and therefore not open to synthesis (Overton, 1984).

If functional analysis is based on common (i.e. similar or identical) function, then research is most likely to focus on the delineation, variation and control of such function, and that, in fact, is the case in developmental research. Although a clear-cut definition of psychological function is not possible, it refers in general to the characteristic action of an entity as part of a system. Piaget (1971) refers to function in two senses: one entails the notion of mathematical function $(y = fx)$—the symbolic representation of an operation that carries out a set of transformations. The other is closer to the sense of a biological function, which refers to the activation or activity of a structure (both physical and psychological). Although Piaget (1971) wrote that functional analysis was the starting point for a structural description and analysis, reflecting the relation of structure and function, functionalists, in the main, simply avoid or reject outright such structural analyses and, as indicated, question the psychological reality of derived structure. Functionalists typically follow the bottom-up approach implied in Piaget's characterisation of his own method and tend to reject top-down theory-driven research strategies. Despite Piaget's claims, they ordinarily interpret Piaget's models to be theory- and not data-driven.

Structuralist theories of the Piagetian, Chomskyan and Levi-Straussian type are characterised pejoratively by functionalists as grand, global and all-encompassing, to indicate that such theories are designed to capture the qualities of universal and invariant structures that cut across large domains of knowledge and function. The reasons for rejecting these views are many. For one, functionalists argue that there is little empirical support for universal structure. If there is universality or invariance, it is likely to be in function (a point of agreement with Piaget and his notion of functional invariants, although not in agreement with Piaget's choice of invariants). Second, in place of universality and cross-domain invariance, functionalists argue for domain specificity. Whatever generalisations are made for behaviour, they are to be made within domain boundaries or across limited domains, and in the form of generalisations close to the data of observation at that. A third claim is that universalist assertions neglect the effect of context on function. Such contexts range from limited task demands to the broadest social, cultural and historical influences, and in developmental contexts to (temporal) generational influences.

Structuralist analysis tends towards constructivism, towards building systems of structure, and is typically—as in the Piagetian case—mapped-on to larger formal (i.e. logical and/or mathematical) frameworks. The preferred methods of functional analysis, at least in functionalisms that carry over elements of earlier empiricist (i.e. behaviourist and association-ist) practice, tend toward methods in which functional systems such as problem solving are broken-down into their functional components, i.e. encoding, memory and representations. The intent is to reduce knowledge of functioning to the smallest and most meaningful units of analysis with the desire to keep as close to the data of observation as possible. In the process, however, they have introduced into their theories theoretical constructs that are identical to the constructs in structuralist theories (e.g. symbolic representation).

In sum, the primary feature that distinguishes the new functionalism and is shared by those in this tradition is an emphasis on functional analysis. The new functionalism also accepts the cognitive tradition's emphasis on mentalist constructs, in a manner reminiscent of earlier functionalism, but the constructs are now more central to their theories. The new functionalism is distinguished further by arguments for domain specificity, for generalisations close to the data of observation, and for bottom-up theory building in preference to top-down theory. Additionally, there is an emphasis on context-related influences on function, although within functionalism there are wide differences in the commitment to contextualism. Lastly, there is the willingness on the part of some functionalists to entertain structuralist constructs and various structuralist assumptions. Although these define the principal commonalities among functionalists, there are important differences among them particularly in the willingness or ability to incorporate structuralist features into their theories.

Within the new functionalism, five groups are discernable: (1) information processing theorists; (2) a group strongly influenced by information processing, but who avoid actual computer simulation; (3) contextualist/ ecological theorists, and (4) neo-nativists. There is another group (5), who are probably best characterised as part of the new synthesis, who attempt to integrate functionalist and structuralist analyses. Included among these are the neo-Piagetians, in and out of Geneva, and a more widely diverse group who wish to retain basic Piagetian insights yet take advantage of newer developments in theory and data collection. I will discuss each of these and delineate their claims as well as their arguments against the Piagetian research tradition, and what I see as their own limitations.

Information Processing Models

Information processing theories had their origins in cybernetics, game theory, communications theory and information theory and reached full fruition with the development of computer hardware and computer programs. The information processing group is itself diverse, but the psychologists led by Simon and Newell are typical. They base their theories and models on a set of suppositions, in addition to those already specified as functionalist. The mind, in their conception, is a processing system in which knowledge is represented in the form of symbols, and processing is fundamentally symbol manipulation. A variety of formalisms are used to characterise cognition and cognitive processing. These take the form of

(1) a computer language with a precisely defined syntax and set of procedures (production systems, which are popular with the Carnegie-Mellon group are typical of such languages); (2) graphic models (such as flow designs and decision trees that represent the temporal course of processing and embody particular assumptions or theories as to the organisation of knowledge in memory), which are extensively utilised; (3) higher-order concepts, such as plans, scripts, schemata and frames that embody larger units of cognitive organisation. Additionally, information processing research is based on the use of a variety of procedures such as chronometric methods, protocol analysis, rule assessment methods and eye movement analysis that offer insight into the processing characteristics of cognition. Recently, these models have come in for serious criticism on the grounds that serial processing models, which are typical of Carnegie–Mellon systems, are a poorer reflection of the nature of many cognitive processes than parallel processing models. Much effort is presently being expended on the development of the latter models.

The information processing approach more than any other aspect of contemporary functionalism shows the extent of departure from past functionalisms, particularly of the behaviourist variety, in their explicit use of a variety of mental constructs. Possibly more surprisingly, these essentially functionalist theories employ a variety of devices more characteristic of structuralist theories. Thus, Boden (1982) is able to point to the commonality between Piaget and computational psychology in their logicist bias and preference for logical and mathematical formalisms. She argues further that some differences between Piaget and information processing theories are more terminological than real, particularly with regard to symbolisation and representation. For example, the Piagetian claim that representational intelligence does not manifest itself until the appearance of symbolic representation is deceptive, she says, since he also claims that the semiotic function makes its appearance in the earliest months of life with the manifestation of the signal and index in a system of signification. Boden's claim is true with respect to the nature of representation in general, but it minimises the Piagetian argument that representational forms are manifest in a developmental sequence and created by distinctively different processes. Although symbolic representation for Piaget is more akin to symbol manipulation in computational psychology, other forms of representation in Piaget's theory are more consistent with proposals made by analogue theorists like Shepard (1978), who claim that imaginal processes are not reducible to propositional (i.e. symbolic) forms of representation. Anderson's (1976, 1978) effort to incorporate perceptual processing components into a propositional (symbol) based processing system aims at retaining the symbolic metaphor, while Kosslyn's (1978, 1980) two-factor theory (both analogue and propositional) comes closer to reflecting Piaget's conception of representation, although it still omits the equivalent of sensorimotor schemes.

The use of formalisms (even those that entail significant structural devices, such as decision trees modelled after linguistic top-down forms, or semantic networks) is not out of keeping with the use by functionalists in the past of—usually mathematical—formalisms. Where the new functionalists differ from earlier functionalists is in the structure-like architectures that appear to embody structuralist assumptions. What is evident, however, is that the assumptions underlying much of information processing theory are associationistic (Beilin, 1983). Production systems operate very much on a modified stimulus–response model. If a condition C (read stimulus) is met, it triggers an action (C→A) (read response), etc. As Fodor (1983) points out as well, defining computation in constructivist associationist terms (i.e. mental life is put together from relatively simple and uniform psychological elements) results in a "shotgun marriage" with inherent contradictions. In traditional associationism, association is a mechanical relation among mental contents, not a computational relation defined over them. (That is, it is characterised in dynamic relations of attraction, repulsion, assimilation, etc., instead of being connected by rule.) Computational theory provides the sort of mental architecture that traditional associationism was in fact designed to replace. The heart of the difficulty with the associationist thesis is its fundamental difficulty in accounting for the ontogeny of mental events, i.e. it lacks a learning mechanism that can profit from experience. Fodor's criticism, however, overlooks the Carnegie–Mellon proposal for self-modifying production systems best represented in a developmental framework in the work of Klahr (1984). Self-modifying production systems "describe the developmental process that yields increasingly sophisticated *quantitative* [my emphasis] knowledge" (Klahr, 1984: 103). The basic model is of a condition–action production system in which three processes are said to operate: (1) discrimination, which entails adding more in its condition side; (2) generalisation, wherein a production is made more general by either reversing a discrimination by creating fewer condition elements, or replacing specific conditions with variables of another class; and finally (3) *composition*—when a set of productions repeatedly fires in the same sequence, they can be combined into a single production, by deleting steps, etc. These mechanisms are said to construct higher-order nodes that correspond to common elements in the combined systems. Klahr (1984) argues that self modifying systems describe developmental processes and not merely learning sequences on the basis that some self-modifying changes occur spontaneously without some external agent instructing, inducing or urging the change. But in an example given by Klahr, change occurs by virtue of repeated firings of a sequence, i.e. repetition, presumably in response to some external demand. Redundancy reduction occurs not by some principled rule, but, as in the development of a skill or a habit such as cycling, by greater economy through deletion. Changes that occur in such systems are said, however, to be qualitative and not merely quantitative, but Klahr's argument in the example given seems to be that changes in procedures that occur through redundancy reduction are quantitative yet lead to qualitative changes in performance. Local changes "yield global effects and from incremental modifications come structural reorganisations" (Klahr, 1984: 131), which is a notion long associated with incremental and atomistic learning theories. Again, although information processing theorists are willing to posit patterning and regularity in development, their theoretical assumptions hark back to associationism and traditional learning principles.

Self-modification ostensibly takes the place of a Piagetian self-regulating system, yet it offers an explanation devoid of indicating the motive force in development, except that implied by "specificity" i.e. an implied law of parsimony and "strength", that which, "has led to the most desirable functioning in the past" (Klahr, 1984: 126), reminiscent of Thorndike's "law of effect". Both notions are intimately tied to associationism. Thus Klahr has succeeded in "mechanising" (Klahr, 1984: 132) Piaget's "reflective abstraction" (at least aspects of it), although again by wedding associationist and learning theory principles to computational theory. The emperor truly does have new clothes, but they are fashioned out of the same old rags he had before. What we are given is a theory that offers us no idea as to what impels the system to run nor what directs it (Kessen, 1984: 10). The program of taking Piagetian concepts such as "reflective abstraction", which neo-functionalists assert is vague, and attempting to specify its nature is clearly a laudable goal. Achieving it by means of a computational strategy may be the most appealing strategy for the moment, but tying it to associationistic learning theory models is a dubious tactic.

Information processing theories make the explicit claim (Simon, 1972) that their models are adaptive systems that take on the shape of the environment. Information processing studies, however, rarely go beyond specification of limited task environments, based on task analysis (e.g. conservation tasks, balance beam problems, chess, samples of expert knowledge). Contextualists fault computational theories on these grounds and on their lack of concern for the effect of context on performance. Before considering contextualist arguments, some comment is in order on a variety of developmental theories influenced by information processing theories.

Computionally Inspired Theories

In this set of theories are the views of investigators such as Nelson,

Mandler, Flavell, Markman, Trabasso, Brainerd, Paris, Siegler, A. Brown and Sternberg. Aside from their common functionalism, these investigators adopt and emphasise limited features of information processing theory. What is also interesting is that often enough the organising constructs of their theories are adapted from structuralist theory, although utilised in a functionalist framework. In current *schema* theories, for example, schemas are conceived by functionalists as dynamically organised representations (as in event representations). Schemata are conceived of as data-driven and environmentally contingent, and their temporal aspects are stressed, in contrast, for example, with the schemes of Piagetian theory that are logically defined organisations. *Rule* systems are another example. As Siegler (1983) uses the concept, they are either representations of behaviour patterns inferred by the experimenter from observations (rule descriptions), or they correspond to what leads to observed behaviour (rule-governed behaviour). As used by functionalist theorists, these constructs are another vehicle for representing the regularities inherent in process-like characterisations of a cognitive system. *Scripts* are structure-like entities that describe predetermined sequences of action that reflect event knowledge and the ordered sequencing of that knowledge. In Nelson's (1985) use of scripts there are three levels of analysis related to one another: event representations, scripts and event (real-world) structure. Scripts in this conception are the functionalist counterparts of categorically and hierarchically (i.e. structurally) organised world knowledge. *Strategies, heuristics* and *hypothesis testing* convey quite directly functions and procedures by which tasks are carried out in systematic fashion; they have been extensively studied in psychology (Bruner, Goodnow & Austin, 1956) as well as in developmental psychology (Gholson, 1980). Furthermore, the emphasis on *skills* within current discussions of cognitive development is extensive. Skills represent more than older notions of habit and allied competencies. They characterise within the current functionalist tradition organised systems that are designed to take the place of the logical structures of Piaget's theory (e.g. Fischer & Pipp, 1984).

What these functionalist constructs have in common is the attempt to devise developmental theories that avoid structuralist–logicist forms of description and explanation. Even as they utilise constructs derived from structuralist theory, they give them a functionalist interpretation. In the case where notions derived from empiricist theory (e.g. skills) are adopted, they give them a more systematic function, without going to the point of giving them a structuralist interpretation.

Contextualism

In the past few years contextualist meta-theory has attracted considerable attention in conceptualisations of cognitive development. The range of adherents to this position is surprisingly broad. What they have in common, as the name implies, is the concern that theories of cognition reflect the effects of context on cognitive function. These theorists include those who are ecologically oriented, such as Neisser (1984) and Eleanor Gibson (1982), who are unsympathetic with the information processing tradition; Zimmerman (1983), who follows Bandura in the social learning tradition; Baltes and his group (Dixon & Baltes, 1986) who are dialectically directed, and finally the neo-Vygotskyans (Bruner, 1980; Cole & Scribner, 1974; Glick, 1985). The contextualist influence is also evident in the use made of Wittenstein's philosophy, as in the work of Rosch (1973, 1978).

The contextualist tradition places its emphasis first on person–environment interactions. In contrast to early environmentalist views that treated the learner as passive, current contextualists consider the individual as active in his encounter with the environment. Context changes the individual; the individual changes the context. Thus, individuals affect their own development (Lerner, Hultsch & Dixon, 1983). This is true even of Soviet psychologists who have retreated considerably from earlier copy–theory views of the origin of thought. Secondly, events are viewed as holistic. Experience is said to consist in events that have the qualities of totalities that are not reducible to discrete elements. This view is shared by some cognitive scientists of a holistic stamp but, as indicated, earlier, not by the majority whose method of choice is to decompose mental processing into discrete components. To holists, concepts are embedded within layers of larger units of experience. The concept of the event, for example, is highly dependent on its content, as well as on features of the environmental setting, i.e. its context-relatedness (Zimmerman, 1983). Against universalism, there is a commitment to at least a weak form of relativism in the assertion that there is no simple elemental form of knowledge, and that knowledge is relative to specific purposes and contexts. The claim is made, too, that other theories neglect individual as well as cultural diversity. Although some contextualists agree with stage theorists that age-related changes are qualitative and discontinuous, they are inclined to argue that these changes are due to age-related changes in social context or to maturational changes, at least in infancy. At the same time, they reject what they consider to be various forms of reductionism: to associationism, even of the mediationist type; to cybernetic processing (of the Piagetian kind); to computer programs, and to logical structuralism (again of the Piagetian type). Phenomenalism represents an important component in these views. The hermeneutical tradition, with its emphasis on the interpretation of historical events, and the move away from causal argument to interpretative analysis has also influenced current contextualist thought.

Although the influence of contextualism on contemporary thought has been considerable, its importance has varied for different theorists and within different disciplines. Within linguistics, for example, contextualist thinking has affected the rise of pragmatics and discourse analysis as against the study of syntax and generative grammars. Emphasis has generally shifted away from the evaluation of truth conditions to the study of meaning; away from causal relations to that of interpretation.

The shift in anthropology away from structuralist theories of the Levi-Strauss type has resulted in a shift back to relativism and contextualism and correspondingly away from the analysis of symbolic forms to emphasis on the significance of cultural practice. Parallel developments are to be found in developmental psychology in the emphasis on cognitive processes as they occur and develop in naturalistic and ecologically significant contexts, and in the differences in cognitive response to differential patterns of cultural or environmental pressure.

Neo-Nativists

The functionalists to be considered next are the most recent to arise on the scene in developmental psychology, or more precisely, to appear again on the scene. They are the neo-nativists, represented, among others, by Keil, Gelman, Spelke, Sternberg and by Carey (1980). Fodor, although not a developmentalist, has much to say about developmental psychology. His position has its origin in Chomsky's nativist claims about language, in particular for universal grammars. Fodor (1983) differs from Chomsky, however, in arguing for the "modularity of mind"—that is, for domain specificity and a computation-like faculty psychology. He rejects Chomsky's consideration of language as a cognitive processing system, except in the most limited sense. Instead, language is seen as a natively specified direct processing system, as is the case with perception, both of which are computational. Fodor believes, however, that thought and belief systems are non-modular and that neither cognitive science nor any psychological discipline has made any progress in their understanding. Chomsky, on the other hand, still holds to the belief in *general* cognitive structures and a nativist account of language origins (Chomsky, 1984).

Nativist accounts of cognitive development currently take the form of discussions on the nature of constraints in development and of developmental change. Typical is Keil's (1984) analysis of a priori constraints in the development of knowledge, while at the same time stressing learning as the focus of developmental change. He emphasises content-bound as against content-free knowledge, and local structural description in contrast to computational routines or general learning procedures. He favours the Fodor view of a relatively small number of specialised cognitive faculties, as well as some more general learning procedures (but not all-purpose learning mechanisms), and limited forms of representation. He favours "pre-storage" (meaning a priori given structures) to computational (i.e. processing) procedures as a model for cognitive development, and he believes that language acquisition data, as well as research on the learning of experts and novices, support these conclusions. Likewise, the recent work of Gelman and her colleagues (Gelman & Baillargeon, 1983; Spelke, 1983) emphasises the nativist origins of number knowledge, and the assumptions underlying Mounoud's (1981; Mounoud & Hauert, 1982) work are consistent with recent nativist trends.[7]

A singular feature of these recent nativist developments is that they are occurring in a generally functionalist framework. Thus, although Keil argues for a shift to understanding more about learning processes, he refers to local learning descriptions and to the presumed biological and structural constraints that exist within a domain. Knowledge of metaphor suggests to him, for example, that when knowledge in a particular domain becomes sufficiently differentiated, new relations are revealed with other domains, through analysing similarities, etc., but not on the basis of any relations that would unite these domains into single or holistic entities by common principle or structure. There are a number of instances in Keil's proposals, however, that indicate a tendency to unite structuralist and functionalist considerations, as in the structuralist organisation of knowledge (tree structures that obey hierarchical constraints) with domain specificity and local learning. Developmental change occurs by virtue of the structure of concepts themselves and not because of shifts to more rule-generated knowledge, i.e. not to general changes in cognitive ability (as is proposed in both Vygotskyan and Piagetian formulations) (Keil, 1984). As we will see, Keil's proposals represent a trend towards uniting structuralist and funtionalist elements into a single theory of cognitive development that has been most evident among the neo-Piagetians to date. This restriction is no longer the case, however.

NEO-PIAGETIAN THEORY

Developments in functionalist thought are increasingly a challenge to the

---

[7] I might myself be placed in the nativist category on the basis of arguments I have made (Beilin, 1971) that some—(probably weak)—form of nativist (i.e. maturationist and preformationist) view of development must hold to account for invariant (universal) orders in development. Some such account also accords best with the apparent triggering of innate structured response dispositions that result from the successful effects of training on conservation derived from *every* form of training designed on either theoretical or pragmatic grounds (Beilin, 1978). I differ from (at least some) nativists in holding that constructivist views are not incompatible with nativism. Thus, innate features of the biological system act to constrain and channel the constructions that occur with experience and actions on the world.

Piagetian tradition, considered as structuralist theory. The idea that functionalism could be wedded to structuralist thinking, however, was evident in the earliest neo-Piagetian efforts to blend Piagetian theory with that of information processing theory. The first efforts were those of Pascual-Leone (1976). Robbie Case's development of Pascual-Leone's theory also provides this approach's most extensive experimental test (Case, 1985). Case's theory (1985: 115–116) is an amalgam of four influences: Piaget's theory, Baldwin's theory, information processing theory and his own contribution. There is some overlap, as expected, between Piaget and Baldwin. What is preserved from Piaget is the stage concept (four stages), with operational structures in equilibrium at the end of a stage ("stable systems"); the differential products of a stage, which when integrated, become the building blocks of the next stage; circular reactions ("control structures") that arise in sequence in infancy; and, the same general progression (vertical decalage) observed in later stages. From information processing comes decomposition ("parsing into components"), means–end analysis, representation (encoding) as inborn capacity, and procedural knowledge. In his own contribution, Case accounts for major shifts in thinking by the coordination of executive structures of similar complexity that differ in function and internal form.

Case's and Pascual-Leone's attempts to integrate Piagetian theory and information processing are approached differently in another effort to integrate Piagetian theory, hypothesis testing theory and information processing (Gholson & Beilin, 1979). There have been many other attempts to integrate elements of Piaget's theory with other theories: with Gibson (Russell, 1984), with Marx (Wartofsky, 1983), and with other elements of information processing theory (Fischer & Pipp, 1984). The integration of structuralist and functionalist theory goes in two directions: (1) some Piagetians integrate elements of other theories with Piaget's theory (e.g. Liben, Scholnick, Dien, Noelting, Laurendeau and Pinard); (2) others integrate Piagetian theory into other theories, principally functionalist in nature e.g. Bower, Harris, Gelman, Neisser and others too numerous to mention).

THE CHALLENGE TO THE PIAGETIAN TRADITION

There is no question that Piagetian theory has, during the past decade in particular, faced some serious challenges. Most of these have come from functionalist theories, although the criticisms have differed depending on whether they come from computational psychologists, contextualists or nativists, as already described. I will summarise these criticisms and follow with an indication of how I feel Piagetian theory can accommodate them, without destroying the integrity of the Piagetian tradition.

Theory change in developmental psychology traditionally takes two forms. On the one hand, changes are positive, in the sense that they represent programmatic and substantive change in prevailing patterns of thought through the introduction or reintroduction of ideas not currently in fashion. Often enough, on the other hand, theoretical change is accompanied by attacks on prevailing theoretical orientations. This was true in the structuralist revolution, with its attack on positivism and empiricism; it is also true of the neo-functionalist's attack on structuralist theory, particularly Piaget's. Along with the attack is the offer of one or another form of functionalist theory. Almost a model of this "the King is dead, long live the King" strategy is Shweder's (1984) review and rejection of the theoretical assumptions underlying developmental theory of the type that Piaget's represents. Shweder's critique is organised around a distinction between "enlightenment" and "romantic" theories of mind. The enlightenment view holds that the mind of man is intendedly rational and scientific, its products are universally applicable and rationality offers a standard for judging validity and worth. Unity and uniformity are its themes. The program of the enlightenment position is to discover universals, based on a conception of deep structure, in which notions of progress and development are central and the history of ideas is perceived as a struggle between reason and unreason.

The "romantic" view is that ideas have their origin neither in logic nor in empirical science and fall beyond the purview of deductive and inductive reason. Instead of being rational or irrational, ideas and practices are *non-rational*. Central to the romanticist thesis is the concept of culture and the arbitrariness of experience. The relation of deep structure to surface content and local context is one of subordination to the latter. Paradigms, cultural norms and the social order provide the "framework" for understanding experience. Action is seen as expressive, symbolic and semiotic. There are strong anti-normative, anti-developmental presuppositions that result in the view that the history of ideas is a sequence of committed ideological fashions (Shweder, 1984). In this view science (especially social science) is 90% ideology.

Piaget, says Shweder, is clearly in the enlightenment tradition in holding that man is by intention rational and scientific, "striving to figure out what causes what in the world, striving to adapt or accommodate intelligence to the demands of common reality, striving for consistency among ideas, striving to build up or 'construct' a set of canons (rules of logic, principles of scientific method) for regulating one's own thought or for deciding whether a piece of one's own thinking is successful or unsuccessful" (Shweder, 1984: 49).

What exercises Shweder most about Piaget's enlightenment views is not that he may be wrong about stage-like development or defining the operational capacities of children and adults, but that he overlooks the elements in children's minds of most interest to romantics. In this vein, he takes Piaget's canons and inverts them. By doing so he defines an alternative canon for a romantic view of the child's mind. Placed in another interpretive framework, the "romantic" tradition is, in essence, functionalist. There are five inversions in this canon. (1) Instead of self-constructed knowledge (Piaget's view), there is other-dependent learning. This is based on the assumption that most of what people know is learned from others; (2) instead of rational man there is non-rational man. The child is immersed in a "framed" universe of constitutive presuppositions, customs, traditions, rituals and arbitrary classifications, which the Piagetian literature completely ignores; (3) instead of progressive development there is frame switching. Growing up is not becoming more rational but entering a new "frame of mind"; (4) instead of personal constraint there is interpersonal constraint. It is not apparent, says Shweder, that the individual mind left to its own devices seeks consistency or integration among ideas. The source of these constraints is a social or inter-personal communicative process; (5) lastly, instead of personal invention there is collective representation. Collective representations, which Piaget himself referred to but did not relate to individual cognitive function, are often decisive for how individuals think. In essence, in the romantic conception of mind, the origin of children's ideas is to a great extent in social discourse.

This one-dimensional attack on Piaget's "enlightenment" theory is considerably modified however, by Shweder, apparently in response to a critical review of his analysis. He says,

> It seems to me misleading to imagine that one must choose, in general, between an enlightenment and a romantic view of the human mind. . . . the human mind is tripartite—it has rational, irrational and nonrational aspects. . . . we will always be able to find some ways in which our ideas are like the ideas of others (universalism) and some ways in which our ideas are different. Sometimes these differences will suggest progress (developmentalism) and often they will not (relativism). The task of the ethnographer is to decide what's rational, what's irrational and what's nonrational and to know when it makes sense to emphasise likeness, difference, or progress (Shweder, 1984: 60).

THE FUTURE OF THE PIAGETIAN TRADITION: WHAT IS DISPENSABLE AND WHAT IS INDISPENSABLE

Shweder's more accommodating stance is a most reasonable and fruitful path to take to an understanding of mind and its development. The romantic rebellion called for by Shweder is concerned with elements of mind that Piaget, by design, depreciated. The child, certainly, receives much diverse information through communicative discourse and other social experience. The question for Piaget was how invariants are constructed from this diverse experience. What is registered in the child's mind are both the transformations (changes, diverse elements, surface contents) and the invariants (universals). On which is one to concentrate? Which is more important, and to what purpose? Rationalists, structuralists and enlightenment figures create a view of mind in one aspect (the universals); contextualists, functionalists and romantics generally the other aspect. There is a third position, however, the *new synthesis* (as I shall call it), which argues for the integration of structuralist and functionalist explanation and theory into a single synthesis (Beilin, 1984). This goal is evident in Shweder's final summing up and in the many recent attempts within developmental psychology to create such a synthesis. I believe this goal was an element in Piaget's program, as is stated in two pieces of evidence. The first comes from his reconceptualisation of equilibration theory. He said, "[equilibration theory] represents a possible synthesis of genetic structuralism, the focus of all our previous work, with the functionalism found in the work of J. Dewey and of E. Claparède, and in many respects in Freudian psychoanalysis" (Piaget, 1985:68). The second piece of evidence is in the radical shifts he made from functionalist to structuralist and again to functionalist emphases in the theory, but always with the attempt to balance the two. The most striking of these shifts, as I see it, was the 1980 declaration in the *Cahiers de la Fondation Archives Jean Piaget* (Piaget, 1980) that his earlier emphasis on extensional logics and truth table relations was in error and that a new "logic of meanings" closer to entailment logic was required in which a "decanted version" of the former logic of operations would emerge. As we know, death cut short the realisation of this revision, but it signals to others concerned with continuing and building on the Piagetian tradition that one should seek those logical and other formal models that best fit the data and not be held to any specific model proposed in earlier Piagetian theory. Whereas the use of formal (i.e. structural) models is at the core of the Piagetian tradition, no specific formal model is so placed (Beilin, 1985).

Does the Genevan interest of the past few years in the analysis of children's problem-solving strategies fully respond to the contextualist's arguments against universals, and for local and domain-specific knowledge? To the contextualists it clearly does not. This is because of an unwillingness on the part of Piagetians to divorce context affects and individual differences in performance from cross-domain generalisation, i.e. structures. In the synthesis view a full characterisation of mind requires some level of cross-domain generality, the abstractness and universality of which is not fully known. One of the principal tasks for contemporary developmental psychology is a clear determination of how much cross-task

and cross-domain generality exists, and generating the appropriate models—
be they information processing, cybernetic, formal or biological at various
levels of generality—that would best fit the data. Even some of the best-
known critics of Piaget's theory (e.g. Flavell, 1982) are loath to fully reject
stage notions in development, despite the recent tendency to question the
"structure d'ensemble" concept, and stage theory generally. Piaget's late
modifications of the stage concept to a spiral model of development, with
"detours of the spiral", retain the essence of the stage concept, probably
because it is critical to the idea that knowledge does not exist in an infinitely
fragmented state either in the world or in the mind (Beilin, 1985).

Is Piaget's constructivism incompatible with contextualism and environ-
mentalism, and with biological preformationism, as Piaget has long
contended in posing his theory as an alternative to other theories? It would
require more space than this chapter allows to pursue the issue, but in my
view constructivism is not incompatible with either of the other positions,
as long as each position is not expressed in radical—extreme—form. On
the one hand, Waddington himself accepted a weaker form of preformationism, one that assumes some form of genetic pre-determinism (see
Koestler & Smythies, 1969). To accept genetic pre-determinism in some
form does not mean that all forms of thought are pre-wired and that
novelty in development is proscribed. It is the task of the sciences to
determine what is genetically pre-wired and what is merely constrained by
genetic limitations. It is counter-intuitive to assume universal order in the
acquisition of cognitive structures and not assume some genetic pre-
determinism. With respect to social and environmental determinism, even
Soviet psychologists (see Leontiev, 1981) have moved from traditional
Marxist–Leninist copy theory to more constructivist views of cognitive
development (although they at the same time eschew idealism). At the
least, one may hold that accounting for environmental influences, particularly of a social, conventional or historical nature, does not in itself define
how the individual acquires knowledge from these influences. There is no
doubt that knowledge (conventional and otherwise) is acquired by means
of direct instruction, through communicative discourse, and through
imitative observation. The fundamental question is how experience is
incorporated and properly represented in mind. Whether it is directly
registered, as is implied by social learning theorists and contextualists, or
whether it has to be reconstructed by the child, as Piaget maintained, is still
an open empirical and theoretical issue. It clearly remains, however, one of
the fundamental presuppositions of Piagetian theory (i.e. genetic epistemology) that knowledge must at some point be constructed or reconstructed by the child. At the same time it should not be forgotten that
Piaget had a place in his theory for knowledge that was not constructed, so-
called physical knowledge (and also biological-instinctual knowledge) that

is acquired by conditioning and other learning processes (or by genetic transmission). There is no reason, then, for the exclusion of conventional knowledge from the repertoire if not acquired by a constructive process nor of knowledge acquired directly through instruction (Beilin, 1981).

The present era in cognitive developmental psychology still appears very much dominated by the search for models of mind that are universal. This is as much on the agenda of artificial intelligence (AI) and information processing theorists, as it is for genetic epistemologists and the new nativists. There is no doubt, however, that in the basic shift toward functionalist accounts of mind the information processing/AI group has retained or incorporated more structuralistic elements than have other functionalists, particularly those of the ecological–environmentalist–contextualist groups. Information processing theory utilises these structures despite their inclination toward the characterisation of domain-specific knowledge. Thus structure-like networks and tree structures and other formalisms are applied similarly to different information contents. Where these differ from the Piagetian constructivist accounts is essentially in their reliance on machine- (i.e. computer-) constrained models rather than on biologically based models of mind. The recent developments in AI (in the new connectionism) reflect attempts to align mental models within the computer-based tradition with biological concepts. This will surely lead to a new class of theories that will probably serve developmental psychology better than the computer-based models of the recent past. Information processing models that introduce self-modifying processes (in an analogue to Piagetian reflective abstraction and constructivism) fall back on associationist-learning theory assumptions whose utility has long been suspect, particularly since Chomsky's classic attack on them. Self-modification or analogous systems, which are clearly required in an information processing theory of development, will surely undergo change as more biologically-oriented versions of AI programs become popular.

There is no doubt that recent interest in non-rational aspects of knowing have greatly expanded knowledge of the functioning of mind, as is illustrated in the study of metaphor and other aspects of language (such as discourse structure and communication), in aesthetics, and in non-rational bases of decision-making and problem-solving. But in each of these domains the problems associated with rational aspects of knowing have not been solved or displaced by increasing knowledge of the non-rational. Thus an understanding of the development of syntax (and other language structures) has not been particularly illuminated by recent studies in linguistic pragmatics. Nor has recent interest in expressive elements in aesthetics displaced cognitive elements of knowing in the arts, etc.

Our agenda, then, should be one of pursuing theory that enables us to understand and explain the development of each facet of knowing—the rational, irrational and non-rational. Our approach should be neither exclusively functionalist nor structuralist, neither exclusively rationalist nor romantic, but a synthesis of these traditions.

REFERENCES

Anderson, J. R. (1976). *Language, memory, and thought.* Hillsdale, N.J.: Lawrence Erlbaum Associates.
Anderson, J. R. (1978). Arguments concerning representations for mental imagery. *Psychological Review, 85,* 249–277.
Angell, J.R. (1908). The province of functional psychology. *Psychological Review, 14,* 61–91.
Beilin, H. (1971). Developmental stages and developmental processes. In D. R. Green, M. P. Ford & G. B. Flamer (Eds.), *Measurement and Piaget.* New York: McGraw Hill.
Beilin, H. (1978). Inducing conservation through training. In G. Steiner (Ed.), *Psychology of the 20th century.* Vol. 7: *Piaget and beyond.* Zurich: Kinder.
Beilin, H. (1981). Language and thought: Thistles among the sedums. In I. E. Sigel, D. M. Brodzinsky & R. M. Golinkoff (Eds.), *New directions in Piagetian theory and practice.* Hillsdale, N.J.: Lawrence Erlbaum Associates.
Beilin, H. (1983). The new functionalism and Piaget's program. In E. K. Scholnick (Ed.), *New trends in conceptual representation: Challenges to Piaget's theory?* Hillsdale, N.J.: Lawrence Erlbaum Associates.
Beilin, H. (1984). Functionalist and structuralist research programs in developmental psychology: Incommensurability or synthesis? In H. W. Reese (Ed.), *Advances in child development and behaviour,* Vol. 18. New York: Academic Press.
Beilin, H. (1985). Dispensable and core elements in Piaget's research program. *The Genetic Epistemologist, 13,* 1–16.
Block, N. (Ed.). (1980). *Readings in the philosophy of psychology,* Vol. 1. Cambridge, Mass.: Harvard University Press.
Boden, M. (1982). Chalk and cheese in cognitive science: The case for intercontinental interdisciplinarity. *Cahiers de la Fondation Archives Jean Piaget,* Nos. 2–3.
Bruner, J. S. (1980). Afterword. In D. R. Olson (Ed.), *The social foundations of language and thought: Essays in honour of Jerome S. Bruner.* New York: Norton.
Bruner, J. S., Goodnow, J. J. & Austin, G. A. (1956). *A study of thinking.* New York: Wiley.
Carey, S. (1980). Maturational factors in human development. In D. Caplan (Ed.), *Biological studies of mental processes.* Cambridge, Mass.: M.I.T. Press.
Case, R. (1985). *Intellectual development: A systematic reinterpretation.* New York: Academic Press.
Chomsky, N. (1959). A review of Skinner's "Verbal Behaviour." *Language, 35,* 26–58.
Chomsky, N. (1984). Changing perspectives on knowledge and use of language. Prepared for Sloan Conference on Philosophy and Cognitive Science, M.I.T. Press.
Cole, M. & Scribner, S. (1974). *Culture and thought: A psychological introduction.* New York: Wiley.
Dennett, D. C. (1984). The logical geography of computational approaches: A view from the east pole. M.I.T. Press. Sloan Conference on Philosophy and Cognitive Science, Cambridge, Mass. (May).
Dixon, R. A. & Baltes, P. B. (1986). Toward life-span research on the functions and pragmatics of intelligence. In R. G. Sternberg & R. K. Wagner (Eds.), *Practical intelligence: Origins of competence in the everyday world.* New York: Cambridge University Press.
Fischer, K. W. & Pipp, S. L. (1984). Processes of cognitive development: Optimal level and skill acquisition. In R. J. Sternberg (Ed.), *Mechanisms of cognitive development.* New York: Freeman.

Flavell, J. H. (1982). On cognitive development. *Child development, 53*, 1–10.

Fodor, J. A. (1983). *The modularity of mind: An essay on faculty psychology.* Cambridge, Mass.: M.I.T. Press.

Gelman, R. & Baillargeon, R. (1983). A review of some Piagetian concepts. In P. H. Mussen (Ed.), *Handbook of child psychology,* Vol. 3: F. H. Flavell & E. M. Markman (Eds.), *Cognitive development.* New York: Wiley.

Gholson, B. (1980). *The cognitive-developmental basis of human learning: Studies in hypothesis testing.* New York: Academic Press.

Gholson, B. & Barker, P. (1985). Kuhn, Lakatos, and Laudan: Applications in the history of physics and psychology. *American Psychologist, 40,* 755–769.

Gholson, B. & Beilin, H. (1979). A developmental model of human learning. In H. W. Reese & L. Lipsitt (Eds.), *Advances in child development and behaviour,* Vol. 13. New York: Academic Press.

Gibson, E. J. (1982). The concept of affordances in development: The renascence of functionalism. In W. A. Collins (Ed.), *Minnesota symposia on child development,* Vol. 15: *The concept of development.* Hillsdale, N.J.: Lawrence Erlbaum Associates.

Glick, J. (1985). Culture and cognition revisited. In E. D. Neimark, R. De Lisi & J. L. Newman (Eds.), *Moderators of competence.* Hillsdale, N.J.: Lawrence Erlbaum Associates.

Hilgard, E. R. (1956). *Theories of learning* (2nd ed.). New York: Appleton-Century-Crofts.

Keil, F. C. (1984). Mechanisms in cognitive development and the structure of knowledge. In R. J. Sternberg (Ed.), *Mechanisms of cognitive development.* New York: W. H. Freeman & Co.

Kessen, W. (1984). Introduction: The end of the age of development. In R. J. Sternberg (Ed.), *Mechanisms of cognitive development.* New York: W. H. Freeman & Co.

Klahr, D. (1984). Transition processes in quantitative development. In R. J. Sternberg (Ed.), *Mechanisms of cognitive development.* New York: W. H. Freeman & Co.

Koestler, A. & Smythies, J. R. (Eds.). (1969). *Beyond reductionism: The Alpbach symposium.* London: Hutchinson.

Kosslyn, S. M. (1978). Imagery and cognitive development: A teleological approach. In R. S. Siegler (Ed.), *Children's thinking: What develops?* Hillsdale, N.J.: Lawrence Erlbaum Associates.

Kosslyn, S. M. (1980). *Image and mind.* Cambridge, Mass.: Harvard University Press.

Kuhn, T. S. (1962). *The structure of scientific revolutions.* Chicago: University of Chicago Press.

Lakatos, I. (1978). *The methodology of scientific research programs.* Cambridge: Cambridge University Press.

Laudan, L. (1977). *Progress and its problems.* Berkeley: University of California Press.

Leontiev, A. A. (1981). *Psychology and the language learning process.* London: Pergamon Press.

Lerner, R. M., Hultsch, D. F. & Dixon, R. A. (1983). Contextualism and the character of developmental psychology in the 1970s. In J. W. Dauben & V. S. Sexton (Eds.), *History and philosophy of science: Selected papers. Annals of The New York Academy of Sciences, 412,* 101–128.

Marr, D. (1982). *Vision: A computational investigation into the human representation and processing of visual information.* San Francisco: Freeman.

Miller, G. A., Galanter, E. & Pribram, K. H. (1960). Plans and the structure of behaviour. New York: Holt, Rinehart & Winston.

Mounoud, P. (1981). Cognitive development: Construction of new structures or construction of internal organisations. In I. E. Sigel, D. M. Brodzinsky & R. M. Golinkoff (Eds.), New directions in Piagetian theory and practice. *Hillsdale, N.J.: Lawrence Erlbaum Associates.*

Mounoud, P. & Hauert, C. A. (1982). The development of sensorimotor organisation in the child. In G. E. Forman (Ed.), *Action and thought: From sensorimotor schemas to symbolic operations.* New York: Academic Press.

Neisser, U. (1984). Toward an ecologically oriented cognitive science. In T. M. Schlechter & M. P. Toglia (Eds.), *New directions in cognitive science.* Norwood, N.J.: Ablex.

Nelson, K. (1985). *Making sense: The acquisition of shared meaning.* New York: Academic Press.

Overton, W. F. (1984). World views and their influence on scientific research: Kuhn-Lakatos-Laudan. In H. W. Reese (Ed.), *Advances in child development and behaviour,* Vol. 18. New York: Academic Press.

Overton, W. F., & Reese, H. W. (1973). Models of development: Methodological implications. In J. R. Nesselroade & H. W. Reese (Eds.), *Life-span developmental psychology: Methodological issues.* New York: Academic Press.

Pascual-Leone, J. (1976). Metasubjective problems of constructive cognition: Forms of knowing and their psychological mechanisms. *Canadian Psychological Review, 17,* 110–125.

Pepper, S. C. (1942). *World hypotheses: A study in evidence.* Berkeley: University of California Press.

Piaget, J. (1971). *Biology and knowledge: An essay on the relations between organic regulations and cognitive processes.* Chicago, Ill.: University of Chicago Press. (First French ed.: 1967).

Piaget, J. (1980). The constructivist approach: recent studies in genetic epistemology. *Cahiers de la Fondation Archives Jean Piaget,* No. 1, 1–7.

Piaget, J. (1985). *The equilibration of cognitive structures: The central problem of intellectual development.* Chicago and London: University of Chicago Press. (First French Ed.: 1975).

Rosch, E. H. (1973). Natural categories, *Cognitive Psychology, 4,* 328–350.

Rosch, E. (1978). Principles of categorisation. In E. Rosch & B. B. Lloyd (Eds.), *Cognition and categorisation.* Hillsdale, N.J.: Lawrence Erlbaum Associates.

Russell, J. (1984). *Explaining mental life: Some philosophical issues in psychology.* London: Macmillan.

Shepard, R. N. (1978). The mental image. *American Psychologist, 33,* 125–137.

Shweder, R. A. (1984). Anthropology's romantic rebellion against the enlightenment, or there's more to thinking than reason and evidence. In R. A. Shweder & R. A. Levine (Eds.), *Culture theory: Essays on mind, self and emotion.* New York: Cambridge University Press.

Siegler, R. S. (1983). Information processing approaches to development. In P. H. Mussen (Ed.), *Handbook of child psychology,* 4th ed., Vol. 1: W. Kessen (Ed.), *History, theory and methods.* New York: Wiley.

Simon, H. A. (1972). On the development of the processor. In S. Farnham-Diggory (Ed.), *Information processing in children.* New York: Academic Press.

Spelke, E. S. (1983). Constraints on the development of intermodal perception. In L. S. Liben (Ed.), *Piaget and the foundations of knowledge.* Hillsdale, N.J.: Lawrence Erlbaum Associates.

Wartofsky, M. W. (1983). From genetic epistemology to historical epistemology: Kant, Marx and Piaget. In L. Liben (Ed.), *Piaget and the formulation of knowledge.* Hillsdale, N.J.: Lawrence Erlbaum Associates.

Zimmerman, B. J. (1983). Social learning theory: A contextualist account of cognitive functioning. In C. J. Brainerd (Ed.), *Recent advances in cognitive-developmental theory: Progress in cognitive developmental research.* New York: Springer-Verlag.

3 Piaget's Natural Logic

Marie-Jeanne Borel
University of Lausanne

INTRODUCTION

The notion of if not the very term of a *natural logic* directs and structures Piaget's whole epistemological enterprise as a philosopher and a logician. Two of his formulae emphasise in a somewhat extreme way the wide span of his postulates, which have both an evolutionist dimension and a structuralist one:

An organism is a mechanism which is involved in transformations.

The logician's thinking is the most elaborate form of human thinking. (Beth & Piaget, 1966: 311)

Let us read these quotations both as an epigraph and as a frame to the following remarks, for they have been a guideline for a new reading of Piaget's writings on logic (see References). As such, they are paradoxical in many respects, since the philosopher here associates without any other modality life and the system, the ideas of creation and permanency, as well as the origin and the end of a Becoming that is viewed from the standpoint of the generation of structures.

Moreover, the notion of natural logic is at the very core of Piagetian psychology. Indeed, in the very first experimental works he carried out in the 1920s, Piaget at once chose as the object of a natural, empirical science this very logical thinking that traditionally seemed bound to be the object of formal analyses.

This chapter was translated from the French by Denys de Caprona.

Nobody should discuss the fact that formal thinking can be studied as a psychological fact (1922, quoted in Ducret, 1984: 740).

We shall briefly recall Piaget's epistemological problem in order to understand better the situation of logic with respect to psychology. We shall mention some aspects of natural logic—a definitely polymorphous notion in Piaget's writings—on which we shall base an attempt to outline some of the problems that Piaget's theses about them may raise nowadays. These problems concern especially the relationships between natural logic and the so-called logicians' logic; they also concern Piaget's use of the latter to "formalise", so he says, the former. In what follows, we shall not investigate the content of Piagetian operatory logic but its very meaning from an epistemological standpoint.

THE EPISTEMOLOGICAL PROBLEM

Piaget's major epistemological problem always was to define the conditions for a *construction of knowledge* and thereby to break away from the prevailing trends, which analysed knowledge from its results. Moreover, Piaget speaks of "valid" knowledge (Piaget [Ed.], 1967:7), a seemingly pleonastic term if we do not at once understand that it refers to the user of knowledge, to the support and actor of a *formation*.

We know that these conditions for a construction are both diachronic—i.e. they are "accessibility" conditions, that is, genetic ones—and synchronic—i.e. they are "constitutive" conditions, that is, either structural when internal or due, when external, to the correlative roles of the "subject" and "object".

Piaget specifically intends "to explain how man's actual thinking may generate science as a coherent system of objective knowledge" (Beth & Piaget, 1966:305). Even more precisely, a "coherent and objective" knowledge is, in the Piagetian viewpoint, essentially a form of knowledge that is "logico-mathematical" or "formalisable" (both terms are equivalent in the texts) insofar as it is "operatory"; and Piaget also asserts that the criterion for the latter is *calculus*.

The epistemological question then becomes to explain how such a "pure" knowledge (as "emptied of its representative content": Inhelder & Piaget, 1964)—which, by definition, does not depend on its contents, nor on the situations, the desires and the debates that motivate it—could possibly be grounded in the natural and human world and exert an efficient action on it. In other words why can we launch a mobile in the cosmos with Newton's equations? Why is logic a form of "morals of thinking" in action, and why is it a condition of a "cooperating" or democratic communication?

Psychology and Logic

In his dialogue or polemic with other philosophies of knowledge, Piaget holds that *disciplinary knowledges* are associated with the kind of reflection that designs the epistemological programme and that they are needed for its realisation. Psychology as an experimental discipline and logic as an exact method of analysis are particularly involved. Instead of speculating, epistemology must explain: its theses make sense in an empirical domain, and the arguments are factual and positive.

Specifically, as soon as the questions of what is "reason", what are "norms", "rules" or "signs", are discussed, an epistemology always involves some psychological presuppositions, i.e. it calls forth questions of *facts*. Now whereas, according to Piaget, reflection only is available to philosophers when they must check their intuitions, psychology offers a field where these hypotheses can be made operational.

Similarly, there can be no epistemology without raising the question of the criteria for knowledge—of its *right* to validity, that is—without investigating the problem of the control of knowledge: knowledge isn't any kind of belief.

Logic must then lend its *tools* of analysis, what Piaget calls the "formalisation procedures". This can be done only if psychology and logic, when their problems "correspond" (Piaget, 1949:14) or when "comparing" their results, keep their own methods and goals and avoid psychologism and logicism, which both establish an illegitimate relationship between fact and right.

The Epistemological Meaning of Facts of Logic

Can Piagetian epistemology, which uses facts for theoretical arguments, be as entirely positive as its initiator wishes it to be? At the outset let us notice that the interdisciplinary nature of its programme would be enough to limit such a hope. Indeed, Kuhn has clearly shown that the "method" commanding an interdisciplinary debate cannot be reduced to any one of the disciplinary methods involved.

A slightly different argument is to emphasise the fact that epistemology, including Piagetian epistemology, is rooted in philosophy; it will be useful for us to lay down this argument in order to better understand Piaget's concept of natural logic.

In that view, any fact that is not interesting in the psychology Piaget intends to elaborate will not be ascribed to the logical analysis he imagines. In the Piagetian endeavour, the only relevant facts are those relating to validity, i.e. the "normative facts", in Lalande's terms. A normative fact is what anybody can both experience and observe on himself; when performing an action, we know that what we are doing imposes itself, cannot be otherwise or must be the way it is. The motives do not pertain to a contingent relationship of the subject to the world but to what Piaget calls, in recent texts, "reasons" (Piaget et al., 1980:47)—i.e. the significant part of an organisation of actions. At a given point in development the child knows *without looking at the facts* that $A > C$ if he knows that $A > B$ and $B > C$; or that there are more Bs than As when A is included in B. According to Piaget, these are facts of natural logic.

For the *psychologist*, however, the way people "have" their reasons is but one fact in many. A "paradigm" could correspond to each stage in development, and no *value* judgement should intervene to balance the observed differences.

A *logician's* position is similar. In his view, a logical system differs from another one according to an agreement as to what should be written and calculated in it; one system is deemed better than another according to a technical or aesthetical criterion.

By contrast, all psychological facts and logical calculi are not equally meaningful. We may thus notice that it was as an *epistemologist* only that Piaget could discern an "immature" logic in the baby's behaviours, speak of logic in terms of a self-regulating development and assess that some logical calculi were more "natural" than others.

The epistemologist only, and only if he is heir to a philosophical tradition that views rationality in a dialectical perspective, could posit rationality as an evaluation principle; and the "self-reflection" ("self-regulation") of reason (even if unconscious or nonverbal) as the *criterion* of knowledge because it is above all its *incentive*.

In its epistemological content, this thesis is fundamental for all that which it makes possible and for the consistency it introduces in reflecting the problem of knowledge. It is, however, of a doctrinal nature, i.e. philosophical in its very status (Borel, 1984). And it goes with two further theses that share the same status but whose content is more liable to discussion.

The first thesis admits of the existence of an "orthogenesis" in the development of reason. In his youth, Piaget thought of elaborating a *biology* of knowledge. In such a thesis, not only do internal norms of knowledge undergo development and changes, but they do so autonomously through an *equilibrating* functional interaction between the living and the environment (or between thinking and the world). Here the epistemologist is opposing the form of relativism that is a natural consequence of any empirical anthropological research on the norms of thinking.

A second and parallel thesis asserts that there is an almost natural hierarchy in the various forms of knowledge. Its apex and ideal lie in the mathematician–logician's thinking. Yet Piaget says that beyond this form of thinking is genius. . . . In our opinion, such theses cannot be separated from *value judgements* that direct the programme of epistemology—hence, in the texts, an oscillation, a strain, between two viewpoints on natural logic which are difficult to conciliate.

On the one hand, Piaget as the outstanding psychologist of child intelligence is sensitive to the specificity, originality and even "incommensurability" of the various forms of thinking at the various stages in the development of knowledge. On the other hand, Piaget the epistemologist is bound by a rationalist tradition and is, in a way, forced to evaluate intellectual abilities in terms of relative limitations on a scale whose, ultimate criterion is the logician's thinking as a model for rationality.

THE NOTION OF NATURAL LOGIC

Contexts

Piaget seems to have begun to use explicitly the term "natural logic" in the 1960s (Piaget, Beth, Grize, Martin, Matalon & Naess, 1962); the term then had relatively standardised uses (Piaget [Ed.], 1967). However, it is rather earlier connotated with a meaning that is polyvalently structured through a whole set of oppositions. An analysis of the contexts where this notion appears, of its denominations and of their paraphrases, would provide interesting data on Piaget's argument, since it represents a central notion within a kernel that remains invariant through all kinds of transformations. The following indicative list provides some of the usual terms by means of which the notion of natural logic is contrasted with the logicians' logic:

a *"sui generis"* "child logic" is contrasted with the "forms logicians know";

"real thinking", "real logic", are contrasted with "formal abstraction", "pure axiomatic";

"natural structures", "natural thinking", "the natural use of operations", are contrasted with "the artefact of logical calculus", "pure formal game", "conventional", "arbitrary";

"naive thinking", "naive logic", are contrasted with "refined thinking", with "rich", "powerful", "very specialised" constructions of the logician, etc.

At least four axes that organise the semantic field of contexts in which Piaget introduces the notion of natural logic can be identified:

natural logic is practised and performed by subjects; it is rooted in their activities, which makes them meaningful; such activities are involved in its factual evidences and necessities.

natural logic is the outcome of a dynamic and temporal, "concrete and living" construction.

it may be assessed in hierarchical terms; it is, in varying degrees, "pure", "rich", "mobile", "systematic", "reflected", and so on. a natural science will take natural logic as a fact, and a formal analysis will deal with it *de jure*.

Contrastingly, the second term of the opposition—i.e. the logicians' logic (initially termed "logistics", then "symbolic logic" in the 1960s)—does not presuppose a subject. For instance, logicians have "forgotten" that "integers are natural numbers" (Piaget et al., 1967:395); such a logic is as "static" and "atemporal" as any set of "conventional", "arbitrary" symbols can be; it is "pure", "rich"; and an abstract, *a priori* reflection bears on it.

Before they are opposed, however, both natural logic and specialised logic are *normative*: a subject may well construct them, he primarily "accepts" them. For this word not to lose its very meaning, what is at stake in any logic is "the validity of noetic constructions and not their causal mechanism" (Beth & Piaget, 1966:140).

Theses and Problems

Beyond the manifold uses of the term and notion of a natural logic, Piaget's works state the theses that are elaborated in the framework of his epistemological programme. Four of them will give us the opportunity to raise a number of problems. Our issue is "Piaget Today". The following thoughts could simply not have been conceived without the contribution of genetic epistemology to considerations on logic. In further elaborating these reflections, however, we are somewhat necessarily led beyond genetic epistemology.

1. In Piaget's view, any intellectual activity internally presents itself in the form of "implications" between linked meanings. A "normative feeling" revealing itself in consciousness is an indication that a "logical experience", a natural logic, exists in the subject. "It must be so", says he: in what he is doing, the subject shows how obvious and constrained are for him certain somewhat systematically or clearly "reflected", "thematised" links.

A first problem arises from noticing a kind of oscillation, in Piaget's texts, between normative facts in a broad sense and in a very restricted sense. The latter is limited to formal validity, which itself comes down to a narrow formalism. Now, can one speak both of a natural "logic of the child" in its own right and of its insufficiently or ill-normed character, with the adult formal thinking as a criterion? "Distinct natural logics" (Piaget et al., 1962:7) are actually sometimes at issue, but a distinction is then immediately drawn between "anonymous constraints" in logico-mathematical thinking, which have more or less incomplete forms, and other constraints originating in communication.

One may also meaningfully point out that the existence of a plurality of logical calculi is, for Piaget, the sign of an "artificiality". Now it may be wondered whether such a plurality would not, on the contrary, indicate a greater variety of operatory properties of logical experience than the use of "mother structures" can account for.

It has been demonstrated (Apostel, 1982) that formal operatory thinking as Piaget views it presupposes at least part of the calculus of predicates—the algebra of which is not any more the Boolean algebra deemed "inconvenient" by Piaget (1942:19)—as well as elements of modal logic.

To investigate the various natural logics without assessing them by the yardstick of formal logic leads to a study of non-formal norms of reasoning. The question is then how one ends up reasoning with "impure" rules, i.e. with rules that depend upon situations and contents, so as to become adapted to a complex and changing world; or to understand how scientific thinking itself advances through procedures when there is no way of using calculus; or how it has historically discussed the types of proofs deemed valid according to the moment in time or to the object it was constructing.

The last stage in Piaget's thinking leads to these questions: A logic of "the meanings of action" is conceived as the "implicative" side of the very causal process of equilibration (Piaget, 1980:12). As far as modelling is concerned, however, everything has still to be done; as for adult thinking, and especially in the field of science, we do not see very well how to deal with this issue if this problem of the articulation of knowledge and discourse (the act of language) is skipped.

2. A second Piagetian thesis on natural logic is that any intellectual activity *externally* presents itself in the form of an organisation of actual and mental actions. According to Piaget, logical experience is explained by postulating highly general coordinations of highly general actions such as reuniting/ separating, seriating or establishing correspondences, which will become operations in the formal structures. An operation can typically be composed in an internal and reversible way. Now the first structure that shows these properties is the structure of *practical* intelligence, which is elaborated before language and which is progressively restructured from stage to stage through a breaking-away from any representative and intuitive element.

Thus, theoretical intelligence originates in practical intelligence. Moreover, the latter is a *model* for the former, for operatory intelligence comprises, at another level of complexity, the most general structural properties of practical intelligence: Theoretical intelligence, i.e. reason, is thereby viewed as instrumental. As opposed to the free activity of calculus, the "figural" as well as the "intuitive" aspects of intelligence are for Piaget the passive, limiting and even "parasitical" side of our cognitive competence.

Yet intuition and figure form the basis of what is called "the intelligence of situations" or "the understanding of others", for instance in a dialogue; and we know the part played, in the scientific discourses themselves, by the spatial properties of all forms of *inscriptions* (graphs, formulae and so on). The problem then is to know to what extent there would not be a *theoretical* risk in reducing understanding to an understanding of what we do, to an explanation of why an action has succeeded or failed, or of how to make it succeed. Indeed, to what extent can we reduce reason to hierarchised routines that combine means and goals and whose procedure pertains to calculus? (Kobsa, 1984.)

3. A third thesis is about the role of language in knowledge: language is useful, but it does not actually contribute to the genesis of cognitive structures; indeed, the whole set of these structures is needed to generate and interpret discourse by using a language.

Piaget devised a specific methodology in order to grasp cognitive structures from an observation of non-verbal conducts. Yet it is as if the very problem of the semiotic function disappeared from the problem of knowledge after "Plays, Dreams and Imitation".

Now, according to Thesis 2, the fact that thinking becomes operatory means that it becomes *formal* and breaks off from any reference to meaning. At this level, however, as thinking has no object, it cannot function without *signs*.

In his texts, Piaget often seems to look somewhat with contempt at the semiological distinctions inherent in the technical concept of formalisation, which blurs the uses he makes of it. Metalogical distinctions are, so he says, secondary because they are linguistic. For example, there is no notion of syntax in his reflections on the logicians' logic, whereas any definition of a formal system would be unthinkable without this notion and the notion of *levels* of language.

By focusing an epistemological programme on the operatory aspects of reason—i.e. on its calculating side—the genetic problem of the construction of a syntactical semiotic competence belonging to any form of calculus is concealed. This may not be unrelated to the fact that the logicist inheritance is what determines the way Piaget conceives the genesis of number, rather than the inheritance of formalistic conceptions where the notion of *recursivity* prevails.

It has also been shown in full detail (Seltman & Seltman, 1985) in what way, in the models Piaget proposed, the lack of any consideration of the syntactic level in a "formalisation" makes the definition of semantics uneasy; one thereby cannot distinguish the formalised statements from the model of "naive" theoretical statements they are supposed to represent.

4. The last Piagetian thesis on natural logic is that there is an *autonomous* becoming of logico-mathematical intelligence. The properties referring to the self-organisation of the living become tools for thinking through *reflective abstraction* which comes first in structuration; this type of abstraction bears on the actions themselves and on operations and not on the world, except when the latter reveals the outcome of *what we have done in it*. From the very sensorimotor beginning of natural logic, an "object" of action is "any" object: Objects are places allowing for a substitution in a structure of actions, and their meaning depends upon the properties of the latter. Yet formal intelligence as the end-point of such a becoming is characterised by the fact that is has become autonomous: as it consists of operations on operations, intelligence once it is completed is not any more directed—or limited—by content. In other words, autonomy in such a becoming is that of a "becoming-autonomous"!

It seems hard to make both assertions compatible. Perhaps the paradox they stress has a conceptual origin. It is difficult indeed not to notice a blind spot in Piaget's theory at the level of his notion of what the "object" is. Once again, an analysis of the contexts and arguments in which the word appears would show a kind of oscillation. Indeed, the same word designates either a meaning in a structure, a "phenomenon" in Kant's terms, i.e. the correlate of an organisation of the subject's actions; or the "thing" in the environment in which the organism lives. Therefore, now the object is *within* what the living *constructs* and now it is *out* of it, that is, in what the living *reacts to*. Do we have here an idealism of the logical analogy or a realism of the biological analogy? The question is whether when understanding Becoming by structures one can *ipso facto* understand structures by Becoming. It seems obvious, however, that in order to understand how thinking gets purified through working on contents and situations which it eventually gets separated from, a representation of what thinking gets purified *in* should be integrated to the theory. The "becoming-autonomous" of natural logic seemingly can only be explained in terms of an interaction which the idea of an autonomy of such a becoming excludes.

To conclude, let us go back to the problem of formalisation. According to Piaget: (1) The various stages of natural logic "converge" (in a "progressive isomorphism") towards the logicians' logic: the adolescent's logic is closer to the latter than to the child's logic. (2) The becoming of logical experience is a "formalisation" process. The logicians' logic is also natural: "the logician is a living being" who codifies in his axioms past operatory logical experiences, which he restructures within historical-social determinations. (3) Therefore, this logic may be used to "formalise" structures that form the basis of natural logics. What is operatory is "formalisable". But what is *formalising* as such? When reading Piaget's texts on logic in the years 1942–1967 (see References), the plurality of the roles with which he endows this enterprise is striking. We shall now list them in the order given by one of the texts (Piaget, 1942:9–12). The same elements appear with no major change in later writings. For the interpreter, they are difficult to coordinate.

According to Piaget, formalising means mathematising the *concepts* of psychology through an analogy with theoretical physics. For example, the biological notion of a coordination between assimilation and accommodation, which is psychologically interpreted by the reversibility of actions/operations, is algebraically conceived in terms of symmetries and inversions.

Formalising, however, is also axiomatising the psychological *theory* itself so as to give logical coherence to its inferences.

Another role of formalisation is in the use of a technical tool, i.e. calculus, to analyse in a precise way the normative logical facts that the psychologist or the historian studies, i.e. to bring "structural laws" out of them: "Logic is the axiomatisation of *thinking* itself" (Piaget, 1942:5). However, this term is equivocal: now the analysis is viewed as a descriptive one ("without any validity judgement") and one tries to construct *models*; now as a normative one, for the logician "assesses the validity of some transformations" in terms of *limitations* (Piaget et al., 1962:5; Beth & Piaget, 1966:227) which he measures with his own yardstick, as both judge and party in development.

Through formalising, at last, one aims at associating formal analysis and empirical experimentation, two independent but parallel endeavours that may compare their results. However, we are again faced with an alternative. Indeed, on the one hand, the results of a temporal and causal production the psychologist describes must be compared *with* the results of formal, atemporal logical analyses; on the other hand, there is a relative kinship, filiation or limitation *among* the results of the formal analysis of some states of development.

It was useful for us to mention the problem of formalisation from the standpoint of the various roles with which it is endowed because it reveals the difficulties in associating, as Piaget's work typically does, the points of view of the philosopher and the naturalist. The former advocates a certain conception of Reason, the very nature of which is to be a "formalising" reason; the latter is guided by its objects, i.e. by the reasons that the actors generate when various cognitive tools are available to them in actions. This rather embarrassing association is heuristically necessary in epistemology.

In the case of Piaget's works, the polysemia in his formalisation ideal also indicates a tension in his thought. Indeed, he wishes to view Reason, formal intelligence and its power to create new *possibilities* as a liberating factor for man. He interprets, however, its form or its norm by means of what partly is the opposite, the instrumentality of calculus that is, as the father of the ELIZA programme puts it, a justification for so many of our industrial nightmares.

REFERENCES

Apostel, L. (1982). The future of Piagetian logic. *Revue Internationale de Philosophie, 36,* 567–611.

Beth, E. W. & Piaget, J. (1966). *Mathematical epistemology and psychology.* Dordrecht: D. Reidel. (First French ed., 1961.)

Borel, M.-J. (1984). Le savoir, un concept contesté. *Etudes de Lettres* (Université de Lausanne), *3.*

Ducret, J.-J. (1984). *Jean Piaget, savant et philosophe.* Genève: Droz.

Inhelder, B. & Piaget, J. (1964). *The early growth of logic in the child.* London: Routledge & Kegan Paul. (First French ed., 1959.)

Kobsa, A. (1984). What is explained by AI models? *Communication & Cognition, 17,* 49–64.

Piaget, J. (1928). *Judgment and reasoning in the child.* London: Kegan Paul, Trench & Trubner. (First French ed., 1924.)

Piaget, J. (1942). *Classes, relations, nombre: Essai sur les groupements de la logistique et sur la réversibilité de la pensée.* Paris: Vrin.

Piaget, J. (1949). *Traité de logique: Essai de logistique opératoire.* Paris: A. Colin, (2nd ed., 1972, established by J. B. Grize, with a new title; *Essai de logique opératoire.* Paris: Dunod.)

Piaget, J. (1952). *Essai sur les transformations des opérations logiques.* Paris: Presses Universitaires de France.

Piaget, J., Beth, E.W., Grize, J.B., Martin, R., Matalon, B. & Naess, A. (1962). *Implication, formalisation et logique naturelle.* Paris: Presses Universitaires de France.

Piaget, J. & Beth, E. (1966). *Epistémologie mathématique et psychologie.* Paris: Presses Universitaires de France.

Piaget, J. (Ed.). (1967). *Logique et connaissance scientifique.* Paris: Gallimard.

Piaget, J. (Ed.). (1980). *Les formes élémentaires de la dialectique.* Paris: Gallimard.

Seltman, M. & Seltman, P. (1985). *Piaget's logic.* London: Allen & Unwin.

Siegel, L. S. & Brainerd, C. J. (Eds.). (1978). *Alternatives to Piaget.* New York: Academic Press.

4 Operatory Logic

Jean-Blaise Grize
University of Neuchâtel

INTRODUCTION

A number of criticisms have been addressed to Piaget's logic. I shall report some of them later, but I would like to start by recalling the context of Piaget's reflection in logic.

Except for Russell—and for all that not the author of the *Principia mathematica* but of the *Introduction to mathematical philosophy* in its French version—he hardly knows more than Edmond Goblot's (1918) and Charles Serrus' (1945) works. Those distinguished scholars wrote manuals but never treatises for logicians. Moreover, we must mention a phenomenon that is typical of French-speaking countries, and France specifically, i.e. their late development of mathematical logic. Despite its title, its date of publication and its publisher, Marcel Boll's *Manuel de logique* (1948) does not quote the *Principia* nor Carnap's and Hilbert's works. It does not draw a distinction between syntax and semantics nor between language and meta-language.

Therefore, since "Piaget Today" is our topic, it seems more important to try to find out what Piaget intended to do, rather than to stress his weaknesses and errors.

I shall follow three steps: (1) I shall first recall some facts. (2) I shall then analyse the well-known INRC group. (3) I shall propose other groups so as to broaden the discussion.

Translated from the French by Denys de Caprona.

A FEW FACTS

We meet three kinds of facts:

1. First of all, Piaget's purpose: He repeatedly said that he had never intended to write a treatise of logic or to make the least technical contribution to mathematical logic. What he wanted to do is clearly indicated in the preface to Inhelder and Piaget's wonderful book, *The growth of logical thinking from childhood to adolescence*: "An operatory analysis of intelligence" (Inhelder & Piaget, 1958).

Why such an analysis? Numerous observations and experiments had shown the simultaneous appearance, in adolescents, of a plurality of operatory schemes: a combinatorial system, proportions, mechanical equilibrium, multiplicative probabilities and so on. Hence a dual concern:

1. to provide a "description of the formal structures that mark the completion of the operatory development of intelligence" (ibid.);
2. to look for "what lies *beneath* the initial operations codified by axioms" (Piaget, 1970).

Now, what lies beneath logical systems is basically an algebraic structure and a lattice structure, which happen to be synthesised in the INRC group, in which N characterises a reversibility by inversion and R a reversibility by reciprocity. Thus, N pertains to groups, rings, fields—i.e. to structures endowed with an equivalence relation—whereas R pertains to order structures.

Another meaningful fact is that, whereas usual presentations of logic start with propositional calculus and then proceed to predicate calculus, Piaget begins with the calculus of classes, goes on to propositional calculus and almost skips predicate calculus. It seems to me that two kinds of reasons led him to this particular approach:

1. First, reasons of a psychological nature: Piaget is primarily interested in the genesis of logic. The child can reason well before he can speak; he therefore manipulates classes well before manipulating propositions, and a characteristic feature of adolescent thinking is precisely that it coordinates the calculus of classes and propositional calculus.
2. Then, a logical kind of reason: Piaget is concerned with grasping logic as it occurs in natural thinking. We never spontaneously think with empty forms: in everyday language, any proposition has a content. Accordingly, Piaget holds that a proposition is never only

either true or false. It is so according to what relation among classes it represents. Thus $p \wedge q$ is true if and only if the class of objects characterised by p has a non-empty intersection with the class of objects characterised by q.

2. Here now are a few algebraic facts. As he confined himself to the calculus of classes and to propositional calculus, Piaget grounded his reflection in the Boolean structure. We know that such a structure can be considered from two standpoints:

1. either as a ring that includes a unit element and idempotent elements;
2. or as a lattice that will be distributive and complemented (Halmos, 1962).

Hence two types of normal forms:

1. In the ring of operations w and $\wedge$ (addition and multiplication),

   $$f(p, q) = \alpha \, w \, \beta p \, w \, \gamma q \, w \, \delta(p \wedge q)$$

   with $\alpha, \beta, \gamma, \delta \in \{0, 1\}$

2. In the lattice of operations $\wedge$, $\vee$ and $^{-}$,

   $$f(p, q) = a(p \wedge q) \vee b(p \wedge \bar{q}) \vee c(\bar{p} \wedge q) \vee d(\bar{p} \wedge \bar{q})$$

   with $a, b, c, d \in \{0, 1\}$

3. Let us finally say a few words about the criticisms that have been addressed to Piaget. They are of three kinds (Seltman & Seltman, 1985):

1. The *Essai de logique opératoire* (Piaget, 1972) contains errors and ambiguities. Alas, this is true, and I can only regret it(!). However, such defects can be corrected and they do not concern the basic problem.
2. Contrary to what he explicitly said, Piaget did not really bring out one single structure, i.e. the INRC group. This group and the lattice of the 16 operations only coexist independently of each other. In what follows, I shall try to show that all this depends on the meaning we give to the words "one single structure".
3. Piaget's propositional calculus does not allow deduction. This old criticism is too basic not to be considered for a while. Indeed, the least we can say about the logical system in which nothing can be deduced is that it is a rather bizarre system! Let us have a look at the reasons for such a situation.

For example, everyone knows that $p \wedge q$ implies $p \vee q$. This is an immediate consequence of the truth tables for each of the propositions (1000 for $p \wedge q$ and 1110 for $p \vee q$) and of accepting that false (written 0) implies true (written 1) as well as false.

Let us examine, however, the normal forms of the propositions when included in the lattice:

n.f. of $p \wedge q$: $p \wedge q$ is present and $p \wedge \bar{q}$, $\bar{p} \wedge q$, $\bar{p} \wedge \bar{q}$ are missing

n.f. of $p \vee q$: $p \wedge q$, $p \wedge \bar{q}$, $\bar{p} \wedge q$ are present and $\bar{p} \wedge \bar{q}$ is missing

According to Piaget, each one of these forms corresponds to a concrete situation of classes. Therefore, to assert that in situation $p \wedge q$ no object is, for example, $p \wedge \bar{q}$ does not of course imply that one may say that some objects are. For Piaget as for a certain common sense, false does not imply true.

I think, however, that to suppose that Piaget did not notice the dead end to which his interpretation led would make him more naive than he sometimes liked to appear. Without being explicit about it, Piaget, under the denomination "operatory logic", actually develops a meta-logic. We must not forget that I, N, R and C are transformations in their own right and that consequently, they allow a progression from one situation to another. It is therefore accurate to say that $p \wedge q$ does not imply $p \vee q$; transformation C, however, really leads to $p \vee q$ when applied to $p \wedge q$.

THE INRC GROUP

I shall take for granted the organisation of the sixteen binary operations through the order relation "to imply" (Fig. 4.1).

The very simple problem I wish to raise is that of the impact that the four transformations I, N, R and C have on the nodes of the diagram.

These transformations are defined as follows:

$I(abcd) = (abcd)$ Identical transformation
$N(abcd) = (a'b'c'd')$ Negation: $RC = CR$
$R(abcd) = (dcba)$ Reciprocal: $NC = CN$
$C(abcd) = (d'c'b'a')$ Correlative: $RN = NR$

in which $a' = 0$ if $a = 1$ and $a' = 1$ if $a = 0$, and similarly with b', c', d'.

This lattice is isomorphic with respect to the lattice of the parts of a set $E = \{e_1, e_2, e_3, e_4\}$ that is organised by the relation of inclusion; it is therefore normal to establish the following correspondence:

$e_1 \rightarrow p \wedge q$ $e_2 \rightarrow p \wedge \bar{q}$ $e_3 \rightarrow \bar{p} \wedge q$ $e_4 \rightarrow \bar{p} \wedge \bar{q}$

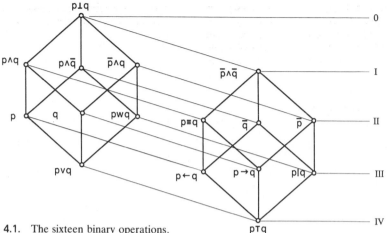

FIG. 4.1.   The sixteen binary operations.
Note:
1. To facilitate reading, I have written down not just the operations—e.g., —but the composed propositions: $p\ q$.
2. If node X is above node Y and if a path links them, then X implies Y (in the logician's sense!)
3. Numbering the levels n shows that the normal form of the lattice has n number 1.
4. $p\,\mathsf{w}\,q$ corresponds to (0110) and p/q to (0111), $p\ q$ to (0000) and $p\mathsf{T}q$ to (1111).

and legitimate to wonder about the effect of an application of the transformations to these four Level I elements. In this respect, we easily obtain the four Level III elements.

We have thus a first-class A1 of operations which includes 8 elements. This corresponds to what Piaget called the quadruples A and B (1972:260). They are characterised by the fact that:

$$I \neq N \neq R \neq C$$

In order to proceed further, Level II operations have to be considered. The transformations prove less productive here. We have:

$$\left.\begin{array}{l} B1 = \{p,\ \bar{p}\} \\ C1 = \{q,\ \bar{q}\} \end{array}\right\}\text{Quadruple B with } I = C \text{ and } R = N$$

$$D1 = \{p\,\mathsf{w}\,q,\ p\equiv q\} \qquad \text{Quadruple C with } I = R \text{ and } N = C$$

As to the remaining levels 0 and IV, they produce:

$$E1 = \{p\ q,\ p\mathsf{T}q\} \qquad \text{Quadruple C}$$

True enough, the operations are grouped according to interesting properties (the quadruples), but we must acknowledge that we are far from having one single structure: the lattice actually splits into five subsets.

Could this have been predicted? The answer is likely to be yes. Indeed, transformations N, R and C are all somewhat related to the general idea of negation, whereas the organisation of the simplex (see Fig. 4.1) pertains to implication. Our problem then is to examine what relations may exist between negation and implication and to see whether or not we reach a kind of unified structure.

Let us start with the classical square of opposition (see Fig. 4.2). We can see at once that it allows a progression from the notion of opposition to the notion of implication. Thus, if two propositions Q and P are contraries, P, will imply $\bar{Q}$. Similarly, if two propositions are subcontraries $\bar{\bar{P}}$ (that is, P) and $\bar{\bar{Q}}$ (that is, Q), $\bar{Q}$ will imply P. Let us try to establish which among the 16 operations of the lattice are contraries and which are subcontraries. Our results are presented in Fig. 4.3. We notice that we meet here all the Level I and Level II propositions.

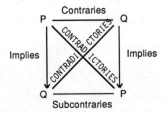

FIG. 4.2.   The square of oppositions. Contraries: not true together; subcontraries: not wrong together; contradictories: one true, the other false.

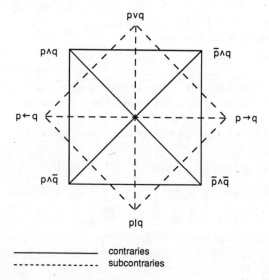

FIG. 4.3.   Contraries and subcontraries.

Let us, then, consider the implications: Each Level I proposition has three contraries, and each Level III proposition has three subcontraries. I shall restrict myself to taking $p\,q$ as an example.

1. $p\,q$ is a contrary of $\bar{p}\,q$; therefore it implies $\overline{\bar{p}\,q}$
   that is, $p \leftarrow q$.

2. $p\,q$ is a contrary of $p\,\bar{q}$; therefore it implies $\overline{p\,\bar{q}}$
   that is, $p \rightarrow q$.

3. $p\,q$ is a contrary of $\bar{p}\,\bar{q}$; therefore it implies $\overline{\bar{p}\,\bar{q}}$
   that is, $p\,q$.

If we now examine on the simplex the three paths that go from $p\,q$ to each of the propositions implied, we observe:

that (1) goes through $p \equiv q$, therefore $p\,q$ implies $p \equiv q$

that (2) goes through q, therefore $p\,q$ implies q

that (3) goes through p, therefore $p\,q$ implies p.

The same deduction is true for $p\,\bar{q}$, $\bar{p}\,q$ and $\bar{p}\,\bar{q}$. The results are shown in Fig. 4.4. The boxes show the intermediate implications at Level II. We notice that, except for the propositions at the two poles, all propositions are thus related in one single structure.

True enough, the role INRC plays is hardly apparent. Transformation R is the only useful one, and for all that it produces only one contrary.

Example: $R(p\,q) = R(1000) = (0001) = \bar{p}\,\bar{q}$

⬈	p v q	p ← q	p → q	p / q
p ∧ q	p	p ≡ q	q	--
p ∧ q̄	p w q	p	--	q
p̄ ∧ q	q	--	p̄	p w q
p̄ ∧ q̄	--	q̄	p ≡ q	p̄

FIG. 4.4.   The implications.

I shall therefore try to broaden the Piagetian notion of transformation so that it can apply to other groups.

SOME OTHER GROUPS

1. Liliane Maury (Laboratoire d'Etude des Processus Cognitifs, EHESS, Paris; director, François Bresson) took up the genetic problem of negation, and she showed that even before the child has constructed the reciprocal R, he negates only one component of the pair. In the example of the conjunction, one observes that:

1. Neg $(p \wedge q)$ is $\bar{p} \wedge q$
2. Neg $(p \wedge q)$ is $p \wedge \bar{q}$
3. Neg $(p \wedge q)$ is $\bar{p} \wedge \bar{q}$ that is, R $(p \wedge q)$

One can easily imagine two transformations G and D such as (if · is any operation):

$$G(p \cdot q) = \bar{p} \cdot q \quad \text{and} \quad D(p \wedge q) = p \cdot \bar{q}$$

G and D are therefore transformations that, in a way, "decompose" R. If we posit:

$$I(abcd) = (abcd) \qquad G(abcd) = (cdab)$$
$$D(abcd) = (badc) \qquad R(abcd) = (dcba)$$

we obtain a new group that is isomorphic with respect to the group of Klein. This group is interesting in that, once it is applied to Level I propositions, it generates all contraries, and when applied to Level IV, it generates all subcontraries.

This may well solve one of the above-mentioned difficulties, yet the two poles remain excluded from the set.

2. Maury's experiment suggested that the model IGDR could be constructed. Even with no experimental data, one is tempted to generalise and to find out ways of "decomposing" transformations N and C. We then obtain two new groups, which again are isomorphic with respect to the group of Klein.

$$I(abcd) = (abcd) \qquad\qquad I(abcd) = (abcd)$$
$$H(abcd) = (a'b'cd) \qquad\qquad X(abcd) = (d'bca')$$
$$B(abcd) = (abc'd') \qquad\qquad Y(abcd) = (ac'b'd)$$
$$N(abcd) = (a'b'c'd') \qquad\qquad C(abcd) = (d'c'b'a')$$

Actually, an application of these groups to the lattice is disappointing: the latter keeps on splitting into several subsets. It seems useful therefore to adopt a new standpoint.

The IGDR, IHBN and IXYC groups are subgroups in a more general structure that I shall not study here (see Leresche, 1976). They are all algebraic in nature. Therefore, it seems reasonable enough to consider the Boolean ring and its two operations w and $\wedge$, instead of the Boolean lattice. When applying these various transformations, we obtain:

$A = \{p \, w \, q, \, p \equiv q, \, p, \, \bar{p}, \, q, \, \bar{q}, \, p \perp q, \, p \top q,\}$ that is, $0 + II + IV$

$B = \{p \wedge q, \, p \wedge \bar{q}, \, \bar{p} \wedge q, \, \bar{p} \wedge \bar{q}, \, p \vee q, \, p \leftarrow q, \, p \rightarrow q, \, p/q\}$ that is, $I + III$

We then produce the lattice by positioning:

p implies q iff $p \wedge q = p$

It is in that sense that we may assert the possibility of a synthesis between the idea of the INRC and the sixteen binary operations of propositional logic.

3. The psychologist has very good reasons to argue that the structure of the group of Klein plays an important part in the development of intelligence. But the mathematician knows another existing group structure with 4 elements, i.e. the cyclic group ISTQ:

I($abcd$) = ($abcd$)

S($abcd$) = ($bcda$)

T($abcd$) = ($cdab$)

Q($abcd$) = ($dabc$)

Can it be used as a model? Our answer is yes. When combined with the IHBN group, it allows for obtaining the same classes A and B we obtained before. (In fact, transformations S and H are sufficient for this.)

CONCLUSION/QUESTION

As far as I know, neither the cyclic group nor the groups that "decompose" N and C have ever been proved to match psychogenetic facts. Is this so for want of a closer look at them, or is it that the role of logico-mathematical models is limited? This question might be an important one for discussion.

REFERENCES

Boll, M. (1948). *Manuel de logique scientifique.* Paris: Dunod.

Goblot, E. (1918). *Traité de logique.* Paris: A. Colin.

Halmos, P. R. (1962). *Algebraic logic.* New York: Chelsea Pub.

Inhelder, B. & Piaget, J. (1958). *The growth of logical thinking from childhood to adolescence.* New York: Basic Books. (First French ed., 1955.)

Leresche, G. (1976). INRC et quelques groupes de transformations logiques. *Revue Européenne des Sciences Sociales, 14,* 219–241.

Piaget, J. (1970). *Structuralism.* New York: Basic Books. (First French ed., 1968.)

Piaget, J. (1972). *Essai de logique opératoire.* Paris: Dunod.

Russell, B. (1919). *Introduction to mathematical philosophy.* London: G. Allen & Unwin. (French transl., 1928.)

Seltman, M. & Seltman, P. (1985). *Piaget's logic.* London and New York: Allen & Unwin.

Serrus, C. (1945). *Traité de logique.* Paris: Aubier.

5 Logical Reasoning, Development and Learning

Barry Richards
University of Edinburgh

INTRODUCTION

Let us begin by declaring two assumptions. We assume that (1) there is genuine cognitive development and (2) the process is psychological in nature. To some these hypotheses will seem bold, if not fanciful, since it is far from clear that there can be a psychological account of cognitive development. To others the assumptions will appear nebulous because there are no secure criteria for discriminating what is cognitive and what is psychological. Despite the broad range of opinion, there would seem to be a certain underlying consensus. It is generally accepted that the problem of cognitive development, no matter how it may be resolved, can only be understood in terms of concepts. If anything develops, it must be concepts; they are the natural measure of development. Accordingly, it is felt that the process of development, if there is such a process, must be interpreted as a process of concept learning.

Given this consensus, we can formulate the "fundamental" question of cognitive development as follows: can there be an explanation of how concepts are learned which is both developmentally interesting and non-trivial? An explanation will be non-trivial only if it indicates how new concepts might be learned without presupposing that they are in some sense already known. It must, in effect, reveal how conceptual development is a coherent, and thus genuine, possibility. Such an explanation will then be interesting if it can demonstrate that the behavioural phenomena of development, when interpreted as concept development, conform to theoretical predictions. To meet these criteria, it will be necessary to have more than a vague idea of what concepts are. Since any adequate theory will have to explain how concepts are built up incrementally, it must inevitably invoke some account of their structure, i.e. of how the parts of a concept are related to the whole. As such, a theory cannot but express a certain philosophical perspective.

With respect to this and other philosophical matters, however, we shall be less than explicit: our immediate aim is not to defend any particular philosophical position, nor to elaborate a comprehensive theory of cognitive development. It is rather to explore one possible explanation of one concrete example, namely the development of the concept of object permanence. The pattern of behaviour associated with this concept is among the most stable and well-documented of all developmental phenomena, and as a result the desiderata that an adequate account must satisfy are unusually clear. Moreover, the nature of the data is sufficiently surprising to induce one to speculate about the details of an explanatory theory. This we have done elsewhere (Richards, 1985). Here we propose to highlight some of the predictions of that theory and indicate one or two of the "promising horizons". The real test of a theory, it is sometimes said, is not only its predictive adequacy but its theoretical richness. A good theory will do more than account for the data under investigation; it will also suggest avenues of enquiry that offer the prospect of new insights.

From a Piagetian point of view development is a special kind of cognitive process, one that cannot obviously be assimilated to other rational processes. If it is a form of learning, it is unlike any of the forms typically studied—e.g. operant learning. From our perspective, however, developmental learning is not unconnected with operant learning. The two work on a common foundation and invoke some of the same cognitive resources. They may, nevertheless, be distinct processes. Once we have characterised the structure of developmental learning, we shall speculate about the nature of the difference.

SOME BASIC IDEAS

Of particular interest in the study of development is the character of "transitional" behaviour—i.e. the behaviour associated with the transition from one developmental stage to another. In the case of the object concept there appears to be a definite pattern that is repeated through each of the substages. When an infant is initially presented with a task, he behaves as if he does not appreciate that there is a task; he seems mystified to the point of ignoring the situation. On later presentations of the task he displays a certain genuine frustration, of a sort that suggests that he is entertaining a paradoxical problem. His behaviour is like that of one who is conceptually stymied. Eventually, he responds appropriately by solving the problem.

Our theory predicts that the process of transition will reflect a pattern of behaviour of this sort and provides an account of the underlying mechanism.

The basic hypothesis is that infants are born rational and that development proceeds in terms of reasoning. To explain the process of development through the substages of the object concept, we assume that infants understand how to reason in terms of three simple notions: conjunction, disjunction and negation. Such an assumption is not unreasonable since these concepts seem fundamental to the possibility of learning and understanding anything. Where there is no appreciation of the conjunction, disjunction and negation of concepts—i.e. of propositions in which they occur—they can hardly be seen to have much content or useful potential. Concepts that cannot themselves be conjoined, disjoined or negated would be so singular as to be curious, if not unworthy, candidates for the name. Since it is also difficult to imagine how conjunction, disjunction and negation might be learned from anything more basic, there seems little alternative but to regard them as primitive. Anyone who does not already grasp them could not, it seems, acquire them. Although this may not be an argument that they are primitive, it is surely a good reason for supposing that they might be.

Taking them to be primitive, however, is not to assume that they are univocal in meaning. It is possible that infants understand them in more than one way. We conjecture, in fact, that infants reason by virtue of at least two different logics, namely the logic of first-degree entailment and classical logic, and thus they understand conjunction (*and*), disjunction (*or*) and negation (*not*) in at least two different (though related) senses. In classical logic a proposition can have only one of two truth values, true (t) or false (f), and this gives rise to one sort of sense of *and, or* and *not*. In the logic of first-degree entailment, on the other hand, there are four possible truth values which a proposition might have: true (t), false (f), neither true nor false ($\emptyset$), and both true and false ($\{t, f\}$).[1] Here the connectives have a somewhat different sense.

Let us first define their classical meanings, for which we use the following diagram:

---

[1] From the viewpoint of logic, the two additional truth values may be chosen arbitrarily, provided they have the proper algebraic significance. This is not to imply, however, that the particular choices will always be without explanatory significance. In fact, the values $\emptyset$ and $\{t, f\}$ will play an important role in our theory, e.g. in linking it to the behavioural phenomena.

To find the value of a conjunction, the diagram is to be read downwards: where A and B are propositions, the truth value of (A *and* B) is the lower of the truth values of A and B if they are different, and otherwise the same as they are. In effect (A *and* B) is true if and only if A and B are both true. In the case of disjunction, the diagram is to be read upwards: the truth value of (A *or* B) is the higher of the truth values of A and B if they are different, and otherwise the same as they are. Thus (A *or* B) is true if and only if A and B are not both false. The interpretation of negation is indicated by the double-headed arrow, which implies that the truth value of *not* A is the opposite of the truth value of A. If A is *t*, *not* A is *f*, and if A is *f*, *not* A is *t*.

Given these definitions, we can formulate logical implication in this way: one proposition logically implies another if the truth value of the former is always lower than or equal to the truth value of the latter. That is, A logically implies B if B is true whenever A is. By way of illustration, let us consider one important pattern of reasoning, sometimes called disjunctive syllogism. The inference from the proposition [(C *or* D) *and not* C] to D is valid in classical logic since it is not possible for [(C *or* D) *and not* C] to be true and D false. Note that the former can be true only if C is false, for otherwise *not* C would be false and hence so, too, would the conjunction. But then D must also be true since the disjunction (C *or* D) can be true only if D is. Thus whenever the conjunction [(C *or* D) *and not* C] is true so is D, which means that disjunctive syllogism is classically valid.

This pattern of reasoning figures prominently in our account of the development of the object concept; we claim that infants use it to solve the two-place hiding problem that characterises substage 4. When infants come to reason classically about the problem, which they do not initially do, they can solve it by invoking disjunctive syllogism. At first, however, they interpret the problem within the logic of first-degree entailment where not all propositions are seen to be either true or false. Since disjunctive syllogism is not valid in first-degree entailment, they cannot use it to resolve their puzzle. For a discussion of the form of the puzzle and the role of disjunctive syllogism see Richards (1985).[2]

To distinguish the meanings of *and, or* and *not* in first-degree entailment, we need the following Hasse diagram:

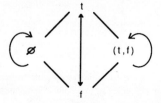

---

[2] See in particular pp. 53–59.

This diagram represents a partial ordering of the set of four truth values: given any two values, one may be lower than the other, or identical to it, or incomparable with it. The values $\emptyset$ and $\{t, f\}$ are regarded as incomparable because neither one is lower than the other. This structure is relevant to the strategy for interpreting conjunctions and disjunctions of propositions. To find the value of a conjunction, the diagram is again to be read downwards: the truth value of (A *and* B) is the lower of the truth values of A and B if they are different and comparable; if they are incomparable, (A *and* B) is false. When A and B have the same truth value, (A *and* B) also has that value. As in classical logic, (A *and* B) will be true if and only if both A and B are true; but when it is not true, it may have a value other than false.

In the case of disjunctions, the diagram is to be read upwards: the truth value of (A *or* B) is the higher of the truth values of A and B if they are different and comparable; if they are incomparable, (A *or* B) is true. When A and B have the same truth value, (A *or* B) also has that value. First-degree disjunction differs significantly from classical disjunction since (A *or* B) can be true even though neither A nor B is true.

The meaning of negation is given by the three arrows. When A is $\emptyset$, its negation *not* A is also $\emptyset$; and similarly when A is $\{t, f\}$, *not* A is $\{t, f\}$. The values t and f are related, as one would expect: if A is t, *not* A is f; and if A is f, *not* A is t.

Logical implication is defined as it was above: one proposition logically implies another if the truth value of the former is always lower than or equal to the truth value of the latter. To help fix these notions, let us show that disjunctive syllogism is not valid in first-degree entailment: from [(C *or* D) *and not* C] one cannot validly infer D. Suppose that C is $\emptyset$ and D is $\{t, f\}$. By the definition of disjunction (C *or* D) will then be t, and by the definition of negation *not* C will be $\emptyset$. As a result, the conjunction of these propositions must be $\emptyset$, since it is the lower of the two truth values. But $\emptyset$ is incomparable with the assumed truth value of D, namely $\{t, f\}$. Hence disjunctive syllogism is not an instance of valid reasoning in the logic of first-degree entailment. As we suggested above, this is crucial to our explanation of the behaviour at substage 4.

Although the logic of first-degree entailment is weaker than classical logic, every inference that is valid in the former is also valid in the latter. That is, the logic of first-degree entailment is properly included within classical logic. It is interesting to observe that the weaker logic has the more complex semantic diagram. By pruning the nodes for $\emptyset$ and $\{t, f\}$ in the diagram of first-degree entailment, one realises the diagram for classical logic. Thus to strengthen the logic it is sufficient to prune the semantics.

Significantly, there is a logic that stands between classical logic and first-degree entailment. This is indicated by the following diagram:

$$
\left(
\begin{array}{c}
\nearrow \ \text{t} \\
| \\
(\text{t},\text{f}) \ \circlearrowright \\
| \\
\searrow \ \text{f}
\end{array}
\right)
$$

The method of interpretation is exactly as before, and so too is the definition of logical implication. The logic defined here turns out to include the logic of first-degree entailment and to be properly included in classical logic. Thus to prune only the node for Ø of first-degree entailment yields a sort of "half-way" house, though one in which disjunctive syllogism remains invalid.[3] This, too, is important to our account of substage 4.

We can now indicate the structure of the process that takes an infant through the substages of the object concept. When the infant first confronts a developmental task, he formulates it within the environment of first-degree entailment. One of the propositions he represents is the solution to the task presented, but he entertains it as having the value Ø, i.e. as being neither true nor false. This reflects his initial attitude that the proposition is irrelevant to the task. Subsequently he comes to suspect that his proposition may not be irrelevant, but he finds himself in a conflict: if it is true, it seems to contradict other things that he supposes to be true. In the circumstance he assigns it a paradoxical status, envisaging that it is both true and false, i.e. $\{t, f\}$. Finally, he conjectures that it cannot be both true and false but must be either one or the other, at which point the proposition becomes "operative" for the task in hand. He can now seek to verify or falsify it, since he entertains it as being either true or false. In the context he is motivated to find out which it is and thereby discovers the solution to the puzzle.

The question is what moves the infant from one phase of the process to the next? What moves him from first envisaging the solution as Ø, to entertaining it as $\{t, f\}$, to concluding that it must be either t or f? Here we invoke the idea of diagram pruning and suppose that the procedure reflects a general developmental strategy. To appreciate the nature of the strategy, one must understand the significance of the truth values Ø and $\{t, f\}$—i.e. the import of entertaining a proposition to be one or the other. When a proposition is taken to be Ø, this is tantamount to seeing it as being *irrelevant*. It is to envisage no state of affairs that could alter the truth value

---

[3] This can be shown by assigning f to D and $\{t, f\}$ to C.

of the proposition. It is, in effect, to regard the proposition as having no definite content. Since there is no point in attempting to verify or falsify such a proposition, it can only be entertained as irrelevant. The situation is radically different when a proposition is taken to be $\{t, f\}$. Here one is virtually entertaining a contradiction and hence something that is compatible with every possible state of affairs. Since any attempt to verify what one entertains will also be an attempt to falsify it, and vice versa, one is envisaging more content than can be justified. For this reason a proposition that is held to be $\{t, f\}$ can only be seen as *paradoxical*. In contrast, a proposition that is held to be either true or false will be seen as potentially verifiable or falsifiable. Depending upon the state of the world, the proposition must be true or false. As such, it may be *relevant*. What makes a proposition developmentally relevant is that the infant represents it in response to a particular task. In the circumstance he is motivated to find out which it is, true or false.

The underlying developmental strategy can be summarised as follows: transform any proposition that is projected as irrelevant into one that is relevant. The mechanism for achieving this is effectively diagram pruning, and the process is tripartite in nature. The infant first envisages the proposition as irrelevant, then as paradoxical, and finally as relevant. The procedure for moving from the first to the second phase involves pruning the four-value diagram of the node for $\varnothing$, leaving the three-value diagram indicated above. This forces a reassignment of truth value; what is initially assigned the value $\varnothing$ will now be assigned $\{t, f\}$. The move from the second to the third phase involves pruning the three-value diagram of the node for $\{t, f\}$, leaving the classical two-value one. Again this forces a reassessment of truth assignment, but here there need be no reassignment; it is sufficient that what was seen as $\{t, f\}$ is now taken to be either t or f.

SUBSTAGE 3

The nature of this strategy, as well as the general outline of the theory, can be more easily appreciated in terms of an example. Let us consider the task at substage 3, which is very simple in form. Here an object that is in the infant's proximate environment and in full view is hidden under a cover, and the task is to discover that in situations like this the object is under the cover. The infant's initial response is usually to behave as one who is confronted with something he can hardly interpret. He does not seem to perceive what he sees as a problem but rather as a phenomenon that is so mystifying as not even to be curious. He simply ignores the task.

How do we account for his behaviour? Roughly speaking, we conjecture that the infant is mystified because he perceives no relation between the object he is attending to and its subsequent placement under the cover. Although he represents the proposition,

1. The object is there (under the cover)

he does not appreciate that it is relevant to the situation in which he finds himself. He has not, as it were, put the pieces together to realise that the object he was attending to can be retrieved from under the cover. His state of mind can be characterised by saying that he represents proposition [1] as being neither true nor false, i.e. as Ø. In effect, he envisages nothing in this situation, nor in any other, which could bear on the truth or falsity of [1]. As such, it is predictable that he will look neither under the cover nor anywhere else. He is so totally mystified as not to entertain the object as being anywhere.

But he does not stay that way. Eventually he becomes frustrated when presented with the substage-3 task. He seems to suspect that the object must be under the cover and yet simultaneously assumes that it cannot be there. It is as if he is confronted with a paradox: while the object can only be under the cover, it cannot be there (since it is nowhere). Given that he entertains [1] as both true and false, it is no wonder that he is frustrated. There can be no point in attempting to verify or falsify a proposition that is $\{t, f\}$ since any state of affairs will be compatible with it. Contradictions are compatible with anything and thus allow nothing to be available for discovery. As a result, the infant is "robbed" of the motivation to look under the cover. Although he surmises that the object must be there, the rational basis for searching is thwarted by the paradox he entertains. Hence the infant will, as before, fail to search anywhere. Although the infant may show a "tendency" to look under the cover, he will in the end look nowhere.

In the final phase the infant seems to free himself from paradox and searches under the cover. We conjecture that he comes to realise that proposition [1] must be either true or false and is thereby motivated to find out which it is. By entertaining [1] as bivalent, i.e. as being necessarily either t or f, the infant envisages [1] as relevant. Not only does he now see it as verifiable or falsifiable, but he does so in the immediate context of the task. In the circumstance he is sufficiently motivated to search.

The strategy that brings the infant to this end is, as we have suggested, tantamount to diagram pruning. The point is to reduce the range of possible truth values so as to allow relevant reasoning.[4] Working within the

---

[4] It should be emphasised that the infant can reason relevantly *in the intended sense* only within classical logic. This may seem strange to logicians who would espouse relevance logic, of which the logic of first-degree entailment is a fragment. Curiously enough, the valuation space of first-degree entailment is not sufficiently constrained to lead the infant to reason relevantly; it admits too many possibilities and hence loses significant semantic structure.

four-value environment of the logic of first-degree entailment, the infant first entertains proposition [1] as having the value $\emptyset$. When this value is pruned away, the infant is forced to assign a new value to [1]. Given his state of mind, he can only choose the paradoxical value $\{t, f\}$. But when this value is also pruned away, the infant can only suppose that [1] must be bivalent, either t or f. Which value it actually has is something he must discover, and for this he has to look under the cover.

Once the infant is able to solve the substage-3 task he has progressed to substage 4. What sort of conceptual advance this represents is discussed at some length in Richards (1985). While this is plainly an issue of central importance to the theory, it is not immediately central to our current objective, which is to explore the theoretical richness of the theory. For the moment let us focus on the most salient prediction, which basically consists of two claims: (1) the initial formulation of a task will be within the logic of first-degree entailment; and (2) the process of transition will be tripartite in nature, with each phase displaying a form of behaviour characteristic of the underlying mechanism. Together, these claims are tantamount to predicting that the order of the phases will be uniform and unidirectional; i.e. the infant will move from first envisaging the solution as $\emptyset$, to entertaining it as $\{t, f\}$, to perceiving it as bivalent. The procedure of diagram pruning is constructed so as to yield this result.

LEARNING AND DEVELOPMENT

The question is whether these predictions coincide with the facts. Does each substage of the object concept emerge through such a tripartite process? In Richards (1985) we show how substages 4 and 5 can be construed so as to reflect an appropriate form: while the tasks are somewhat more complicated, the process of transition is uniformly tripartite. Piaget's investigations of the object concept lead naturally to the conjecture that the transition from one substage to another is typically a tripartite process, although not of the sort that our theory adumbrates. He supposes that the mechanism is non-logical since the ability to reason logically is itself something that develops. This underscores the fact that there are really two issues that we must confront, one phenomenological and the other theoretical. If the process of transition proves to display the predicted phenomenological structure, does it do so for the reasons we suggest?

Here it is useful to note another prediction of the theory, one that is in direct opposition to Piaget's theory. He sees action to be an essential ingredient in the process of development; action provides the basis for reflective abstraction and, hence, infants who cannot act on their environments do not have the means to develop. While we would agree that action might be an aid to development, our theory would predict that it is not essential. Since the underlying mechanism is logical in nature, i.e. works by virtue of logical structures, the means by which new concepts emerge does not rest on an ability to initiate appropriate action. Thus physically handicapped infants are not seen to be restricted in their potential for conceptual development; they have all the potential that any normal infant has, although that potential may be more slowly realised. How severely impaired infants actually develop is therefore of considerable significance. If their conceptual horizons are severely limited, Piaget's account will be the more compelling. But if the course of development is otherwise—i.e. if it proceeds more or less normally—his explanation can only be found wanting, indeed necessarily so. This is not to say, of course, that our explanation must then be the correct one, even though it would coincide with the facts. But the case would become somewhat more compelling if there were independent evidence for the basic assumption, namely that infants possess an innate capacity to reason logically.

To this end we shall consider a task situation that is unconnected with the development of the object concept, and apparently with any other aspect of development. The environment is intended to explore operant learning in infants who are approximately 4 months old. Here the task is to learn the connection between a simple state of affairs, where the process of association might perhaps be explained by a stimulus-response theory. In contrast, the tasks that "measure" the emergence of the object concept are typically felt to require a different form of learning. Since our theory purports to capture its distinctive characteristics, it may be thought that non-developmental learning will be non-logical in nature, although not necessarily of a stimulus-response sort. But this is not what our theory would predict. On the assumption that infants are endowed with the ability to reason logically, we would expect to see evidence of its application across different and unrelated task domains, e.g. in simple operant environments. This is just what appeared to emerge from certain pilot studies caried out in Edinburgh. Infants sometimes seemed to approach operant tasks by invoking a pattern of reasoning that was plainly logical. There was no evidence, however, that the process of discovery was tripartite in structure. This would suggest that operant learning, although perhaps logical in nature, may still be different from developmental learning. We shall have one or two things to say about this below.

Let us now sketch the experimental environment used in the pilot studies.[5] The infant is seated in a reclining chair in front of a screen on which is projected a brightly coloured mobile. A photoelectric beam is

---

[5] The work referred to here was done by David Wallace and will be reported in his Ph.D. thesis, which is to be submitted jointly to the Centre for Cognitive Science and the Department of Psychology.

placed so that when the infant raises one or both of his legs to full extension, the beam is broken. The mobile is wired to rotate when the beam is broken. It is assumed that the projection of the rotating mobile is a sufficient stimulus to engage the infant in the task. How the task is conceived by the experimenter depends upon how the stimulus is controlled. If the mobile is rotated on occasions other than those on which the beam is broken, the most that the infant can discover is that when he extends his leg(s) appropriately, the mobile moves. This is not to say that in such circumstances the infant will necessarily be uninterested in what happens when he does not extend his leg(s). Since he does not know exactly what the task is, he may in the course of events consider both possibilities—that leg extension may not only be *sufficient* for mobile movement but also *necessary* for it.[6] The pilot studies would suggest that this could well be the case.

Perhaps the most revealing aspect of the studies was the way infants reacted to and explored the environment. It was observed that while they were initially attracted by the stimulus itself, their interest was not long sustained by that alone. Where they displayed no suspicion that they might have some control over the stimulus, their attention quickly wandered. But when their suspicion was galvanised, they seemed to anticipate the possibility of having complete control. That is, they seemed to project that leg extension might be both necessary and sufficient for mobile movement. Since the actual state of affairs was unclear, this was obviously a useful strategy.

It is not obvious, however, how the infant could test both possibilities, at least not without a little logical reasoning. To test whether leg extension was sufficient the infant could stick his leg(s) out and see what happened. If the mobile did not rotate, his hypothesis would be falsified; if it did rotate, he would have reason to think that it might be true. What he would be testing for on a given occasion can be formulated as follows: "If my leg(s) are extended on that occasion, the mobile will rotate on that occasion." For convenience let us abbreviate the proposition in this way, with o being a parameter referring to the relevant occasion.

2. *If* L(o) *then* M(o).

It should be noted that the intended sense of *if–then* is here the truth functional one; there is no need to appeal to any sense stronger than this. Thus [2] is equivalent to

3. *Not* [L(o) *and not* M(o)].

The equivalence is important, since it implies that [2] can be understood by infants who are assumed to know the truth-functional meanings of *and, or*

---

[6] The concepts of being necessary and sufficient are here understood in the logical sense.

and *not*. We shall, nevertheless, use [2] rather [3] since it is somewhat more perspicuous. Now what could the infant do to test whether leg extension was necessary for mobile movement? For a given occasion he must find out whether the following is true:

4. *If* M(*o*) *then* L(*o*).

Plainly, there is no obvious way in which he could make the antecedent true so as to see what the consequent would be. What he could do, however, is make the consequent false and see what the antecedent would be. If it is true, he would have falsified the hypothesis; if it is false, he would have reason to think that it may be true.

But to invoke this strategy he must either use the logical rule of *modus tollens* or infer from [4] that

5. *If not* L(*o*) *then not* M(*o*).

It does not matter which he opted for, since they are effectively equivalent. What is significant is that they are both instances of logical reasoning and, it so happens, valid in all three of the logics that are used to explain development.[7] One infant in the pilot studies showed a particularly striking pattern of behaviour. After extending his legs a number of times and watching the mobile rotate, he tucked his legs right under the chair and waited to see what happened. The sequence was repeated. It was hard to resist interpreting his behaviour as an attempt to make the consequent of [4] false, with a view to investigating the effect on the antecedent. What more obvious way to make the consequent false than to stick one's legs way back under the chair? Natural though it is to assume this, it must be admitted that it is far from a secure hypothesis. Still, it is highly suggestive and worthy of further enquiry. If it can withstand closer scrutiny, it would help to "vindicate" the basic assumption underlying our theory of development. It would also point to an interesting possibility.

Within our theory it might be possible to characterise the difference between development and operant learning. While both involve logical reasoning, only development invokes a "meta-theoretical" strategy. As we have illustrated, the process of transition from one substage to another is explained by a strategy that works over the semantic structures of three different logics. The strategy is appropriately seen as a meta-theoretical procedure since it is not strictly part of any of the logics but is rather defined over them. The situation may be different in the case of operant learning. Here the process may be explicable wholly within the logics

---

[7] It is sufficient to show that they are valid in the logic of first-degree entailment since this entails that they are also valid in the other two logics. One can verify their validity in the four-value diagram, and hence the proof is left to the reader.

themselves. In the particular case of the pilot study there was no appeal to the meta-theory of the three logics that might be involved. Both the rule of *modus tollens* and the principle of contraposition belong to the logics themselves, not to any part of the meta-theory. Since they are valid in all three logics, it does not matter which one the infant is taken to be working in. Hence the learning process will be the same in each case. Given that it does not involve the meta-theoretical procedure used in developmental learning, one would expect that it ought not to be tripartite. And in fact there was no evidence that it was. As a consequence, one may conjecture that the distinction between operant learning and development may be of some genuine interest.

We should emphasise that we do not claim to have established this to be so. We have, rather, pursued a line of speculation with a view to indicating the potential richness of our theory of development. Such a logically based theory seems not without empirical import, or fruitful predictions. In the circumstance further research may not be unjustified

REFERENCE

Anderson, A. & Belnalp, N. (1972). *Entailment*. Princeton: Princeton University Press.

Beth, E. W. & Piaget, J. (1966). *Mathematical epistemology and psychology*. Dordrecht: D. Reidel.

Bower, T. G. R. (1974). *Development in infancy*. San Francisco: W. H. Freeman.

Brainerd, C. J. (1976). *Piaget's theory of intelligence*. Englewood Cliffs: Prentice-Hall.

Fodor, J. A. (1976). *The language of thought*. Brighton: Harvester Press.

Furth, H. G. (1981). *Piaget and knowledge*. 2nd ed. Chicago: University of Chicago Press.

Makinson, D. C. (1973). *Topics in modern logic*. London: Methuen.

Piaget, J. (1954). *The construction of reality in the child*. New York: Basic Books. (First French ed.: 1937.)

Piaget, J. (1967). *Six psychological studies*. New York: Random House. (First French ed., 1964.)

Piaget, J. (1970). *Genetic epistemology*. New York: Columbia University Press.

Piaget, J. (1971). *Biology and knowledge*. Chicago: University of Chicago Press. (First French ed., 1967.)

Piaget, J. & Inhelder, B. (1973). *Memory and intelligence*. London: Routledge & Kegan Paul. (First French ed., 1968.)

Richards, B. (1985). Constructivism and logical reasoning. *Synthese, 65*, 33–64.

Wishart, J. G. (1979) The development of the object concept in infancy. Unpublished doctoral thesis. University of Edinburgh.

6 The Value of Logic and the Logic of Values

Seymour Papert
Massachussets Institute of Technology

First I would like to clarify some double meanings of the words "value" and "logic" and the way they enter into thinking about intelligence. The relevant distinction has been made many times about logic. Most recently, Henri Wermus reminded us that we should distinguish between two ways in which logic might figure in Piaget. Sometimes Piaget uses logic to talk about a domain of knowledge used by the subjects he is studying; sometimes he uses logic as the theoretical construct, as the matter out of which his representations are modelled. The first sense studies the child's logic just as it studies the child's geometry. The second uses logic to study the child's intelligence in all its departments. One could call the two senses "the subject's logic" and "the psychologist's logic". I would have intervened yesterday to say that these two are not that separate. Nevertheless, as a first approximation, it is good to see them as pulling in opposite directions even though they are tightly unified.

Where the subject's logic and the psychologist's logic are not so separate is when Piaget talks about logic that is explicitly present in the child's reasoning. If the child said "p or q", then we would know it was logic. There would be no question of distinguishing between the subject's logic and the psychologist's injection of logic. In fact, the child never does say "p or q", so interpretation is always present. But direct interpretation of the child's discourse as an exercise of logic is quite different from what I understand Piagetian theorists like Grize (Chapter 4, this volume) to be saying, where you do not even pretend that there is anything vaguely like logic in the surface structure. Instead, logic is entirely in some kind of deep

101

structure; it is a material out of which other things are made. I will return to this later.

Part of my "Piaget diatribe" is that he often makes things much more difficult for himself, for us and for the rest of the world with an extra layer of logical interpretations. If he had separated the two a little more, you could see the commonsensical aspects of what he is saying far more clearly. It gets tangled by being buried in logical roots.

Except for my "diatribe", there is nothing new in noting this distinction about logic. It is less familiar when applied to values. One might be talking about value judgements made by the subjects, or about the values that are built into the psychologist's thinking. I want to suggest that making models of certain sorts does carry implications about values. To illustrate these ideas, I shall talk about Carol Gilligan's (1982) very important work in criticism of Larry Kohlberg's models of moral development. I will recapitulate, in a highly over-simplified form, some of the issues that come up in this debate.

Kohlberg picks up on Piaget's stage theory. He asks what are the stages of development of moral judgement, just as Piaget asked what were the stages of numerical reasoning. The stages that Kohlberg discerns start with value judgements of a highly egocentric form. In the earliest stages, judgements of what is good or bad are referred to the subject: what I like is what is good. Then there is a decentering process—the criteria move out to other people. Now I say something is good because it is good for somebody else, or it is bad because it hurts somebody else. But even within that, there are subdivisions that one could make. For example, why do I think that something is bad? Because if I hurt you, you might hurt me sometime. This is somewhat decentered, but still tinged with egocentrism. From here, the stages are progressively more detached; they do not refer back to oneself. Finally, the highest stage of development is having moral *principles*. At this stage, if I ask whether I should kill, I do not say, "I don't kill because I might be killed back, or because it might hurt someone". I say, "I don't kill because killing is bad". It is an abstract principle, reduced to the analytic.

Kohlberg's stages resemble Piaget's in another way too: not everyone eventually adopts the forms of reasoning characteristic of what the theorists postulate as the "highest stage". What does one do in the face of such data? One might deduce that the theorist is wrong or one might deplore the fact that many people do not reach the ultimate heights of development. Gilligan's book "*In a Different Voice*" presents a compelling case for the thesis that many people whose moral reasoning does not qualify for Kohlberg's highest stage are nevertheless to be counted as highly sophisticated, highly moral people. They are not stuck in an inferior stage of development; they have followed a different speaking path, as it were, in a different voice.

Gilligan's position is made more poignant—and perhaps given greater depth—by its relation to gender issues. She does not assert anything as blunt as "all men follow the Kohlberg pattern while all women speak in her different voice." However, she does find (at least in this generation of American culture) a significant tendency for women to deviate from the Piaget–Kohlberg expectation that abstract and absolute principles mark the highest level of human intellectual development. In their discussion of moral principles, women are far more inclined to "contextualize" the discussion. The ultimate criterion for the morality of the act is not its conformity to categorical imperatives but a weighing up of its human consequences. If she is right, Kohlberg must be regarded as describing not the stages of human development, but the stages of male development. Could this be true of Piaget as well?

I suggest that the debate between Kohlberg and Gilligan goes further than moral principles. I believe that something like Gilligan's two voices can be heard in all domains, including the logical and mathematical. Her critique of Kohlberg suggests a critique of all theories based on a vision of the abstract as the ultimate. It leads us to ask whether we have been carried away by a tacit assumption that the formal stage is somehow higher, better, farther along than the non-formal.

One experiment that questions this assumption in the domain of morals is described by Gilligan (Gilligan, 1982:25–32). Two 11-year-olds are presented with a moral dilemma: "Should Heinz steal a drug which he cannot afford to buy in order to save his wife's life?" The boy is sure that Heinz should steal the drug, and equally sure that a judge's thinking would be based on the same logical steps and would therefore arrive at the same conclusion.

> Constructing the dilemma, as Kohlberg did, as a conflict between the values of property and life, [the boy] discerns the logical priority of life and uses that logic to justify his choice.... His judgment... rests on the assumption of agreement, a societal consensus around moral values that allows one to know and expect others to recognize what is "the right thing to do". Fascinated by the power of logic, [he] locates truth in math, which, he says, is "the only thing that is totally logical".

The girl, on the other hand, says that "there might be other ways besides stealing it, like if [Heinz] could borrow the money or make a loan or something, but he really shouldn't steal the drug—but his wife shouldn't die either". She sees in this dilemma

> ...not a math problem with humans but a narrative of relationships that extends over time. [She] envisions the wife's continuing need for her husband and the husband's continuing concern for his wife and seeks to respond to the druggist's need in a way that would sustain rather than sever connection....

Just as [the boy] is confident the judge would agree that stealing is the right thing for Heinz to do, [the girl] is confident that "if Heinz and the druggist had talked it out long enough, they could reach something besides stealing".... Both children thus recognize the need for agreement but see it as mediated in different ways—he impersonally through systems of logic and law, she personally through communication in relationship. Just as he relies on the conventions of logic to deduce the solution to this dilemma, so she relies on a process of communication, assuming connection and believing that her voice will be heard.

It is much harder to question the sequence when you are discussing logic than when you are discussing morality. More people are inclined to say— once they have seen the point—that they understand Gilligan, that Kohlberg has been an exaggerated formalist, and maybe it is good not to be formalistic in morality. But when you talk about logic, the idea of relativity in logic is not so easily accepted. Yet there are many people who do not use formal logic. They do not deny the principles of formal logic, they simply prefer to think in another way. If you give them a problem, they will use this other way and tests may show them as "not formal". It is not that they could not have done the formal reasoning, they just felt uncomfortable with it. I will give some concrete examples to show what might happen.

I would like to start with an old story that I have gradually followed over a long time. Every now and then I come back to it and collect more data. This line of investigation started with Wertheimer, who carried out a very interesting experiment related to the concept of what is difficult and what is easy in mathematics.

I think everybody knows the story of how Gauss was supposed to have discovered the principle of summing $1 + 2 + 3 + 4 \ldots$ up to 100, by the usual trick of writing it backwards underneath and noticing that it gives you 101 every time, so you have 50 times 101. Gauss is said to have discovered this when his teacher gave this task to the entire class in order to keep them busy, thinking it would take them a long time to add all the numbers. He was very surprised when Gauss produced the answer almost instantaneously. This is quoted very often as an example of precocious childhood genius.

Wertheimer tried it out—he put many children in the situation where they might have discovered this, and found that a fair proportion will discover something like this, even though they have not been taught it in any way. That has a lot to do with your perception of what is difficult and what is easy in mathematical discovery. It is very difficult to have an accurate assessment of what is easy and what is difficult for anybody except yourself, or people sufficiently like you.

My second example comes from my own work and is described in detail in *Mindstorms* (Papert, 1980: 197–202). The subjects here were college-aged and older, but one can obtain similar results for children. They were asked to prove that the square root of 2 is irrational. This proof also has a history—like the Gauss story—of being regarded as fantastically difficult, and Euclid's proof was a kind of monument of mathematical elegance and a unique event.

Many people with very little mathematical knowledge can discover Euclid's proof if emotionally supportive conditions encourage them to keep going. Many also discover another proof, one that is seen by some as better than Euclid's. It is quite interesting to ask why G. H. Hardy, for example, who wrote a lot about it, made much of the supreme elegance of Euclid's proof, and did not think of the other one. The theorem is that $\sqrt{2}$ is irrational; that is to say that it is impossible to have

$$\sqrt{2} = p/q$$

where p and q are whole numbers.

To prove that this is impossible, we assume it is true and try to deduce a contradiction. We note at this point that if such numbers p and q exist at all, then there is a pair of numbers which are not *both* even. So we can assume that either p or q (and possibly both) is odd.

Almost everybody who knows some school algebra multiplies both sides by q, and then squares both sides to get

$$p^2 = 2q^2$$

That is an easy transformation, motivated by the heuristic "get rid of the square root". Incidentally, it casts the same problem in another form (which was probably the Greek form of it), namely: could you have two squares, one of which is exactly double the area of the other? I will present two different proofs that $p^2 = 2q^2$ is impossible.

You can see that p^2 is even because it is twice something, so p must be even too. (The squares of even numbers are always even, the squares of odd numbers are odd.) You can write:

$$p = \text{twice something,} \quad \text{let's say } 2m$$

But in that case, I can substitute $(2m)^2$ for p^2 to get:

$$4m^2 = 2q^2$$

Now I can cancel out the 2 on both sides:

$$2m^2 = q^2$$

And, since q^2 is even, q is even—but that is a contradiction.

The other proof uses a very different process which is much less "sequential". It has to do with having a picture of numbers in terms of the prime number theorem. For example, 6 has two factors: 2 and 3. You can think of 6 as its two prime factors. Every number is uniquely represented as its prime factors. This sort of image is fairly well-rooted in our culture. I am not interested in where it came from, I am interested in what people do with it.

They say, "What about a square number?" (such as p^2). If 6 is 3,2, then 6 squared is 3,3,2,2. When you square the number, you double up the factors. So square numbers always have an even number of factors. But $2q^2$ has an odd number of factors: 2 and the factors of q^2. How can p^2 equal $2q^2$ when the first has an even number of factors and the other has odd? That is also a proof.

It is interesting to see people's reactions to this. Some think the first proof is terrible, others think the second is terrible.

The second proof uses a different voice of doing mathematics. The first is far closer to the model of logical deduction. I do not mean to say that you cannot formalise the second proof, simply that it does not feel like a formalised process. If you pursue the discussion of why they like the second one better, some people will say, "You can try it with specific numbers, you can play it through and see it more clearly".

This example shows different psychological styles or ways of thinking. Such differences appear not only in doing mathematics, but in problem solving generally. I think that psychological style is related to fairly clear and definable personality traits. There are people who like the feeling of giving up control to the outside process, and people who are softer, more negotiational. You can interpret, you can concretise it, you can make it your own. (Obsessives are like the first, and hysterics like the second.)

I stated the difference between the two proofs in terms of "control", but it could be cast equally well in terms of *logic*. I do not mean that the second proof is not "logical", simply that it does not demand the kind of step-by-step reasoning of traditional logic. The two styles are more strikingly separable when we look at mathematics as a creative activity in which "proof" is only a facet. (Actually, we can see the difference even when we look at proof, but this is not where it is most apparent.)

I now turn to some examples of children doing constructive mathematics, and describe some work we have been doing at M.I.T. with children. The most detailed writing about this work appears in *The second self* (Turkle, 1984), Chapter 3 of which describes the context of one school in which a "computer culture" developed. Two elements were essential to this process: the children had free and open access to the computers, and they were sufficiently ahead of their teachers to develop their own style of how to program the computer. This is very important in that context. Not that all of them did, but some did, and we were looking for those who did.

When children deal with number as it exists in our culture, it is not surprising that they construct their own version of number before they encounter the official one. When you give them the chance to play with computers, you might expect them to develop their own notion of computing or programming. Indeed, we see more variations here than we do with ideas of number.

The reason I am talking about computers here is that we have that wonderful situation where children are dealing with something that is new. Fairly mature children build constructs quite rapidly, so we do not have a long developmental process. The material lends itself to being put together in more than one way, and thus can be a window to different voices, to different styles of intellectual development.

I will describe two ways children program, as interpreted by Sherry Turkle: hard and soft programmers. (This distinction was meant to be a "natural" one, but unfortunately there are other connotations to these words—such as hard associated with boys and soft with girls.) I will take two extreme cases of how to program, and I will talk about their differences and how they fit into this other issue.

This work took place at the time the first space shuttle went up, and on that Monday, shuttle mania had reached the point where almost everybody in the school wanted to do something related to it. ("Even the girls!" as one girl remarked. Until then, spaceships were found far more often in the boys' work than in the girls'.) Graphic programming was very easy to do on the computers there. In particular, we were using Sprite Logo in which it is very easy to make dynamic objects move. A lot of children got involved in the same project—simulating a space shuttle on the screen—so we could see how different people approached the same task in different ways.

A caricature of the difference is that "hards" follow our culture's model of what programming is: logical and highly structured. When they write a program, they break their task down into sub-tasks and plan it all out. In fact, "planner" might be a better name than "hard". The "softs" are very different. They do not show any sign of wanting to plan and organise. It is not a question of whether they are able to do it or not; they just do not want to. They can reach the same result as the "hards", but they use a radically different process to get there, one that is very different from our culture's image of programming. Where "hard" is reminiscent of the mathematician following the structure of a step-by-step proof, "soft" corresponds more to the artistic process of painting. There is interaction, a negotiation between you and the thing.

Negotiation versus logic is what I want to emphasise here. One of these ways of programming lends itself more than the other to be modelled as logic. When we asked the teachers which children were doing good things with the computer, we got a list of the "hard" programmers—those who fit the projective model of the right thing to do. That model is a highly logical model. This is reflected in different ways by people who say that the computer is good for children because it teaches them to think logically.

This a popular belief. I present it not as a misunderstanding, but as a datum about the sociology of superficial knowledge. It tells us something about the way that the culture mediates in the establishment of logical models: for these teachers, it was obvious that hard mastery represented the highest stage.

The high value placed on logic has important implications. The teachers' valuing of logic blinded them to the other; they literally could not see it. Similarly, I think that Kohlberg was not particularly sexist in any conscious sense. He too was genuinely blinded by a deep-seated assumption that the abstract is best. That is the glass through which our culture makes us see intellectual development.

Where do these differences in programming style come from? This question is obviously very complex. When you look at the hard and soft styles, you can relate them to numerous other attempts to understand thinking. There are many such dichotomies: the left and right brain, the field dependent and field independent, the visual and verbal, etc.[2] Hard/ soft can be associated with many other dichotomies, possibly all of them. I do not mean to imply that the other dichotomies do not have a lot of importance, for they do. I simply do not want to get sidetracked into the issues of how these different dichotomies might reinforce one another. There are many mechanisms that can make them act together.

In her book, Turkle did develop one dichotomy that I want to pursue: the hypothesis that in a certain sense hards are thing-oriented and softs are people-oriented. The hard knows what he or she wants and pursues it. When you see hards making programs, it is more like the way you manipulate things, and the others are more like the way you manipulate people. I want to point out that in a certain sense, what we call logic is the logic of things. Even Grize (Chapter 4, this volume) said that, although he may have meant it in a slightly different sense. But I think there's a lot in what he said—that the logic of things is not the logic of people—for that you need a different way of thinking.

So it is not arbitrary to say that there are differences. For the softs and for Gilligan's "different voice", the role of logic (in the sense that it is usually understood) is very different from the usual one. Even if logic turns out to be relevant to modelling both kinds of behaviour, the way in which logic will enter into them is surely very different.

My last example is an analysis of Piaget's style of thinking about mathematics. He is often "accused" of being too taken with logic. But, in fact, one can see him as more related stylistically to the softs than to the hards, and closer to the prime factors proof than to Euclid's.

---

[2] Such dichotomising is probably an important process in itself, something essential to the evolution of a theory just as the things Piaget talks about are essential to children's intellectual development. They may even be a form of the same thing.

Pierre Greco once said that the most remarkable thing about Piaget's book on number was his courage in writing a book about number in which he says very little about number. It is about other things. He talks about order and ordering things, about nearness, farness and topologising things, about algebrising things. What Piaget says is very simple and very profound and very commonsensical. I want to detach this commonsensical aspect from an extra phase that goes beyond common sense into logic and that—as I said in the beginning—makes Piaget harder to understand.

Why is Piaget's concept of number important? If we jump ahead in history, we discover a close analogy between what Piaget said here in the 1930s and something that mathematicians who called themselves Bourbaki were doing in France much later. I'd like to compare Bourbaki with a different approach to number, that of any formalist such as Peano or Hilbert.

The important difference is that Bourbaki says that the way you make a structure like numbers is by separately axiomatising certain meanings for sub-structures. You axiomatise these separate, simpler structures—and then you put them together. In this picture, the structure of number is made up of parts that are separately meaningful structures, like the structure of ordering. In the Peano–Hilbert model, the axiomatisation is not represented as parts. You present a minimum set of axioms, and any subsets of them are just nonsense. This model does not give insight into the nature of number.

The difference between Bourbaki and Peano is a fundamental one. The same kind of difference exists between Piaget's ideas of how to represent number psychologically and the pre-existing idea in both philosophy and psychology—which is still there—which in essense says that numbers have a definition or that there is such a thing as the concept of number. The emphasis here is on seeing number as having parts—as both Piaget and Bourbaki did.

Psychologists probably did not conceptualise number that way because it requires some quite deep mathematical sophistication to be able to go along with that. It is not obvious to break numbers into parts. So it is interesting that Piaget found it.

The relationship between Piaget and Bourbaki comes from the fact that Bourbaki's mathematical way of breaking number up into sub-structures yields what are in fact psychologically simpler things than number. So you can think of the child learning order by working in a little universe of putting stones one on the other, or arranging sticks or dolls. There are many ways in which you can establish a mental horizon. I call this making a micro-world. By working in a micro-world, you work in a simplified piece of reality. Such pieces can be exercised and built up separately. This is what I mean by a very commonsensical interpretation of why number might emerge.

The next step in Piaget's story is analogous to the project that Grize presented to us in his chapter. The way Grize takes the formal structures and works on unifying them is incredibly beautifully elegant. He got that from Piaget. Piaget says to himself: "Okay, we've got these three things called 'groupement', we must have a unifying formalism." And there you are in that other branch of activity which asks for a unifying formalism—lattices, groups, logic, extension, intention.

I do not want to judge what is good about these two aspects of Piaget. I simply want to draw a line between them and say there is the soft aspect and the hard aspect; they are distinct—two separate enterprises. I do not talk about Piaget's theory of number itself. In any case, it is not time invariant, nor is it end-project invariant in Gruber's sense of project. There are two different projects. One results in seeing and thinking in terms of sub-systems: appropriable, learnable, developable pieces that are complete in themselves. The other is to formalise and unify the sub-systems.

I claim that the formalisation is the less important project. I will not say that it is useless heuristically, but, in terms of its immediate role, you can rip it out and you have a better theory—better because you are more relaxed about what the sub-systems are and do not have to force them into a procrustian sort of improved state-of-being.

My point is this: Piaget can be separated into two distinct voices. One speaks in the soft register, the other booms in the hard register, very determined (for reasons we could speculate about) to stay in that hard register and never drop it. This hard voice runs straight through Piaget's life until the "prise de conscience" when he sort of weaned himself from this hard enterprise. In short, Piaget disguised himself as a hard—but when he allowed himself to think as a soft, that freed him from the bonds that limit many people in a culture that values "hard" intellectual enterprises.

REFERENCES

Gilligan, C. (1982). *In a different voice: Psychological theory and women's development.* Cambridge, Mass.: Harvard University Press.

Papert, S. (1980). *Mindstorms: Children, computers, and powerful ideas.* New York: Basic Books.

Turkle, S. (1984). *The second self: Computers and the human spirit.* New York: Simon & Schuster.

7

The Masculine Authority of the Cognitive

John M. Broughton
Teachers College, Columbia University

The purpose of this chapter is to present a speculative vision of the Piagetian tradition that might suggest ways in which that phenomenon could be reinterpreted, broadening its scope. Piaget's work represents the genetic wing of the functionalist movement within twentieth-century psychology, that movement which has culminated in the investiture of cognition with the robes of paradigmatic monarchy. Any tradition has a cultural significance, and by acknowledging this in the case of cognitive developmental psychology we may restore to consciousness the social meaning that this psychology currently embodies. By admitting that monarchy is always partly pomp, partly circumstance, we may also rediscover the political character of the theory and its practice.

It is my particular concern to situate the distinguished Piagetian approach to scientific thought in relation to the technological imperative of our post-modern era, with its inventive forms of objectification and its innovative forms of authority. Moreover, it is my contention that a close examination of these connections reveals an extensive circuitry of power and knowledge that is implicated in and energised by recent shifts in the relationships between men and women.

I shall draw our attention back to Piaget's early attraction to molluscs, and postulate that, for the adolescent retreating to nature to escape his own biology, these creatures provided a convenient symbolic condensation

I should like to dedicate this essay to my friend Maxine Greene, in memory of her beloved daughter. Maxine's love of freedom has helped keep many of us, men and women, alive.

111

of male and female—an alternative title for the present chapter might have been "Bisexuality and the bivalve". Piaget's enthusiasm for malacology may have been more than just a case of youthful serendipity. It may have afforded a precious glimpse of emancipatory insight into the workings of modern political psychology. This glimpse was not made less real just because Piaget devoted the rest of his life to the active construction of an elaborate system designed to erase it from memory.

COGNITION AND THE DEVELOPMENT OF THE SELF

The Epistemological Self

Larry Kohlberg rescued me from the infancy fad of the 1960s and convinced me to transpose my romantic interest in the genetic epistemology of the object concept of the pre-linguistic era (e.g. Bower, Broughton & Moore, 1971) into a concern with research on the emergence of a theoretical reality in the adolescent construction of reflective epistemology. I had hoped to provide evidence of a single, iconoclastic discovery of epistemology, corresponding to the revelation of object permanence in infancy. Indeed, this is what we had all been led to believe must be the case by the speculative writings on adolescence by Inhelder and Piaget (1958).

Instead, I was surprised to find a multiplicity of epistemologies, a series of qualitatively emergent theories of knowledge, progressively displacing each other across a 15-year period (Broughton, 1978). Moreover, despite the prediction by Kohlberg and Gilligan (1971) that there was just one birth of the reflective "self", each epistemology in this seriated order was found to be accompanied by a distinct and innovative "epistemological self" (Broughton, 1975). It was not so much a matter of demonstrating that there was a genetic epistemology after childhood, as a documentation of the *genesis of epistemology* itself.

In addition, the findings of my cross-sectional interview study indicated a lack of support for the theoretically generated expectation that formal thought would lead naturally to a theory of knowledge (Broughton, 1977a). Conceptually and empirically, it appeared, Inhelder and Piaget had been overly hasty in equating reflective thought and self-consciousness with the logical recursiveness of formal operations.[1] Rather, what was indicated was that the cognitive self needed to rise above second-order logic and hypothetical scientific reasoning to a higher plane of the insights and illusions of philosophical rationality, a step that reflective abstraction of a logical kind alone could not provide.

---

[1] Instead, my findings provided empirical support for Blasi and Hoeffel's (1974) challenge to the Inhelder and Piaget position on formal operations and adolescence.

Thus, given the prevailing argument for equating adolescence with the potential for theoretical thought (Gruber & Voneche, 1976, Gillieron, 1979), the acquisition of formal thinking skills had to be abandoned as the developmental marker for the end of childhood (Broughton, 1979a). A further consequence of this discovery was that stage theories, such as Kohlberg's (1969) and Furth's (Furth, Baur & Smith, 1976), formulated conceptually in terms of an "underpinning" of the phases of social and moral development by the Piagetian sequence of logico-mathematical structures, would also have to rescind their claims to explain the boundary between childhood and adolescence (Broughton, 1983).

The Metaphysical Self

With a certain hindsight gained from a more detailed analysis of the data on adolescents in the light of a re-reading of Baldwin and Hegel, I came to the realisation that it was not epistemology that was central to these developments but *ontology* (Broughton, 1977b, 1981a). Despite the claims of Inhelder and Piaget, and Kohlberg and Gilligan, it was the metaphysical status of the subject, not its emergence as a knower, that was central to the adolescent concept of the self (Chandler, 1978). At the core of transformations in the metaphysical self were the interlinked issues of substantiality, morphology, and phenomenology: mind–body, inside–outside, and reality–appearance. At Teachers College, we have found that even personal issues such as identity and illness and social relations such as love and aggression are grounded in ontological presuppositions (Broughton, Honey & Wootten, 1982; Golden, 1984; Shohat, 1985; Zarem, 1985).

Later longitudinal and cross-sectional research with Barbara Schecter (see Broughton, 1979b; Schecter and Broughton, submitted) suggested links between mind–body concepts and reflective understanding of biological and psychological existence. Moreover, transformations in the concepts of animate–inanimate and sensate–insensate turned out to be closely connected to the emergence of literal and metaphorical understandings of texture in organic and inorganic bodies, particularly qualities such as "hard" and "soft".

In tune with the various critics of idealism, I moved toward the programmatic definition of a primary developmental domain of *genetic metaphysics*, one in which the Piagetian and Kohlbergian spatial epistemology of "perspectives", "role-taking", "egocentrism", and "decentration" were preempted by conceptually prior ontological notions of persons and reality (Broughton, 1980). In sum, formal theories based on the subject–object dualism of Descartes, the traditional Euclidian metaphors for knowing, and the pragmatist stress on instrumental action were found less tractable, both empirically and conceptually (Broughton, 1983), than a metaphysical approach to development closer to post-Hegelian ontology (Merleau-Ponty, 1963).

DEVELOPMENT OR FORTIFICATION OF THE SELF?

The claim that Piagetian theory is a formal theory of comprehensive scope (see, for example, Cowan, 1978; Furth, 1986; Marcia, 1980; and the papers collected in Broughton, Leadbeater & Amsel, 1981) led to a series of studies at Teachers college on the relationship between the development of logico-mathematical reasoning and the development of personality. While structural developmental phenomena appeared to be identifiable in the domain of self or identity (Golden, 1984), empirical relations between logical development and identity development did not materialise either in the United States (Weiss, 1984,) or in Ghana (Afrifa, 1983). Moreover, a detailed review of the literature suggests no clear empirical support for the claims made by Kohlberg and Gilligan (1971) and others concerning an orderly relationship between logical and moral development (Broughton, 1983).

Development in the realm of the social and personal does not seem to conform to the principle of an increasingly scientific rationalisation of life (Broughton, Honey & Wootton, 1982). Rather, as indicated by a number of clinical studies (e.g. Shapiro, 1965; White, 1975), the extension of scientific reasoning to personal and social life would appear to represent a defensive manoeuvre. Piaget (1952: 238) described it, in his own case, as an attempt "to take refuge," (Voyat, 1980).

Commonly called "intellectualisation" (A. Freud, 1948), this repressive distortion of consciousness can be characterised as a desperately clever attempt to substitute autonomy for memory. The self "frees itself"; the subject is dissociated from its living by turning life into an anonymous and exclusively theoretical object.[2] In the mythopoetic interiority of personal, intrapsychic life, science symbolises a purely rational autonomy, the "freedom from" constraint achieved by mastery over nature. This dominance is effected by a psychic coordinator—an agent actively (one might say, hyperactively) constructing the most general order of things. Symbolically, such an instrumental agent stands in opposition to the psychic humanist—an interpretive and communicative subject (Habermas, 1975) that surrenders its control to the meaning of particular understanding or insight, thereby attaining a "freedom to", an enlargement of the domain of realisable possibilities for the subject (Rapaport, 1958; Holt, 1965).

---

[2] There is an aggressive element involved in this isolation of the self, an emotional rejection of the non-objective: "I started to forego play for serious work very early; this I obviously did as much to imitate my father as to take refuge in a private and non-fictitious world. Indeed, *I have always detested any departure from reality*"(Piaget, 1952, p. 238, emphasis added).

The need for an individuality based on "freedom from" the other entails magnification of the self through domination of otherness. As such, it serves to buttress the rigidity of compulsively vigilant neurotic systems that are designed to predict and eradicate potential perturbations of the stable order—systems of what Sullivan (1954) termed "security operations". Shapiro's (1981) recent volume, *Autonomy and rigid character*, has documented the detailed features of this constellation of traditional individuation.

Cross-sectional and longitudinal interview research and clinical case studies reveal that this rigidity of personality, the so-called virtue of "ego-strength", tends to manifest itself as a morphological preoccupation with fortified structures, with impenetrable defensive and offensive containers, such as castles or tanks (Broughton, 1979b; Reich, 1949, and Lacan, 1949). In its extreme, paranoid form, obsession reaches deeper to generate grand theorising. Here, the omnipotent self is religiously identified with a monolithic, invulnerable yet intractable *Weltanschauung* (Freud, 1933), the ultimate negation of otherness (Freud, 1923).

As Shapiro's (1981) account makes clear, the constructive *activity* of the subject *per se* is no indication of mental health or development. Activity may be adaptive; it can just as easily be maladaptive. We know from clinical research (see, for example, Shapiro, 1965) that some of the most active subjects are those busily preoccupied with the construction and elaboration of their defensive apparatus. Such a subject is concerned primarily with preventing disturbances of the equilibrium already established in his or her intellectually controlled system. A certain compulsive busy-ness or "hyperactivity" is, in fact, symptomatic of a variety of neurotic disorders; it is diagnostic of a self-protection against depression or schizoid fragmentation (Guntrip, 1969). Similarly, when an individual's behaviour exhibits an exaggerated "toughness" it usually leads us to suspect a magnified sense of vulnerability in his or her subjective experience: "methinks he doth protest too much", to borrow Shakespeare's pre-Freudian diagnosis. As long as "activity" is not distinguished from "reactivity", it is impossible to distinguish action from *reaction formation* (Freud, 1949), a defensive reversal of the self's *passivity*. The fact that new middle-class ideology tends to promote a high level of busy-ness (Bernstein, 1975; Kanter, 1972) most probably serves to stabilise socially what would otherwise be discerned as a maladaptive trait.

Biological metaphors serve to conceal the possible dynamic meaning of activity as defence because we tend not to think of animals and other sub-human organisms as possessing any internal life of an emotional sort. We are also well disposed to accept into the definition of life some unquestioned notion of activity in order to permit an easy distinction to be made between animate beings and inanimate objects. In so doing, we prefer to ignore the fact that living beings are quite capable of being or becoming passive, even if they do not become inanimate.

DEVELOPMENT OR RATIONALISATION?

Cognitive developmental theories claim to identify sequences of qualitatively discrete structures or "stages". However, as we know from sociology (Gouldner, 1970; Habermas, 1971; Giddens, 1976), the qualitative and structural pretensions of functionalist approaches are always precarious and tend to dissolve into unitary, quantitative adaptation to the environment. So, for example, empirical research tends to reveal ever more interstitial sub-stages and mixtures of different stages, while few instances of outright psychological conflict are found, suggesting a substantially continuous underlying process of change. It is to the credit of Piaget—in contrast to Kohlberg, for example—that he acknowledged, toward the end of his career, the reality of this underlying functional continuity, by shifting from his "structural" model to a more or less cybernetic one (Gruber & Vonèche, 1977).

Rather than mapping a number of series of "discoveries", I have argued (Broughton, 1983, 1986a) that these "developmental" trajectories actually represent a single, homogeneous acquisition of prevailing political ideology—a socially functional process of psychological reproduction via a progressive elaboration of one and the same world view. As Kaplan (1967) has warned us, the *telos* of a developmental theory, its final destiny, is not unknown or variable; it exerts a single, magnetic influence—backwards, so to speak—through the preceding stages. Moreover, there is a discernible tendency for the unitary acquisition process that moves so inexorably towards this fixed end-point to result in an increasingly closed and sterile cognitive system (Vonèche, 1982; Gruber, 1982).[3] In the face of the burgeoning obsession with activity, a sedentary passivity accumulates. As both malacologist and gastronomist would assure us (Broughton, 1966), with an old oyster, you get more shell and less oyster.

Cognitive developmental psychology subscribes to the "psychology of more" (Looft, 1971). The "leap" from concrete operations to formal operations does not represent a true transcendence but, rather, gives us more of the same. "Development" here consists of nothing other than a rational reconstruction of the same old operationism at a greater level of abstraction, raising it to a higher power. The same holds for Kohlberg's

---

[3] This phenomenon would appear to apply in the domain of personality development as well as cognitive development. Broughton and Zahaykevich (1980) and Broughton (1986b) point to the increasing authoritarianism of higher stages in ego and faith development, while Josselson (1980) has noted that the achievement of "identity" entails a *loss* of, not a gain in, vitality in the personality.

"post-conventional" level, which does not rebuild morality on new foundations but merely jacks up the old liberal structure of role-taking one more floor (Broughton, 1983). In neither theory does the elevation of individuality and rationality lead to any reconsideration of individualism or rationalism. In this sense, cognitive developmental theories are theodicies of adaptation that glorify conformity and stagnation; they provide us with directions for how to get nowhere fast. They are blueprints for fossilisation, in the guise of plans for evolution.

The paralysis of subjectivity and agency brought about by this model of psychological individuation converges neatly with the needs of an insecure nation state obsessed with stability. At this point, the fortification of the ego and of the state attain a triumphant coincidence. The bounded self finds narcissistic satisfaction in its mirror image, the society of bondage.

OBJECTIVISM AND MALE DOMINATION

Central to cognitive psychology in general (Sampson, 1981), and cognitive developmental psychology (including Piaget's genetic epistemology) in particular (Broughton, 1986c), is a thoroughgoing *objectivism*. Following Descartes, the present, cognitivist incarnation of evolutionary functionalism segregates "reality" from consciousness and rejects the subjectivity of the latter in favour of that "objectivity" that grasps and represents the former (Strauss, 1958; Jones, 1975).

As a metatheoretical position, objectivism has come under intense critical scrutiny by recent feminist psychology (e.g. Dinnerstein, 1977; Chodorow, 1978; Baumrind, 1980; Benjamin, 1980, 1981, 1986) and feminist philosophy of science (Keller, 1985). These researchers have argued, using sociological and historical evidence as well as psychological findings, that the subordination of subjectivity promoted by objectivist scientific meta-theories is linked to the social and psychological structure of male domination.

According to this feminist interpretation, the traditional development of men requires that, as boys, they attain sex-appropriate autonomous individuality by repudiating as "opposite" their mothers, femininity, and all feminine sex-typed characteristics. The latter centre around intimacy: love, attachment, sensitivity, expressiveness and intraceptiveness (psychological-mindedness)—in other words, subjectivity.

Central to this masculine gender identity is a committed *over-differentiation*: a definition of self in terms of separateness and self-sufficiency. This emphasis on boundary is transposed into the psychological sphere, valorising the "hard", scientific, cognitive faculty governed by two-valued logic, analytic decision-making, and instrumental-rational justification, at the expense of a devaluation of the "soft" focus on personal understanding and insight, expressive communication and interpersonal relatedness (Gilligan, 1982; Broughton, 1984; Papert, 1985).

Benjamin's work has underlined the *political* nature of early individuation, since it constitutes a quest for *freedom*, not just an acquisition of individuality. Rejecting individualism and objectivism and following the account of the "master–slave dialectic" in Hegel (1952), she assumes the fundamentally inter-subjective nature of liberation. She traces the phases of personality development in which the *desire for independence from the other* struggles to free itself from the *need for recognition by the other*. This struggle is hopeless, since autonomy presupposes the attachment it seems to escape. The vision of freedom as liberation from authority is illusory since in the absence of an authoritative other, there would be no reliable source for the acknowledgement and legitimation of that very freedom.

Benjamin identifies not one, but two alternative developmental outcomes in this struggle. The traditional "masculine" resolution—typified by the Freudian oedipal paradigm but reflected also in the Piagetian, Kohlbergian and Loevingerian paradigms of moral and ego development—is patriarchal in character: it postulates heteronomy as a necessary and inevitable step in the acquisition of individual autonomy. According to this model, the solution to an intractable battle of wills between two subjects is for one to submit to the authority of the other, and to internalise that authority. In return for a lengthy delay of gratification, the internaliser receives a promissory note permitting him to take up the role of authority later, at a point of greater maturity. In founding itself upon an exchange of present slavery for future mastery, this resolution requires a *polarisation of autonomy and attachment* in which the satisfaction of needs for intimacy is given up, the needs themselves being repressed and even disowned as "immature" and "impulsive".[4]

The alternative, one might say "post-feminist", resolution is to acknowledge the *dependence of autonomy on attachment*, and to distinguish this mature, voluntary dependence from the helpless, involuntary dependence of the immature infantile state. When the other as subjective being is included in the development of the self in this way, the universal objectification of the animate and inanimate world is displaced by a "subjectification." (Kaplan and Broughton, submitted). Objectivity is no longer seen as necessarily requiring the elimination of subjectivity, but as presupposing subjectivity.

The traditional, "masculinist" developmental path, which we normally assume to represent the obligatory course pursued by the subject in the

---

[4] The implicit authoritarianism of the cognitive developmental model is pointed out by Buck-Morss (1986), and documented in detail by Broughton and Zahaykevich (1980), in prep., and Broughton (1981b, 1983, 1986a, 1986b, 1986d).

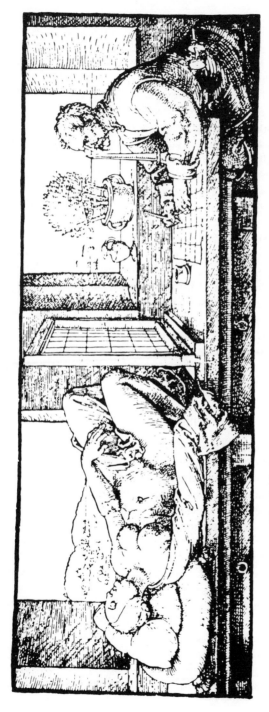

Albrecht Dürer: *The Artist's Model* (*Treatise on Measurement*, 2nd ed., 1538, Formschneider).

developmental quest for autonomy, is, therefore, a *false* individuation resulting in a "false self" (Winnicott, 1965). The obsessive pursuit of autonomy produces freedom in an ersatz form. This corruption involves not just a disowning of the self's spontaneous needs, but an estrangement from all relatedness.

What is the motivation for such "rigidity of self-direction" (Shapiro, 1981:5), for independence purchased at the expense of relatedness to self and other? Shapiro's clinical case material indicates that it is an "abhorrence of 'weakness'" (ibid.:71), a reaction against "the impulse to a 'female' surrender of will that is abhorrent to a rigid, prideful 'masculine' point of view" (ibid.:166). Yet discovery and invention, in intelligence or personal life, require precisely that moment of "female" surrender—a submission of the self to the expressive and creative impulse embodied in one's own wilfulness.

A recent study of cognitive development in boys, carried out at Teachers College (Bragonier, 1985), has provided initial empirical confirmation for Benjamin's account. Latency-age male subjects reared in homes structured by a traditional, polarised and hierarchical gender arrangement exhibit a personality constellation and perceptual orientation regulated by the ideal of objectification of self and other. Socio-economically comparable subjects of the same age, but reared in "post-feminist" homes where gender polarisation and hierarchy have been largely attenuated, exhibit a markedly greater capacity for appreciating the existence and legitimacy of subjective life, in women as well as in men.

INJURY AND SAFETY

We have now compounded our first critique of the Piagetian tradition with a second one. Not only does the ideology of cognitive development celebrate psychodynamic defences and promote the accommodation of the child to the rationalisation of social life, but it also buttresses a gender hierarchy in the order of social life and the division of domestic and public labour. The authoritarianism embodied in genetic epistemology is not only anti-democratic, it is pre-feminist. Cognitivism in general and cognitive developmental psychology or genetic epistemology in particular follow exactly the objectivist, male-supremacist paradigm that feminist thinkers have identified.

However, an ideology critique of this psychology and epistemology would be a pale shadow of dialectics indeed if it were to fail to find the suppressed obverse—the subjective side of the objectivist and misogynist urge lurking somewhere within the Piagetian system. In order to locate this dialectical moment of self-negation and so display that reversibility that always eluded Piaget's own theory of intelligence, we need to fish in childhood waters.

The undiscovered pearl of wisdom in Piaget's otherwise oppressive systematisation lies in the spontaneous delight of his early choice of molluscs as an object of study. These creatures, whose bodies are soft and easily damaged (not to mention, at least in French-speaking countries, cooked and eaten), require a system of defence, and so they continually secrete around themselves an inert shell that serves as a protective barrier. Only the opening of the shell, a tiny window of vulnerability, remains. "Soft" and "hard", "vulnerability" and "defence", these were metaphorically crystallised in the very foundational studies of genetic epistemology. When Piaget devoted his life to the study of life, he also acknowledged, implicitly, the omnipresence of death.

We, too, secrete ourselves within increasingly complex and sophisticated mechanisms of defence. In human beings, defence and offence are not easy to differentiate. Safety itself turns injurious when it becomes an obsession (Scarry, 1985). The technology of the late nineteenth and early twentieth centuries made possible the military discovery of the "shell", the projectile in the nominal guise of the protectile. As the end of the twentieth century approaches, our advanced technology now promises to render us as invulnerable as the gods, via a molluscan enterprise of fantastic proportions, the Strategic Defense Initiative ("Star Wars"), itself a disguised offensive weapon.

The nature of men and women was a central concern of the early Piaget, as his autobiography discloses. Little surprise, then, to find gender in the symbolic objects selected (so "naturally") for those first studies of his. As Hegel's *Phenomenology* describes, human civilisations always construct their inner and outer, their public and private, their toughness and tenderness, along gender lines. Science and technology—the latter the publicising of the achievement of the former—are outwardly turned, like the shells they generate. Their mechanisms, their objectivity, and their extroversion, have always been associated with the masculine gender (Keller, 1985, in press; Haste, in press). That which is protected within is the sphere of intimacy and domesticity, otherwise known as the feminine. As we know from the studies using Osgood's "Semantic Differential", if not from our own experience, the signifiers "masculine" and "hard" cluster together, as do those of "feminine" and "soft" (Hudson, 1968; Papert, 1985).[5]

Although Piaget the youth strove manfully to eliminate gendered beings from the sphere of his operations, the repressed returned in the symbolic content of his concerns. Those that engender and those that defend, the

---

[5] On the psychological development of the literal and metaphorical distinction between "soft" and "hard", and the implications for concepts of life and consciousness, see Schecter and Broughton (submitted).

symbols of Eros and Thanatos, found their rightful place at the hidden heart of cognitive developmental psychology.

Perhaps I was wrong when I once called for an advance "beyond Piaget". Possibly, what we need is not to displace Piaget but to rejuvenate him. A new Piaget is needed to return to the youthful scientist's study of molluscan life, but in its human, cultural and symbolic form. Is it too much to hope for that men and women might cooperate in the conceiving and nurturing of a critical developmental psychology that might, however sluggishly, bring shell and flesh into a new, vital relation instead of the usual fatal one?

REFERENCES

Afrifa, A. (1983). *The relationship between cognitive and identity development in Ghanaian secondary school seniors*. Unpublished doctoral dissertation, Teachers College, Columbia University.

Baumrind, D. (1980). New directions in socialization research. *American Psychologist, 37* (7), 639–652.

Benjamin, J. (1980). The bonds of love: Erotic domination and rational violence. *Feminist Studies, 6* (1), 144–174.

Benjamin, J. (1981). The Oedipal riddle: Authority, autonomy, and the new narcissism. In J. P. Diggins & M. E. Kann (Eds.), *The problem of authority in America*. Philadelphia: Temple University Press.

Benjamin, J. (1986). The decline of the Oedipus complex. In J. M. Broughton (Ed.), *Critical theories of psychological development*. New York: Plenum.

Bernstein, B. (1975). *Class, codes, and control*, Vol. 3. London: Routledge and Kegan Paul.

Blasi, A. & Hoeffel, E. C. (1974). Adolescence and formal operations. *Human Development, 17*, 344–363.

Bower, T. G. R., Broughton, J. M. & Moore, M. K. (1971). Object permanence of infants as manifest in tracking behaviour. *Journal of Experimental Psychology, 11*, 182–193.

Bragonier, P. (1985). *True and false differentiation in latency age boys from traditional and non-traditional families*. Unpublished doctoral dissertation, Teachers College, Columbia University.

Broughton, J.M. (1966). Brainless but pure: The oyster. *Daily Telegraph*, Oct. 21, 17.

Broughton, J. M. (1975). *The development of the epistemological self in the years 10–26*. Unpublished doctoral dissertation, Harvard University.

Broughton, J. M (1977a). "Beyond formal operations": Theoretical thought in adolescence. *Teachers College Record, 79* (1), 87–98.

Broughton, J. M. (1977b). *The metaphysical and epistemological selves*. Paper presented at the Jean Piaget Society, Philadelphia.

Broughton, J. M. (1978). The development of concepts of self, mind, reality, and knowledge. In W. Damon (Ed.), *New directions in child development, No. 1: Social cognition*. San Francisco: Jossey-Bass.

Broughton, J. M. (1979a). The limits of formal thought. In R. A. Mosher (Ed.), *Adolescents' development and education*. Berkeley: McCutchan.

Broughton, J. M. (1979b). Structural developmentalism: Without self, without history. In H. K. Betz (Ed.), *Recent approaches to the social sciences*. Winnipeg: Hignell.

Broughton, J.M. (1980). Genetic metaphysics: The developmental concept of mind–body concepts. In R.W. Rieber (Ed.), *Body and mind*. New York: Academic Press.

Broughton, J. M. (1981a). The divided self in adolescence: Laing's David. *Human development, 24*, 13–32.

Broughton, J. M. (1981b). Piaget's structural developmental psychology, Parts I–V. *Human development, 24* (2–6), 78–109, 195–225, 257–285, 320–346, 382–411.

Broughton, J. M. (1983). The cognitive-developmental theory of adolescent self and identity. In B. Lee & G. G. Noam (Eds.), *Developmental approaches to the self*. New York: Plenum.

Broughton, J. M. (1984). Not beyond formal operations but beyond Piaget. In M. Commons, F. J. Richards & C. Armon (Eds.), *Beyond formal operations: Late adolescent and adult cognitive development*. New York: Praeger.

Broughton, J. M. (1986a). The genesis of moral domination. In S. Modgil & C. Modgil (Eds.), *Lawrence Kohlberg: Consensus and controversy*. Brighton, England: Falmer.

Broughton, J. M. (1986b). The political psychology of faith. In B. Wheeler, C. Dykstra & S. Parks (Eds.), *The faith development theory of James Fowler*. Birmingham, Ala.: Religious Education Press.

Broughton, J. M. (1986c). Piaget's conception of the self. In P. Eisendrath Young (Ed.), *The book of the self: Ego, identity and subjectivity*. New York: New York University Press.

Broughton, J. M. 1986d). Introduction to critical developmental psychology. In J.M. Broughton (Ed.), *Critical theories of psychological development*. New York: Plenum.

Broughton, J. M., Honey M. & Wootten, J. (1982). Concepts of health and illness in minority adolescents. Paper presented at Downstate Medical Center, Brooklyn.

Broughton, J. M., Leadbeater, B. & Amsel, E. (Eds.) (1981). Reflections on Piaget: Proceedings of the Jean Piaget Memorial Conference. *Teachers College Record, 83* (2), 151–217.

Broughton, J. M. & Zahaykevich, M. K. (1980). Personality and ideology in ego development. In V. Trinh van Thao & J. Gabel (Eds.), *La dialectique dans les sciences sociales*. Paris: Anthropos.

Broughton, J. M. & Zahaykevich, M. K. (in preparation). From authoritarian personality to ego development: ideological features of Loevinger's theory. In B. Seidman (Ed.), *Theories of adult socialization*.

Buck-Morss, S. (1986). Piaget, Adorno, and dialectical operations. In J. M. Broughton (Ed.), *Critical theories of psychological development*. New York: Plenum.

Chandler, M. J. (1978). Adolescence, egocentrism, and epistemological loneliness. In B. Presseissen (Ed.), *Topics in cognitive development*, Vol. 2. New York: Plenum.

Chodorow, N. (1978). *The reproduction of mothering*. Berkeley: University of California Press.

Cowan, P. (1978). *Piaget with feeling*. New York: Holt, Rinehart and Winston.

Dinnerstein, D. (1977). *The mermaid and the minotaur*. New York: Harper & Row.

Freud, A. (1948). *The ego and the mechanisms of defence*. New York: International Universities Press.

Freud, S. (1923). *The ego and the id*. London: Hogarth Press.

Freud, S. (1933). The question of a Weltanschauung. In *New introductory lectures on psychoanalysis*. London: Hogarth Press.

Freud, S. (1949). *Three essays on the theory of sexuality*. London: Hogarth Press.

Furth, H. G. (1986). *Knowledge as desire: An essay on Freud and Piaget*. New York: Columbia University Press.

Furth, H. G., Baur, M. & Smith, J. E. (1976). Children's conception of social institutions: A Piagetian framework. *Human Development, 19*, 351–374.

Giddens, A. (1976). *New rules of sociological method*. New York: Basic Books.

Gillieron, C. (1979). La pensée de l'adolescent. *Totus Homo, 11*, 11–24.

Gilligan, C. (1982). *In a different voice: Psychological theory and women's development*. Cambridge, Mass.: Harvard University Press.

Golden, R. (1984). *The development of critical consciousness in upper middle class high school students.* Unpublished doctoral dissertation. Teachers College, Columbia University.

Gouldner, A. (1970). *The coming crisis of western sociology.* New York: Basic Books.

Gruber, H. E. (1982). Piaget's mission. *Social Research, 49,* 239–264.

Gruber, H. E. & Voneche, J. J. (1976). Reflexions sur les opérations formelles et la pensée. *Archives de Psychologie, 44,* 45–55.

Gruber, H. E. & Voneche, J. J. (1977). *The essential Piaget.* New York: Basic Books.

Guntrip, H. H. (1969). *Schizoid phenomena, object relations, and the self.* New York: International Universities Press.

Habermas, J. (1971). Theorie der Gesellschaft oder Sozialtechnologie. In J. Habermas & N. Luhmann, *Theorie der Gesellschaft oder Sozialtechnologie: Was leistet die Systemforschung?* Frankfurt: Suhrkamp.

Habermas, J. (1975). *Legitimation crisis.* Boston: Beacon.

Haste, H. W. (in press). Brother Sun, Sister Moon. *New Ideas in Psychology, 5.*

Hegel, G. W. F. (1952). *Phänomenologie des Geistes.* Hamburg: F. Meiner.

Holt, R. R. (1965). Ego-autonomy reevaluated. *International Journal of Psychoanalysis, 46,* 151–167.

Hudson, L. (1968). *Frames of mind.* London: Methuen.

Inhelder, B. & Piaget, J. (1958). *The growth of logical thinking from childhood to adolescence.* New York: Basic Books. (First French ed., 1955.)

Jones, B. (1975). *Cartesian preconceptions in the shift from behaviourism to cognitive psychology.* Paper presented at Cheiron: The Society for the History of the Behavioural Sciences, Ottawa, June.

Josselson, E. (1980). Ego-identity in adolescence. In J. Adelson (Ed.), *Handbook of adolescent psychology.* New York: Wiley.

Kanter, R. M. (1972). The organization child: Experience management in a nursery school. *Sociology of education, 45,* 186–212.

Kaplan, B. (1967). Meditations on genesis. *Human Development, 10,* 65–87.

Kaplan, M. M. & Broughton, J. M. (submitted for publication). The mother herself: Subjectivity, resistance, and development in modern women's parenting.

Keller, E. F. (1985). *Reflections on gender and science.* New Haven: Yale University Press.

Keller, E. F. (in press). On the need to count past two in our thinking about gender and science. *New Ideas in Psychology. 5.*

Kohlberg, L. (1969). Stage and sequence: The cognitive developmental approach to moralization. In D. Goslin (Ed.), *Handbook of socialization theory and research.* Chicago: Rand McNally.

Kohlberg, L. & Gilligan, C. (1971). The adolescent as philosopher. *Daedalus, 100,* 1051–1086.

Lacan, J. (1949). The mirror phase as formative of the function of the "I". *New Left Review, 3,* 71–77.

Looft, W. R. (1971). The psychology of more. *American Psychologist, 26,* 561–565.

Marcia, J. (1980). Identity in adolescence. In J. Adelson (Ed.), *Handbook of adolescent psychology.* New York: J. Wiley.

Merleau-Ponty, M. (1963). *The structure of behavior.* Boston: Beacon.

Papert, S. (1985). *Values inherent in the logical cybernetic models of the notion of development.* Paper presented at the Cours Avancé, Archives Jean Piaget, University of Geneva, September.

Piaget, J. (1952). Autobiography. In C. Murchison (Ed.), *A history of psychology in autobiography.* Worcester, Mass.: Clark University Press.

Rapaport, D. (1958). The theory of ego-autonomy: A generalisation. *Bulletin of the Menninger Clinic, 22,* 13–35.

Reich, W. (1949). *Character analysis*. New York: Farrar, Straus, & Giroux.

Sampson, E. E. (1981). Cognitive psychology. *American Psychologist, 36,* 730–743.

Scarry, E. (1985). *The body in pain*. New York: Oxford University Press.

Schecter, B. & Broughton, J. M. (submitted for publication). Metaphor and concepts of life and consciousness in childhood and early adolescence.

Shapiro, D. (1965). *Neurotic styles*. New York: Basic Books.

Shapiro, D. (1981). *Autonomy and rigid character*. New York: Basic Books.

Shohat, L. (1985). *Concepts of war and peace in Israeli children and adolescents*. Unpublished doctoral dissertation, Teachers College, Columbia University.

Strauss, E. (1958). Aesthesiology and hallucinations. In R. May (Ed.), *Existence*. New York: Simon and Schuster.

Sullivan, H. S. (1954). *The psychiatric interview*. New York: Norton.

Vonèche, J. J. (1982). Evolution, development and the growth of knowledge. In J. M. Broughton and D. J. Freeman-Moir (Eds.), *The cognitive-developmental psychology of James Mark Baldwin*. Norwood, NJ: Ablex.

Voyat, G. (1980). Piaget on schizophrenia. *Journal of the American Academy of Psychoanalysis, 8,* 93–113.

Weiss, R. (1984). *The relationship between cognitive, moral, and identity development in late adolescence*. Unpublished doctoral dissertation, Teachers College, Columbia University.

White, R. (1975). *Lives in progress*. New York: Holt, Rinehart, and Winston.

Winnicott, D. W. (1965). Ego distortion in terms of true and false self. In *The maturational processes and the facilitating environment*. New York: International Universities Press.

Zarem, S. (1985). *Concepts of love in female children and adolescents*. Unpublished doctoral dissertation, Teachers College, Columbia University.

8 Sociology of Science and Sociogenesis of Knowledge

Rolando García
Institúto Politecnico Nacional, Mexico

In the very first volume of the *Etudes d'épistémologie génétique* (Beth, Mays & Piaget, 1957), Piaget defines genetic epistemology as follows:

> the empirical as well as theoretical positive science of the becoming of positive sciences *as* sciences.[1]

This definition is followed by a very clear-cut statement:

> As a science is at the same time a social institution, a set of psychological conducts and a *sui generis* system of signs of cognitive behaviours, a rational analysis would bear on the three aspects jointly. There will be a primacy of the epistemological aspect, since this aspect is the phenomenon whose laws and explanation must be elucidated.[2]

Ten years later, in a well-known volume of the *Encyclopédie de la Pléiade* (Piaget, 1967),[3] he adds something else. After stating that an epistemologist cannot clarify the meaning of what he calls "a system of

---

[1] la science positive aussi bien empirique que théorique du devenir des sciences positives en tant que sciences.

[2] une science étant une institution sociale, un ensemble de conduites psychologiques et un système *sui generis* de signes de comportements cognitifs, une analyse rationnelle de cette science porterait donc sur ces trois aspects conjointement. L'aspect épistémologique aura la primauté puisqu'il constitue le phénomène dont il s'agit de dégager les lois et l'explication.

[3] See the chapter "Les méthodes de l'épistémologie", by Jean Piaget, pp. 105–106.

127

notions or a method", [*"un système de notions ou une méthode"*] without retracing historically its formation, he adds:

Reconstituting the development of a system of operations or experiments is first of all establishing its history. The epistemological goals thus pursued could even be fully reached by using the historical–critical and socio-genetic methods if such methods were complete, that is, if they could go beyond the history of science and back to the collective origin of notions, i.e. to their prehistoric sociogenesis.[4]

I have taken these quotations, which are representative of a Piagetian way of thinking that is very often forgotten both by those who defend Piaget and by those who attack him, in order to bring forward three points. Firstly, one of the primary aims of epistemology for Piaget is the understanding of the development and the structure of science. Secondly, if, as Piaget says, we were in a position to know the development of science in detail from the very beginning, then probably genetic psychology would never have been born.

The third point is that in the above quotations there is an implicit assumption or hypothesis: if it is true that we may appeal to psychology in order to understand the development of science itself, i.e. the development of human cognitive systems, it means—and this is the hypothesis—that there are common mechanisms underlying both individual development and the development of science. However, let us say very strongly that this hypothesis has nothing to do with the classic idea of a relationship between ontogenesis and phylogenesis, nor can it be taken as any sort of "psychologism".

The point made in the last quotation I took is that it would be sufficient for epistemology to use a "historical–critical" and socio-genetic analysis if this could be done in depth with all necessary information. But what is meant by sociogenetic analysis? Very often, and this book is not an exception, people react against Piagetian epistemology because he did not emphasise enough the need for cultural considerations, for social considerations, and so on. Nonetheless, we very rarely—if ever—find the same people giving a clear statement or analysis of the ways in which society enters into the development of the cognitive system.

In the book *Psychogenèse et histoire des sciences* (Piaget & García, 1983), we try to show that there are at least two components in the field of

---

[4] reconstituer le développement d'un système d'opérations ou d'expériences, c'est avant tout en établir l'histoire, et les méthodes historico-critiques et socio-génétiques suffiraient même entièrement à atteindre les buts épistémologiques ainsi poursuivis, si elles pouvaient être complètes, c'est-à-dire remonter en deçà de l'histoire des sciences elles-mêmes jusqu'à l'origine collective des notions, donc jusqu'à leur sociogenèse préhistorique.

the relation of society with science. One component has to do with society itself—its evolution and characteristics. Certain societies, at certain historical moments, depending on the social structure and on political and economic factors, develop a certain kind of science in the sense that they provide a directionality to scientific research. We have called this the *sociological component*. It has to do with the sociology of science.

There is, however, another component: the way in which the actual content of science is developed goes along, in general, with a certain conception of the world—a certain *Weltanschauung*—which has a direct influence on the content of science, i.e. the way in which concepts are developed and theories shaped. I call this the *socio-genetic component*.

On this subject, one finds, in general, a good deal of confusion among those who claim that Piaget failed to take "society" into account when describing the development of the cognitive system. They, not Piaget, fail to distinguish between the influence of the socio-economic and political structure of the society on the direction taken by scientific research in a certain period, and the socio-genetic component that has to do with the content itself of science. Most of those who appeal to society in order to understand the development of science make reference only to the first component.

I often take the development of science in the nineteenth century to illustrate what I have stated above. The nineteenth century is a very special period that offers a real epistemological laboratory for analysing how the development of science takes place. In that period, science becomes science-as-we-know-it-now. Various branches of physics are established: thermodynamics is born, as is the electro-magnetic theory. Chemistry "emerges" as a science. Biology becomes a science. The social sciences are established.

There are many studies about this period. Some of them show the sociological component very clearly. Merz (1907)[5] provides one of the best examples in this regard. We shall very briefly summarise the findings of such studies. French science, German science and British science are characteristically different during the first half of the nineteenth century. They emerged that way from the eighteenth century due to marked differences in the socio-economic and political history of the three countries. French science was dominated by rationalism and was mainly Newtonian science. Newton was born in England, but his mechanical theory took on its final form in France. People like Clairaut, for example, gave the final mathematical shape to the theory. Moreover, science developed much more in France than anywhere else. It became a profession in France from the beginning of the eighteenth century. This

---

[5] The preface is dated November 1896. I have access to the Third Unaltered Edition, 1907.

was not true in other European countries. British science went in an entirely different direction. It was not rationalistic, as in France, but it had a strong empiricist bias. And in Germany, which was not yet Germany, a number of movements had a direct impact on the conceptions that held sway in the numerous small states and cities that were later to become Germany. All this is quite clear. The extent to which this was due to socio-economic and political factors can best be seen by a reference to the birth of the social sciences.

The French sociology of Comte is very characteristic of French sociology for two reasons. First of all, Comte is a product of the *Ecole Polytechnique*, with a strong mathematical background. Secondly, the aim of sociology in France was shaped by the French Revolution: the destruction of the old institutions created a strong pressure to reconstruct legitimate government and "order". That was the main aim of sociology for the French. It was entirely different for the British. They did not have such a problem. Thanks to the Industrial Revolution, Great Britain had emerged as the first power in the world, and the most important element to be studied in the newly born social sciences was the economy. *The wealth of nations* by Adam Smith reveals the kind of problems that were typical of the British but not of the French.[6] Finally, the way in which metaphysics and philosophy of history take a predominant role in German thinking also reflects the history of Germany at that moment.

The socio-economic and political context contributed a great deal to shaping the orientation of science in each country. This is a factor that no one could ignore. But this alone does not explain the actual content of science in each case, the building of its conceptual framework, the structure of the theories. How do we jump from considerations concerning the Romantic movement and the "Sturm und Drang" in Germany to the kind of science that was developed in that country? This jump is made without warning in most cases by people who insist on condemning a history of science that fails to take into account society, culture, economic conditions and so on. I agree that all this is important. But, first, they should be able to indicate the "what" and the "how"; secondly, such factors do not explain the whole story. To avoid speaking vaguely, I shall take a very concrete example.

My analysis will be based on the historical material presented in a well-known paper by Kuhn (1977) entitled "Energy conservation as an example of simultaneous discovery".[7] It is a very serious study, exceptionally well documented and, undoubtedly, the work of a professional

---

[6] There was, no doubt, a strong influence of the French *physiocrates* on Adam Smith, but this fact does not invalidate this assertion.

[7] The paper on energy conservation, originally published in 1959, is reprinted in chapter 4 of Kuhn (1977).

historian. Notwithstanding this, and despite the author's authority in the field, the problems posed in the paper are in my opinion left without an answer. There are few papers with such a wealth of historical information and such a profound intention of providing meaning to this mass of data. And yet, I am not betraying Kuhn at all when I say that the analysis remains insufficient.

In the history of the energy conservation principle as reconstructed by Kuhn, he finds a number of pieces that do not quite fit together. He makes this plain more than once in the text. My claims are, first, that no amount of new "facts" will suffice to "close" the picture; and, second, that we have to appeal to an epistemological analysis if we want to introduce order in the mass of data handled by Kuhn. I am well aware that most historians of science—including Kuhn—have no taste for such an incursion of epistemology into history. In this respect Kuhn sets a limit to his own inquiry. In the book *The essential tension* (Kuhn, 1977:12), he clearly states his opinion of this subject. He says: "I do not think current philosophy of science has much relevance for the historian of science". He believes, however, that "much writing in philosophy of science would be improved if history played a large background role in its preparation". I will maintain, contrary to Kuhn's assertion, that the reciprocal is also true. In this connection, I would like to remind you of a distinction made by the distinguished Dutch historian of science, E. J. Dijksterhuis, who says that there are two ways of doing history of science. One way is to take history as the memory of science. The other way is to take history as the epistemological laboratory of science. I believe that Kuhn recognises in his papers that he is doing the first, not the second. He does not believe that epistemological analysis has a role to play in the history of science. I believe, with Piaget, that without such an epistemological analysis, it is very difficult to make sense of the evolution of scientific thought. I shall take Kuhn's study on energy conservation as a paradigmatic example to show it.

Kuhn starts his paper by stating that "between 1842 and 1847 the hypothesis of energy conservation was publicly announced by four widely scattered European scientists—Mayer, Joule, Colding and Helmholtz—all but the last working in complete ignorance of the others". In addition to these four scientists that I shall call *Group A*, Kuhn mentions two other groups (that I shall call *B* and *C*):

Group B: "Sadi Carnot before 1832, Marc Séguin in 1839, Karl Holtzmann in 1845, and G. A. Hirn in 1854, all recorded their independent conviction that heat and work are quantitatively interchangeable, and all computed a value for the conversion coefficient or an equivalent".

Group C: "Between 1837 and 1844, C. F. Mohr, William Grove, Faraday, and Liebig, all described the world of phenomena as manifesting but a single 'force', one which appears in electrical, thermal, dynamical, and many other forms, but which could never, in all its transformations, be created or destroyed".

After listing the three groups, Kuhn adds: "the history of science offers no more striking instance of a phenomenon known as a simultaneous discovery". Strangely enough, when he starts to ask what was meant by this "discovery", he begins by softening this very strong statement. He says, for example, "no two of our men said the same thing . . . most of them will not understand what the other said and many of them will not believe that what the other said had something to do with what he said." He is, therefore, obliged to admit that though the phrase "simultaneous discovery" points to the central problem of his paper, "it does not, if taken at all literally, describe it". With this clarification he formulates his problems by asking how it happens that in such a short period of time, so many people came up with "something that we may call" the discovery of the principle of energy conservation.

Kuhn's problem is to explain "the rapid and often disorderly emergence of the experimental and conceptual elements from which that theory [of energy conservation] was shortly to be compounded". Among the enormous complexity of factors that "caused the individual pioneers to make the particular discoveries that they did", he identifies a sub-group of three factors that seem more significant than the others. They are called "availability of conversion processes", the "concern with engines" and the "philosophy of nature". There is no question about the three factors being important. There is no objection to the choice. Our discrepancy relates to the role they play in the "emergence" of the principle of energy conservation.

Let us now analyse Kuhn's "factors". We shall start with the second one. Group B is the one mainly referred to as the people concerned with engines. Through their interest in engines, so Kuhn seems to imply, they develop the idea of analysing how much heat we put in a steam engine and how much work we get out, and, from this, they came up with the idea of "conversion" and arrived, finally, at energy conservation.

I do not agree with this apparent logical sequence. In particular, it does not seem right to say that "that question—how much work for how much fuel?—embraces the notion of a conversion process" (Kuhn, 1977:92). However, the concern with engines did play an important role as one of the three "factors" selected by Kuhn. Let us see then, what its role was.

Our first question is, why were the French more interested in engines than anyone else?[8] This interest in engines did not come "naturally", in the way that little girls are "naturally" interested in dolls. Frenchmen did not like playing with engines rather than with dolls. There was a very deep reason why this happened in France and not elsewhere. The interest in engines in France at this period is a question to be answered by the sociology of science[9]. Look at the dates. During the French Revolution and the Napoleonic wars, France and Britain were without communication. They were isolated from each other. And it was in that period that the British produced the peak of their Industrial Revolution. When the Napoleonic wars finished, communication was re-established. Among other things, there was an active exchange of scientists. The British discovered French science, and the French discoverd to their amazement that industrialisation had put Great Britain miles ahead of any other country in the world. The source of her wealth was to be found in thousands of steam engines working throughout the country. It was imperative for the French to catch up with the British. In this battle, the pragmatic, purely empirical approach of the British was going to be confronted with French science. So, it is not *par hasard* that Carnot asked the question: what is the maximum amount of work we can get from a steam engine out of a given amount of fuel? The question was far more pertinent in France than in Britain. The scarcity of coal in France made the difference. And Carnot made the fantastic discovery that no matter how you build a steam engine—no matter what materials you use, or the mechanism, or whatever—there is a maximum amount of work you can get with a certain amount of heat and that maximum is determined by only one factor: the difference in temperature of the two sources between which the engine works. There is always a transfer of heat from the source of the steam at high temperature, through the engine, to the condenser at a lower temperature. In this transfer, a certain amount of work is produced. The fantastic discovery was that in order to calculate the maximum possible efficiency of the engine, only the difference in temperature matters and nothing else. The leading idea behind this research was one that preoccupied the whole country: how to get more efficient engines in order

---

[8] Kuhn does not discuss the origin of such a "concern with engines". He only refers to it "as an aspect . . . whose existence I shall now take for granted as a well-known by-product of the Industrial Revolution" (Kuhn, 1977:83). I think, however, that it is necessary to make the sort of analysis I very briefly summarise in the text in order to make it evident that the role of this "factor", when we consider it from the epistemological point of view, is quite different from the other factors pointed out by Kuhn.

[9] French studies in mechanics and in engineering related to engines have other sources not directly linked to the Industrial Revolution. Here I refer only to those aspects that were predominant at the time of Sadi Carnot.

to catch up? The motivation was rooted in a deep socio-economic–political reason. But such a motivation *directs the question, not the answer. It directs the kind of research, not the structure of the theory that may eventually emerge.* It should be clear, however, that this group did not really come up with the principle of energy conservation. Carnot discovered his maximum efficiency cycle and gave a proof of it for the wrong reasons. In fact, he applied the analogy of a waterfall that produces work by moving a turbine. The drop of the water from an upper to a lower level produces a certain amount of work. He compared the difference in height with the difference in temperature and made a wrong extrapolation, as children do when they discover something and extend it beyond the limits: the amount of water is conserved, therefore, the amount of heat—which was considered as a fluid—is also conserved. This was wrong. But the fact that only the difference of temperature matters—like the difference of levels in the waterfall—was true. It was the basis for the development of thermodynamics, but *no conversion principle was involved.* What was, in fact, involved was another principle, which is very often mistakenly taken as equivalent to energy conservation: the impossibility of perpetual motion. The latter does not necessarily imply either conversion or conservation.[10] Notwithstanding this, Carnot's theory, in the Clapeyron version, did provide one of the elements that led, in the late 1840s, to the precise notions of "conversion" and "conservation", as we shall see later.

Let us now turn to the third "factor". It involves mainly—but not only—Group C. This group was strongly influenced by the philosophical movement, called *Naturphilosophie*, which originated in Germany.[11] It should be remembered that this movement was the continuation of a line of thought that had started long before. Leibniz was part of it, but during the period we are concerned with, it found its maximum expression with Goethe, Schiller and, particularly, with Schelling. I am not going to dwell on it. I shall only refer to a central idea that is relevant to our discussion: *what is important in the world is not matter, but force.* When we press the table—they used to say—we believe that we touch matter, but in fact we only feel forces; force, rather than matter, is the underlying reality. The *Naturphilosophie* reacted in this way against French rationalism that "explained" everything—even thought!—in terms of matter and motion.

The force or "power", as it was called, was assumed to take many forms but to be *one* single force that manifests itself in all the different

---

[10] The best analysis I know of the underlying logic of Carnot's *Réflexions sur la puissance motrice du feu* is the article by Philip Lervig (1972).

[11] The influence of the *Naturphilosophie* is not only restricted to Germany. English Romanticism was also influenced by this philosophical movement, particularly after the voyage of Samuel Taylor Coleridge to Germany. Grove was a friend of Coleridge, and there is a clear influence of *Naturphilosophie* in his "Correlations of Forces".

phenomena we know. A number of important discoveries were made at that time that seemed to corroborate this idea. For instance, Oersted, who had been a student of Schelling, discovered that electricity produces a magnetic field. William Herschel discovered that there is a relationship between heat and light in the infra-red. Ritter found a connection between light and chemical affinity. Seebeck discovered that there is a relationship between heat and electricity: when two different metals are joined to make a circuit, if the two junctions are heated at different temperatures, a difference of potential is produced. Then Peltier discovered the reverse effect. Such discoveries favoured the idea that there is only one force, and that this force manifests itself in different ways. It would be a mistake to call them "conversion processes". Grove was more cautious and called all those phenomena "the correlation of forces"; and he was right. The most they could say with such experiments is that they showed a correlation of forces; but this does not mean that people thought at that time that electricity is "transformed" into something else, into heat; or that light is "transformed" into heat. There are three notions involved here that need to be carefully distinguished: correlation of forces, conversion processes and conservation. The first does not imply the second, nor does the second imply the third.

Carnot's "proof" of the maximum efficiency of his famous cycle is a clear example of a "correlation" (between the heat transformed from the higher to the lower temperature sources, and the work produced) that does not imply "conversion" (because, in his proof, heat is assumed to be conserved). Thomson, before 1849, as we shall see later, did not believe in conversion either. His change of opinion presents an important epistemological problem that Kuhn leaves untouched.

The people belonging to the Romantic tradition of "only one force" did not think of conversion processes, much less of conservation. They were making a purely metaphysical statement: that there is one force in the universe and that this force manifests itself in different ways. It is true that this way of thinking gave a strong impulsion to the search for correlations between electricity and magnetism, between heat and light, and so on. However, the search for correlations did not succeed in all cases. Faraday, for instance, tried to find a correlation between gravity and electricity. The results were negative, and he abandoned them, not without declaring that "they do not shake my strong feeling of the existence of a relation between gravity and electricity". Even with such failures, this kind of *Weltanschauung*—the idea of a single force in the universe—had a lot to do with the discoveries of "correlations". And these discoveries are an important step in the development of the subject we are talking about. There is a long way, however, before making the jump from here to anything near energy "conservation" or even "conversion". By this, I do not intend to minimise what they did, but rather to put it in the proper context.

This is not, however, the whole story of the role of the "factor" we are considering. What we have shown so far is, so to speak, the positive influence of *Naturphilosophie*. There is, however, a negative influence not considered by Kuhn, and one that is of utmost importance for epistemological analysis. The tradition of Schelling—*Naturphilosophie*—the idea that there is only one force in the Universe, the rejection of matter, the reaction against French rationalism and against Newtonian science and so on, meant a reaction against all sorts of measurements. And we have a striking example of this. Ohm, in Germany, discovered the first quantitative law in electricity—the fact that the intensity of the current and the resistance of the conductor are related to the difference in the voltage in the two extremities of the conductor. Ohm's Law $(V = IR)$ became a standard subject in the High School, but it took a long time. In 1827, Ohm published his book *The galvanic circuit mathematically treated*. Nobody in Germany paid any attention to it. The reaction of the *"Natur"*-philosophers was very consistent: What was the point of "measuring" such phenomena? Electricity is something very immaterial—how can one measure it? Experiments and mathematics were considered entirely irrelevant to obtaining a true understanding of Nature. Remember that Goethe wrote a book on optics where he rejected the Newtonian idea of analysing light by using a prism in order to produce the spectrum of colours. Goethe said that light is a unity; we have to go out and look to discover what light is. The prism destroys light, i.e. it destroys the unity, the essence of light.

This was the *Weltanschauung* involved in the Romantic movement, and this is the reason why all the people in Group C rejected measurements. Ohm was recognised in England, he was honoured by the Royal Society, and the British started using his methods. The Germans did not. Why? Because their *Weltanschauung* was against measurement, against any quantitative evaluation. In this case, a particular cultural pattern enters in a very concrete way into the shaping of science in a particular society at a particular time. In the case we are considering, it acts as an epistemological obstacle, to use Gaston Bachelard's expression. Here, the social component is not merely providing directionality to scientific research; it enters deeply into the conceptualisation of science. It is not a "sociological" component. It has to do with the *sociogenesis* of science. This socio-genetic component explains why, although people in the *Naturphilosophie* movement played all the time with what we now call "conversions", they never reached the principle of invariance. Because "invariance" means an *invariant quantity*.

We now turn to Great Britain at a somewhat later time, in the late 1840s. Here the story is taken up by two main personages. The first of them, John Prescott Joule, the leading figure in Kuhn's Group A, made a very important experiment that consisted of an isolated recipient containing some water, and a mechanism to agitate the water. When agitation is introduced, the water is heated, and that amount of heat can be measured by the change of temperature. The work can also be calculated. So Joule was able to say how much work produces so much heat. This is taken by Kuhn to be a conversion process. It was considered so by Joule, as we shall see, but it was not readily accepted as such by the scientific community. The experiment was presented by Joule at a meeting of the British Association for the Advancement of Science in Cambridge, and summarised in a letter to the Philosophical Magazine. A paper was then submitted to the Royal Society, who sent it to a referee (probably Faraday). The comments of the referee emphasised that we cannot say that any one of these powers is the cause of the others, but only that all are connected and due to one common force. Faraday, or whoever it was at the Royal Society who wrote this judgement, was quite aware of the fact that getting so much heat from so much work does not necessarily mean a *conversion* of work into heat.

Joule again brought up his experiments on the "mechanical value of heat" at the Oxford meeting of the British Association in 1847. At this moment, another man enters the scene, a man who is crucial in this history, and who is not even mentioned by Kuhn[12] as having something to do with the discovery of energy conservation: William Thomson, one of the greatest physicists of the nineteenth century. He was a graduate of Cambridge but went to France to study with Regnault and so became much influenced by the French. He knew Carnot's work through Clapeyron who made Carnot's theory known and elaborated the mathematical form of Carnot's cycle. On this return from France, he brought Carnot's theory with him. When Joule spoke at Oxford, Thomson was there.[13] He was shocked by Joule's results. He repeated the experiment himself, just to be convinced, and found that the results could not be explained with Carnot's theory. Thomson found a true contradiction, which worried him for the next couple of years. And it was this contradiction that, in my view, produced a "disequilibration"—in Piagetian terms—of the whole system

---

[12] The ironic remark made by Kuhn about Lord Kelvin (who was not yet Lord Kelvin but simple W. Thomson at that time) in his note 98 shows, in my opinion, the shortcomings of Kuhn's study due to the lack of epistemological analysis.

[13] The account given by Joule himself of that (by chance!) historical session is highly interesting. He first says that in his former presentations, with few exceptions, "the subject did not excite much attention", and then adds: "so that when I brought it forward again at the meeting in 1847 the chairman suggested that, as the business of the session pressed, I should not read any paper, but confine myself to a short verbal description of my experiments. This I endeavoured to do, and discussion not being invited, the communication would have passed without comment if a young man had not risen in the session, and by his intelligent observations created a lively interest in the new theory. The young man was William Thomson".

that was restructured a few years later in an entirely different manner.

In 1848, Thomson wrote a paper commenting on Joule, saying that the conversion of heat into work is "probably impossible and certainly not demonstrated". But he is puzzled by the experiment. In 1851, he wrote another paper accepting the conversion of work into heat. What had happened in-between the two papers? First of all, the contradictions between Carnot and Joule and within each theory constitute the motor of what happened after the 1848 paper: the principle of the impossibility of perpetuum mobile; the principle of conservation of caloric; the constant rate of heat production by work; the transmission of heat without producing work. How to put all these contradictory ingredients together in a coherent theory?

In 1848, Thomson, in accordance with Carnot's theory, still regarded heat as a kind of a fluid.[14] This was the epistemological obstacle that prevented him from accepting Joule's experiments as "conversion" processes. How could a motion be converted into fluid? And yet Joule seemed to be right: his experiments can only be explained by accepting a true conversion of work into heat. It was, therefore, necessary to give up the "caloric" theory. The conversion could be understood if heat itself was also a kind of motion. Thomson thus arrived at the dynamic theory of heat.[15] When he came up with the idea that heat is the motion of the molecules, and he was able to show that such a motion could produce the kind of phenomena known as thermal phenomena, then he became convinced that there were, indeed, conversion processes in Joule's experiments. From then on the whole perspective changed. So here again a certain Weltanschauung had played a decisive role: the Newtonian tradition—so vigorously repudiated by Naturphilosophie—according to which only the motion and the interactions of particles had any meaning, and everything else could be reduced to them.

This is not, however, the end of the story. Thomson at once saw the difficulties. By simply resorting to the dynamic theory, the problem was not solved. If the conversion processes are all subject to dynamic laws, they

---

[14] It is true that, as pointed out by Kuhn, Carnot abandoned the caloric theory of heat. However, he only left a record of these later thoughts in his posthumous manuscripts. Carnot died in 1832. His brother sent those manuscripts to the Académie des Sciences as late as 1878. The Académie published them the same year, in the Comptes Rendus. Therefore, it is clear that they had no influence on our story. What Clapeyron, Thomson and Clausius knew as Carnot's theory was only what was contained in Réflexions sur la puissance motrice du feu (1824).

[15] Of course, Thomson did not invent the theory at that moment. The theory was rather old and had been referred to and used by several researchers, although not in the way Thomson did. This subject would require a quite different treatment, perhaps much longer than the present one.

must be reversible. There could be no loss or waste in nature. In fact, nature could go backwards. There were other difficulties, but we cannot dwell on them here. Joule alone could not explain the processes. In order to reach a satisfactory explanation, it was necessary to go back to Carnot's theory, removing from it the spurious idea of *heat* conservation, which played no role in the theory.

The synthesis between Joule's and Carnot's theories was carried out by Thomson in England and by Clausius in Germany, with some interactions between them. Only then did it become clear that there were two principles, not just one, involved in the conversion processes. The notion of energy emerged as a clear-cut and enlarged concept not to be confused with force, and Carnot's discovery was solidly founded in a second principle providing an answer to the problem of the non-reversibility of natural phenomena.

Now we are in a position to see clearly why we cannot accept that any one of the groups mentioned by Kuhn arrived at the conservation principle.[16] The reason is that in order to have conservation, you need a system of transformations and an invariant in the system. Energy is not "force" as Helmholz said, because force is not conserved. There was confusion during this period between the non-conservation of force and "something" that should be conserved. It was through Thomson and Clausius that this idea—that they were dealing with transformations which leave an invariant (namely energy)—finally took shape. And at this moment, the principle of conservation was born. Not before.

As to the *jump* from "conversion of forces" to energy conservation, it is true that Kuhn recognises it when he asserts that "the notion of a universal convertibility of natural powers does not imply their conservation". He is conscious that it is not the same thing. "However", he says, "the remaining steps are small and rather obvious". I am going to argue that this is epistemologically wrong. Indeed, the remaining steps are extremely important and very difficult. They become obvious for us when we look back, but they were not so at that time. The situation is quite similar to that of a child who has just arrived at the notion of the conservation of volume in fluids. At that moment it becomes obvious to him. A few months before, it was far from obvious and, in fact, he considered it to be wrong.

I believe that this picture, which cannot be elaborated here in extenso, is very much in line with what we tried to develop in the book *Psychogenèse et histoire des sciences*. Piaget and I mentioned there that we found in several fields that the construction of a theory goes, in general, through three different moments: a moment when a number of isolated facts are known, identified and analysed independently of each other; another moment when these facts are found to be connected by transformations

---

[16] The only exception is Helmholtz, but he requires a separate study.

that leave something invariant; and a third moment when you have a structure that explains the transformations and the invariance, and each particular case. We have called these three steps "intra", "inter" and "trans". The analysis summarised here shows very clearly that before 1850 there was a period when a number of particular cases were analysed quite independently; this is the "intra" period. Some of them were not even meant to be real conversion processes, but some were. Then, there was a jump: the known experiments became conceived as real conversion processes, and the links among them were established as being particular cases of a system of transformations. And I call it a "jump" because it means that a new concept had to be introduced to designate the quantity that remains invariant during the transformations. This was *energy* (an old concept that acquired a new meaning). This is the "inter" period. And this was the work of Clausius and Thomson. On this basis, I may venture the opinion that they were the people who really discovered the principle of the conservation of energy.

I would like to emphasise two things. First, the jump from "intra" to "inter" is neither small nor obvious, as Kuhn maintains. The discovery of a new function that is invariant in a system of transformations is not trivial and cannot be called a small and obvious step. It requires nothing less than a complete reorganisation of physical thinking. And this complete reorganisation does not occur as a continuous change. It means that at a certain moment, a process of reconceptualisation takes place, and the explanatory framework is reorganised. This, I submit, is a re-equilibration in strictly Piagetian terms.

Second, even the clear idea of energy conservation as an invariant in a system of transformations ("inter") did not suffice to explain the complexity of the phenomena involved. The new step was the mathematical formulation of what became known as the two principles of thermodynamics, accomplished by Clausius and Thomson. Only *then* were the "transformation" processes and related phenomena clearly understood. This was the "trans" period.

REFERENCES

Beth, W. E., Mays, W. & Piaget, J. (1957). *Epistémologie génétique et recherche psychologique*. (Etudes d'Epistémologie Génétique, Vol. 1). Paris: Presses Universitaires de France.
Kuhn, T. S. (1977). *The essential tension*. Chicago: The University of Chicago Press.
Lervig, P. (1972). On the structure of Carnot's theory of heat. *Archive for the History of Exact Sciences, 13*.
Merz, J. T. (1907). *A history of European thought in the nineteenth century*. Edinburgh and London: W. Blackwood and Sons.
Piaget, J. & García, R. (1983). *Psychogenèse et histoire des sciences*. Paris: Flammarion.
Piaget, J. (1967). Les methodes de l'épistémologie. In Piaget, J. (Ed.): *Logique et connaissance scientifique*. Paris: Gallimard.

9 Theory Change in Childhood

Susan Carey
Massachussets Institute of Technology

It is perhaps of some surprise to Genevans that the current debate of Piaget's theory in the United States almost exclusively surrounds the stage theory. That is, the proper characterisation of pre-operational, concrete operational and formal operational thought is debated, and, even more fundamentally, the very existence of domain-general changes in the course of cognitive development is discussed. That Piaget's position has been identified with a commitment to domain-general developmental differences is shown by the use of the term neo-Piagetians. So-called neo-Piagetians such as Case, Pascual-Leone and Halford dub themselves as such because they hold that there are domain-general developmental changes, although they conceive of these changes as increases in information-processing capacity, rather than as changes in inferential structure or power. On the other hand, others deny the existence of stages, in either the information-processing or inferential structure sense, and therefore consider themselves non-Piagetians.

This debate concerns the proper *description* of development. How does the child at time 1 differ from the child at time 2, time 3 and time 4? The debate about stages concerns the correct level of abstractness to describe cognitive development. A commitment to stages is a commitment to there being a domain-general—i.e. conceptual content-free—level of description of what changes in the course of cognitive development. In the course of his long career, Piaget, of course, tried several different domain-general characterisations: the young child is egocentric; the young child cannot represent true classes nor linear orderings, and so on. The information-processing characterisation of the young child as possessing less working

141

memory than does the older child is domain-general in the relevant sense, which is why adherents to such characterisations of development see themselves as neo-Piagetian.

An oversimplified example can give a flavour of the debate about domain-general changes. Any psychometrician knows that memory span develops between ages 5 and adulthood—doubles, in fact. Digit span is 3 plus or minus 1 at age 4 and 7 plus or minus 2 at age 16. How long a list of randomly chosen digits a child can remember is a reliable indicator of "mental age." This fact is the historical basis of "processing efficiency" descriptions of cognitive development, which see the child at time 2 as having more chunks of short-term memory, for example, than does the child at time 1. Such a developmental change is intended to be domain-general (i.e. independent of cognitive content). If this description is correct, the cause of the developmental change would surely be maturational. Thus, we see how a descriptive claim constrains a search for "causes".

But is the descriptive claim true? The robust phenomenon is actually that digit span doubles and letter span doubles. But the 5-year-old is a rank amateur, an extreme novice, in the worlds of numbers and letters, compared to an adult. Perhaps the developmental change should be located not at the abstract level of digit span itself, but at the level of increasing knowledge of letters and numbers.

In a too-little cited review, Chi (1976) showed that the ratio of memory span between adults and 5-year-olds is a function of the discrepancy in their knowledge of the domain of stimuli to be remembered. The ratio falls when the stimuli are nonsense figures, which are meaningful neither to a 5-year-old nor an adult. Similarly, the ratio falls when the stimuli are high-frequency concrete nouns, which are equally familiar to 5-year-olds and adults. Thus, even though some memory *spans* double, it is not memory capacity itself that is changing between age 5 and adulthood. Rather, what is increasing is knowledge of each of the domains from which the materials to be remembered are taken. Accepting this redescription of what is changing leads to an entirely different search for causes of development. Now, instead of a maturational mechanism yielding greater processing efficiency or capacity, we seek learning mechanisms yielding greater knowledge of digits, letters and word meanings.

Recent arguments about Piagetian stage theory have a parallel form. For those who do not know this recent bit of intellectual history, let me sketch it. Piaget presented us with hundreds of phenomena that diagnosed (so the story went) the fundamental differences between the young child's and the adult's thought processes. Most of these phenomena have been replicated literally thousands of times. The debates are rarely about the phenomena themselves. Take the period of childhood between ages 4 and

10. In addition to the conservations, and other changes in physical concepts, this period witnesses changes in moral reasoning, classification tasks, childhood animism, children's appreciation of the requirements of communication, acquisition of algebraic and geometric concepts, etc.

As Americans see it, Piaget's program was to bring order to this bewildering catalogue of differences between pre-school children on the one hand, and 10-year-olds on the other. He sought an abstract, simplifying characterisation of how pre-school children's thinking differed from that of late-elementary-school children's thinking. He tried many different formulations: the 4-year-old child can focus on only one dimension of a task at once, the 10-year-old can coordinate two dimensions; the 4-year-old cannot represent linear orders, cannot form representations of classes nor of the inclusion relation among classes; the 4-year-old cannot distinguish appearance from reality; the 4-year-old has no notion of physical causality; the 10-year-old has attained each of these capacities. These are all domain-general characterisations, just as is "the 4-year-old has one less slot of short-term memory than does the 7-year-old."

Piaget's descriptive claims about what changed in development included a precise and radical characterisation of conceptual restructuring. He attempted to formalise the inferential capacities of the child at time 1 (e.g. age 4), time 2 (age 10), and time 3 (age 16). According to his theory of operational development, thought processes themselves are restructured in the course of cognitive development.

Consider the conservations. It does seem that the young child fails to distinguish appearance from reality, where the older child succeeds; it does seem that the older child coordinates two dimensions, where the young child focuses on just one. So, too, all the other phenomena I listed above— each putatively exemplifies one or more of the general shifts in thinking that occur in the first decade of life.

So how does the debate about Piaget's abstract characterisation of what is changing run? Each claim—e.g. that young children cannot represent the class inclusion relation—has been subjected to intense scrutiny. And for each reconstruction of what each claim could mean, in representational terms, the claim that young children are incompetent in that particular way has been denied. This denial has always taken the same form: a positive demonstration that pre-school children have the representational or computational capacity in question. This is shown by their success at some task requiring that capacity. In the case of class inclusion, for example, 3- and 4-year-olds are seen to be able to make transitive inferences that depend upon representing the inclusion relations among concepts, including appreciating the asymmetry of the relation (e.g. Smith, 1979). A second part of the denial is coming up with an alternative explanation for the

Piagetian phenomena that had previously been taken as evidence that the young child lacked the capacity in question. In most cases, but not all, the alternative explanation involves the attainment of domain-specific knowledge in some particular content domain.

The upshot of the past two decades of American research is the progressive denial of the putative domain-general changes in the child's reasoning or thinking skills. The denial states that the 4-year-old is not a different computational device from, does not have different inferential capacities than, the 10-year-old or adult. I do enter into this debate here. Recent reviews of the issues can be found in Gelman and Baillargeon (1983) and Carey (1985a). While I feel that the current evidence weighs on the side of denying domain-general developmental changes, I do not consider the issue closed by any means. Furthermore, this descriptive problem is of utmost theoretical importance, for finding the correct level of abstractness to characterise what is changing constrains our search for the causes of development, as I indicated above. Rather than enter into this debate, I will make three points. First, the denial of domain-general changes seems to have grave consequences for developmental theory. Second, the concentration on the stage theory has resulted in a neglect in the United States of another important thread in Piaget's work, especially in his latest work with García—namely, Piaget's searches for parallels between ontogenetic and historical development. Third, focussing on these latter issues may provide one solution to the problems caused by abandoning the stage theory.

THE COSTS OF ABANDONING THE STAGE THEORY

Many cognitive developmental psychologists have resisted the pendulum swing towards more domain-specific descriptions of what changes in the course of development. It is perfectly obvious why. Piaget's theory characterised the *systematic*, domain-general, differences between the young child and the older child—just a few systematic differences at that (e.g. the groupings of concrete operations or, earlier, the shift to non-egocentricity, coming to draw the distinction between appearance and reality, attaining powerful, domain-general causal schemata, etc.). This short list supposedly captures how 4-year-olds differ from 10-year-olds in a way that enables us to understand the 4-year-old's limitations in reasoning about morality, spatial perspective, physical quantities, games of marbles, friendship, number, geometry, etc. By giving up this short list, we seem to be abandoning hope for a theory of cognitive development.

Let me put the dilemma in another way. There is no problem at all in finding differences between 4-year-olds and 10-year-olds. Indeed, it is news when children of such different ages perform the same on some task. But then 4-year-olds know less about just about anything you can mention, have less experience in almost every domain of endeavour of a child. Does the abandonment of a search for domain-general characterisations of what is changing mean that there is nothing *unifying* in the description of cognitive development? Is there no order to the thousands of piecemeal domain-specific developmental changes?

THE ALTERNATIVE

I have a counterproposal. With Piaget, I maintain that there are far-reaching reorganisations of knowledge that unify the description of what might otherwise seem myriad piecemeal changes. These reorganisations are content-specific, not content-free. They can best be thought of as theory changes or, more precisely, as the emergence of new theories out of earlier ones. I have completed case studies of two such theory emergences. One charts the acquisition and reorganisation of biological knowledge over the ages of 4 to 10 (Carey, 1985b); the other charts the construction of naive theory of matter over this same time period (Smith, Carey & Wiser, 1986; see also Piaget & Inhelder, 1941).

There are at least two broad types of theory changes in the history of science. In one, a well-developed domain of endeavour—say, mechanics—undergoes revolution, as in the transition from the impetus theory to Newtonian mechanics, or from Newton's to Einstein's theory. In the other, a new theoretical domain emerges from a parent domain (or domains), as evolutionary biology, logic, psychology and chemistry emerged as new domains of science in the nineteenth century. Even the second is a type of theory change, because theory emergences build on well-developed scientific traditions, and because some of the phenomena that motivate the new domain are studied earlier within a different scientific tradition. The developmental cases I have studied both fall into this latter type of theory change, those that witness the emergence of new theoretical domains. As in historical cases of the emergence of new theories, three developments are intertwined—a new domain of phenomena is encountered, a new explanatory apparatus is developed and new concepts come into being. Insofar as the new domain overlaps that of older theories, the changes in explanatory framework and concepts constitute a theory change of the impetus theory/Newtonian theory variety. That is, these phenomena are articulated in terms of new concepts and explained in terms of new laws and causal mechanisms.

Perhaps this will become clearer if I sketch one of my case studies—the study of the emergence of the domain of biology from the domain of psychology. Let us look at all three kinds of change—domain, explanatory framework and core concepts.

Domain

There is no domain of phenomena that is strictly biological for the 4-year-old. Four-year-olds do not know the biological functions of eating, breathing, sleeping, having babies, having hearts and so on. Activities such as eating, and breathing and sleeping are part of the domain of human activities. They are phenomena of the same sort as playing and bathing. Important facts about eating include when one is allowed to eat candy, the difference between breakfast, lunch and dinner, whether one is allowed to eat spaghetti with one's fingers, etc. The young child's knowledge about parts of the body is integrated into these same concerns—the child knows one eats through one's mouth, that one's stomach get full, even to the point sometimes of aching, etc. These activities and facts about people constitute a theoretical domain, because the child has an explanatory framework that accounts for them.

The Explanatory Framework

The explanatory structure in which these phenomena are embedded is social and psychological. The whys and wherefores of these matters, as the child understands them, include individual motivation (hunger, tiredness, avoiding pain, seeking pleasure and approval) and social conventions. Asked why people eat, 4-year-olds answer "because they are hungry," or "because it is dinner-time." They might also say, "to grow", or "to be strong", but the ultimate explanation is still in terms of wants and beliefs—growing and being strong are desirable. The child knows no bodily mechanism whereby eating affects growth or strength.

Biological explanation, while also teleological, is not intentional. Supporting life is a bottom-line goal; biological functions and bodily organs are explained in terms of their role in supporting life. The way eating, breathing, having babies, and so on are understood in terms of biological explanation in the 10-year-old's conceptual system is different from the way these are understood in terms of intentional explanation in the 4-year-old's conceptual system. Thus, if my analysis is correct, the changes in both domain and explanatory structure characteristic of theory emergences are exemplified in this case study.

CHANGES IN INDIVIDUAL CONCEPTS

Sometimes theory changes involve changes in the core concepts that articulate the theories. The clearest cases are differentiations—as Newton's distinction between mass and weight; Black's between heat and temperature. Coalescences also occur—Galileo collapsed the Aristotelian distinction between natural and violent motion. Conceptual change entails cutting nature at different joints and sometimes abandoning certain ontological commitments. For example, Aristotle was committed to "natural places" and "natural states" in his explanations of motion—such notions played no role in Galilean or post-Galilean mechanics. The emergence of an intuitive biology by age 10 involves conceptual change. The most radical is the coalescence of two distinct ontological types—*animal* and *plant*—into a single ontological type, *living thing*. For the 4-year-old, animals are fundamentally behaving natural kinds, like people; plants are fundamentally non-behaving natural kinds, like rocks. By age 10, both animals and plants are fundamentally the same kinds of things—living things. Differentiations also occur—the 4-year-old does not distinguish between two different senses of "not alive"—the sense of *dead* and the sense of *inanimate*. Indeed, every core concept in an intuitive biology, including *animal, living thing, growth, death, baby* and the very notion of *species*, changes over this period. The status of people as animals also changes dramatically over these years. Such are the simultaneous, mutually supportive, readjustments that constitute historical cases of conceptual change as well.

EVIDENCE

Several different methods yield a variety of phenomena that support the claim that an intuitive biology emerges during these childhood years. Six are briefly described below.

The Six Phenomena

1. Inductive projection
We constantly make inferences that are not deductively valid. Taught that people have membranes called omenta that hold our digestive organs in place, most adults infer that all mammals have omenta. Some infer all vertebrates do, and some infer even more widely. Adults do not think that dolls have omenta, even though in many ways dolls appear more similar to people than are, say, dolphins. One role of our theories (naive or otherwise) is to constrain inductive projections of this sort. Our biological theory tells us that dolphins are similar to people in the relevant respects, while dolls are not. Because this is so, patterns of inductive projections provide evidence about the theories held by the person making the inferences.

Four-year-olds, no less than adults, make sensible projections of newly taught biological properties. For example, when given some vague information about a new internal organ (such as that a spleen is a round, green thing found inside people), subjects at all ages between 4 years and adulthood projected the new organ to other animals, with decreasing likelihood from mammals, through birds, through insects, through worms. At all ages there was significantly less attribution (usually none) to inanimate objects and plants (see Fig. 9.1). Apparently, even for 4-year-olds, enough information had been given for spleens to be interpreted as internal organs, and even 4-year-olds expect only other animals to share internal organs with people.

Despite these constancies throughout development, patterns of inductive projection provided the best single piece of evidence that the 4-year-old's knowledge is organised differently from the adult's. The relevant data came in part from two other conditions in the same study. Other groups of subjects were shown a dog as the example of a spleen-haver (or omentum-haver, in the case of older children and adults). Still others were shown a bee. As Fig. 9.2 shows, in these cases, 4-year-olds did *not* project spleens to other animals more than to inanimate objects, not even to other mammals (e.g. an aardvark) or insects (e.g. a stinkbug). As Table 9.1 shows, 4-year-olds projected more from people to aardvark than from dogs to aardvark. They also projected more from people to the stinkbug than

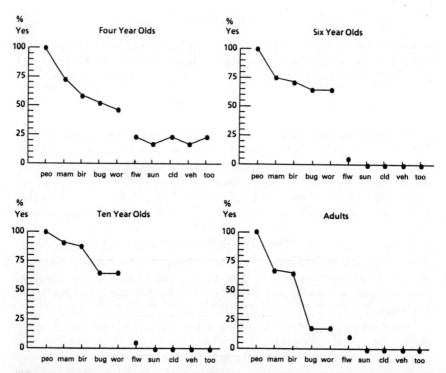

FIG. 9.1. Subjects' projection of spleens from people to other objects: people [peo]; mammal [mam]; bird [bir]; bug [bug]; worm [wor]; flower [flw]; sun [sun]; cloud [cld]; vehicle [veh]; tool [too].

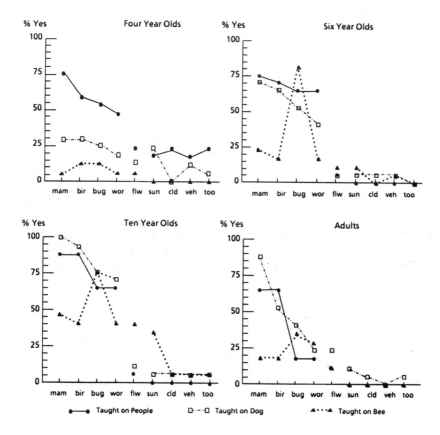

FIG. 9.2. Subjects' projection of spleens from people, from dogs, and from bees, to other objects.

TABLE 9.1
Age 4—Projection of Spleen

	To new mammal (aardvark)	*To new insect (stinkbug)*
From people	71%	53%
From dog	24%	12%

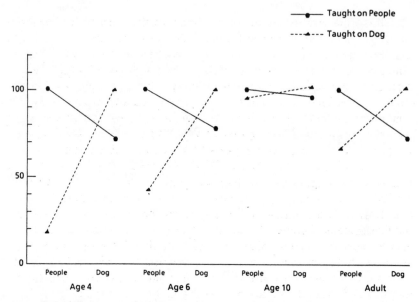

FIG. 9.3. Projection of spleen from people to dogs and from dogs to people.

from the bee to the stinkbug. Figure 9.3 represents the developmental change most clearly. At all ages spleens were projected significantly from people to dogs. But at ages 4 and 6 there was much less projection the other way around, from dogs to people. By age 10, there is no longer any asymmetry between dogs and people as exemplars of the havers of some previously unknown internal organ.

The shift from total asymmetry of projection (greater from people than from other animals) at age 4 to none at age 10 reflects restructuring of knowledge about biological properties. Apparently, for young children, these properties are fundamentally properties of people and only second-arily properties of other animals also. Only if new knowledge can be integrated into the child's knowledge of humans and human activities will the 4-year-olds project it sensibly to other animals. By age 10, people are only one mammal among many with respect to biological properties, and there is no longer an asymmetry of projection from people and from dog.

2. Patterns of attribution of biological properties

If 4-year-olds' knowledge of biological properties such as eating, sleeping, breathing, having hearts, having bones, and having babies is structured in terms of the role of each in human intercourse, then they should not differentiate between those properties all animals must have from those that only some animals share with people. This prediction follows from the assumption that a child of this age does not know the biological functions of these properties.

Children were probed as to which things in the world eat, breathe, sleep, think, have babies (always asked "Does x have baby x's?"), have hearts, have bones. To a first approximation, the 4-year-old's patterns of attribution of all these properties were identical to each other (Carey, 1985b). In each case, attribution was virtually 100% to people and fell off thereafter according to similarity to people. Indeed, the patterns of attribution were the same as those for spleen. It seems that 4-year-olds answer the question, "Does an x breathe?" by recalling that people breathe and then projecting breathing to other objects, according to similarity to people. These patterns of projection reflect paucity of biological knowledge in various ways. There is a drop in attribution of about 20% between people, on the one hand, and mammals such as dogs and aardvarks, on the other—for having hearts, breathing, etc., as well as for having spleens. People are not just one mammal among many with respect to these properties. Also, properties of all animals such as having babies, breathing and eating are greatly under-attributed to peripheral animals such as bugs and worms. The 4-year-old does not know enough biology to infer that all animals must eat, breathe and reproduce.

By age 10 none of these generalisations is still true. The patterns of attribution of the various properties are sharply differentiated from each other and from the pattern of projection of newly taught properties. Ten-year-olds know that all animals eat, breathe and have babies, and they restrict bones and hearts largely to vertebrates. Any property of people is also attributed to other mammals. Ten-year-olds resemble adults in this respect; 7-year-olds are intermediate between 4- and 10-year-olds.

The differences between the 4-year-olds, on the one hand, and the 10-year-olds, on the other, provide insights into just what biological knowledge is acquired in these years. But much more important to the present argument is the evidence these differences provide for knowledge restructuring. As in the case of the asymmetries of projection reviewed above, the evidence comes from the different information-processing models that account for the responses of subjects of different ages. Young children (4- and 5-year-olds) decide which animals eat, breathe, etc., on the basis of an inductive projection from knowledge that people do these things. Older subjects are capable of reasoning of this sort and use it when they have no other information to go on (as in the projection of omenta described above). However, 10-year-olds and adults use two quite different processes to generate their judgements about breathing, eating, having babies, having bones, etc. They base their judgements on deductive inferences from category membership (e.g. worms eat because worms are animals and all animals eat; worms do not have bones because they are not vertebrates, and only vertebrates have bones) or from reasoning about knowledge of biological function (e.g. worms must breathe because any living thing must burn oxygen for energy, and must therefore have a way of obtaining oxygen from the air). These information-processing differences in turn reflect differences in the organisation of knowledge. Four-year-olds' knowledge of what for us are biological properties is organised around their knowledge of people. Biological function does not affect the similarity metric underlying the projection of these properties to other things. By age 10 there is no evidence that knowledge that people have the properties in question is playing any role whatsoever in the child's attribution of these properties to other objects.

3. Projections from two animals

Suppose that instead of being informed that a dog is one of the things in the world that has a spleen, or a bee is one of the things in the world that has a spleen, the child is told "and here are pictures of two of the things in the world that have spleens," at which point pictures of both a dog and a bee are produced and spleens drawn inside each. Adults might be expected to reason that if two such disparate animals share some unknown internal organ, then all animals of some minimal complexity must have that organ. Four- to 6-year-olds, in contrast, would not be expected to have this form of reasoning available to them, because they do not know the biological functions of internal organs and do not understand that because some biological problems are universal, some aspects to the solution to them are also widely shared. How might young children decide whether some new object (say, a bird) has a spleen, given that they know that dogs have spleens and that bees have spleens? They might retrieve the known spleen-haver most similar to a bird, and then judge according to similarity to that spleen-haver. If this is how children do it, the pattern of projection from dogs and bees will be the intersection of the projection curve from dog alone and of the projection curve from bee alone.

The data from 17 six-year-olds are given in Fig. 9.4. They almost perfectly fit the intersection pattern. Except in the case of projection to worm, projection to new animals is no greater from dog and bee than from dog alone (to people, another mammal, and a bird) or from bee alone (to another bug). Knowing that dogs *and* bees have spleens makes it no more likely to a 6-year-old that aardvarks do than knowing only that dogs have spleens. Analyses of individual patterns of projection showed that 6-year-olds were no more likely to judge that *all* animals have spleens, given that dogs and bees do, than they were to judge that all animals have spleens given that dogs alone do (or that bees alone do). In all three of these cases, about 5–10% of the subjects attributed spleens to all animals. Adults, in contrast, were significantly more likely to judge that all animals have omenta when taught that dogs and bees have omenta (about 50% of the time) than when taught that dogs alone, or bees alone, have omenta (5–10% of the time).

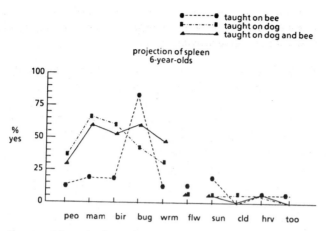

FIG.9.4. Six-year-old's projection of spleen from bees, from dogs, and from dogs *and* bees.

One way to characterise this developmental difference is to say that the concept "animal" constrains inductive projection by 6-year-olds differently than it does for adults. That is, the concept "animal" constrains inductive projection in some sense even in the youngest children tested. As we saw above (Fig. 9.1), when taught that people have some internal organ, even the youngest children project it almost exclusively to new animals. However, the concept "animal" seems available as an inductive base in another sense by adulthood. Taught that dogs *and* bees have some animal property, the 6-year-old does not assume that all animals have that property, while adults do (at least sometimes). This is yet another difference between young children's and adults' inferential processes. This third reflection of restructuring provided by differences in information-processing models is interpretable as were the first two. Only when children understand some of the biological functions of activities like breathing and eating and of organs like stomachs and hearts can they begin to understand that there are some basic problems every living organism must have successfully solved in order to exist. Armed with this under-standing, the child can discover that some aspects of the solutions reappear throughout the biological kingdom. With such knowledge, the information that dogs and bees both share a biological property provides prima facie evidence that all complex animals do.

4. Clinical interviews
The above discussion assumes that young children do not know the biological function of bodily processes and internal body parts. This assumption is supported by a vast literature on the young child's concepts of death, growth, gender, reproduction, illness, internal body parts and

bodily processes such as digestion. Almost without exception, the method used in this literature is the clinical interview. The child is asked a structured, semi-standardised set of questions about his or her understanding of the issue under study. And without exception the young child (4- to 6-year-olds) conceives of these matters differently from the 10-year-old, who usually (but not in all cases) has achieved the naive adult conception.

This literature is much too vast to summarise here (see Carey, 1985b, for a review). It reveals the pre-school child's ignorance of what is inside the body (4-year-olds commonly mention blood, food and bones). Insofar as internal organs are known, they are assigned functions on the principle: one organ—one function. The stomach is for eating, the heart is for making blood, the brain is for thinking, etc. Processes such as death, growth, reproduction, and ingestion are conceptualised in terms of the behaviour of the whole person, and its consequences for the whole person. Thus, the 4-year-old might well know that if you eat too much dessert you will get fat, or that eating vegetables will keep you healthy. What the 4-year-old decidedly does not have is any knowledge of any mechanism by which the body mediates these input–output relations.

All this has changed by the age of 10. Ten-year-olds know of many internal body parts and have constructed a model of how the integrated functioning of these internal organs supports life, growth and reproduction (Crider, 1981). The first model (achieved by age 9 or so) has substances being passed around—air, food, blood—and being used by the body. Different body parts are containers or conductors of these substances along the way. Only later does the child understand how the body breaks down and transforms substances. Even the first model, however, allows conceiving death as the cessation of internal bodily processes and allows all animals to be seen as fundamentally alike in ways that do not involve being behaving beings. It also allows the conceptualisation of plants as being like animals. Finally, it allows the formulation of the general biological problems to which each animal is a solution, and therefore enables the child to see that the real nature of each animal is to be found in its unique solution to these problems. This leads us to the fifth phenomenon I would like to discuss.

5. Species as natural kinds
At least since John Locke, philosophers have distinguished between natural-kind terms, such as *tiger, gold, water, proton, star, gene* and so on, and non-natural-kind terms, such as *box, thing, table,* and so on. While the distinction is easy to appreciate, it is not easy to state precisely, partly because many competing analyses have been offered in the philosophical literature. One thread running through the literature since Locke is that natural-kind terms refer to kinds that have essences that are the proper

business of science to discover. The essence of a natural kind is that property that kind must have in order to *be* that kind. The essence of water is being H$_2$O; the essence of gold is being the element with atomic number 69; the essence of tigers is presumably to be stated in terms of genetic structure. Note—we can believe that some kind is a natural kind, and therefore that its members have essences, without yet knowing the essence. Such is the case for tigers. We do know which science will discover the essence of tigers—namely biology—but we can only guess at the nature of the tiger's essence. We can see, then, that the specification of natural kinds is closely tied to our theories of the world. A rough-and-ready test for non-natural kinds is that they play no role in scientific theories. There is no essence of a box, a thing, or a table to be discovered; none of these is likely to play an important role in any present or future scientific theory.

When people treat a term as a natural-kind term, they are willing to grant that those properties they know of things to which the term applies do not actually determine category membership. That is, they may have a prototype of members of the kind, but they are ready to defer to experts or to their own theory building to discover that their prototype is wrong. This is why if I show you a fruit with nubbly skin the size, shape and colour of an orange, but *tell* you that it grew on a lemon tree, you are happy to conclude it is a funny-looking lemon. Our current theories of the essences of biological kinds, being tied to genetics as they are, lead us to weight parentage very heavily. If something that looked exactly like a cactus had the genetic structure of a grapefruit, could cross with prototypical grapefruits, and so on, we would be surprised, but we would accept that it is nonetheless a grapefruit.

Recently, Frank Keil (1986) has asked at what age words for individual animals, such as "skunk" and "racoon", fruits, such as "lemon" and "grapefruit", and plants, such as "cactus" and "palm", become natural-kind terms in this sense. He used two converging paradigms. One pitted his best guess of the child's views of the nature of individual species' essences against his guess of what the child would consider merely characteristic features. The other left entirely open what the child might consider the essence. In the first experiment the child was shown a picture of an animal—say a skunk, as in Fig. 9.5—and told various things about the behaviour of that animal, such as that it was active at night, squirted smelly stuff when it was attacked or frightened, and so on. In other words, both its appearance and behaviour fit the prototypical skunk. The child was asked what he thought it was a picture of, and of course ventured it was a skunk. He was then told that scientists had studied this particular animal in great detail and had discovered that its parents had been racoons, that its babies had been racoons, and that its heart, brain and blood were like the heart,

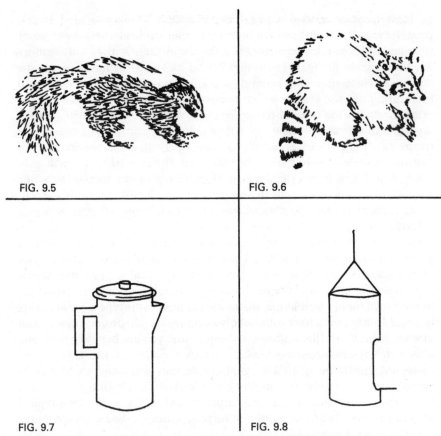

FIG. 9.5   FIG. 9.6

FIG. 9.7   FIG. 9.8

Stimuli for Keil's natural kind and artifact studies.

brains and blood of racoons. He was then asked what the animal was—a racoon or a skunk. Subjects were 5-year-olds and 9-year-olds. The younger children insisted that the picture depicted a skunk; 9-year-olds said it was a racoon that merely looked like a skunk.

As mentioned above, this study depended upon a guess as to what the child's views of the underlying essences of species would be like—parentage and internal organs would loom large. The second study depended on no such guess. As before, the child was shown a picture such as that in Fig. 9.5 and asked what he thought it was—skunk again being the answer. He was told that some veterinarians had taken that animal and shaved off all its fur, replaced it with black and brown fur, made it much fatter, removed its tail and replaced it with another, and so on, until the result looked as in Fig. 9.6. The question was what Fig. 9.6 depicted. Five-year-olds were adamant that it was a racoon, 9-year-olds equally sure that it was a skunk that merely looked exactly like a racoon.

An important control is to see that this shift does not occur for terms that do not refer to natural kinds. Parallel controls were carried out for the two studies; I will describe those for the second study only. Subjects were shown a picture such as that in Fig. 9.7, and all agreed it was a coffee pot. A transformation was described, where various parts were rearranged, excised and added until the final result was as in Fig. 9.8—a bird feeder. The question is what the resulting object is—a coffee-pot or a bird-feeder. Here children of both ages agreed that it is a bird feeder. There is no general tendency for 9-year-olds to conserve kind across transformations such as these.

Keil used many different examples, taken from the plant as well as the animal kingdom and from various types of non-natural kinds as well. He saw his data as reflecting a shift, between the ages of 5 and 9, in the nature of all the terms for biological species. For 5-year-olds these terms are non-natural-kind terms, like coffee pot, while by age 9 they are natural-kind terms. There is another way of describing the shift that is perhaps more familiar to developmental psychologists: the 9-year-olds make a distinction between appearance and reality that the 5-year-olds do not. These two ways of describing the change are, in fact, closely related. Essences are the ultimate reality, the real nature of the things in nature, and are usually deeply hidden. It is the business of science both to discover essences and to discover deeper realities underlying surface appearances.

Keil does not argue for a general shift between these ages such that all terms that refer to natural kinds as far as adults are concerned begin to do so around age 9. Whether a term is a natural kind or not is a function of two factors: the world (*is* there a kind in nature picked out by the term?) and the user's knowledge (does he realise that the objects referred to have an underlying essence?). Thus, the words "atom" and "elm" may function as natural-kind terms for me, but not for my 6-year-old daughter. Similarly, there is no general emergence of the appearance/reality distinction around age 9. Children as young as 3 command the distinction in some contexts (Flavell, Flavell & Green, 1983). After that, grasp of the distinction develops in two respects: the child comes to appreciate it on a meta-conceptual level (Flavell et. al., 1983), and the child comes to know, through domain-specific conceptual change, more and more cases where surface appearances do not accord with deeper reality (Carey, 1985a). Keil's phenomenon is an instance of the latter sort.

The discovery of the essences of the things in nature and the discovery of deeper realities underlying surface phenomena are two of the goals of theory development. Rudimentary biological knowledge is being acquired and restructured in the years between 4 and 10. The reflections of this process described above provide some insight into Keil's phenomena. What for the adult are basic biological functions and crucial biological organs are seen by the 4-year-old in terms of their place in human activity. Other animals have these basically (for the child) human properties only insofar as they are similar to people. Suppose I am right that children do not understand these properties in terms of their biological functions until around age 10. Perhaps they cannot conceive of each animal or plant species as a unique solution to a basic set of common biological problems until then. In other words, if hearts, blood, stomachs are fundamentally properties of people, then the very notions of the heart of a skunk, the blood of a skunk, the brain of a skunk, and so on, are not meaningful to a 5-year-old.

6. Childhood animism

The sixth phenomenon that reveals acquisition and reorganisation of biological knowledge between ages 4 and 10—childhood animism—is well known to developmental psychologists, although not usually interpreted in this light. Asked what things in the world are alive, young children include various inanimate objects—the sun, the moon, cars, fires, stoves, clouds, rivers, the wind, televisions, rocks rolling down hills, and so on, have all been judged alive by many animistic young subjects (Piaget, 1929; Laurendeau & Pinard, 1962; Carey, 1985b). Childhood animism disappears almost completely by age 10.

Piaget (1929) placed the phenomenon of childhood animism in the context of the child's notions of causality. He claimed that the pre-school child had only one causal schema—human intentional causation. Lacking any notions of physical causation, the child interprets cases of one inanimate object's affecting another in terms of the intentions and goals of the active object. The active object is seen as causal agent, as in the sun's warming a person, the fire's cooking food, the rolling rock's knocking loose another, and so on. Active agents, in turn, are endowed with life. Hence childhood animism. As Gelman and her collaborators have shown, the key presupposition of Piaget's account is false. The pre-school child does *not* lack a notion of physical causality (e.g., Bullock, Gelman & Baillargeon, 1982; see also, Shultz, 1982). Thus, although Piaget is right that young children do attribute intentional causal agency to inanimate objects, the reason for this cannot be that the child lacks any other causal schema. The root of childhood animism must be found elsewhere.

Here let us restrict our attention to developmental changes in the meaning of the word "alive." In my monograph I argue that one major factor in the animistic attribution of life to inanimate objects is lack of biological knowledge. My argument is much too lengthy to go into here, but I can give a flavour of a part of it. Suppose that the child knows, because he has been told, that plants and animals are alive. Given that children under 7 do not yet know the biological functions of eating, breathing, growing, and so on, such that they do not even realise that all animals must share these functions, they could have no basis for rationalising the inclusion of plants and animals in a single category. Having no basis for seeing why animals and plants are alike, other objects might be included among the living. Two results directly support this line of reasoning. First, a new property (having golgi) was taught as were spleen and omenta in the studies described above, only the child was told "and here are pictures of two of the things in the world that have golgi— dogs and flowers." By hypothesis, the 6-year-old does not have the concept "living thing" available as an inductive base, and so should sometimes include inanimate objects among projected golgi-havers. As Table 9.2 shows, this is what happened. Thus, it is possible to produce patterns of attribution like those for judgements of what is alive or not merely by telling the child that an animal and a plant share some property and asking him to judge what else might. Second, when tested in the standard Piagetian interview, 4- to 7-year-olds gave animistic judgements *only* when they judged that plants were alive. If they judged animals to be alive, but not plants, they also did not include inanimate objects among the living (Carey, 1985b). In sum, one source of animistic attributions of life is not having the biological concept "living thing" available to rationalise the inclusion of animals and plants into a single category. The concept "living thing" becomes available as biological functions and properties become differentiated from general knowledge of people. As we saw above, this happens in the years between 4 and 10.

TABLE 9.2
Projection of Golgi to Inanimate Objects at Age 6

	Inanimate objects attributed golgi (%)	Subjects making at least 1 attribution to an inanimate object (%)
taught on dog and flower	38	44
	a	c
	11 b	19 d
taught on flower		
	4	15
taught on dog and bee		

a: $p < 0.10$, t-test, l-tailed.
b: $p < 0.10$, t-test, l-tailed.
c: $p < 0.10$, ^{2}, corrected for continuity, l-tailed.
d: $p < 0.05$, ^{2}, corrected for continuity, l-tailed.

CONCLUSIONS

If these phenomena do, indeed, plausibly reflect the emergence of a new theoretical domain, then such childhood cases of theory emergence involve restructuring of knowledge of just the same sort as occurs in the history of science. Insofar as there are only a very few intuitive theories represented by the child, and insofar as these intuitive theories encompass wide domains of phenomena, the study of theory changes in childhood will provide one source of unity in our description of development. Thus, if these two assumptions are correct, an undesirable consequence of abandoning the stage theory is avoided. We are not to be reduced to describing thousands of piecemeal developmental advances.

In Piaget's last work, he returned to questions that might be seen as the core of genetic epistemology—the relationships between the ontogenesis of scientific knowledge in childhood and in the history of science. In this context, the question of stages should be differentiated into two questions: (1) Are there developmental constraints on the types of theories children can construct? (2) Within any given theoretical domain, is ontogenesis characterised by large-scale restructuring? If so, must we characterise the restructuring in cases of historical theory change in the same terms as we would characterise the restructuring in the case of individual development of scientific concepts? Some have taken scale structural reorganisations as the hallmark of stages. This is merely a semantic issue; any theorist is free to use the word "stage" however he or she pleases. But if "stage" is taken in the domain-general sense adopted in this chapter, a commitment to there being stages is a commitment to an affirmative answer to the first question. Here I would simply like to point out that the answer to each of these two questions constrains the other. Insofar as there are developmental constraints on the kinds of theories children can construct, the parallels between the characterisation of conceptual change in childhood and in the history of science are limited. Insofar as the same representational and computational machinery is needed to characterise conceptual change in both cases, the role of domain-general developmental change in childhood is limited. Thus, there is a certain tension between Piaget's work on the domain-general characterisation of changes in representational and inferential capacities and this work on the parallels between ontogenesis in the history of science and in childhood.

One example may make clear that these two questions are distinct. The difficulty in getting a child past a Piagetian hurdle is well known. Indeed, the hallmark of most of Piaget's phenomena is that it is nearly impossible to get the child to perform as would an adult. Upon seeing a non-conserving child for the first time, most people's initial response is that the child is failing to understand the question, for some trivial reason. The intuition is that given 20 minutes with the child, you could make clear what is wanted and straighten the kid out. The literature is littered with failed attempts to do just that. So-called training studies just do not work—unless the child is "ready" to be trained. This is to be understood on the assumption of domain-general stages, since being "ready" meant having attained a new way of thinking or new information-processing capacity—only if you have passed into the new stage will you be able to benefit from training. But this is also to be understood on the theory change story.

Theories resist change. Discrepant phenomena are assimilated or ignored. Given the restructuring involved, it is no accident that the process is protracted—over a 5- or 6-year period—and it is not surprising that short training studies fail. Indeed, the science education literature now has myriad examples of failures of curricular materials to dislodge misconceptions, where the source of each misconception is alternative conceptual frameworks—intuitive theories—novices bring to science learning. A year of college-level mechanics does not replace the pre-Newtonian ideas the college student brings to the physics class (see Chi, Glaser & Rees, 1983, for a review.)

I am arguing here that conceptual change in childhood must be analysed in the context of theory changes in childhood. This commits me to the view that children, even babies, represent theory-like conceptual structures. Of course I embrace this commitment; indeed, I believe that we will need to appeal to intuitive theories in any attempts to specify constraints on induction, ontological commitments, and causal notions. And, as I have tried to sketch in this talk, appeals to theory change may provide some descriptive unity to diverse developmental changes and may help us understand resistance to learning in at least some cases.

Just what is meant by "theory", and is it plausible to impute theories to young children? A theory is characterised by the phenomena in its domain, its laws and other explanatory mechanisms, and the concepts that articulate the laws and the representations of the phenomena. Explanation is at the core of theories. It is explanatory mechanisms that distinguish theories from other types of conceptual structures, such as restaurant scripts. To see this, consider such questions as "Why do we pay for our food at a restaurant?" or "Why do we order before the food comes?" The answers to these questions are not to be found within the restaurant script itself; the answer to the first lies in the domain of economics, where questions of exchanges of goods and services sit, and that to the second in the domain of physics, where questions of the directionality of time sit.

The distinction between theory-like structures and other types of cognitive structures is one of degree. Probably all conceptual structures provide some fodder for explanation. My intuition, however, is that there are only a relatively few conceptual structures that embody deep explanatory notions—in the order of a dozen or so in the case of educated non-scientists. These conceptual structures correspond to domains that might be the disciplines at a university—psychology, mechanics, a theory of matter, economics, religion, government, biology, history, etc. On the view of development put forward in this chapter, the child begins with many fewer such domains—perhaps only a naïve mechanics and a naïve psychology. Conceptual development consists, in part, of the differentiation of a new theoretical domain from these beginning ones, as in the differentiation of biology from psychology previously described.

I have not shown, of course, that theory-like structures are relatively few in number, and that such structures can be distinguished from other conceptual structures along the continuum of explanatory depth. Rather, I have attempted to make these claims at least plausible, so that they may be subject to further scrutiny and test. I hereby confess that the ultimate interest of the arguments in this chapter depends on these claims being cashable.

One final caveat—many will recognise that I have opened a can of worms. I have tried to show that developmental psychologists are up against the same set of problems that arise in the general problem of understanding theory change—but what kind of step forward is this? All I can say is that I think it is important to know just what can of worms we are in.

REFERENCES

Bullock, M., Gelman, R. & Baillargeon, R. (1982). The development of causal reasoning. In W. J. Friedman (Ed.), *The developmental psychology of time.* New York: Academic Press.

Carey, S. (1985a). Are children fundamentally different thinkers and learners from adults? In S. F. Chipman, J. W. Segal & R. Glaser (Eds.), *Thinking and learning skills, 2.* Hillsdale, NJ: Lawrence Erlbaum Associates.

Carey, S. (1985b). *Conceptual change in childhood.* Cambridge, Mass.: M.I.T. Press.

Chi, M. T. H. (1976). Short-term memory limitations in children: Capacity or processing deficits? *Memory & Cognition, 4*, 559–572.

Chi, M., Glaser, R. & Rees, E. (1982). Expertise in problem solving. In R. Sternberg (Ed.), *Advances in the Psychology of Human Intelligence.* Vol. 1. Hillsdale, N.J.: Lawrence Erlbaum.

Crider, C. (1981). Children's conceptions of the body interior. In R. Bibace & M. Walsh (Eds.), *Children's conceptions of health, illness and bodily functions.* San Francisco: Jossey-Bass.

Flavell, J., Flavell, E. & Green, F. (1983). Development of the appearance–reality distinction. *Cognitive Psychology, 15*, 95–120.

Gelman, R. & Baillargeon, R. (1983). A review of some Piagetian concepts. In J. H. Flavell & E. M. Markman (Eds.), *Carmichael's manual of child psychology.* Vol. 3. New York: Wiley.

Keil, F. C. (1986). The acquisition of natural kind and artifact terms. In A. Marrar & W. Demopoulos (Eds.), *Conceptual change.* Norwood, NJ: Ablex.

Laurendeau, M. & Pinard, A. (1962). *Causal thinking in the child: A genetic and experimental approach.* New York: International Universities Press.

Piaget, J. (1929). *The child's conception of the world.* London: Routledge and Kegan Paul.

Piaget, J. & Inhelder, B. (1941). *Le développement des quantités chez l'enfant.* Neuchâtel: Delachaux et Niestlé.

Schultz, T. R. (1982). Rules of causal attribution. *Monographs of the Society for Research in Child Development.* Chicago: University of Chicago Press.

Smith, C. (1979). Children's understanding of natural language hierarchies. *Journal of Experimental Child Psychology, 27,* 437–458.

Smith, C., Carey, S. & Wiser, M. (1985). On differentiation: A case study of the development of size, weight, and density. *Cognition 21,* (3), 177–237.

10 Cognition in Its Relationship to Total Development in the First Few Years of Life

Sybille K. Escalona
Albert Einstein College of Medicine, New York

My primary research interest has been and still is to elucidate developmental processes in infancy and early childhood. Most of our research has tried to take into account that what develops is not cognition or perception but children who perceive, who cognate, who feel, who simultaneously act upon the environment and are acted upon by the social and material forces and conditions in which they grow and to which they must adapt. The fascination lies with the manner in which diverse conditions, events and intrinsic characteristics combine and interact in such a way as to result in lawful developmental sequences that characterise the species as a whole and yet ensure enormous individual differences; no two children develop in the same manner.

Study of the intertwining of cognitive, affective and social components of development requires factual knowledge and workable theory in all of these areas. Decades of research by Piaget, Inhelder and the entire Geneva group have created an extraordinarily explicit, systematic and empirically based theory of cognitive development. For the area of personality development the equivalent does not exist. However, psychoanalytic ego psychology deals with what Piaget called affectivity in structural and dynamic terms. In its own way it maintains a close connection with concrete and observable phenomena. As Greenspan (1979) has described in some detail, an affinity between Piagetian theory and psychoanalysis exists, despite enormous differences in the two approaches. Psychoanalytic theory can serve as an overarching framework, in part because the stages of development as envisaged by current ego-psychoanalytic scholars encompass the evolution of thought, deal with the manner in which

165

children adapt to reality, postulate internal regulating structures and allow for the interplay between biological, psychological and environmental components and determinants of development. It is also the only theory that deals with intra-psychological events and plausibly relates them to overt behaviour. What is to be said here will sound crude in comparison to the erudition with which cognitive development can be discussed, and also by comparison to sophisticated psychoanalytic discourse. I hope to show that these deficiencies arise precisely *because* we try to interpret our data with full recognition of the complexities they mask.

During early phases of development there are certain nodal points at which decisive transformations in cognitive development are intimately interwoven with equally important developments within the ego. It is then that the links between cognitive, affective and social components can be traced with some clarity. I shall speak of two such nodal points, one taking place during the first 6 or 8 months and the other late in the second and during the third year of life. For each I shall first state what I have in mind and then provide some of the data and observations from which these tentative conclusions were derived. The first might be called the importance of the distance receptor systems for the development of sensorimotor intelligence and the importance of mother (read mothering persons) in that connection. Sensorimotor intelligence is distilled from the infant's transactions with or, as Piaget would put it, actions upon the environment. It is the behavioural arousals that occur as the alert infant is attentive to the environment that mediate the evolution of increasingly differentiated and increasingly complex schemes. Much research has demonstrated three different things: (1) that alertness and the proclivity to engage with aspects of the environment differ among infants and that such differences are related to the rate of cognitive advance; (2) that infants tend to be at their most alert, and to display the most mature behaviour patterns of which they are capable, while in close interaction with a caretaking adult—in our culture, that adult tends to be the mother or whoever has responsibility for the baby's care; (3) that the nature of the infant's responsiveness while in contact with less familiar persons, and especially the sensorimotor activations that occur while the baby plays when alone, are greatly influenced by the style in which mothers habitually interact with their babies. Obviously, the actions that build sensorimotor intelligence depend on many other things as well: the state of the infant; intrinsic characteristics of the organism, including whatever makes for intellectual endowment, temperamental dispositions, and much more. Nonetheless, sensorimotor activity is always influenced by what the environment has to offer and by the kind of actions it invites and cultivates.

So much by way of recapitulating familiar ground. A number of our research projects, and in particular an endlessly detailed observational study of two infants from birth to their second birthday, have shown that one of the pathways through which the nature and quality of sensorimotor activity is established is the relative emphasis mothers place on the distance as contrasted to the near receptors (Escalona & Corman, 1971, 1974). It is the distance receptors, sight and sound, that are primarily employed when attention and behaviour are focused upon the environmental field, and it is the distance receptor systems through which the inanimate environment is apprehended. It can also be shown that, at least for much of the first year, the differentiation, combination and integration of sensorimotor schemes is facilitated primarily by action upon manipulable objects in the environment (rather than upon persons or their own body). I think that cultivation or "exercise" of the distance receptor systems early on enhances sensorimotor intelligence. Although all babies use every sense modality and are responsive to all aspects of the relevant environment, the relative prominence of different universal schemes, and the most responsive sense modalities, vary greatly among babies. Furthermore, mothers differ from one another in behaviour style. We have found that mothers are remarkably consistent in terms of the sense modalities they themselves employ and which they tend to stimulate in their babies.

Whether a mother is a toucher, one who relies heavily on sound, or one who looks and shows has a good deal to do with central aspects of personality. To oversimplify: persons who are interested in and concerned with the broader social and cultural environment are likely to emphasise and behaviourally value sight and sound in the absence of touch or kinesthesia. Those whose outlook is narrower, focused on the family and on more concrete and immediate things, are more likely to accompany sight and sound by touch or movement, as if to enhance and make more vivid that which is looked at or listened to. Behavioural preference among the sensory systems is a personal attribute, but also one associated with social class. Needless to say, there are enormous variations within social class. Yet, up to this point, some sort of supra-personal orientation to life in general was seen in every woman who went in massively for the distance receptor systems while interacting with her babies.

Now for some supporting data about two babies, one of whom developed more rapidly than the other and later proved to be intellectually precocious, while the other developed at an average rate and, at the age of two, obtained an MDI of 108 (Fig. 10.1). Figure 10.2 requires some explanation. To describe the methodology as a whole would be impossible. What you do need to know is that two trained observers visited these babies in their homes once a week. Independently, they recorded the child's behaviour and the context in which it occurred. Visits were timed so that we covered the baby's entire day, from awakening in the morning to being put to bed at night. Neither observers nor the families could tolerate more than two hours at a time, so it required six weeks to obtain an

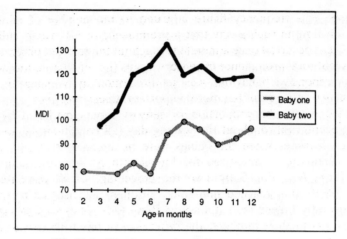

FIG. 10.1. Developmental test scores for two infants.

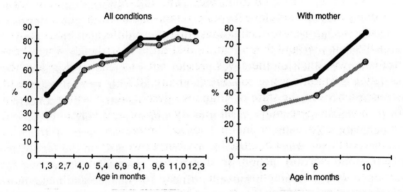

FIG. 10.2. Sensory input: percent prominence by distance receptors.

approximately representative sample of the infant's day. The narrative observational material was then coded and computer processed for each six-week period—the bottom line shows the age span being summarised.

Insofar as the observers were in agreement, the narrative data were scored in a great variety of ways. These included what, for want of a better word, we called sensory inputs—the sensory modalities through which the infant became aware of some change or spectacle in the environment and to which the infant made a distinct response. If he looked at a curtain swaying in the breeze, the input would be visual and the source would be scored as inanimate. If mother approached the child speaking to him, and he gazed and cooed at her, the input would be visual/auditory, social, mother. And so for all possible combinations of modalities and sources, but always *only* if the infant was roused to some sort of coordinated action by the spectacle. Fleeting gazes, sounds and motions were not counted.

Prominence is a frequency figure adjusted to the number of minutes' observation time in such a way that a prominence of 100 would indicate that the event occurred once a minute throughout the relevant observation time. Percent total prominence of sensory inputs (i.e. of all occasions when an overt responsive behaviour was set in motion by a change in the environment) proved to be more important than frequency as such. Figure 10.2 shows the proportion of sensory inputs mediated by the distance receptors throughout the waking day (all conditions) as well as at only those times when the babies were in direct contact with their mothers (the latter summarised for four-month periods to secure sufficiently large *N*s). For Baby Two the percentage of all responses to external events that reached him solely through the distance receptors was consistently higher than it was for Baby One. However, when the babies were with their mothers, the difference in this respect was more pronounced.

So far I have illustrated that there are differences in the relative distributions of near- and far-receptor systems involved in spectacles that set in motion sensorimotor activations, that these differences persist over at least the first year and that a feature that differed strikingly when these babies were with their mothers was present but to a smaller degree when all situational conditions are combined. Figure 10.3 substantiates some of the consequences of the state of affairs we described for Babies One and Two. It shows the percentage of all sensory *outputs* directed at portions of the inanimate environment in the mother's presence as well as in all situations when she was not close by. By output we meant that the infant initiated some sort of action spontaneously, i.e. when nothing had occurred to draw his attention to the object. For instance, a baby might suddenly focus on a teddybear, coo and smile at it and finally reach for it, although the toy had been sitting there all along and nothing had happened in the environment. When they were in direct contact with their mothers both babies were equally attentive to things in their environment. But on their own, or with non-mother persons, the difference between the infants was striking after 4 months of age, largely because in mother's absence Baby Two became more attentive to the inanimate surroundings than in mother's presence. Baby One, on the other hand, lost interest in the world of things when mother was not there to reinforce it. A brief look at the lower graph of Fig. 10.3 gives another measure of the pattern of sensorimotor activity. In this case I used prominence, i.e. relative frequency and, as can be seen, it was Baby Two who busied himself manipulating objects far more than did Baby One.

The clue to how these and related differences came about is the fact that Mother One was given to touching her baby a great deal. She stroked, tickled, kissed and pinched with abandon. Furthermore, when showing the

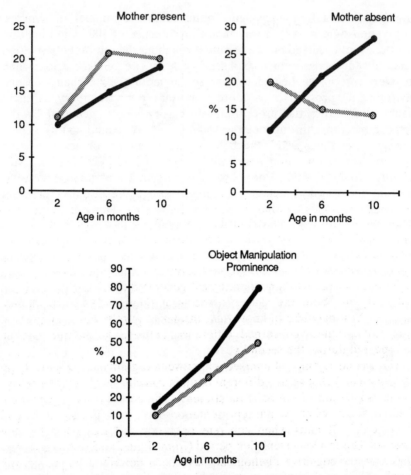

FIG. 10.3.   Sensory output: percent prominence to inanimate environment.

baby a toy or when inviting her social attention, she tended to reinforce sight and sound by also touching the baby's hand or face. We had found in previous studies that, in mother's absence, very young infants tend to re-create whatever actions and sensations had been prominent and pleasurably arousing while they were with mother (Escalona, 1968). Figure 10.4 is one example of this tendency. It shows the relative frequency with which the babies touched their own skin more than transiently; this refers to such actions as stroking and rubbing their own body, hair and ear pulling and, in the case of Baby One, energetic scratching and pinching. On the right-hand side of the same figure we show, for the same time span, how frequently these babies used the tactile modality to explore objects. Most often, the babies would look at something they were holding and at the

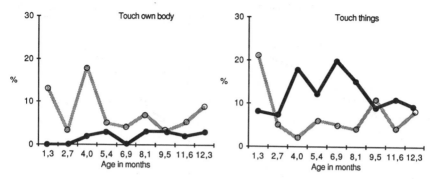

FIG. 10.4.   Tactile sensory output: percent prominence.

same time finger and stroke it, or bring it to their lips or cheek alternately with visual regard. (The tactile aspect of holding or manipulating something was not scored under this rubric. It had to be some sort of savouring and prolongation of tactile sensations the object could evoke.) Both graphs together indicate that the amount of self-generated tactile exploration that occurred was about the same; it was what they tended to touch that differed. You may like to know that, insofar as purely sensory aspects of input and output are concerned, differences between the children virtually disappeared during the second year.

The second instance of intersection between cognitive development and developmental change in a different domain coincides with the emergence and consolidation of symbolic functioning. The period of pre-operational thinking begins when mental representations have been formed at the end of stage VI. It ends when concrete operational thinking has become possible. This is a long transition period (from about 2 to 5 or 6 years). The phase-specific cognitive phenomena have been described. However, the massive changes that occur do not lend themselves to the kind of formal, logical and structural analysis that was made of the preceding and the subsequent stages. The hallmark of this stage is the emergence and flowering of the semiotic function. Other major characteristics specify what, by comparison to the next stage, has *not yet* evolved—for instance, reversability on the level of mental representations. Other major characteristics such as egocentrism and animism are defined by their similarity to the preceding stage. The child must learn anew, on the level of mental representations, what he had already mastered on the sensorimotor level.

Possibly this relative opaqueness came about because rational thought is hardly the hallmark of the toddler and early pre-school years. It is no accident that *Play, dreams and imitation in childhood* (Piaget, 1951) is the only major work in which Piaget offers explicit formulations in the area of affectivity and motivation. In essence, what he had to say was that at this age the newly acquired semiotic abilities make the child aware of the huge universe of which he is a small part and of the multitude of social regulations by which it is governed. Yet his cognitive capacities do not enable him to comprehend and integrate these complexities. Therefore he needs periods during which he is free to modify reality and, on a symbolic level, to structure and master his experience.

Parenthetically, one reason why psychologists have so resisted the notion of animism and magical thinking outside the play situation is that the manner in which this information is obtained is somewhat artificial. Ordinarily, children take for granted the phenomena by which they are surrounded. Seldom if ever do they spontaneously wonder whether the sun knows where it is going, where dreams are located or what is alive. When queried in a respectful and conversational manner, they will do their anthropomorphic best.

Psychoanalysis, on the other hand, sees the toddler and early pre-school age as a period during which structure formation is the central issue. It also emphasises the transition to symbolic functioning and its consequences for cognition and for awareness of the self as a small entity in a large world. Psychoanalytic ego psychology proposes that the intra-psychic ego structures that support more mature modes of adaptation, of which cognitive and other symbolic functions are an integral part, evolve in the course of sequential stages in the mother–child relationship. When this relationship is adequately satisfying, it facilitates the growing child's disposition to act upon the environment, to explore, and the host of other tendencies summarised as striving for mastery. The more autonomous and effective the toddler's behaviour, the more it creates awareness of his physical and psychological distance from the mother. Simultaneously, mastery activities broaden the youngster's awareness of the environment. Inevitably, as was also pointed out by Piaget, toddler exploits lead to conflict with the mother, who must restrain, limit and direct him. What neither analysts nor Piaget have emphasised enough is that the energetic doings of young children constantly bring them into conflict with the physical world as well. Hot stoves burn; sharp corners hurt; and balls refuse to hit their target. Thus the pursuit of action impulses becomes doubly dangerous. The child's cognitive map includes the possibility of bringing pain, whether due to his own reckless action or to mother's disapproval. It is on this basis, combined with the surging desire and ability for independent action, that the young child is forced to recognise his dependence on the mother. In a sort of vertical decalage the heedless and as it were innocent toddler enterprises change in nature. He now needs to know that mother is nearby; he ventures more readily with her support; when anxious he clings to her, and so forth. The need for mother's closeness and the need for self-directed activity create conflicting feelings and thus ambivalence in the mother–child relationship. It is precisely at this point, that Mahler called the phase of *rapprochement* (Mahler, Pine & Bergmann, 1975), that the semiotic function begins to flourish. (Incidentally, I believe that this universal ontogenic experience of lost innocence lies at the root of the theme of a Paradise Lost, which looms so large in religion and in myth.) At any rate, for some time to come, the young child struggles with the necessity to control his impulsivity. It is specified that delay capacity, intentional delay between an impulse and its execution, is a pre-requisite for cognition on the symbolic level.

This may have been a fragmentary and bowdlerised account of psychoanalytic thinking on the matter but it will serve to indicate an area of overlap between it and Piagetian formulations. In Piaget's version, the relevant cognitive advance depends on the process of decentering, which creates increasing distance between the acting subject and the acted-upon object. No classification or other simple concept formation can occur without such distancing—this being the term Heinz Werner preferred for the same thing.

It follows that a degree of impulse control (delay capacity) must be present before thought proper—i.e. the use of symbols to denote mental representations—can take place. Impulse control evolves chiefly in the context of interpersonal transactions in the family. It is only after internal regulating structures have operated in daily life for some time that decentering can take hold in the more neutral area of cognition. Impulse control demonstrably depends on the maturation of the central nervous system, but, given that, it is massively influenced by the social climate in the home and the pattern of the mother–child relationship.

In a research project involving the longitudinal study of premature infants and their families, whom we followed from birth to three-and-a-half years, we had occasion to examine the links between the emergence of impulse control, cognitive development and the child's day-by-day experience. Once again, the methodology cannot be described. What you do need to know is that in this study, which we called "Critical issues in the development of infants at biologic risk", we focused on family life style as much as upon the cognitive and psycho-social development of the children. Standard tests of intelligence (Bayley Scales of Infant Development, and the Stanford Intelligence Test) were given every 6 months. A good many other standard procedures to reflect cognitive and personality development were added, as were procedures to assess the progress of the mother–child relationship. Throughout the biannual research visits, which lasted for at least half a day, the child and the accompanying adults were observed by two staff members. To learn about the child's everyday experience, and about the cultural and material environment in which he grew, lengthy interviews were held with the mother and other relatives. These were prolonged, detailed, entirely informal and made possible by the fact that much of the research effort was devoted to developing a good relationship with our subjects. (It may be mentioned that with our population, which consisted predominantly of the urban poor, this was achieved by going all-out to meet their convenience, by respecting their privacy and reserve, by being genuinely interested in anything they had to say and, last but not least, by avoiding direct questioning.) While impulse control was assessed in a number of ways, the most important measure was a rating of the level of impulse control at each age level between 28 and 40 months. In the belief that ego control is demonstrated (and also learned) during socialisation procedures and other situations in the home, this rating was based entirely upon the child's typical behaviour in his own milieu and thus almost independent of what office observation showed. These ratings were not impressionistic. They were based on a scoring manual that listed, for each age, behaviours in many different situations, indicating various levels of control.

The sample consisted of 106 infants, of whom 21 showed neurological pathology and an additional 26 had such severe behavioural difficulties as to be classified as "deviant". Analyses were done separately for each of these groups. We found, as has everybody else, that IQ scores and other

TABLE 10.1
Mean IQ for Each Impulse Control (IC) Rating at Three
Ages (Intact Group)

Age^a	IC	N	IQ	S.D.	F
28	1	1	66.0		
	2	12	77.1	7.85	
	3	23	94.1	10.13	0.000
	4	9	100.2	13.94	
		45	90.4	13.89	
34	1	0			
	2	10	74.9	19.32	
	3	19	93.8	14.79	0.007
	4	8	97.8	12.11	
	5	1	73.0		
		38	89.1	18.85	
40	1	0			
	2	11	86.0	12.85	
	3	24	94.6	a12.45	0.005
	4	9	105.7	14.08	
	5	1	73.0		
		45	94.3	14.42	

^{a} In months.

cognitive appraisals are massively influenced by socioeconomic status, beginning during the second year. For the intact children, the mean IQ at 40 months ranged from 78 in the lowest SES quartile to 106.3 in the highest. Our expectation was that the rate at which impulse control emerges differs as a result of the experience of each child; that patterns of experience conducive to impulse control would be found less often in poor and ill-educated families than in the others, and that therefore, at very early ages, impulse control is one of the mediating variables between social class and cognition. This assumes that levels of impulse control (IC) are associated with IQ, and Table 10.1 shows that this is the case. An IC score of 1 denotes a near-absence of control; 2 indicates that impulse control fell below that shown by the majority of peers; 3 means that the child showed the age-appropriate balance between control and impulsivity; 4, that impulse control was tighter and more pervasive than is at all common at their age; and 5, the atypical pattern of children who vacillate between over- and under-control in the absence of moderate control. Since 1 and 5 were almost never seen in the intact group, it is best to focus on the fact that mean IQ rises with the shift from an IC rating of 2 to 3, and again with the transition from 3 to 4.

To avoid misunderstanding, I wish to emphasise again that the association between relatively weak and relatively strong impulse control and IQ is pronounced at ages two, three and four, while restraining structures are in the process of being formed. Later such an association exists at the extremes, but excellent cognitive performance can and does occur when ego control is at the lower extreme of the normal range (Block & Block, 1980).

Figure 10.5 shows that the relationship between IC and IQ applies

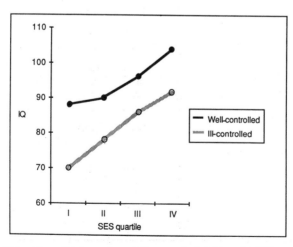

FIG. 10.5.   Mean IQ for well- and ill-controlled children by SES quartile.

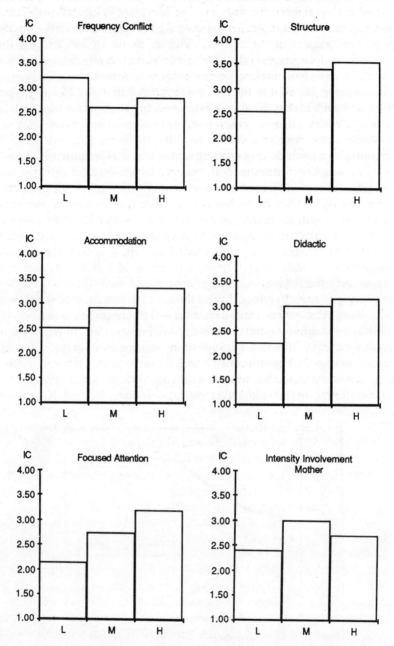

FIG. 10.6.   Mean IC for different ratings on various patterns of experience.

within social class. Note that impulse control does not by itself facilitate cognitive development. The difference between the low and higher SES groups is as great for the well-controlled as for the children who were ill-controlled.

An elaborate analysis of what we call stable patterns of experience was required. By this term we refer to enduring aspects of each child's experience of the kind that permeates daily life—for example, whether a child's life was highly structured or whether fluid and at times chaotic event sequences predominated, or how much open conflict occurred between the child and the adults with whom he lived. Figure 10.6 gives a rough idea of the degree to which the presence or relative absence of such experience patterns was related to impulse control. Whether a given pattern received a rating of Low, Medium or High was determined by independent ratings of two investigators. Again, criteria for each rating at each age had been specified, pre-tested and embodied in a manual. Clearly, structure, accommodation, how much teaching the child received and how often he was the sole focus of adult attention had a great deal to do with impulse control. Note that it was when these experience features were minimally present that IC scores fell well below the age-appropriate (3) level. Whether one of these patterns was extremely dominant or present to about the same degree seen in the majority made relatively little difference. It turned out that the absence or minimal presence of IC-related patterns was a great deal more frequent in the two lower SES quartiles than in the upper ones (where some of them were always present).

If it is indeed poor impulse control that constitutes a major impediment to appropriate cognitive advance, this relationship should hold for deviant children also, including those whose lack of control is due to neurologic deficit. Figure 10.7 shows the distribution of IC scores for all three subject groups. In each it is close to a normal curve. For intact children the peak is at the age-appropriate 3 level, more or less by definition. The children with behaviour difficulties peaked at the 2 level, denoting relative immaturity in this respect. Where neuropathology had been diagnosed, the distribution may at first seem surprising. For obvious reasons, near-absence of control was seen more often than in the other groups. Yet the great majority showed stronger and more pervasive control than is expected at their age. Those familiar with neurologically impaired children know that, if the pathology is fairly mild, these youngsters are troubled by their impulsivity and often work so hard to subdue it as to suppress it to an undue degree. Observation of these children left no doubt about the effort they expended to hold themselves in check. Figure 10.8 compares the IQ distribution of well- as compared to poorly controlled children. We see that the majority of poorly controlled children with behaviour difficulties functioned at the borderline retarded level (70–80 IQ), and 22% had IQs below 70.

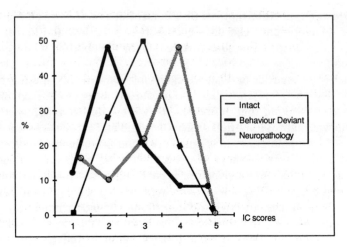

FIG. 10.7. Distribution of IC scores for three groups.

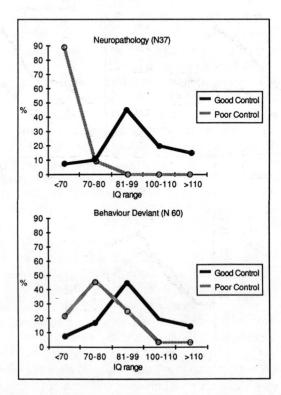

FIG. 10.8. Distribution of IQ scores for well- and-ill-controlled children.

However, a few members of this group had superior IQs—something we did not find among the intact children. The distribution for the well-controlled children in this group was very similar to that of the intact group. Among the neurologically impaired, impulse control was *the* decisive factor. Of those with poor control, 90% had IQs below 70, and none was able to go beyond 80. Of those with good control a minority (19%) fell below 80; the majority functioned in the average and/or superior range. It should be made explicit that adequate control does not in and of itself facilitate cognitive advance. In every group some children with excellent control were nonetheless retarded. What we had expected and were able to confirm was that relatively poor impulse control is frequently an impediment to normal and optimal cognitive development at toddler and pre-school age in deviant as well as intact children.

Lastly, I want to demonstrate that impulse control and cognitive progression maintain their correspondence within social groups for the entire sample (see Fig. 10.9). To plot mean IC scores against mean IQ is an

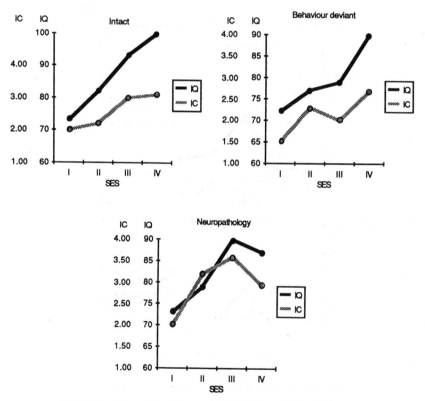

FIG. 10.9. Mean IQ and mean IC by SES quartile for three groups.

arithmetic oddity, but it does show that when one goes up, so does the other. Note that in the behaviourally deviant group, where child characteristics make a large contribution, the ascent in mean IQ from one SES quartile to the next is not as regular as for intact children.

A word needs to be said about the complexities and perplexities inherent in this approach. Or, rather, the difficulty is inherent in the problem once one decides to look for the intertwining of different facets of development. The major aim was to demonstrate that experience patterns, developmental changes in non-cognitive domains and the rate and pattern of cognitive development bear a systematic relationship to one another. The first example I presented concerned maternal style of interaction with the infant as a co-determinant of sensorimotor intelligence. The mediating variable proposed was the selective emphasis on some sense modalities as compared to others. The second instance was the emergence of impulse control as largely influenced by the growing mother–child relationship, which brings in its wake the development of ego structures that serve to modulate and restrain immediate action impulses and thus allow decentering to occur. In consequence, appropriate cognitive advances within the pre-operational stage will take place, provided the environment offers sufficient aliment. These are some of the lawful and necessary relationships between extrinsic circumstances, which we crudely reflected by social class, intra- and interpersonal development and cognition. None of these relationships is of the cause-and-effect variety. If parental practices and aspects of the mother–child relationship are to some extent determined by life circumstances and traditional values, these same experience patterns are also co-determined by inborn and acquired characteristics of the child. For instance, impulse control is affected by experience; but it is equally true that the level of control that has been reached at a given time will affect patterns of experience, if only because a child's interpretation of and response to given circumstances will not be the same when control is poor as when it is well-established. The same applies to cognitive level. A bright child will experience whatever may befall him differently than does a dull one, so that cognitive level is both a product and a determinant of experience. Circularity prevails and, for this reason, tried and proven methods of quantitative analysis are inapplicable to data such as these. I think that such apparent circularity, which in fact is a complicated set of reciprocal interactions, constitutes the very essence of the developmental process. In psychology the tendency has been to continue doing what we do best, with the result that many central issues are not addressed. I believe that the more skilful we can become in elucidating interactions and interrelationships, the closer we will come to understanding the development of the child organism in its habitat.

REFERENCES

Block, J. H. & Block, J. (1980). The role of ego control and ego resiliency in the organisation of behaviour. In A. Collins (Ed.), *Minnesota symposium on child psychology, XIII*. Hillsdale, N.J.: Lawrence Erlbaum Associates.

Escalona, S. K. (1968). *The roots of individuality: Normal patterns of development in infancy*. Chicago: Aldine Press.

Escalona, S. K. & Corman, H. H. (1971). The impact of mother's presence upon behaviour: The first year. *Human Development, 14*, 2–15.

Escalona, S. K. & Corman, H. H. (1974). Early life experience and the development of competence. *International Review of Psychoanalysis, 1*, 151–168.

Greenspan, S. L. (1979). *Intelligence and adaptation*. New York: International Universities Press.

Mahler, M. S., Pine, F. & Bergmann, A. (1975). *The psychological birth of the human infant*. New York: Basic Books.

Piaget, J. (1951). *Play, dreams and imitation in childhood*. Melbourne, London: Heinemann. (First French ed., 1945.)

11 Origins of Intentional Strategic Memory in the Child

Cesare Cornoldi
University of Padova

The contribution of the Geneva school to the study of the development of memory is, in many respects, still very relevant today. Perhaps the main idea underlying the work on memory by Piaget and Inhelder (1973) is the need to connect the general development of intelligence with the specific development of memory. This idea goes against one that was peculiar to the Ebbinghaus tradition, where one attempted to study the associative laws of memory at a pure level by abstracting them from all intervening variables. In this respect, Piaget and Inhelder (1973:360–362) point out:

> One may understand that, in order to study the effects of temporal factors (short learnings performed at intervals, or grouped learnings, etc.), nonsense syllables, numerals and so on, are useful, so as to neutralize as much as possible the attribution of meanings which may vary from one individual to the next. However, this suggestion reflects a double bias, namely: that it is possible to effect a maximum dissociation between memory and intelligence, as if there were a "pure" or an autonomous memory and that meanings may be eliminated. The first disadvantage of all such attempts ... is that they blur the distinction between reconstitution and recollection.... But there is a second and even more serious disadvantage: no matter what material we present to our subjects, we are invariably inviting them to engage in mental co-ordinations based on a regard for order, resemblances and contrasts, spatial structures etc., and including the affective aspects....

This paper was supported by a CNR grant. The author is deeply indebted to Dr. Kail Goodman for her help.

It is, in fact, essential to bear in mind that, no matter what material we present, the subject's intelligence necessarily intervenes during the three essential phases of mnemonic activity.

Among the ideas proposed by Piaget and Inhelder (1973, first French ed., 1968), I wish to emphasise the distinction between memory tasks and memory systems. These authors distinguished between activities involving the subject's system of knowledge (called "mémoire au sens large") and those involving the retrieval of specific episodes (called "mémoire au sens strict") (such a distinction is similar to the one proposed by Tulving, 1972, four years later). Examples of the "mémoire au sens large" are the perceptive recognition of a stimulus and also the relearning activity as schematic knowledge is used by the subject in the task. Examples of the "mémoire au sens strict" are the recall or memory recognition of specific information characteristic of time and space. There are, however, great differences between recall and memory recognition tasks. Memory recognition is more primary and cognitively simpler than recall and is present in inferior invertebrata. In addition, it varies only moderately with development, since it does not require the support of higher attentive and expressive functions. Recall ability, on the other hand, appears later and requires a clear search effort and the use of expressive-communicative channels that testify what the subject has retrieved. As Piaget and Inhelder observe, there is a close relationship between memory and semiotic mechanisms of both a figurative nature (images, symbolic play, etc.) and of other kinds (language), because these mechanisms are based on memory, and recall especially requires that the subject masters them at least partially.

MEMORY STRATEGIES

In agreement with these ideas, empirical data show that the general improvement of memory abilities with age is not extended to all memory tasks, since in some cases (recognition tasks, memory for location tasks) children's performance can be equal or even superior to that of adults. One of the most accepted explanations of the improvement of memory with age is based on the notion of "memory strategies". It is well known, in fact, that on the one hand memory strategies such as rehearsal, mediation and organisation improve memory, and, on the other hand, such strategies, at least in the typical laboratory memory tasks, appear late in the course of children's development and that their use increases with age. The rehearsal strategy, i.e. the tendency to name stimuli either overtly or covertly, inferred by an explicit repetitive activity or by primacy effects, may sometimes appear at 5 years of age. However it is between 10 years of age and adulthood that subjects become increasingly proficient in this activity (see, for example, Hagen & Stanovich, 1977). The objective organisation strategy, i.e. the tendency to group randomly presented stimuli belonging to the same categories, also appears later (see, for example, Moely, 1977; on the developmental trends, see also Cornoldi, de Beni & Martini, 1985). One could object that these strategies are too sophisticated and structured to be found in children, as they require the use of competency in abstract contexts. Yet, other researchers (see later) have also found different forms of strategic memory behaviours in very young children.

In the field of memory strategies, there are some terminological and conceptual points that are not clear at all and may hamper the discussion. A first indefinite point concerns the word "strategy", which, in its Greek etymology, relates to the general ability to lead [*agein*] the army [*stratos*] and can be distinguished from the word "tactics" which is related to the ability of disposing [*tassein*] the army during the battle. But, if we consider the typical memory strategies, we can find closer relationships with procedural routines. If we consider the literature on memory we could specify a "memory strategy", starting with the simple definition by Salatas Waters and Andreassen (1983) and following the observations by Cornoldi (1985) and Kail and Bisanz (1982). Its typical characteristics are as follows:

A strategy is an activity that is not simply "a necessary consequence of doing the task" (Salatas Waters and Andreassen, 1983).

A strategy is a set of well-defined operations that must be completely carried out in order to succeed, and that are typically repeated in the same way by the same and by other subjects.

A strategy is connected to (but is different from) a strategy attitude.

A strategy is different from a plan, which is a more general programme (typically implicit and in progress) concerning the range of activity that has to be done during the task.

Usually a strategy requires a large use of attentional resources.

A strategy is used in interaction with characteristics belonging to the material, task, context and subject.

In this respect, a "memory strategy" should be distinguished from a "strategic attitude", which involves general aspects such as planning ahead, predicting outcomes, monitoring activity, checking the results of an action, using feedback in order to modify plans and activities, and specific aspects related to the use of strategies. The specific aspects of a strategic attitude are:

PT-G

1. behaving in a specific way in an intentional task;
2. being able to use strategies (following instructions);
3. understanding the connection between use of strategies and memory success;
4. knowing strategies;
5. using strategies spontaneously;
6. inspecting task characteristics so as to make a choice between strategies.

Comparison between Incidental and Intentional Memory Tasks

If we make reference simply to the definition already mentioned by Salatas Waters and Andreassen (1983), we have a basis from which we can begin to search for early strategic behaviours. In fact, we can suppose that they are present whenever the child, facing a memory requirement, behaves in a specific, different way, with respect either to a situation without memory requirement (as is the case when intentional and incidental memory tasks are contrasted) or to one with a different memory requirement. Flavell and Wellman (1977:7) stress that the child "must learn to differentiate a future-oriented memorisation instruction from a present-oriented perception instruction". The distinction is not clear at all if we consider that a good perception can enhance memory. The authors do specify, however, that "early in development, both might be treated as requests merely to perceive the items in an idle, essentially purposeless fashion". Even with this clarification, the distinction is not completely devoid of ambiguity and vagueness as, in some cases, the reasons for a greater perceptive activity cannot be wholly understood. Nevertheless, the definition by Flavell and Wellman (1977) of planful, deliberate intentionality as a "preparation for future retrieval" has the advantage of great generality and of a reference to the distinction between perception and memorisation. But, in our opinion, we also have to differentiate between *continuous* and *dis-continuous* memory tasks. In the former kind of task there is a continuity between the presentation of the object to be memorised to the subject and the beginning of the test. The subject remains in the same room and can maintain his direction of thought and maybe his visual focus on elements related to the object: in such cases, the subject is not wholly involved in a typical memory task since his mental effort is devoted to maintaining the object (as in a perceptive or, eventually, in a short-term memory task) rather than to preparing himself to retrieve it. On the contrary, in dis-continuous memory tasks, the disappearance of the object to be memorised cannot be avoided because there is a break between the presentation of the objects and the beginning of the test. It is clear that adequate behaviours can be revealed more easily and earlier on in continuous tasks, but it is important to analyse how the subjects generalise them to the remaining tasks.

In continuous tasks, the subject is particularly involved in the effort to maintain the perception. In a continuous task, furthermore, the elements of the memory test are anticipated, because the memory requirement is not only imminent but is implicitly present, and the place and the modalities of the test are described by the context. In this respect they help the subject to understand the nature of the memory task. In recent U.S. experiments, strategic behaviours appear early, especially with tasks that are not only continuous but also require not the recall of symbols such as the names of the items, but of spatial positions, a task notoriously easy for the child. For example, De Loache, Cassidy & Brown (1985) submitted children of 18–24 months of age to a few trials with a hide-and-seek game where a stuffed animal was hidden in a room and a child was invited to play a different game during a 4-minute interval. This stimulus was apparently not too distracting since the children showed many memory behaviours during this interval, and in particular spoke about the toy or the hiding place or looked towards them. When the basic memory task was modified so as to remove the memory demands from the child, very few strategy-like behaviours occurred, indicating that they were specific to the intentional context. De Loache (1984), in a review of her research on early strategic memory behaviours, focussed particularly on the following other behaviours: (1) the exploitation of an informative stimulus (at 26 months of age the child may be helped by the presence of a well-defined object close to the hidden one); (2) the persistence of the search when a hidden object was surreptitiously moved without the child's knowing (such a behaviour is present at 27 but not at 21 months of age). Wellman, Ritter & Flavell (1975) studied the behaviour of 3-year-old children in a multi-trials memory task involving the location of a hidden object, but this time the hiding place could not be remembered on the basis of its characteristics— the object being hidden in one of several identical cups—but only on the basis of its position. The experimenter told the children a story about the object, put it under a cup and then left the room on some pretext for 40–45 sec. Half of the subjects had to "wait for the hidden toy", whereas the others had to "remember where it was". In two studies by Wellman et al. (1975), children who received specific memory instructions produced more memory behaviours, such as touching, looking at the hiding place or making it distinctive while they waited for the experimenter to return. Furthermore, there was a correlation between the memory performance and the memory-relevant behaviour. In addition, Acredelo, Pick & Olsen (1975) found that with 3-year-old children the performance in an intentional condition was superior to that in an incidental situation. In the experiment, children were taken on strolls, exposed to an event and later required to find the spot where the event had taken place. This task is similar to the one just mentioned in that localisation and only one item are involved in both, but it is different because it is not really continuous. Nevertheless, this type of task is very easy for children (see, for example, De Loache et al., 1985) and we are more surprised by the poor performance of the incidental group than by the good performance of the intentional group. A localisation task involves not only information of a specific nature but also retrieval processes of a specific nature. It is in fact more like a recognition task because the child has to choose among different positions, which he can see. This is the case if the child is not required to recall those positions without seeing them, as in the MVHS game (modified version of the hide-and-seek game) we are using, which includes a free-recall task. As many authors have suggested, this point is very relevant from a developmental point of view (see, for example, Hasher & Zacks, 1979; Perlmutter & Lange, 1978; Piaget & Inhelder, 1973). However, it is strange that in order to study the development of memory strategies and their relations with the age, a task has to be chosen where no clear difference can be found between children and older subjects as far as memory is concerned.

The hide-and-seek game could be made more difficult by modifying it as we did, both by creating a long break between the presentation and the retrieval and by asking a free recall of the names of the hidden objects and of the places before coming back to them in the experimental room.

According to Istomina (1975), who studied the free recall of items, the development of voluntary memory requires three conditions to be satisfied: firstly, the mnemonic goals have to be meaningful for the child; secondly, these goals must have concrete reality, since memory operations are formed by discrete, conscious acts; and, thirdly, the child must have some means at his disposal to carry out the voluntary acts. Istomina created these conditions by engaging the children in a play context where the memory requirement was meaningful and concrete. In one room, the game consisted of simulating a kindergarten and in another room of simulating a grocery store. Different children and adults played different roles. When the fictitious grocery store was opened, the adult who played the kindergarten leader invited the child to go to the grocery store on errands to buy things for the kindergarten, by saying "Here's a permission slip to go to the store; go and buy...". The child would then be given the permission slip, money and a basket for the purchases (see Istomina, 1975:10).

This experimental situation is an intermediate case between continuous and dis-continuous tasks since the context varies with the room and the people involved, but there is no completely different interpolated activity.

Furthermore, the context is considerably complicated, since the subject is involved in a game with roles, rules, required activities (e.g. behaviour required in the grocery store and use of the permission slip, of the money and of the basket), and this can hamper the child. Istomina observed that children recalled more items in a play context than in a laboratory context. In the laboratory context, the experimenter would call a child to come "for a lesson" and would ask him to listen attentively to the words and to try to remember them later (after a short pause of 60–90 seconds). For example, children between 3 and 4 years of age recalled a mean number of 0.6 items in the laboratory context, whereas the mean number was about 1 in the play context. In fact, both values seem to underestimate the memory capacity of the child; we have observed 3-year-old children who, after hearing the story of the "imprisoned princess", easily recalled 3 items (see later). Furthermore, the results obtained by Istomina are not directly related to the variable represented by the presence/absence of a deliberate voluntary act of memory. Other variables, which can explain the difference between laboratory and play performances in her research, are the interest of the situation, the social responsibility given to the child, the social–communicative feature of the situation, the fact that the success in the task is a necessary condition for the continuation of the game and not simply an end per se, the possibility (not clear in the description of the experiment) that some items could be seen in the store and, finally, the fact that the items to be remembered were part of a general grocery-store script.

If we continue with the research analysis by Istomina, we find a very interesting review of the memory behaviours shown by children during the presentation and retrieval phases (Istomina, 1975). However, such behaviours are infrequent in 3- to 4-year-old children, whereas they appear clearly in those of 5-year-old children.

The Relationship between Metamemory and Memory

Despite Istomina's (1975) idea that voluntary memory requires some form of meta-memory knowledge, the debate concerning the relationship between meta-memory and memory has not produced any clear results. The question is also complicated in this case by conceptual and terminological ambiguities, since meta-memory is referred to both as what we have called "strategic attitude" and as the "knowledge that a subject has on memory in general, with specific reference to his own memory, independently of whether he is involved in a memory task or not". This second and more specific aspect of meta-memory can be studied independently within the framework of the studies on the acquisition of knowledge. Cavanaugh and Perlmutter (1982) notice that this kind of research would seem to reflect one of the most genuine aspects of the Piagetian approach and gives substance to the question: "is there a relationship between meta-memory and memory behaviours?" If the definition of meta-memory does include strategic aspects involved in memory behaviours, then the question becomes tautological.

A direct connection between a subject's meta-memory and choice/use of plan and strategies is shown in the diagram in Fig. 11.1. We think that such a connection is largely indirect and confused, even in the adult, due to the existence of two main factors. First of all, only part of meta-memory knowledge is clearly delineated, perfectly conscious, readily available in

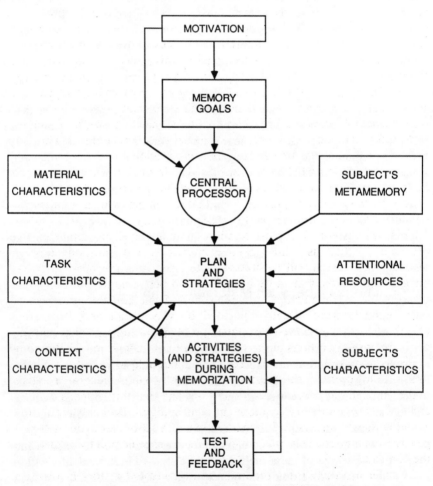

FIG. 11.1   Schematic diagram of memory plan and strategies.

practical contexts. Secondly, human beings may behave at different levels of rationality and decide to use only a part of their knowledge.

In many cases, the child is probably not aware of the reasons why he does what he does, or he is not able to tell us about them, or he avoids some forms of communication and self-analysis. The problem of awareness is connected to that of the relationship between meta-memory and memory, which, as we stressed in the first part, does not follow impelling rules. Flavell and Wellman (1977:23) speak about a type of meta-memory knowledge that "consists of knowing that the variables that form a memory problem can be related in a representational scheme consisting of an initial state, a goal state and the means for transforming the initial state into the goal state". In children, some forms of understanding of means–end relations are very precocious, but in the case of a memory task the point is complicated because the goal state does not only concern concrete to-be-remembered items, but also the more abstract evaluation concerning the knowledge that the subject has about them. This evaluation can also affect the memorisation activity and means that the subject must understand that he could fail, that he decides to evaluate, plan the evaluation and obtain some value regarding his actual and future knowledge states.

In a research with 5- to 10-year-old children, Cavanaugh and Borkowski (1980), for example, did not find clear evidence of a relationship between memory and meta-memory. In fact, they observed that both meta-memory and strategic memory behaviours increased with age, but when they looked for more specific relationships within a specific age group, they found no strong evidence supporting the idea that a subject with a good meta-memory also has a strategic and successful memory.

One reason for this partial failure may involve the limits of the procedure, which uses introspective interviews and questionnaires. A second point, which will be stressed later, concerns the possibility that meta-memory affects memory behaviour and performance more in some respects and in some contexts than in others. Some limits of introspective questionnaires were already indicated by Cavanaugh and Perlmutter (1982) when they reviewed the classic problems of introspection and the danger that the questions put to the child are not understood, or that they are suggestive, or yet again that the child is not able to verbalise what he thinks. In my opinion, the questionnaire raises two more general problems in the sense that it poses abstract questions and that this happens out of a context where a memory requirement is meaningful. Probably a question would be better understood if children could think of a situation where a general memory problem was involved and the specific point was raised in the context.

In order to satisfy these requirements, we created a story involving a general memory problem and inserted some simple questions into it. In the story, during a long journey, a prince must remember three pieces of information that will help him to liberate a princess. The child must decide whether the prince will be able to remember them, why he forgets and what he could do to remember better. The main purpose of the story concerns the following ideas, which the child may or may not have:

1. that something can be forgotten;
2. that success in a memory test is not an ineluctable event but that it depends on certain factors;
3. that there are some specific activities in particular which can be done by the subject and help him in a memory test.

There are also many problems in such a procedure. For example, the child may be aware of the possibility of forgetting but be sure that the prince will not do so. Or, the questions may be suggestive, producing answers that do not reflect the child's real knowledge. But these problems can be overcome by repeating the questions in different contexts and forms and on different days, and by examining their reliability and consistency. Our first observations show that relevant information can be drawn from such a procedure.

The Knowledge of the Requirements of a Memory Task

A central aspect in the development of meta-memory is represented by the ability to identify the peculiarity of a memory requirement, and eventually behave in a specific way so as to improve performance. Such an identification of the task directly implies neither that children decide to behave in a specific way nor that they improve this performance. On the contrary, specific behaviours and improvements in performance cannot be interpreted as indices of good meta-memory. Childrens' capacity to make a deliberate and effective effort to memorise is the result of a slow and laborious process. This process cannot be inferred on the basis of differences in performance alone, e.g. by observing that a child's ability to recall in an intentional task is greater than in an incidental task. We should not, in fact, be surprised when a 6-year-old child does not perform better on an intentional task, if we consider that similar results can sometimes be observed in adults also (see, for example, Smirnov, 1973), and we cannot infer from such results that neither the adult nor the child possesses the capacity to discriminate the tasks and develop different activities. Salatas Waters and Andreassen (1983) observed, for example, that children performed better on an incidental task (where the orienting task suggested semantic processing of the items) than on an intentional task.

It is necessary, therefore, to distinguish between the subject's meta-memory (i.e. his knowledge on memory requirements) and the adequacy of behaviour during a memory task. Appel, Cooper, McCarrel, Sims-Knight, Yussen & Flavell (1972) have compared the performance of 4-, 7- and 11-year-old children in memory tasks. They observed that the youngest children did not reveal any sign of memory intentionality, whereas some indices were present in 7-year-old children but were not associated with better performance. What they found at 7 years could also be found with tasks with younger children. It must be added that the absence of better performance on the intentional task can be due either to the inadequacy of the specific behaviours or to the inability to profit from adequate routines, as suggested by Smirnov (1973). In Smirnov's study, a correct semantic strategy was not useful when it was used voluntarily by pre-school children, thus showing that the children did not profit even when a correct strategy was employed. Bearing in mind the distinction between meta-memory, memory behaviours and memory performance, we suppose that there are different levels representing each of these three variables. A sketchy synthesis of this point follows. It includes the description of four levels of meta-memory and three levels of memory behaviour and memory performance with respect to the subject's know-ledge of the requirements of a memory task and to the experimental differentiation between incidental and intentional situations.

Meta-memory

A1. The child doesn't understand the request at all.

A2. The child simply understands that he must pay particular attention and/or must engage in a particular (but not clear) effort.

A3. The child understands that he must not "lose" the object (in a continuous task).

A4. The child understands that he has to prepare for future retrieval.

Memory Behaviours

B1. The child does not behave in a specific way when a memory requirement is given.

B2. The child behaves in a specific but inadequate way (inadequate from the point of view of the strategies that were used).

B3. The child behaves in a specific and adequate way.

PT-G*

Memory Performance

C1. Performance is lower in the intentional condition than in the incidental one.

C2. Performance is equal in the two conditions.

C3. Performance is higher in the intentional condition.

Looking at Figure 11.2, we can see how all these levels can be combined to produce 36 cells, some of which are impossible and some possible.

In view of the connections existing between the development of meta-memory and the modifications of the child's behaviour in the social context, it is not easy to sketch the phases that characterise his acquisition of the idea of memory; some of these phases, maintaining the difference between more intuitive levels (A2 and A3 above) and the highest level also described by the Flavell and Wellman (1977) definition, are shown below.

	B_1			B_2			B_3		
	C_1	C_2	C_3	C_1	C_2	C_3	C_1	C_2	C_3
A_1	−	⊗	−	−	−	−	−	−	−
A_2	−?	−?	−?	?	?	−?	−?	X?	−?
A_3	−?	−?	−?	?	?	−?	−?	X?	−?
A_4	−?	−?	−?	?	X	−?	?	X?	⊗

FIG. 11.2 Possible combination of different levels of meta-memory (A1–A4) memory behaviours (B1–B3) and memory performance (C1–C3). The cells containing a dash are considered to be impossible (when a question mark is added, the case is not impossible, but improbable). The cells with a question mark are uncertain, whereas the cells marked with a cross were clearly observed.

The Development of Knowledge Concerning the Requirements of a Memory Task

The study of the development of children's knowledge on memory is a challenge for Piagetian researchers, because it provides the opportunity to establish connections with the acquisition of other forms of knowledge. Some possible steps in the development of knowledge concerning the requirements of a memory task are:

a1. The word "remembering" (or similar) is not devoid of sense for him (remembering = knowing?).

a2. He distinguishes between a declaration, a state question and a knowledge question.

b. He grasps some characteristics of the retrieval task (involving knowledge or ability, requiring effort etc.).

c. He evokes an image or anticipatory representation of the test during the presentation of the material to be remembered.

d. He comprehends the relationship existing between activities done during the memorisation and success at the retrieval.

e. He identifies specific strategic activities.

Some of these steps clearly need to be better analysed. Step (b) appears particularly central and shows how actual experience with memory situations can influence meta-memory. The nature of the memory task will probably be better understood on the basis of what happens during the test than on the basis of what is said during the presentation. The solicitations to memorise given to the young are not too frequent (Horn, 1980), but they are especially more abstract than the memory requirements given at the moment of the test. We find therefore that the conceptual notion of the memory task is specifically produced in connection with memory tests. The adult usually comes to a better understanding of the nature of the task and the problems of memory, for example, during the test, experimenting whether he knows certain things, has forgotten other things and whether, perhaps, a different attitude during the presentation could help his memory.

The intentional memory instructions can be considered as a requirement to the subject to anticipate the events of a memory test. In this respect, two fundamental conditions must occur: (1) the subject must understand the nature of the test, and (2) he must be able to anticipate the test when certain cues are given. The first condition relates to the child's ability to discriminate between a declaration and a question, a distinction that appears very early in the development of child language (Horn, 1980) and has many different implications. Furthermore, different kinds of questions must be distinguished. Typically, the mother asks her child questions designed to assess his problems ("Are you hungry?" etc.) which simply require the description of a state. But, in other cases, the child's knowledge is tested, such as when the child's vocabulary is examined ("What is the name of this object?", "Do you remember the name of Uncle George's dog?" etc.). The verb "to remember" is, in its general meaning, understood by the child early on, although it can simply imply the fact of possessing the information or not (as the result of an ineluctable fate). In a second phase, this knowledge is enriched with the idea that

"I don't know but other people could know."

which appears early on, too.

Other forms of enrichment of the notion of a memory test can concern the levels of knowledge and the understanding of the causality relating memory to the activities carried on by the subject. Relative to the levels of the knowledge, the subject can anticipate conditions such as:

1. "I don't know, but I knew it."
2. "I don't remember at the moment, but I could remember at another moment."
3. "If you help me (e.g. by giving a list of items for a recognition task), I could remember."

Such knowledge has a direct effect on the subject's attitude in the intentional task. When the child comprehends that the possibility to remember also depends on what he does, he has an intuition concerning the causality of the events in this field. From a theoretical point of view, we distinguish between simple behaviours guided by the effect law, in which the subject repeats the behaviours that produced memory results, and behaviours that are guided by causality intuitions. In our opinion, these intuitions appear very early on and are the result of different conditions, including the fact of being aware that a particular behaviour produces a positive effect. Other conditions concern the activity involved in the continuous memory tasks and the activity involved during retrieval. Relative to the continuous tasks, we have already made reference to the effort devoted to maintaining the persistence of the object. For retrieval, the empirical study is complicated by the fact that the child does not like to be engaged in a mental effort that can be unsuccessful, but if the above-mentioned ideas [conditions (2) and (3)] are in some way grasped, they could produce an intuition such as the following:

4. "Now I don't remember, but on another occasion I could remember. However, by making a particular effort (thinking about the question) or finding the right way, I could remember".

The intuition of a causal connection between the activities of memorisation and remembering could be related to the observation of differences within the subject and between subjects:

B1. "There were some things I remembered better and some others I remembered less well."

B2. "I was not able to remember but Mary was."

If the subject is asked about the causes of the two events "Why did it happen that...?", he could show an understanding (or understand directly) that different degrees of effort and different activities were made in the different situations. Even if this does not happen, the intuition of the mnemonic causality will very probably appear shortly, as we will suggest below.

Coming back to the second basic condition for the use of the test experience in approaching memory tasks in a specific way, we can observe that the anticipatory ability is basic in cognitive development. This has been deeply studied by the Piagetian school and can offer a great contribution to the understanding of these points.

In this case, the anticipation of the critical aspects of the memory test can consist of the retrieval of similar past experiences (rather than of the creation of new states), and, in this way, it is specifically based on reproductive memory. Following general memory rules, we can expect that success in the retrieval of preceding experiences will depend on their recency and on the appropriateness of the cues given to the subject. For example, if a subject is required to do a memory problem twice in a row, the first experience will help him to anticipate some elements of the second test. Nevertheless, we note that despite the child's memory knowledge, this situation does not necessarily mean that he will develop more appropriate behaviours; De Loache et al. (1985), for example, have observed that 18 to 24 month-old children who have experienced an easy memory test show less self-involvement and fewer strategic behaviours the next day. Furthermore, the efficacy of the cues for the retrieval of past memory test experiences can depend on the sameness/similarity of contextual elements, rather than on similarities in the nature of the specific task.

THE CHOICE OF THE MEANS FOR REACHING THE MEMORY GOAL

The choice of the means depends on the continuity of the task and on the possibility of using concrete means directly connected with the object to be remembered. In a continuous task, the goal concerns not only the future but also the present, because there is something that must not be lost. Furthermore, when the memory task concerns a concrete object, the subject can operate on it directly as a memory aid. For example, in a situation described by Kreutzer, Leonard and Flavell (1975), subjects are engaged in a dis-continuous but concrete task. The interview question was the following: "Suppose that you are going ice-skating with your friend after school tomorrow, and that you want to be sure to bring your skates. How could you be really sure that you will not forget to bring your skates along to school in the morning? Can you think of anything else? How many ways can you think of?". This kind of question has the limitations that we have already mentioned, partly because it suggests what the subject was not yet ready to think and partly because we are not absolutely sure that meta-memory should be reflected in actual behaviour. Nevertheless, it is interesting because it allows us to discover how children of different ages conceptualise a memory situation that is absolutely dis-continuous (tomorrow is very far from today!). The concreteness of the object to be remembered explains why the highest proportion of answers (43%) is centred on the skates themselves, especially by making the skates serve as their own retrieval cue. In general, the subjects at all age levels examined (4-, 6-, 8- and 10-year-olds) gave their preference to external aids, but it is surprising to find at all ages (even in infant-school children) several "note" answers, especially in the form of a written reminder, rather than the use of strategies requiring others to help them to remember.

SOME OBSERVATIONS ON THE CHILD'S META-MEMORY

The memory function in the written text is probably as evident to children as it is to adults, as is shown in the following example of A. When A was 4.6 years old, her father told her a story before she went to sleep, but he also told her that there was another, related story.

"Please, tell me that story too," said A.
"No, tomorrow. You must remind me to tell you the other story tomorrow evening."
"No, daddy, I can't remind you because I always forget things."
"Oh well, and what could we do so that we don't forget?"
"We'll take a piece of paper and write on it that you must tell me that story, and we'll put it on the wardrobe" (which is near A's bed).

Similar forms of conceptualisation can be found with the story of the imprisoned princess. The preceding example concerns the memory of "partial" action (telling a story) in a real concrete world, whereas the story of the "imprisoned princess" is the opposite because the prince must remember concrete actions in the context of a symbolic event (a narrated story). Furthermore, in this story, the need for a positive memory activity emerges when the prince has to return for the correct information after his first failure to remember. The question "Can the prince do anything to remember this time?" is comparable to the question by Kreutzer et al., but it concerns the imaginative world rather than the real one. The answer of a child who has no means–end representation would probably be "nothing" in connection with the idea that there is no possibility of modifying a memory event. In this respect, the answer, "I don't know. Please tell me" given by 3-year-old children could represent the acceptation of the means–end relationship, although great caution is necessary here. The following example reflects the most competent behaviour of A, when she was 4.10 years old.

"Do you think the prince will remember the things he has to do?"
"I don't think so."
"Why?"
"Because the road is too long, and he will forget."
"In fact, that is so. Do you remember what he has to do?"
"He must take a flower, a branch and a leaf and put them against the
    door of the castle."
"OK. Now, you must know that when the prince fails, he decides to
    come back to the old man. . . . Can the prince do anything to
    remember this time?"
"Oh, he can take the old man with him?"
"But the old man doesn't want to go."
"Then, the prince can write."

Our research with the story of the imprisoned princess has revealed that the meta-memory of a 5-year-old child is surprisingly advanced. And, in fact, the research by Kreutzer et al. does not reveal variations in the type of memory aids chosen for the "skates" question at different ages, although it does show considerable fluctuations in the classes of the answers. The differences found with age concerned the presence of clearly goal-oriented activities and the overall number of aids indicated (the subjects were invited to indicate as many aids as they could). The high presence of "external" aids to memory is typical at all ages; this is probably not very different from what happens with adults who say they use more external aids than internal ones in daily memory situations (Harris, 1980). To acquire awareness of and describe an external strategy is really easier than to do so for an inner mental process (and it can produce a lower report of internal aids), and this should be still more true for children than for adults.

We expect from our research and that of others that a better knowledge of the child's conceptualisations on memory will be developed. In our opinion, relevant conceptualisations can also be observed in very young, 2- or 3-year-old children. In addition, child meta-memory must be studied, but separately from memory behaviour; and memory beliefs must be considered separately from their effects on memory. Methodologies for studying such forms of conceptualisations can largely follow the ideas and procedures followed by Piaget's school in various forms of "clinical interview". In the case of the memory conceptualisations, we must avoid two dangers: getting too little information, either because the child is unable to understand the question or to express his ideas; and getting too much information, because the questions are suggestive. In this chapter, we have given some examples that in our opinion may over-ride these problems. Future research will tell us to what extent the child's beliefs concerning memory can be known and how such beliefs influence memory behaviour and performance.

REFERENCES

Acredelo, L. P., Pick, H. L. & Olsen, M. G. (1975). Environmental differentiation and familiarity as determinants of children's memory for spatial locations. *Developmental Psychology, 11*, 495–507.

Appel, I. F., Cooper, R. G., McCarrel, N., Sims-Knight, J., Yussen, S. R. & Flavell, J. H. (1972). The development of the distinction between perceiving and memorizing. *Child Development, 43*, 1365–1381.

Cavanaugh, J. C. & Borkowski, J. G. (1980). Searching for metamemory–memory connections: A developmental study. *Experimental Psychology, 5*, 441–453.

Cavanaugh, J. C. & Perlmutter, M. (1982). Metamemory: a critical examination. *Child Development, 53*, 11–28.

Cornoldi, C. (1985). Riflessioni sulla nozione di memoria strategica. In W. Fornasa & Manfredi M. Montanini (Eds.), *Memoria e sviluppo mentale: Studi in onore di P. Tampieri*. Milan: F. Angeli.

Cornoldi, C., De Beni, R. & Martini, A. (1985). Strategie di memoria nel bambino. *Saggi, 1*: 12–18.

De Loache, J. S. (1984). Oh where, oh where: Memory based searching by very young children. In C. Sophian (Ed.), *Origins of cognitive skills*. Hillsdale, N.J.: Lawrence Erlbaum Associates.

De Loache, J. S., Cassidy, D. J. & Brown, A. L. (1985). Precursors of mnemonic strategies in very young children's memory. *Child Development, 56*, 125–137.

Flavell, J. H. & Wellman, H. M. (1977). Metamemory. In R. V. Kail & J. W. Hagen (Eds.), *Perspectives on the development of memory and cognition*. Hillsdale, N.J.: Lawrence Erlbaum Associates.

Hagen, J. W. & Stanovich, R. E. (1977). Memory: Strategies of acquisition. In R. V. Kail & J. W. Hagen (Eds.), *Perspectives on the development of memory and cognition*. Hillsdale, N.J.: Lawrence Erlbaum Associates.

Harris, J. E. (1980). Memory aids people use: Two interview studies. *Memory and cognition, 8*: 31–38.

Hasher, L. & Zacks, R. T. (1979). Automatic and effort processes in memory. *Journal of Experimental Psychology: General, 108*, 356-388.

Horn, H. R. (1980). The role of social context in memory development. *New Directions for Child Development, 10*, 49–67.

Istomina, Z. N. (1975). The development of voluntary memory in preschoolage children. *Soviet Psychology, 13*, 5–64.

Kail, R. & Bisanz, J. (1982). Cognitive strategies. In C.R. Puff (Ed.), *Handbook of Research Methods in Human Memory and Cognition*. New York: Academic Press.

Kreutzer, M. A., Leonard, C. & Flavell, J. H. (1975). An interview study of children's knowledge about memory. *Monographs of the Society for Research in Child Development, 40*, 1–57.

Moely, B. E. (1977). Organisation factors in the development of memory. In R. V. Kail & J. W. Hagen (Eds.), *Perspectives on the development of memory and cognition*. Hillsdale, N.J.: Lawrence Erlbaum Associates.

Perlmutter, M. & Lange, G. (1978). A developmental analysis of recall recognition distinction. In P. A. Ornstein (Ed.), *Memory development in children*. Hillsdale, N.J.: Lawrence Erlbaum Associates.

Piaget, J. & Inhelder, B. (1973). *Memory and intelligence*. New York: Basic Books. (First French ed., 1968.)

Salatas Waters, H. & Andreassen, C. (1983). Children's use of memory strategies under instruction. In M. Pressley & J. R. Levin (Eds.), *Cognitive strategy research*. Psychological foundations. New York: Springer-Verlag.

Smirnov, A. A. (1973). *Problems of the psychology of memory*. New York: Plenum Press. (First Russian ed., 1966.)

Tulving, E. (1972). Episodic and semantic memory. In E. Tulving & W. Donaldson (Eds.), *Organisation in memory*. New York: Academic Press.

Wellman, H. M., Ritter, K. & Flavell, J. H. (1975). Deliberate memory behaviour in the delayed reactions of very young children. *Developmental Psychology, 11*: 780–787.

Spatial Reasoning in Small-size and Large-size Environments: In Search of Early Prefigurations of Spatial Cognition in Small-size Environments

Gerhard Steiner
University of Basel

This chapter focuses on the construction of large-size environment representations and their use in adults and children. We also look at early childhood in an attempt to determine whether we find precursors to these large-size environment representations in the spatial cognition processes used by very young children in their typical home environment. The home environment is both a small- and, in a certain sense, a large-size environment. I shall not go into details here about small-scale space, i.e. about models of the real environment; instead, emphasis will be put on real, everyday situations, although some experimental (even artificial) situations will be mentioned.

PROCESSING LARGE-SIZE ENVIRONMENT INFORMATION OR MAPPING THE LARGE-SIZE ENVIRONMENT IN ADULTS

The question of how adults map their real environment has been largely investigated (see e.g. Downs & Stea, 1973; Siegel & White, 1975; Gaerling, Böök & Lindberg, 1984, 1985—or the earlier work by Lynch, 1960; Appleyard, 1970; or Ladd, 1970). There are several ways in which one can assess individual spatial representations or cognitive maps, drawing a sketch map being the one used by most investigators. Another possibility would be to have the subjects compare certain distances within the represented district, city or other kind and size of environment.

One of the important results of almost all studies is that the representations of large-size real environments are not, as might have been expected, mental maps, where the spatial information is read off as from a printed map. Spatial representations considered as mental maps are not just visual; they are somewhat fragmented representations, distorted in some individual way, like a jigsaw puzzle, where some parts are complete and others as yet incomplete, and, if one refers to the results obtained by the developmental approach of the Geneva school to spatial cognition (Piaget, Inhelder & Szeminska, 1960; Piaget & Inhelder, 1967), it is perhaps surprising to find that even adults do not always retain elementary topological or projective relations—let alone Euclidean ones—in their externalised spatial representations (Appleyard, 1970; Lynch, 1960). Results like these—which, incidentally, look exactly the same as those obtained with kindergarten children who were asked to replace pieces of furniture in a classroom model from memory (Schadler & Siegel, 1973)— might be interpreted as showing that spatial representations, even for adults, are not static like a picture, painted once and for all, but rather that they are dynamic configurations, which change when repeatedly drawn and never accomplished. (We should not forget that experimental test situations normally impose certain time limits on the subjects, so that the map sketches possibly suffer from a lack of time!) Obviously, the given situation constraints may be as much a factor of performance as the level of cognitive development—even for adults! (I shall not go into the problem of décalages!)

When looking at the performance of the above-mentioned subjects, one may ask oneself whether sketching a map is an adequate proof of the mental representation people have of their environment; whether their current mental representation would not suffice for all the activities that life requires of them—for example, finding their way, i.e. not getting lost even at night; judging which of several ways is shortest, least dirty or least dangerous; showing, when asked, the directions of certain locations that are not visible; knowing a detour in case of an accident or traffic jam, etc. The deep meaning of spatial representations is definitely to enable someone to survive, not to make drawings!

To be sure, what interests the cognitive psychologist is not the survival of his fellow creature, but his ability to code and structure his experiences in his natural habitat or setting. Thus, what processes do adults use when spatially representing both the near and the more distant environment?

1. First and most important: When adults are in an unknown environment, they focus on particular landmarks, visually attractive places, buildings or objects (like, for example, brightly coloured letter boxes); they develop a certain landmark knowledge. Landmarks either lead to a

decision to change the direction of locomotion or they are a "course-maintaining device" (Siegel & White, 1975:23).

2. Adults learn routes, i.e. they connect landmarks in certain sequences according to the time that elapses between the different places they move through. Route learning can, therefore, be described as the organisation of landmark node information around the decision nodes. A route is learned if one is able to anticipate all the landmarks of a certain trajectory, one after the other in the correct order. Routes are characterised by their terminal points. There are often several routes between two points, but sometimes only a few or even only one is functionally useful. Many authors assume that landmarks are primarily visual, whereas routes are primarily sensorimotor. At a first glance, this assumption would seem to be correct. But if we define routes as sequences of landmark expectations (in the sense of hypotheses) and confirmations of these expectations, it is obvious that the "iconic" characteristic is dominant, even for routes. This is even more true for an internal scanning of a certain route (Kosslyn, 1980:42f).

3. When routes are connected, specific spatial configurations form in the adults' minds. Route knowledge can be more or less integrated into a holistic, probably network-like, representation. This network-like representation has some analogue characteristics (in the sense of the imagery debate: see Kosslyn, Pinker, Smith & Schwartz, 1979; Rumelhart & Norman, 1983; Steiner, 1987) and is supposed to preserve, to use the terms of Piaget and his collaborators (Piaget & Inhelder, 1967), the topological, projective and even Euclidean relations. The above-mentioned example with adults from a study by Appleyard (1970) reminds us that there is a developmental progress (even in adults) from route maps to survey maps. Although this development is often mentioned in the literature, it is not too clear what the crucial processes of integrating routes into networks are. Several factors are considered to be responsible: a growing information-processing capacity (which allows processing of very dense route information that is already partially interconnected); repeated experience with the spatial features of an environment; the integration of route information in the course of time; or, the continuously preserved meaningfulness of the spatial situation. I assume that networking in adults is certainly based on these factors but that, on a finer level of detail, it consists of the gradual growth of single, partial networks that, while growing, touch or overlap each other, forming more and more integrated structures. The partial networks have to "approach" each other from "the correct side", i.e. there has to be something like an overall organising process. This is an overall reference system that allows the hierarchical integration of parts of spatial structures, each of these being marked by an outstanding landmark (or,

alternatively, by the mental representation of it). Survey maps (mental spatial representations) are said to be Gestalt-like and to be meaningful totalities. The question here is what "meaningful" means, and who can define the meaningfulness of a survey map. There is certainly much more meaning in it than just the spatial meaning, and this is even more important as far as children are concerned.

CHILDREN'S REPRESENTATION OF THEIR LARGE-SIZE ENVIRONMENT

For children, the elements of a spatial representation are basically the same as for adults: landmarks and routes. The major difference is (1) the way in which they acquire information about these elements and (2) the extent to which they further process them, and whether and how they integrate them into more coherent spatial representations.

What objects can be landmarks for a child of 4 or 5 years in a complex urban area? Which of its features are coded, recognised on later occasions and recalled when heard about later at home? Although much research has been done on the development of children's spatial cognition (e.g. Cohen, 1985; Altman & Wohlwill, 1978; Siegel & White, 1975; Liben, Patterson & Newcombe, 1981), relatively little is known about the spontaneous selection of landmarks and about the amount of information concerning the elements which is processed once they have been chosen. This will not be just visual information but will also concern the function of a particular landmark (e.g. the baker's store) and its emotional connotation (the friendliness of the baker's wife or alternatively the angry man's house). The younger the child, the greater the quantity of information having an emotional connotation that enters the encoding of a landmark. These landmarks thus function as "multimedial" representations, the often-mentioned particularly strong iconic representation of children's land-marks being just one of the aspects. With regard to the iconic representa-tion, it is not quite clear how much of the spatial context of a landmark is also part of a representation. For the structuralist, the question is of some importance; it is less so for the functionalist. For the latter, it is sufficient to know that the recognition of a landmark and its later representation will be the basis of a decision to maintain or change the direction of locomotion. We have to bear in mind the general developmental progress of the child and be aware of the fact that the "decision-relevant features of a landmark" may change during development. With a growing repertoire of assimilation schemata or, later on, of conceptual knowledge and experi-ence (enlarging the child's world knowledge), the child will process the information offered by a landmark differently.

Route knowledge is constructed from real movement (e.g. Shemyakin, 1962, cited in Siegel & White, 1975). This accords with the early work by Piaget et al. (1960) on the change of position. These authors state the following about the child's activity in space: (1) "When dealing with a route, they think of their own actions first as though these were some kind of absolute, and the various landmarks are fixed in terms of them, instead of vice versa" (Piaget et al., 1960:6). (2) In recent studies emphasis is put on the organising and guiding function of landmarks: they organise and guide the child's visual and motor exploration of the terrain (Siegel & White, 1975:39–40). The fact that landmarks are indeed not just fixed in terms of the child's actions but also the other way around, may be seen from landmarks that are too far away to be "fixed" on an own action but which, nevertheless, serve as a guide of that action (e.g. as a confirmation of being on the right track!).

Like the adult, the child learns a series or a sequence of landmarks as confirming or decision points for a route, but as Piaget and his collaborators say: "[children's] landmarks are not organised in terms of an objective spatial whole; the links between any two are conceived of as being independent of the system as a whole;" (Piaget et al., 1960:6)—i.e. the integration into a coherent network-like representation or, in Piaget's term, the construction of a "topographical schema or plan" has not taken place and will take place only years later at stage IIIA, when they form sub-systems of reference or, as other authors say, "multiple mini-maps" of parts of the environment (Siegel & White, 1975; but see also Hart, 1981). Some of the mini-maps are partially coordinated by using common landmarks, but others remain uncoordinated. This kind of spatial representation that is partially but not fully coherent has been shown in several experimental studies where children had to transfer their real environment into a small-scale model of it (e.g. Schadler & Siegel, 1973). Kershner (1971) and Duncan and Eliot (1973) showed that route knowledge was not yet integrated into a whole reference system by asking children to reconstruct the route a toy truck had taken when the model city was rotated (supporting exactly what Piaget et al. had found in 1960).

Astonishingly enough, Piaget et al. (1960) anticipated the most crucial points concerning the appearance of survey maps or topographical schemas: these become possible constructs when both well-established routes and an objective reference frame exist.

Stage IIIB subjects are able to construe topographical schemata according to a two-dimensional coordinate system. Thus, topological and projective relations are established; angles and distances or proportions— the Euclidean features—are not always fully correct yet, but the basic complete coordination is achieved. The same findings emerge from Russian studies (run at about the same time; Shemyakin, 1962) where 12-

year-olds made drawings that showed the environment "in the form of a closed aggregate".

Again, we do not know exactly what transfers route maps into survey maps. The explanation whereby there is a transfer from associations to structure—where route maps are taken to be associations, and survey maps structures—by means of growth of the information-processing capacity in the child is not quite satisfactory. To be sure, that kind of growth is necessary, but it is in my view not sufficient. It is probably not just a question of being able to keep more items at once in one's working memory, but rather of what the child is able to do with the growing number of elements that are accessible at one time (or at least within a very short time!). The child or the adolescent must be able to chunk his spatial elements specifically, and probably to chunk his landmark and route knowledge hierarchically. Little is known about these processes, which have a more qualitative impact. We do not know either what role certain configural elements, such as outlines, graphic skeletons or figural metaphors (Siegel & White, 1975), play in the construction of coherent spatial representations or survey maps—whether, for example, the whale-shape of the city of Berne is important for children or not!

IN SEARCH OF EARLY PREFIGURATIONS OF SPATIAL COGNITION IN SMALL-SIZE ENVIRONMENTS

The parallels between adults' and children's constructions of spatial representations are quite obvious. Let us now have a look at smaller children, 1- or 2-years-old, in their real environment: their home. The home—an apartment or a house—is a rather small-size environment compared to the neighbourhood as a whole. Everything is within walking or crawling distance. What makes the home similar to any large-size environment, however, is the fact that it cannot be looked at from one vantage point. For the small child, the home is the realm of several important kinds of experience, one of these being spatial experience!

In what follows, I try to trace back further the developmental lines of spatial reasoning we have begun to follow. I am going to present our preliminary remarks, reflections and speculations about very early spatial performances of small children in a highly familiar small-size environment where a child's spatial behaviour is altogether perfect. This has led us to ask whether most developmental psychologists do not underestimate a child's spatial cognition.

Let us begin with landmarks: What are the landmarks in the home that will become decision-relevant elements for route learning in the home? How does a small child select important landmarks? How does he represent them? A preliminary question may be "What is the spatial knowledge that a small child has of his home?" The very young child who is carried by his parents or siblings knows "places" rather than landmarks. Being carried means—spatially—being transported from one box-like section of the home to another one. Entering a new section is clearly marked by a door that has to be opened and perhaps closed again. Spatial knowledge of these places is strongly connected with habitual activities, i.e. with the function of the particular section: where one eats, where one sleeps, where one gets cleaned up, where mother regularly does interesting things, where parents and siblings seem to hide themselves and reappear after a while, where one only passes through, etc. Some sections are bright with windows, others are dark and have to be illuminated by switching on the light. The main features of these places are determined by their function, i.e. for the child, by their assimilability. Early on, the question of where a place is located is certainly a subordinate question. But once the function of a locality or place is assimilated, i.e. understood, it may gain a certain interest as a goal, because, for example, in the locality there is a special object, such as the refrigerator, the TV set, the toy box etc. Goals may be places where one wishes to go but also places one wishes avoid— places with certain objects that are loved, hated or feared, i.e. connected with emotions of all kinds. As soon as places become goals, the spatial aspect—i.e. their whereness—comes into focus: how to get to this place from any point in the home? This is obviously the prerequisite for a child to construct actively a spatial representation of a home without any help from a psychological experimenter.

To get to a certain place, what landmarks become important, and what is the landmark selection process? One important landmark, namely the mother, is a very unstable one as far as spatial definition is concerned, but a very stable one as far as social impact is concerned. The child crawls or walks after his mother. A route is where his mother goes. I shall come back to the routes later! What is learned is an orienting activity after a guiding element. This is a special kind of observational or imitative learning! But mother will sometimes be faster-moving—she does not wait for the child. She will go out of sight, but the child will probably hear her doing something, and this will reinforce his memory of where his mother went.

Mother disappeared within or from a certain spatial (or home-geographic) context. What remains—visually—is that context: a relatively distant part of walls, perhaps doors, pieces or furniture and the like. Since the child makes a correct spatial decision and also turns at the point where mother turned the corner, some elements of that perceived situation (poorly-structured in cognitive terms) obviously act as landmarks. If an object such as an umbrella stand is there, it could be the landmark—at least if it can be assimilated by the child. Otherwise, it may be the whole visual impression that this part of the home makes on the child. We do not know what kind of cognitive process corresponds to this kind of rather general impression formation, but it could be what Livingston (1967a, 1967b) has called a "Now Print!" process (see Siegler & White, 1975). The "Now Print!" process involves neural activity: if a perceived situation in the environment of a person is biologically meaningful or even important—which is certainly the case when the small child wants to watch his mother's activities in a remote room of his home—several different neuronal patterns are aroused. Livingston (1967b) suggests several steps: (1) The reticular system recognises the novelty (maybe the relative novelty only) of a situation (a percept); (2) the limbic system makes a discrimination of the biological meaning of the situation for that particular individual at that particular point in time; (3) there is a limbic neuronal discharge into the reticular formation; (4) the discharge of the reticular formation, in turn, is diffusely projected into both hemispheres, and this widespread discharge is the "Now Print!"—so to speak an order for several encodings in memory. (5) "All recent brain events, all recent conduction activities will be "printed" to facilitate repetition of similar conduction patterns" (Livingston, 1967b:576; cit. in Siegel & White, 1975:27).

Such a model could explain the fact that small children do, indeed, have certain "landmark-prints"—i.e. multi-medial information, though primarily visual, that is certainly not yet cognitively well-organised (because of a lack of assimilation schemata) but which is sufficient to be recognised in context if met with again and again while locomoting through the home. The greater the number of (visual) assimilation schemata acquired, the better these "prints" will be organised cognitively.

Siegel and White assume that "the figurative core of a spatial representation could exist on the basis of a flashbulb going off (an orienting response made ...), leading to 'recognition-in-context' memory of landmarks" (Siegel & White, 1975:28). If these authors mean that the small child is acquiring landmark knowledge in his home via a flash bulb procedure, I would argue that this is probably not the case. Let us take a close look at what goes on during the acquisition of landmark information. The very small child is crawling towards the place where his mother disappeared around a corner. In a "Now Print!" process, he takes in some information, mainly a complex visual pattern. As he approaches the spot, its optical appearance changes, of course. Every new "Now Print!"—or at least any further perception of that particular landmark—will be different from the first one, so that the child needs several "prints" at least to obtain information about a certain landmark. The adult has the possibility of encoding a landmark symbolically, e.g. by naming it verbally, whereas the small child has to construct a perceptual invariant of his decision-relevant landmarks. It could be that small children choose landmarks that are already (at least to a high degree) perceptual invariants such as, for example, a door surface that looks more or less the same from most directions. What certainly helps the child to integrate several "prints" into a kind of unified landmark knowledge is his slow locomotion.

We do not know a lot about these very first and elementary processes of landmark knowledge acquisition, but they certainly do occur. They could be tested experimentally by changing something in the environment, and controlling the effects of these changes (acting startled, slowing down locomotion, etc.) as dependent variables.

We have to assume that even small children can and do recognise landmarks from different viewpoints as invariant (as identical objects) even before they can name them verbally. This is probably a prefiguration of a form of perspective integration (that can certainly not be tested by asking the children to choose a particular picture, but that is sufficient for a decision in route finding).

Let us turn now to route learning. Locomotion is an essential element of route learning. This has been stressed by many authors (e.g. Cohen & Cohen, 1985; Gaerling et al., 1984). Indeed, locomotion as a temporal process allows the child to seriate the cues or landmarks along a certain walking or crawling route. But this is not to say that route learning is primarily "enactive" (to use Bruner's term), whereas landmark learning is primarily visual. It is probably correct that slow locomotion helps the construction of the sequence of landmark information. But it is certainly not the locomotion process per se that is crucial for representing the route spatially. Locomotion has a subordinate function that is the intake of visual information from different angles of vision, in a particular learned sequence. The serial learning process is fortunately helped and not hindered by locomotion, and it is the internalised (visually imageable) series of encodings (or "prints" to use a different term according to Livingston's neurological hypothesis) that is crucial for later wayfindings. Of course, the small-size environment of the child's home reduces the number of landmarks to be kept in mind when finding a certain place in the home or an object in a certain room.

To "have" a route or to have constructed particular knowledge about a route means that one is able to expect a landmark or certain features of it, i.e. to activate a certain representation or expectation, to test the expectation, to respond to that test result and to decide about continuing the route. It should be possible to assess the existence of route knowledge even in very young children, again by altering or modifying various features along his route and observing whether he remarks the discrepancies with his existing (certainly unspoken) knowledge. This, of course, leads us to query Piaget's suggestion that the child forms behaviour patterns of coordinated sensorimotor schemata, or at the least it means that the "sensori" part of that sensorimotor process should be stressed.

Now let us go one step further towards the coordination of route knowledge. As everybody knows, children have no problem in finding their way back to a starting point in their home; in other words, it is no problem for them to reverse a certain route. What are the characteristics of this reversibility? First of all, children do not reverse a route in their home as they would in an experiment. Whenever they go back to a starting point, they do it for some non-experimental reason, e.g. because they have been interrupted there in their playing activities. Crawling back, on the other hand, can occur only if this route is also known. We have to be aware of the fact that this reverse route looks quite different from the direct route: it has a different set of landmarks. Several landmarks along the route will be recognised as familiar, but they appear on the opposite side of the crawling route (to the left instead of to the right of the child as previously!). The two routes are, therefore, completely different and not only with respect to their serial representation. We realise, in fact, that it is impossible to reverse a route exactly. (This, incidentally, is also true for adults in difficult regions, e.g. while climbing a mountain where the view upwards is quite different from the one downwards; it is not just a 180-degree rotation of a set of elements!) For a certain time, the young child probably has a set of route knowledge items where back and forth routes are represented as two different entities. But very soon they overlap or coincide. We know little about how this takes place, but the small-size environment has one special connecting element that may help to interconnect the two routes mentally, namely the floor (e.g. the carpet) that is felt by the child as he crawls over it!

What I want to stress here is that a motor interpretation of this kind of spatial learning is not sufficient and that we are probably in the presence of some of the very earliest interconnecting processes of partial structures of spatial information into higher-order structures. This kind of early interconnection of partial structures might be the prerequisite for a later symbolic representation of route knowledge.

Let us turn now to the final question of whether the small children we are focusing on here have a survey map of their home—or at least some form of one—in their heads. Whenever we try to test them by asking them to draw a sketch map or arrange a model home, the answer is apparently no. It is generally maintained that children under four years of age cannot construct a survey representation of their environment. But did anybody ask the children the appropriate questions or set them appropriate test tasks?

It should be borne in mind that we are observing the child in his home, i.e. in a very restricted, although fairly complex, spatial area! We have to ask what conditions would have to be fulfilled by the child (and the environment) for him to be able to construct an overall (survey) spatial representation. The following list shows some of the important conditions (although they overlap somewhat). The first three focus primarily on the environment, while the last three focus strongly on the child's cognitive activities:

1. a challenging situation, involving the meaningfulness of the spatial-task demands throughout the task;
2. salient landmarks;
3. unrestricted activities (perceptions, locomotions, etc.);
4. an information-processing capacity large enough to handle the cues in the home, including the ability to organise (chunk) spatial information hierarchically and to integrate it into a frame of reference;
5. a high density of stored route information, including or stemming from the temporal integration of route knowledge while (slowly) locomoting; and
6. repeated experience, i.e. adequate learning, including modelling, appropriate feedback and contingent reinforcement.

I shall just make one very brief remark concerning the first point. It might be said that the spatial behaviour of a small child is performed for reasons other than spatial ones! But even if this is true, the child's behaviour shows that spatial knowledge is nevertheless present; it has probably been learned incidentally, and it has imposed itself because it was biologically as well as socially necessary.

Concerning points (2) and (3), let us hope that these conditions are fulfilled in the child's home.

Point (4) is most important. In the everyday activities of the child, the home is a spatially rather restricted (though not simple) area and does not overload his information-processing capacity. As far as his organising capacity is concerned, it can be seen that there are not only sequential or additive spatial processes, but also hierarchical organisations with an important spatial aspect: the child is able to find the scissors in mother's room, in the topmost drawer of the cupboard close to the window! This is actually a very natural (ecologically valid) parallel to finding a physician's office on the seventh floor of a large building at 18th Street in Lower Manhattan in a real large-size environment. Why should the child not go beyond interconnecting direct routes and their reverse? Why can he not interconnect direct routes—leading, for example, from several bedrooms to the bathroom, or from the living room where the family has the TV to different bedrooms—that may start out the same but which split off when approaching the different doors. A small child certainly possesses this kind of route knowledge since he is able to discriminate the routes leading to his own bedroom and to his sister's, and this is nothing other than a cluster or configuration of slightly differing route representation, i.e. the basis for a "mini-map" or even more.

I think that small children reach at least this level of spatial representation. Whether we admit that they have an at least partially holistic representation depends largely on the tests we make them undergo.

After our preliminary (no more than that!) observations, we could blindfold small children, bring them to a certain point in their home and have them indicate with their arm where other specific places are located. Or we could direct or "tune" them, still blindfolded, to a certain place (and to a certain direction) and ask them to indicate other places, as before. We could also ask them to tell us where particular, unfamiliar sounds are coming from, etc. Whether the spatial representation observed by this kind of experimentation is one that is based mainly on topological relations, or on topological and projective or even Euclidean relations, is a question that deserves serious empirical as well as theoretical investigations. I have no ready answer.

Finally, in point (4), there is one more problem. Establishing an integrated survey map involves, according to Piaget and his collaborators and to several other researchers in the area (e.g. Pick & Lockman, 1981), integrating partial spatial structures or mini-maps into a more encompassing reference system. A home offers a reference system, e.g. in its orientation to the stairway or to the door that leads into the backyard. Observations with children who had just moved into a new home showed that they started by taking the views from the windows on the two sides of the apartment as reference frames: one window looked towards a neighbouring building, the other, on the opposite side, towards a meadow and a forest. This reference worked as long as the doors that allowed the view out of the window remained open and as long as there was no furniture in the new home.

The condition formulated in point (5) is filled inasmuch as children can reach any place in their home from any starting point. Thus, there is a very dense set of routes, and these, in my opinion, do not remain isolated but form a mobile, coordinated set of paths from which one at a time may be chosen. Of course, most of these routes are clearly defined and unambiguous. There are usually few alternatives for reaching a certain room or object in a home. To prove the presence of survey maps in small children, we need homes with rooms that are accessible from more than one side. This would enable us to see how the children use alternatives, i.e. detours to particular places.

As far as learning is concerned (point 6) it can be seen, first of all, that everything is highly over-learned by repeated execution. It might be early observational learning that led to the very first route knowledge. This kind of learning has also been shown in young children who had to find a way across a model village in an experimental setting (Cohen & Cohen 1985). One of the advantages of a home is that the small child can ask for feedback when trying to find his way by calling to his mother or someone else. Furthermore, learning is far from being restricted to visually encoding the spatial information; there are other encoding possibilities such as auditory and tactile ones. Finding a certain point in a house is, for the child, self-rewarding; thus reinforcement has a very direct intrinsic effect and depends very little on other persons. Not finding the way to a certain room or a certain object immediately sparks off the search for feedback information.

To sum up, it would seem that within the small-size environment of a home, the prerequisites for constructing survey spatial representations seem to be fulfilled. If these representations could be proved empirically, which is what we hope to do, we would have to revise our standard image of the development of spatial cognition. This would be replaced by the developmental steps of first being able to recognise landmarks, later on routes and finally survey maps that guide spatial behaviour, and it has the advantage of taking the situational contraints more into account.

REFERENCES

Altman, I. & Wohlwill, J. F. (1978). *Children and the environment.* New York: Plenum Press.

Appleyard, D. (1970). Styles and methods of structuring a city. *Environment and Behaviour, 2,* 100–118.

Cohen, R. (Ed.) (1985). *The development of spatial cognition.* Hillsdale, NJ.: Lawrence Erlbaum & Associates.

Cohen, S. L. & Cohen, R. (1985). The role of activity in spatial cognition. In R. Cohen (Ed.), *The development of spatial cognition.* Hillsdale, NJ.: Lawrence Erlbaum & Associates.

Downs, R. M. & Stea, D. (1973). Cognitive maps and spatial behavior: Process and products. In R. M. Downs & S. Stea (Eds.)., *Image and environment.* Chicago: Aldine, pp. 8–26.

Duncan, B. & Eliot, J. (1973). Some variables affecting children's spatial conservation. *Child Development, 4,* 828–830.

Gaerling, T., Böök, A. & Lindberg, E. (1984). Cognitive mapping of large-scale environments. *Environment and Behaviour, 16,* 3–34.

Gaerling, T., Böök, A. & Lindberg, E. (1985). Adults' memory representation of the spatial properties of their everyday physical environment. In R. Cohen (Ed.), *The development of spatial cognition.* Hillsdale, NJ: Lawrence Erlbaum Associates, pp. 141–184.

Hart, R. A. (1981). Children's spatial representation of the landscape: Lessons and questions from a field study. In L. S. Liben, A. H. Patterson & N. Newcombe (Eds.), *Spatial representation and behavior across the life span.* New York: Academic Press, pp. 195–236

Kershner, J. R. (1971). Children's acquisition of visuo-spatial dimensionality: A conservation study. *Developmental Psychology, 5,* 454–462.

Kosslyn, S. M. (1980). *Image and mind.* Cambridge, Mass. Harvard University Press.

Kosslyn, S. M., Pinker, S., Smith, G. & Schwartz, S. P. (1979). On the demystification of mental imagery. *The Behavioral and Brain Sciences, 2* (3), 535–581.

Ladd, F. C. (1970). Black youths view their environment: Neighborhood maps. *Environment and Behavior, 2,* 64–79.

Liben, L. S., Patterson, A. H. & Newcombe, N. (Eds.) (1981). *Spatial representations and behavior across the life-span.* New York: Academic Press.

Livingston, R. B. (1967a). Brain circuitry relating to complex behavior. In G. C. Quarton, T. Melnechuk & F. O. Schmitt (Eds.), *The neurosciences: A study program.* New York: Rockefeller University Press, pp. 499–514.

Livingston, R. B. (1967b). Reinforcement. In G. C. Quarton, T. Melnechuk & F. O. Schmitt (Eds.), *The neurosciences: A study program.* New York: Rockefeller University Press.

Lynch, K. (1960). *The image of the city.* Cambridge, Mass.: MIT Press.

Piaget, J. & Inhelder, B. (1967). *The child's conception of space.* New York: Norton. (First French ed., 1948.)

Piaget, J., Inhelder, B & Szeminska, A. (1960). *The child's conception of geometry.* New York: Basic Books. (First French ed., 1948.)

Pick, H. L. & Lockman, J. J. (1981). From frames of reference to spatial representations. In L. S. Liben, A. H. Patterson & N. Newcombe (Eds.), *Spatial representations and behavior across the life span.* New York: Academic Press, pp. 39–62.

Rumelhart, D. E. & Norman, D. A. (1983). *Representations in memory.* University of California, San Diego. Cognitive Science Laboratory, Chip 116, June 1983.

Schadler, M. & Siegel, A. W. (1973). *Young children's knowledge of a familiar spatial environment.* Paper presented at the meeting of the Psychonomic Society, St. Louis, November 1973.

Shemyakin, F. N. (1962). Orientation in space. In B. G. Anan'yev et al. (Eds.), *Psychological science in the USSR, Vol. 1, Part 1.* (Rep. No. 11466). Washington DC: U.S. Office of Technical Reports, pp. 186–255.

Siegel, A. W. & White, S. H. (1975). The development of spatial representations of large-scale environments. In H. W. Reese (Ed.), *Advances in child development and behavior, Vol. 10.* New York: Academic Press, pp. 10–55.

Steiner, G. (1987). Analoge Repräsentationen. In H. Mandl & H. Spada (Eds.), *Wissenspsychologie.* München: Urban & Schwarzenberg.

13 Mental Development: Construction in a Cultural Context

Hans Aebli
University of Bern

If one adopts Piaget's constructivist point of view, one is faced with the following questions: where do the construction processes take place, and what are they like? In other words, this raises the double question of the psychological and cultural *context* of constructions in development and of their *nature* insofar as this is influenced or determined by the said context.

Ad hoc Constructions During Piagetian Experiments

In his early works (e.g. *The child's conception of the world*, 1929) Piaget wondered whether some children's interpretations of reality might not be generated *ad hoc*, in the course of the experiment. Piaget gave up this idea thereafter, and tacitly assumed that the experimenter's questioning has but one function: to bring to light cognitive structures that pre-exist in the child's mind. There is no "elaboration", but a mere bringing out of mental structures, built up outside the experiment in the child's natural environment.

This tacit assumption by Piaget is apparent above all in his notion of transitional reactions. In these exceptional cases, construction is said to continue at least partly during the experiment. As a rule, however, construction is completed when the experiment starts. The child's stage is then marked by equilibrium, e.g. by variant or invariant judgements on physical quantities or number. The experiment activates equilibrated and completed structures.

Such an attitude has important consequences (Aebli, 1963). If the only function of the experiment is to reveal what was previously constituted, then the nature of the problem that the experimenter devises, the characteristics of the experimental set, the experimenter's reactions to the child's answers and, more generally, the social interactions during questioning, will be of little importance.

A whole series of data contradict such a conception. Let us briefly sum them up. First, there are the *"horizontal décalages"*. An interpretation in the Piagetian framework will have to assume for each variation of a concept—e.g. invariant substance, weight or volume—a separate constructive process and an independent sequence (Wohlwill, 1973; Hoppe, Schmid-Schönbein & Seiler, 1977). Such an interpretation is onerous. Moreover, it is well known that new *"décalages"* can be produced almost at will by varying the experimental procedure; introducing, for instance, facilitating or complicating elements in the structure of the problem or in the presentation of the data. The mere hypothesis of the *ad hoc* construction of judgements and of the underlying cognitive structures by the child accounts for the same facts much more parsimoniously.

A second series of observations bears on the *instability* of children's judgements. It has often been observed that their judgements on quantities, spatial relations and physical phenomena are unstable and that the same child may generate responses that belong to different stages, even when the instructions are the same. (For a summary, see Gelman & Baillargeon, 1983; Rest, 1983). Piaget tends to interpret such events by the instability of intermediate stages. However, it is equally plausible to assume that such fluctuations result from the fact that the structures are elaborated in the course of the experiment and that the child's judgement reflects the instability of a recent, *ad hoc*, construction. This idea is supported by the often reported fact that children's justifications contradict their judgements (Seiler, 1966; Bruner, Olver, & Greenfield, 1966).

Such facts are well known. An experiment we are presently carrying out at the University of Bern (Riesen & Aebli, in prep.) also supports the hypothesis of an *ad hoc* elaboration of cognitive structures. It bears on cases where variant judgements are *not* transferred to relevant practical situations. The basic idea is simple. With children who have just emitted variant judgements on physical quantities (e.g. after transfer of liquids, deformation of clay balls, spacing of discrete objects), *a need to increase the quantity is created* (e.g. the child will need more tea, more clay, or a greater number of glasses). We observe that a fair majority (83%) of the children do not think of using the transformations as a means to produce such an increase in quantity. Even if we *suggest* that method, 22% of the subjects deem it inappropriate and reject it.

Finally, two methods are proposed and contrasted: The child may either transform (e.g. by transferring the liquid into a higher and narrower container, by lengthening the clay ball, or by spacing the discrete objects), or add something. Of the two methods, 86.4% of the children chose the latter method, and only 13.6% the former, even though they had just said that the transformation causes the quantity to increase. The child's recent judgement does not seem to have any effect on behaviour. Transferring liquids, deforming clay and spacing glasses are not considered means for increasing quantity or number (Fig. 13.1).

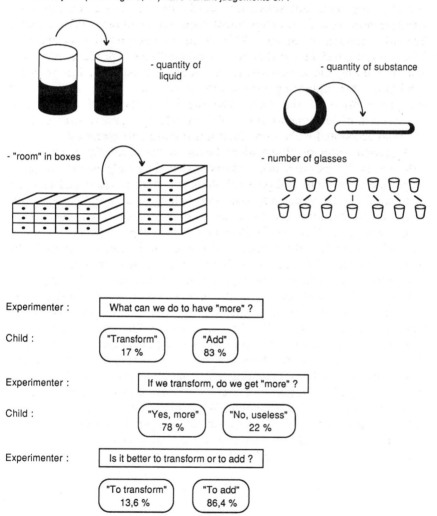

FIG. 13.1. The non-application of judgements on physical and numerical quantities by pre-operatory children.

These results appear all the more important if we consider the fact that constructions in everyday life occur in a similar context of action. If children do construct concepts in such a context, they should apply them when the action context is re-created in an experiment. The non-occurrence of such a transfer seems to indicate that children do not ask the constancy questions in everyday life. In other words, their variant quantity hypothesis was generated *for the first time* in the experiment. It is quite natural for a newly elaborated judgement not to be applied.

Provided that these data and their interpretation are valid, we have good reasons for undertaking a careful study of the processes that take place in the course of developmental experiments. The site of construction lies before us, what goes on is open to our study. The present author has made proposals to that effect (Aebli, 1963; 1978).

Constructions in Everyday Life Situations

Even though important construction processes take place during the experiment, children have a different cognitive repertoire at different age levels. Some kind of development clearly takes place outside the experiment. There is construction in everyday life. A double problem arises: How does natural development take place and what kinds of additional constructions occur during experimental sessions? And what are the major domains of development in everyday life?

To date, developmental psychology has little to say about these problems. Hardly anybody has observed the work site, at least from the standpoint of cognitive construction. However, a few directions of enquiry can be made out. We should not adopt Rousseau's anti-cultural attitude, which influenced Piaget. It would be wrong to look for the child's extra-experimental construction in the spontaneous and individual activities only. Indeed, social exchanges, including those which take place in the context of school, give rise to important constructions. Developmental psychology should investigate them, even though many of them do not succeed. Constructive processes, actuated by social and didactic exchanges might even bear a great resemblance to the exchanges occurring in Piagetian experiments. The latter are more didactic in nature than we might think: Prestructuring of a construction by a concrete problem that the child is able to grasp; genuine reflection on interesting phenomena; subtle directions given to help the child solve the problem; urging children to produce the best answers they can give in a pre-established problem context.

Such thinking leads beyond Piaget. It tends towards a rigorous analysis of *ad hoc* constructions by the child. Which of them occur in everyday life? The problems of invariance do not seem to be among them. They seem to be almost completely lacking in spontaneous verbal exchanges. Are they implicit, or are they non-existent? Thoughts are expressed, however. They relate to family activities and occur in the context of child–child and adult–child exchanges about practical facts of everyday life. The stories told to children and the picture books they look at, often with adults, are important. Once children are able to read books, these become another major source of constructions.

The problem then is to find adequate formalisations for such constructions. Piaget's formalisations are not very helpful. They are devised for an analysis of specific operations and cognitive systems. The domain of application of such formalisations is limited, and their compositions are very abstract. They are mathematical in nature and bear on addition, multiplication and the successive performing of actions. In Piaget's late writings (Piaget, Grize, Szeminska, & Vinh-Bang, 1977), mappings that prepare the concept of mathematical function are added to them. The cognitive systems resulting from these compositions are very sophisticated. Only Grize (1960), Steiner (1973), Wittmann (1973), and a few others, have established satisfactory formalisations. Specifically, Piaget never took into account, in his psychological writings, that group structures require a preliminary determination of a set of elements for which the composition of random pairs always generates new elements of the basic set.

Formalising Constructions that Occur in Everyday Life and at School

Any realistic example of the construction of a concept in everyday life or at school will suffice to see that it cannot adequately be described by Piagetian formalisations. If construction is the basic fact in development, then a formalisation for everyday qualitative constructions is required. To demonstrate how Piagetian construction can be extended, to account for qualitative conceptual development, we shall now take up a Piagetian construction—the construction of *a bi-dimensional concept*—and then change it, step-by-step, into a construction of the kind we find in the child's everyday life.

In pre-operatory thinking, says Piaget, the child's judgement on quantity takes into account one dimension only (e.g. in the conservation of substance, the child equates quantity with length or thickness). Two general requirements for construction are fulfilled: (1) the elements of the to-be-executed construction are present in the child's repertoire; (2) these elements are not yet composed.

At the next step, the two dimensions (e.g. length and thickness) are composed, in Piaget's words, "coordinated", "related", which gives rise to

Stage 2: quantity = length · thickness. ("·" stands for "logically multiplied by".)

A new way of looking at these facts follows from the work of such scholars as Fillmore (1968); Kintsch (1977); and Rumelhart, Lindsay, and Norman (1972). Their descriptive tool is propositional formalisation:

$$\cdot \ (l, th) \ [= q_s]$$

where "·" stands for multiplication, "l" for length (F1), "th" for thickness (F2), and "q_s" for quantity of substance.

The predicate in the proposition relates the elements. The arguments are the elements related. The operation endows the elements with a definite role: they become factors (F1, F2), and the operation generates q_s. Next, we follow Piaget who tells us that operations are derived from *concrete actions*. So, let us look in the same way at a concrete action:

GIVE (D: John, R: Mary, OG: dollar)

Once again, the action attributes a role (the *case*) to the elements. We shall call them the "participants in the action". They are: D = donor; R = recipient; OG = object given. Therefore, the predicate represents the *action scheme* as a possible, available action, with slots for the participants in the action.

To account for the *richness of qualitative constructions*, let us see how new objects and relational concepts are constructed:

1. As to the construction of new elements, as just mentioned, the basic process consists of attributing a new role to an element that participates in an action: the dollar becomes an "object given" or "gift", Mary "the one who receives", and John gives himself the role of the "donor". One can easily imagine how objects and persons acquire new qualities through participation in actions and operations, or—more fundamentally— how objects are constituted (or constructed) through participation in actions.[1]

2. How is the repertoire of relational terms generated? Let us ask a more elementary question: How are new actions (or predicates) constructed? Through a combination of simpler actions. An example of this, represented in the spirit of Gentner's (1975) work, is shown in Fig. 13.2. It bears the form of a network. The combination of two elementary action

---

[1]Incidentally, this is orthodox Piaget: in *The origins of intelligence in children* (1952), he shows how objects become "suckables" and "graspables" when the actions of sucking and grasping come to bear on them.

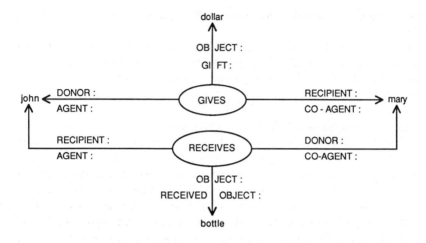

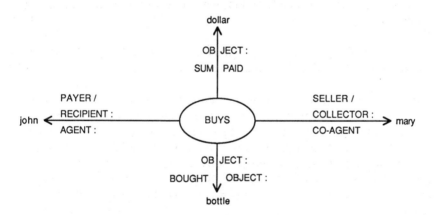

FIG. 13.2.   Two action schemes are being combined into a new scheme: BUYING.

schemes, GIVING money and RECEIVING an object, make up the new action scheme of BUYING.

In this very simple example, we use the language of action schemes. These can be translated into verbal symbols, the actions and perceptions being their meanings. The result is *concept formation through verbal explanation*. Let us sketch, as an example, the construction of the concept of "witness", in a propositional format:

1. COLLIDES (A: motorbike, WITH: car)
2. DAMAGES (A: motorbike 1, O: car 1)
3. OBSERVED NOT (A: cyclist, O: traffic rules)
4. OBSERVES (A: person, O: non-observation 3, accident (= 1,2))
5. DESCRIBES (A: person 4, R: judge, O: observation 4)
6. person 5 = "WITNESS"

This construction is hierarchical[2]. It is, moreover, a "multi-level" construction. The numerals after arguments indicate the references. We notice
various "objectivations" that change whole propositions into objects, on
which new actions can bear. This theory of construction is detailed in Aebli
(1980/81).

Such a structure is likely to be stored in the subject's memory in two
different forms: (1) as the *conceptual hierarchy*, just described, and (2) as a
non-hierarchical *knowledge network*, a *Wissensnetz* (semantic network—
see Fig. 13.3).

With regard to individual concepts, the semantic network plays the
same role as Piaget's grouping with respect to operations and Tolman's
(1932) cognitive map with respect to individually chosen paths: A large

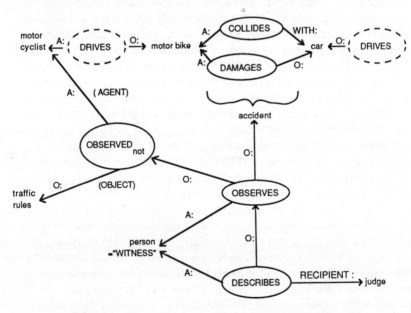

FIG. 13.3.   The semantic network for the notion of "witness".

---

[2]It is a "complexion" (Dörner, 1974) or "intensional" hierarchy—not an abstraction
hierarchy.

number of new structures can be generated from a network-like knowledge basis.

The Role of Mental Representation of Conceptual Structures in Development

Considering the Kosslyn–Pylyshyn controversy on modal or non-modal representation of human knowledge (Kosslyn, 1975; Kosslyn & Pommerantz, 1977; Pylyshyn, 1973) and the stand of Karl Bühler (1907/08) and his colleagues of the Würzburg school, one may ask what is Piaget's attitude towards the representation of thinking and towards the role of such representation in mental development. His stand is not easy to define. In his great syntheses (see, for example, Piaget, 1947), he assumes that the early structures of the child's thinking are inherent in his actions and iconic representations. If Piaget had used Bruner, Olver, and Greenfield's (1966) terminology, he would have said that the young child's knowledge is *enactive* and *iconic*. But how are the structures of concrete operations represented? The very term "concrete operation" points to an intuitive basis which is close to action (Piaget, 1950: p.146). But the notion of a "basis" is not much more than an analogy. Piaget seems to be hesitating. He seems to admit that thinking gradually becomes *amodal*.

The same problem arises with formal thinking. At times he seems to think that it is amodal. Piaget's exact stand is hard to determine, for he did not explicitly attack the problem of how structures are represented. He never really assimilated the idea that knowledge needed a medium of representation, clearly stated by Bruner in the 1966 book. To a certain extent, this is understandable. Bruner dealt with the representation of knowledge and experience, not with the representation of cognitive structures, which was Piaget's problem.

Looking at things more generally, the structuralist is faced, at this point, with a new and important problem: Can the structures of human thinking do without a medium of representation, or do they always require such a medium? In concrete terms: When children (or adults) think of such concepts as the triangle, justice, or acceleration, must they utter, internally or effectively, the *name* of the concept, evoke its *mental image*, or externally or effectively perform the corresponding *action*? Or can they conceive the notion in an amodal way? Deciding for modality does not necessarily imply the acceptance of Bruner's threefold taxonomy of representation media. The repertoire of their various forms might be more diverse.

The problem of representation is important for developmental psychology, but it is even more so for its didatic applications. Just as children do not construct a conceptual repertoire all by themselves, so also do they depend on their socio-cultural environment for the provision of their representations. Developmental and instructional psychology should therefore co-operate in the examination of the support that different types of representation lend to the child's learning and development. Cross-cultural comparisons may provide evidence for important differences in that respect, as Bruner et al. (1966) have already shown. Diverse forms of representation seem to lead to diverse forms of memory storage, of reproduction and of power of transfer in the child.

Staying within the framework of Piagetian psychology, the theory of "décalages" and stages will gain if we incorporate the Brunerian concept of representation. The age at which a given structure can be constructed can only be determined if its mode of representation is defined. A given structure may be attained earlier or later, according to whether the representational mode is favourable or not. Besides structural complexity, medial representation is the major factor determining the difficulty of an act of thinking.

In my introduction, I asked what processes take place at the site of mental development. The answer now must be: Not only construction, but also elaboration of representations for structures. Once the latter are constituted, numerous medial transformations and translations take place. Medial development accompanies structural development.

We constantly meet this process in our own research on *text problem solving* (Aebli, Ruthemann, & Staub, 1986; Aebli & Ruthemann, 1987). A text problem is first assimilated by children as a story. As comprehension progresses, they mentally reconstruct a complex action system. Its structure and representation conform to the logics and modalities of action. Solving the numerical problem raised by the text then requires a new and more abstract representation of the relations involved. It is no longer carried out in the syntactic format of the sentence. The child initially uses qualitative concepts and eventually replaces them with mathematical variables. The representational system consists of algebraic or arithmetical symbols. Yet another type of representation uses figurative schemata. The structures are simultaneously elaborated on several levels: On the level of specific relations, and on the meta-levels of planning and of executive control (Brown, 1978; Flavell, 1979; Kluwe, 1982; Weinert, 1984). Solving a problem thus includes many structural and representational transformations, starting with concrete action and ending in a mathematical formula represented by an artificial symbolism.

Development Through Equilibration?

Piaget elaborated a general theory that was meant to explicate the driving forces in development. His *equilibration* concept is aimed at explaining the rise of motives of development, the term of "motives" being taken in the etymological sense. In this view, the child modifies his action schemes and his modes of representation when disequilibria occur in thinking or action. The resulting accommodation processes resemble the way equilibrium is restored in thermodynamic systems.

What is the psychological meaning of equilibria, and how do equilibrating forces arise? Four possible disequilibria are found in Piaget. They stem from a double dichotomy, which states (1) that the subject can either *act* on reality or *describe* (interpret or explain) it; and that these activities get complicated when (2) assimilation either *fails* or *ends up in contradictions*. Therefore, these two categorisations generate the following cases:

1. cases of failed actions (e.g. to fail to grasp an object, to fail to apply an operation to a term);
2. cases of contradictory action (e.g. trying to have the cake and eat it);
3. cases of failed descriptive or explanatory assimilations (e.g. to fail to predict the relative positions of three mountains seen from a new standpoint); and
4. cases of contradictive descriptive statements (e.g. to claim that a rolled-out clay ball is heavier because it is longer, and lighter because it is thinner).

According to Piaget, man dislikes failures and contradictions in his assimilative activity and hence develops a need (or motive) to accommodate his procedural and presentative schemes. He will thus overcome the contradiction of thesis and antithesis by attaining a synthesis that will embrace or differentiate them.

This equilibration theory has found many supporters. They seem to find it attractive because it is a theory of *intrinsic* motivation. It says that the driving forces in the child's development are not external ones. As the child attempts to incorporate objects and phenomena into action and representative schemes, so the child creates the field forces through which the limitations of those thoughts are overcome. This view is close to some *Gestalt* theories, in particular Wertheimer's (1945), in which the vectors that drive individuals to restructure their thinking stem from tensions within ill-formed *Gestalts*.

Despite its attractiveness, equilibration theory has two weaknesses: It is under-determined, and it reflects a narrow view of human motivation.

1. Equilibration theory is under-determined insofar as it does not tell at what moment disequilibria start triggering learning and development. In this respect, two observations are easy to make: (1) Many children and adults do not suffer at all from holding contradictory views. In many cases, the contradictions must be pointed out to them by a third person. When

obvious contradictions occur in the field of action, they can always be resolved by discarding one of the alternatives, or by finding a compromise. Neither of these solutions implies "augmentative" or constructive equilibration. (2) Once the child's thinking or action has reached a given level of equilibrium, months or years are often needed before a new construction appears. Why does such a construction not appear immediately? Obviously, additional mechanisms must be postulated. They should necessarily occur within equilibrated cognitive structures. Staying within the framework of Piagetian theory, one might think of consolidation or saturation processes. These might prepare the search for new constructions.

In our opinion, Piaget's model must, however, undergo a deeper modification. The view of man that is contained in equilibration theory is *conservative* and *defensive*. Overcoming it is not only philosophically and educationally desirable. It may also lead towards a better understanding of the driving forces in mental development.

2. According to Piaget, a number of assimilation schemes are available to people as they try to cope with the situations they encounter. The first impulse will be to do so without modifying them. The same is true for the representative schemes through which the individual describes or interprets reality. The spontaneous tendency is to do this without modifying their structure. The individual will only modify them if they prove non-efficient in overcoming the disequilibria. Otherwise, existing modes of reaction are conserved and defended. This is what we call a conservative and defensive conception of the deep motives of children.

Development: Cognitive Socialisation and Acculturation

Contrary to Piaget, we see more positive motives in the child's and adult's behaviour. Their vital source is *curiosity* in the field of knowledge and a *need for activity* in the field of action. These motives constantly induce children to try kinds of action and attend to phenomena that they have never thought of or understood. Thus, children will set themselves goals without knowing how to reach them. They will try to get at them, using the available cognitive and action schemes. This leads to the construction of new schemes. The corpus of available means and acquired truths constitutes the starting platform for the construction process.

As an example, let us examine the case of a boy who intends to build a soapbox car. He is able to conceive the goal because he has the notion of a racing car. Building the car requires not only that appropriate materials and tools be available to him, but also that practical schemes be present in his subjective repertoire. Such schemes permit him to plan and perform the work. To the practical availability of material means corresponds, psychologically, the availability of behavioural means that will provide the elements for the conceptual construction. New material and/or mental structures will result. For the child, attaining them means developing (Aebli, 1980/81).

Analogous processes are found in the field of knowledge. What is a hypothesis? It is a proposition whose truth is not yet secured. We verify it deductively, using our available cognitive schemes. In addition, we must link it to the corpus of corroborated truths. Such a conceptual construction represents the theoretical equivalent of the construction of a practical action (Aebli, 1984).

For example, the child asks the parent: "Do fish breathe?" The question is meaningful for the child, who knows what breathing is, and what a fish is. The question could have been put in the form of a hypothesis to be corroborated ("All fish breathe"). Like any other proposition, the child generates this hypothesis by using his or her conceptual repertoire. However, the ensuing process will then modify and expand the child's knowledge. They will learn that water contains a component of air, in a soluble form, and that the fish's gills absorb it in the same way as the lungs absorb air. The elements of the cognitive repertoire from which the construction proceeds are therefore: water, air, components, form, gills and lungs. They are connected by the relational terms TO CONTAIN, TO SOLVE (soluble), TO ABSORB and SAME WAY AS. Although the truth of the propositions that compose the explanation is not proved to the child, they are more elementary and, therefore, more plausible to the child. So, the question, a hypothesis, is linked to the corpus of corroborated truth. A cognitive structure has been constructed, in continuity, from the corpus of existing knowledge.

This is one of the major ways in which cognitive development is achieved. Its starting point is not dissonance or disequilibrium, but hypothesis formation; in other words, by asking questions, and by having project ideas. Generalising from the cases of building actions and of hypothesis validation, one may state that mental development is achieved as the child generates performing or descriptive acts that are not yet linked to the corpus of their procedural or presentative knowledge. Mental development takes place when this link is constructed, mediating between the corpus of consolidated and corroborated acts, and the practical or theoretical goal.

These are basic assumptions to a constructivist theory without equilibration. It can be developed into a theory of motivation. The reader will find this elaboration in our 1984 paper (Aebli, 1984).

Such a theory still shares one weakness with Piaget's theory, in that it is based on the postulate of *autonomous development*. It is a projection on child development of Rousseau's ideology of independence and autonomy. Children are seen as developing like little Robinsons. (*Robinson Crusoe* was one of Rousseau's favourite books.) To overcome this limitation, the theory of constructive linkage should be extended in a social and cultural dimension. This can be done by noting that it is not by autonomous decision that children set all the goals that rule their activity. In fact, many are suggested by the socio-cultural environment. Often, the child is not even attracted by objective goals, but by the promise of rewarding social exchanges with adults or elders. The child takes up and internalises goals for action and knowledge manifested by "significant others". This process takes place through such identification and imitation processes as described by Bandura (1969). Also, significant others provide the child with the support and instructions that are required for a constructive attainment of goals.

A child starts out by establishing an affective identification with the parents and social environment, and it is on this basis only that the mechanisms of goal setting and its constructive linkage are triggered. It remains that children must carry out this construction process by their own means. That is Piaget's important message. But it is possible to prompt, to support and direct the child's activity at a structural as well as at a motivational level.

We believe that this view of development is realistic. It goes beyond an ideology that wishes to create autonomy through autonomy, finding no room for education. Man is a cultural being. Society, civilisation and language play a fundamental role in the child's and adolescent's mental development.

It is in this area that developmental theory should go beyond Piaget. Admittedly, it is in that same area that major unsolved problems of developmental psychology arise. Even if cultural and social factors have been integrated into the picture of development during the last 20 years, Bruner and his collaborators having played an important role, the new ideas still have to be elaborated. Theoretical alternatives to Piagetian ideology of equilibration and autonomous construction must be developed.

The following statements may sum up these ideas. The motives to development appear whenever children and adults "have ideas", whenever they enter new fields, setting new goals for action and thinking, and attaining them through the construction of new structures. Such goals are not set in an autonomous way. They are suggested to the child by the cultural and social environment, which, moreover, supports their constructive linkage to acquired knowledge. From a motivational standpoint, the process starts when the objective goals are activated, or when interesting exchanges with adults are initiated.

The last decades of the twentieth century might witness the fall of a psychology of autonomous and individual development, and the rise of a pedagogical psychology that will integrate traditional child psychology. A period that started 200 years ago with the publication of Rousseau's *Emile* (1762), may have come to an end with Piaget's *The equilibration of cognitive structures* in 1975. This date might mark the end of an illusionary view of natural development separated from culture and socialisation. Psychology may be on the verge of realising that there is one single development, which is construction, socialisation and acculturation.

REFERENCES

Aebli, H. (1963). *Ueber die geistige Entwicklung des Kindes.* Stuttgart: Klett.
Aebli, H. (1978) Von Piagets Entwicklungspsychologie zur Theorie der kognitiven Sozialisation. In G. Steiner (Ed.), *Piaget und die Folgen.* Zürich: Kindler.
Aebli, H. (1980/81). *Denken: Das Ordnen des Tuns. Vol. 1: Kognitive Aspekte der Handlungs theorie. Vol. II: Denkprogresse.* Stuttgart: Klett.
Aebli, H. (1984). What is intentionality and who has intentions in a structuralist model of knowledge, action and thought. *Dialectica, 38,* 231–243.
Aebli, H., Ruthemann, U. & Staub, F. (1986). Sind Regeln des Problemlösens lehrbar? *Zeitschrift für Pädagogik, 32,* 617–638.
Aebli, H. & Ruthemann, U. (1987). Angewandte Metakognition: Schüler vom Nutzen der Problemlösestrukturen überzeugen. *Zeitschrift für Entwicklungspsychologie und Pädagogische Psychologie, 19,* 46–64.
Bandura, A. (1969). *Principles of behavior modification.* New York: Holt, Rinehart and Winston.
Brown, A. L. (1978). Knowing when, where, and how to remember: A problem of metacognition. In R. Glaser (Ed.), *Advances in instructional psychology,* Vol. I. Hillsdale, N.J.: Lawrence Erlbaum Associates, pp. 77–165.
Bruner, J. S., Olver, R. S. & Greenfield, P. (1966). *Studies in cognitive growth.* New York: Wiley.
Bühler, K. (1907/1908). Tatsachen und Probleme zu einer Psychologie der Denkvorgänge: I. Ueber Gedanken. *Archiv für die gesamte Psychologie, 9,* 297–305. II. Ueber Gedankenzusammenhänge. *Archiv, 12,* 1–23. III. Ueber Gedankenerinnerungen. *Archiv, 12,* 24–92.
Dörner, D. (1974). *Die kognitive Organisation beim Problemlösen.* Bern: Huber.
Fillmore, C. J. (1968). The case for case. In E. Bach & R. T. Harms (Eds.), *Universals in linguistic theory.* New York: Holt, Rinehart and Winston.
Flavell, J. (1979). Metacognition and cognitive monitoring. A new area of cognitive-developmental inquiry. *American Psychologist, 10,* 906–911.
Gelman, R. & Baillargeon, R. (1983). A review of some Piagetian concepts. In P. H. Mussen (Ed.), *Handbook of child psychology. Vol. III.* New York: Wiley, pp. 167–230.
Gentner, D. (1975). Evidence for the psychological reality of semantic components: The verbs of possession. In D. A. Norman & D. E. Rumelhart, *Explorations in cognition.* San Francisco: Freeman.
Grize, J.-P. (1960). Du groupement au nombre. In P. Greco, J.-B. Grize, S. Papert & J. Piaget (Eds.), *Problèmes de la construction du nombre.* (Etudes d'épistémologie génétique, vol. XI). Paris: Presses Universitaires de France, pp. 69–96.
Hoppe, S., Schmid-Schönbein, C. & Seiler, Th. B. (1977). *Entwicklungssequenzen.* Bern: Huber.
Kintsch, W. (1977). *Memory and cognition.* New York: Wiley.
Kluwe, R. H. (1982). Kontrolle eigenen Denkens und Unterricht. In B. Treiber & F. E. Weinert (Eds.), *Lehr-Lernforschung.* München: Urban & Schwarzenberg.

Kosslyn, S. M. (1975). Information representation in visual images. *Cognitive Psychology,* 7, 341–370.

Kosslyn, S. M. & Pomerantz, J. R. (1977). Imagery, propositions and the form of internal representations. *Cognitive Psychology, 9,* 52–76.

Piaget, J. (1929). *The child's conception of the world.* London: Kegan Paul, Trench, Trubner. (First French ed., 1926.)

Piaget, J. (1950). *The psychology of intelligence.* London: Routledge & Kegan Paul. (First French ed., 1947.)

Piaget, J. (1952). *The origins of intelligence in children.* New York: International Universities Press. (First French ed., 1936.)

Piaget, J. (1985). *The equilibration of cognitive structures.* Chicago: The University of Chicago Press. (First French ed., 1975.)

Piaget, J., Grize, J.-B., Szeminska, A. & Vinh-Bang (1977). *Studies in Genetic Epistemology,* Vol. 23: *Epistemology and psychology of functions.* Dordrecht: Reidel. (First French ed., 1968.)

Pylyshyn, Z. W. (1973). What the mind's eye tells the mind's brain: A critique of mental imagery. *Psychological Bulletin, 80,* 1–24.

Rest, J. R. (1983). Morality. In P. H. Mussen (Ed.), *Handbook of child psychology,* Vol. III. New York: Wiley, pp. 556–629.

Riesen, M. & Aebli, H. (in preparation). *Die Nicht-Anwendung varianter Urteile über physikalische und numerische Mengen.* Universität Bern: Abteilung Pädagogische Psychologie.

Rousseau, J.-J. (1762). Emile ou de l'éducation.

Rumelhart, D. E., Lindsay, P. H. & Norman, D. A. (1972). A process model for long term memory. In E. Tulving & W. Donaldson, *Organization of memory.* New York: Academic Press.

Seiler, Th. B. (1966). *Die Reversibilität in der Entwicklung des Denkens.* Stuttgart: Klett.

Steiner, H.-G. (1973). Mathematische Präzisierungen und didaktisch relevante Modelle zum Piagetschen Gruppenbegriff. *Didaktik der Mathematik, 3,* 210–225.

Tolman, E. Ch. (1932). *Purposive behavior in animals and men.* Berkeley: University of California Press.

Weinert, F. E. (1984). Metakognition und Motivation als Determinanten der Lerneffektivität. In F. E. Weinert & R. Kluwe (Eds.), *Metakognition, Motivation und Lernen.* Stuttgart: Kohlhammer.

Wertheimer, M. (1945). *Productive thinking.* New York: Harper.

Wittmann, E. (1973). The concept of grouping in Jean Piaget's psychology—Formalization and applications. *Educational Studies in Mathematics, 5,* 125–146.

Wohlwill, J. F. (1973). *The study of behavioral development.* New York: Academic Press.

14 The Coordination of Values— Current Relevance of the Piagetian Concept of Philosophy

Reto Luzius Fetz
University of Fribourg

I try to show in this chapter why the definition of philosophy proposed by Piaget in his famous little book, *Insights and illusions of philosophy* (Piaget, 1971b) seems to me to be still of interest today. This book created a considerable stir when it was first published in 1965, and it was at the centre that year of a debate at the Union Rationaliste in Paris in which Paul Ricoeur, among others, participated (Piaget, Ricoeur et al., 1966). Ricoeur tried to show that the definition proposed by Piaget implied more than what Piaget was prepared to admit with regard to philosophy. In the second edition of this book, Piaget added a postscript in which he examines the questions raised by Ricoeur: but if the two are compared, one has the impression that the central question was left open. In the first part of this chapter, I briefly describe the exchange of views between Piaget and Ricoeur, starting with Piaget's definition of philosophy. I then recall the principal objection raised by Ricoeur to Piaget's conception, and the reply Piaget gave in the postscript to the second edition of his book.

I

Piaget's definition of philosophy can be considered as consisting of two elements—one very traditional, the other very modern. In the traditional view, philosophy is defined by its object, which is the totality of that which exists. Piaget writes, "Philosophy takes up a rational position to the whole

---

Translated from the French by Angela Cornu-Wells.

of reality" (1971b:39). Philosophy, unlike science, is not limited to one particular field but must include everything that man encounters; to use the German expression, it is a sort of *Totalitätsvernunft*. I shall not retrace the history of this concept of philosophy, which goes back to Aristotle and which is found again with philosophers like Hegel or Leibniz. Philosophers who openly wish to include the whole of reality are a rarity today. Nevertheless, almost all philosophers agree that there is an inalienable moment of philosophy to which a new meaning has to be given. What then is this modern, up-to-date meaning that can be given to this relation to the whole, which nevertheless characterises philosophy? An answer to this question is provided by the second definition of philosophy given by Piaget. It is a "functional" definition, considering philosophy as a "coordination of values". In this expression, the term "value" doubtlessly has a neo-Kantian origin. "Values" in the plural refers to the different spheres of reality and the acts that relate to it: scientific knowledge, moral, aesthetic and religious experience. German neo-Kantians thus speak of *Wertbereiche* or *Wertsphären*. The specifically Piagetian term is "coordination", and it is his definition of philosophy as a "*coordination* of values" that marks the originality of his approach. This "coordination" is the form in which this "taking of a rational position to the whole of reality" (1971b:39)—the definition that Piaget gives of philosophy—takes place.

It should be noted that Piaget talks of a "rational position" (1971b:39) and not of "knowledge" of the whole of reality, as was the case in traditional philosophy. This is because, for Piaget, "knowledge" refers only to *scientific* knowledge in the modern sense of the term. This scientific knowledge is one of the values of which philosophy is the coordination: science is the supreme representative of "cognitive values" (1971b:65, 116). But, for Piaget, the coordination of values itself no longer has a scientific status; it is not real knowledge, but at the most a wisdom, i.e. a personal approximation based on a commitment. Here, we touch upon the central "thesis" of the book, i.e. "that philosophy, as its name implies, is a 'wisdom', which man as a rational being finds essential for coordinating his different activities, but is not knowledge properly so-called, possessing safeguards and methods of verification characteristic of what is usually called 'knowledge'" (1971b:xiii).

The great problem with the Piagetian notion of philosophy is that it constitutes a "wisdom" and that Piaget refuses it the status of "knowledge". The real difficulty is not that Piaget distinguishes philosophy from "strict knowledge" (1971b:65), i.e. from science. Science delimits the problems it deals with and uses specific methods of deduction and verification. Everyone recognises the specificity of experimental science among the different forms of human knowledge, and it is obvious that it would be difficult to grasp the "whole of reality" with a scientific approach of this type. But does this mean that one has to reject the possibility of "knowledge" existing prior to science or alongside it? To answer this question, one would have to re-examine Piaget's criticism of different philosophical notions, such as the world of daily experience (*Lebenswelt*), "intuition" and "reflexion". This is not our purpose here; rather, we will show the ambiguity of Piaget's position. Nothing is more revealing than his use of the term "cognitive". When Piaget, referring to a problem such as the meaning of life, asserts that "a problem that does not have a present meaning from the cognitive point of view is, nonetheless, in many cases a problem having a permanent human meaning, [and] is consequently a legitimate philosophical problem" (1971b:41), it is obvious that "cognitive" is used here in the sense of "scientific". But how can such a problem be "central" for the "thinking subject" (1971b:43), for a subject who "necessarily tries to construct a general conception" (1971b:43)? This "thinking" and this "general conception", are they not of a "cognitive" nature even if they do not share all the privileges of scientific knowledge?

It is precisely this point that is at the centre of the debate between Piaget and Ricoeur. Ricoeur first sets out the points on which he and Piaget agree and then goes on to develop those on which they disagree. He agrees with Piaget's functional definition of philosophy as the "coordination of values". Ricoeur considers it as a minimal definition, but valid in philosophy. But, for him, if this definition is to mean anything, if it is not just a commitment based on a simple decision, then one has to admit that there is a form of thought that of course takes into account the contribution of science but which is not exhausted by the work of scientific knowledge. Ricoeur thus thinks that a philosophical reflection is necessary, but one having a true cognitive value that cannot be reduced to the special cognitive order characterising science. And since Piaget spoke of commitment, of decisions that have to be taken when faced with different values, Ricoeur recalls that, in addition to the theoretical reason of the scientist, there is a practical reason in the Kantian sense of the term—a reason that gives a justification—which is a real form of thought, even if it is different from the one characterising science (Piaget, Ricoeur, Fraisse, Zazzo, Jeanson & Galifret, 1966:55–59).

Piaget (1971b) goes more thoroughly into this question in the postscript to the second edition of his book. Ricoeur had said that this philosophical reflection which he postulates as a condition for the "coordination of values" is "the grasping of meaning, of all the concepts that make it possible for man to exist" (Piaget et al., 1966:58). Piaget wonders about the meaning of this "meaning". He quite rightly finds it ambiguous and feels that a distinction needs to be added. "Meaning" has two meanings: an "epistemic" one and a "vital or praxic" one. The "epistemic" meaning is nothing other than the scientific significance of a question. The "vital or praxic" meaning is connected with praxis—i.e. with what "man must do and can hope" (1971b:220). "In short," says Piaget, "a 'meaning' and moreover 'for man' has always at least two meanings, one cognitive and the other vital" (1971b:220). Of course, what shocks the philosopher is the fact that the "cognitive meaning" is considered identical to the "epistemic meaning" and that it is yet again associated solely and exclusively with science. Thus, not only does Piaget not take Ricoeur's additions into account, but he also abandons Kant, to whom he referred as "the father of us all" (1971b:220). As we said, Kant distinguishes between pure or theoretical reason and practical reason, but there can be doubt that for Kant, practical reason is a theoretical reason of the practical or the praxis, since it acts on the basis of principles that it gives itself.

The question that remains open, then, in this debate is the "cognitive" status of philosophy considered as the "rational coordination of values" (1971b:116, 217). Piaget admits himself that "concerned above all to defend knowledge" [once again considered as the equivalent of science], "I may have given the impression that there is a radical opposition between wisdom and truth" (1971b:217–218). He wants, however, "to establish the closest possible connections between wisdom and reason" (1971b:218), and he asserts that "the coordination of values or beliefs presupposes reason and thought" (1971b:220). But is there really room for a philosophical reason and thought when "wisdom's" role compared to that of "knowledge" is reduced to a "factor of decision or of engagement" and to a "set of hypotheses" (1971b:218)? Was not Ricoeur right to insist on all the conceptual and logical work that this "coordination of values" presupposes? If the philosophy–wisdom advocated by Piaget is not to be reduced to a blind engagement or belief, to a pure and simple decisionism, then there must exist a "logic of philosophy", which, if not a "logic of the answer" to the same extent as science, is, nevertheless, to use Ricoeur's expression, a "logic of the question" (Piaget et al. 1966:55–56)?

The position I wish to defend will be obvious from the above. I maintain that the definition of philosophy as the "coordination of values" is an excellent modern functional definition, and I would like to show why. But I also agree with Ricoeur when he says that this coordination requires a reflection of a cognitive order sui generis, and that this cognitive order cannot be reduced to that of science. And I shall try to create a paradox at the end of the chapter by showing that Ricoeur is right, while using a typically Piagetian argument drawn from the theory of equilibration.

II

The modernity of Piaget's definition of philosophy becomes obvious when we refer to Max Weber's analyses of modern mind (see Habermas, 1981:205–366). Weber analyses what he called "Western rationalism". I do not have time, unfortunately, to go into one of the major questions that Weber dealt with—to wit, whether this Western rationalism is a particular cultural phenomenon, specific to the history of Europe, or whether the laws underlying its historical development are universal. I shall also leave aside the social, institutional and economic aspects and concentrate on Weber's analysis of the culture. Weber's main thesis is that modern mind was formed by a process of differentiation, which resulted in an autonomous science, morality and art, each forming an independent cultural sphere. The culture of earlier eras—particularly that of the Middle Ages—formed a whole, where all the fields that later became autonomous were integrated into a single metaphysical and religious view of the world. Simply stated, one can say that in the Middle Ages, art was directed by a religious vision, that morality was based on metaphysical or religious conceptions and that science and philosophy were subjected to religious dogma. This is particularly obvious on the institutional level, especially as regards institutions of a cognitive order: the universities, which were the scientific institutions *par excellence,* were controlled by the ecclesiastical authorities, as was morality and art whenever they touched on questions of doctrine.

The processes that lead to the modern mind can thus be described as processes of differentiation and autonomisation, by which science, morality and art free themselves from external authorities. Science frees itself from theology and philosophy; the search for objectivity becomes a goal in itself, whatever the results of this search. Science thus becomes its own judge and no longer accepts the judgement of an external authority. The important thing is that the results be obtained in accordance with the methods used by science itself, and not that they agree with doctrines from other sources, such as divine revelation. The university gradually becomes an institution that devotes itself entirely to the search for truth, independently of all religious or political authority. If science can thus be characterised as the search for *cognitive* values as such, art is the search for *expressive* values. Its aim is, so to speak, expression itself and no longer the expression of such and such a *content* predetermined by religious beliefs. Its autonomous institution is to be found in those temples of art that are the museums. Finally, morality evolves in a similar way: it is no longer based on a metaphysical, religious conception of man, but on principles of justice and equality, expressed in the fundamental rights of liberty. According to Weber, all these processes have in common the fact that each cultural sphere develops according to its own laws; the contribution of each sphere is considered valid inasmuch as it conforms to the canons of each of these fields and is specific to them.

Before examining the position of philosophy in the modern mind, I would like to use this Weberian framework to place Piaget's work and genetic epistemology in particular, but also the other attempts that, like Kohlberg's, are based on the same approach, and use more or less the same methods but apply them to different fields. One cannot help being struck by the fact that these different attempts study, from an ontogenetic view, the same processes of differentiation and autonomisation that Weber analysed from a historical point of view. Genetic epistemology, which is the prototypic example of this current, approaches the development of science by means of scientific methods and not just purely philosophical ones. It constitutes the last step of this now autonomous science, to wit, the reflection on its own development, using the methods and the canons that science has given itself. Kohlberg's work, which has been greatly influenced by that of Piaget, is devoted to the second modern cultural sphere described by Weber—i.e. moral development—and it is not a coincidence if the outcome of this development is an autonomous morality based on the principles formulated by Kant, the classical philosopher of modern morality. And after the genetic approach to the subject of science and the moral subject, we now find interest turning to the aesthetic subject (Gablik, 1976 and others). Even religion has become the subject of the genetic approach (Fowler, 1981; Oser & Gmünder, 1984); and it is not surprising to find that the authors who have taken this direction are confronted with the same crucial question that Weber raised concerning religion's right to existence in the modern mind. In philosophy too, we find advocates of a genetic approach: one of the major tasks of philosophy is the analysis of "ontological" development, which Piaget himself (1930:210–212) distinguished from "logical" development, i.e. the development of "real categories" that shape our conception of reality (see Fetz, 1982; Broughton, 1981). But in order to understand the only aspect that concerns us here—the role of philosophy as a "coordination of values"—we must examine the relationships between these different attempts.

Do these attempts have anything in common or not? There are most certainly deep connections between them, in view of the fact that they are all derived from the basic paradigm of genetic structuralism. This shows the extent to which Piaget's way of thinking has enriched fields beyond the scope of genetic epistemology, which was voluntarily limited to the development of knowledge and more specifically to that of science. The interdependences between these different developments gradually become apparent. One well-known example is provided by Kohlberg, for whom the development of the logical structures of thought is the condition sine qua non of moral development—although this "necessary" condition is not "sufficient" to explain what happens in the field of morality. Similar findings can also be observed in other fields. All the attempts in the fields of morality, of philosophy, of art and of religion thus derive from the pioneering work carried out by Piaget in the most general field of development—that of formal structures ("formal" should be taken here in the broad sense of the term, and without taking position on the crucial point of to what extent these different fields depend on the same formal development or the same formal structures).

But none of this seems sufficient to formulate, yet alone solve, the problem of the unity of the different developmental lines that we have just mentioned. This is a real problem, and it boils down finally to the problem of the unity of a culture, especially modern culture.

It is quite remarkable that Piaget and Weber attacked this problem from the same angle—that of a theory of symbols—although, in Weber's writings, we find the idea that the different modern cultural spheres form as many forms or systems of symbolisation. But it is Ernst Cassirer (1923–1929, 1944) who comes up with the idea that a theory of culture can and must take the form of a comparison of different cultural spheres, considered as "symbolic forms". Piaget drew his inspiration from the Saussurian idea of a general semiology: for Piaget too, it is the study not only of science, but also of mythology, art, religious and philosophical creations as symbolisation systems that offers the broadest scope for comparing different aspects of culture (Piaget, 1972:277–278, 353–357). If, in addition, we consider the importance given by Piaget to what he called the "semiotic function" that manifests itself in numerous spheres, e.g. imitation, play, language, etc., which are all necessary for the development of the child (Piaget, 1951: Piaget & Inhelder, 1969:51–91), if we also consider that genetic epistemology was only interested in these symbolic forms to the extent that they contribute to the development of knowledge that later becomes *scientific* knowledge, it is obvious that the broadest programme that one could imagine applying the genetic approach to all cultural spheres would be that of a *genetic semiology*. This would study not only the development of science—as genetic epistemology has done—but also that of art and all other forms of higher symbolism. Such a genetic semiology would provide a synthesis of what we learn from the different attempts mentioned above on moral, aesthetic and other developments; it would analyse what these different symbolic forms, including science, have in common, how they differ and why they can be complementary (see Fetz, 1981).

This sort of genetic semiology is faced with problems both of a diachronic and of a synchronic nature. The history of humanity, in particular, raises diachronic problems: how should one interpret the order in which these symbolic forms appear—the fact, for example, that mythical explanation preceded scientific explanation? (But is it not also true on an ontogenetic level that narrative explanation precedes causal explanation in the strict sense of the term?) And what is the meaning of the differentiation of scientific modelisation and artistic expression—and yet other symbolic spheres—that characterise the modern era, compared with the archaic cultures that seem to form a whole? Modern man cannot be conceived without science—he can, however, appreciate contemporary art and at the same time be deeply impressed by myths, religious or otherwise, from far-off times (note how frequently ancient myths reappear in modern artistic works). Thus, symbolic forms of different eras and origins can cohabit in modern man without this preventing him from participating in contemporary knowledge, and without his ceasing to have the mentality of a modern being. A modern man, for whom a primitive myth has a meaning, does not return to the state of a primitive. This is where the "synchronic"problem of the different symbolic forms arises. If they are to coexist in one and the same mind, then they must be coordinated. It is through what one might call the "coordination of symbolic forms" that we touch again upon this "coordination of values", which is, according to Piaget, the "permanent function of philosophy" (1971b:44). But how can philosophy fill this role today?

In the development of modern mind, there have been times when philosophy believed that it could claim the role of supreme judge of scientific and artistic work, and of the moral and religious life of an era. This was mainly due to the fact that in view of the conflicts dividing science and religion, or alternatively the political establishment and new ideas of freedom, philosophy alone seemed to have the necessary competence to judge all the questions of principle and to be submitted to no authority, i.e. to reason alone. Kant is the classical representative of a philosophy that sets out to establish impartially, on the basis of reason alone, the principles of legitimate knowledge, of moral action and of valid aesthetic judgment. Hegel goes even further. He believes that he can show the particular "truth" of each historical moment in the development of knowledge, of morality, of art and of religion, and that he can locate these moments within the logic of a universal and absolute mind that only philosophy allows us to understand. These attempts to find an all-inclusive philosophical system dominating everything are discredited in philosophy today. And science, morality and art no longer accept philosophy as supreme judge. This is undeniably the probably irreversible result of the autonomisation processes that make up the modern mind. What, then, is the place and function of philosophy—especially if one wants to maintain this relation to the whole which belonged to it traditionally?

A reply that takes the Weberian analyses explicitly into account has recently been given by Jürgen Habermas (1983). Philosophy, for Habermas, has two roles. He starts by showing that philosophy has been integrated into the analysis of the development of modern mind. We can refer here to the role philosophy played for Piaget. For Piaget (1971b:231), philosophy provided the position of the problems he studied, which did not prevent him from trying to solve them by scientific means. This is even

Kohlberg, who refers explicitly to the moral philosophy of Kant and of Rawls when he justifies the normative aspect of his theory. Kohlberg (1971:222–223) declares that only a moral philosophy can justify why a stage of moral judgement may be considered superior (and not just subsequent) to the preceding one; but only empirical research can show how moral development really takes place. Moral philosophy, which is a normative theory, and the psychology of moral development, which is an empirical theory, must be kept apart, but they are complementary. This "thesis of complementarity" proposed by Habermas (1983:46–48) and accepted by Kohlberg (1984:222–224) shows that, in the field of morality, the cooperation between philosophy and reconstructive science (which tries precisely to "reconstruct" the development of modern mind) is not only possible but already a fact. Such a trend could and should be generalised. If one accepts that the "theses" of the classical Kantian and Hegelian philosophies concerning the structure and development of mind could be used as "hypotheses" for the reconstruction of the development of the mind, as suggested by Cassirer (1922:7, 17) and reasserted by Habermas (1983:23), then the primary role of philosophy would be to formulate questions of universal scope, which can be tackled by empirical research.

If we accept that philosophy plays this first role—and the example of Piaget and Kohlberg shows that it has effectively played this role—then one has to admit that it is already present in the reconstructive sciences. But philosophy is especially necessary when it acts as an interpreter and mediator between the different spheres of modern culture. Once these cultural spheres have become independent, they, of course, no longer need philosophy in order to be what they are: it is not necessary to have an explicit philosophy to do excellent scientific work, to be a great artist, or to work for greater justice. Philosophy has no right to intrude into these fields. However, these fields sometimes become imperialistic and assert their own rights at the expense of the others. The best-known example of this sort of imperialism is the negation of human liberty—the basic principle of modern morality—by a mechanistic-type science. It is, therefore, important to recognise the status and the contribution of each of these cultural spheres. It is also important not to let these spheres become isolated, esoteric, accessible only to experts. Scientific representations, artistic expressions, all the higher forms of symbolism that make up the wealth of a tradition must be connected to what Habermas (1983:24–27) calls everyday communicative practice. In short, the processes of autonomisation and differentiation, which have led to modern culture, require that the different spheres that have emerged from them be connected—and this connection may be referred to, in Piagetian terms, as the "coordination of values".

But this answer only leads to another question: how can philosophy play the role of interpreter with a view to the coordination of values? What sort of language do we need to link the different cultural spheres and everyday life? Do we need elaborate philosophical systems, or would ordinary language do (provided we consider it as a meta-theoretical language when used to refer to our theories on science, art, morality)? We shall not go into all the possible solutions here. Since we have looked at the problem from a Piagetian point of view, is there not a Piagetian way in which to solve it? In our view, such a way exists, and this would be a genetic approach to the "coordination of values". This is not only of great educational importance, but it could also throw light on questions on which professional philosophers are presently working.

III

We would like, in fact, to draw attention to the fact that a "coordination of values" of the type we have just described—i.e. as the establishing of relationships between different cultural spheres or different symbolic systems—is by no means the concern of professional philosophers alone. It is a task that devolves on each child and on each adolescent as soon as he is faced with a rich-enough cultural heritage. Only a unilateral or unidimensional education centred on technological know-how alone might mean that this confrontation does not take place. But we believe—and it is also Habermas' opinion (1983:26)—that a child's education should bring him into contact with the principal modes of symbolisation—mythical, literary, religious, or other—that have formed a culture. This does not mean that this is a simple matter, as we shall now see.

An empirical research project on how young people of our culture develop a world-view enabled us to see what happens when these children and adolescents—for the most part of Judeo-Christian background—acquire the elements of a scientific explanation of the world (Fetz & Oser, 1986). Our subjects were Swiss children and adolescents aged between 5 and 20 years. One of the topics they were questioned on was the origin of the world. The following answer was often given by children aged around 9 to 11 years: At the beginning, there was a big explosion; big bits flew through space. God saw one of these bits, and he thought it would be a good idea to make it come alive, so in one day he made plants, the next day he made animals, and the third day he made man. It is obvious that this account is a hybrid mixture of the scientific theory of the "big bang" and of the biblical account of creation. This mixture can be explained by the fact that the two explanations had been presented to the children at school, but no one had thought to point out that a biblical account is not the same as a scientific explanation. Children of this age spontaneously combined the two explanations—or rather the two belief systems—and the combination one finds is usually quite original and not very orthodox. Many children, for example, do not accept that God created the universe since the universe is infinite and not even God could make something that has no end. Such a hybrid mixture cannot make sense for long. As soon as the child—or, rather, the adolescent—understands some of the elements of the theory of evolution, he finds it difficult to see what God had to do with all this. Either the subject drops the biblical belief system or he gives it a new meaning, which agrees with his scientific knowledge. Both cases involve a coordination of values, which takes the form here of a coordination of two belief systems. In the first case, this coordination involves the acceptance of one belief system and the negation of the other: scientific knowledge leads to the negation of what is written in the Bible. In the second case, the two belief systems are maintained but their meaning and their scope are redefined.

We shall give another example, where the subject's main preoccupation is to coordinate his scientific knowledge and his moral intuitions. A 17-year-old sixth-form boy told us clearly that in material nature, God did nothing and could have done nothing; everything is governed by mechanistic laws. God—who, for this subject, is not a person but something inside us—only appears when someone wants to carry out a morally good deed and especially when the person holds back his aggressivity, does not wish to kill. This discourse was founded on a dualistic metaphysics and ontology produced by the adolescent himself, according to which reality is composed of two sorts of entities: those that owe their existence to other entities, and those that exist in their own right. Those of the first type are material in nature, the others are spiritual. The relationship with seventeenth-century philosophies is obvious, even though this 17-year-old sixth former knew nothing about them.

This research on the development of a world-view also provided us with the opportunity to study the difficulties a child or an adolescent has to coordinate two representational systems or two different symbolic systems. We examined the way in which they reconciled the "Heaven" of religion with the "space" of physics (Fetz, 1985). The data collected enabled us to distinguish three major levels: At a first level, whose archaism is striking (a heavenly vault made of stones, and other such ancient conceptions), the child views the world as being divided into regions by an absolute vertical axis: the high and the low are fixed polarities, and heaven, which is the summit of this axis, is inaccessible to man and qualitatively different from the earth. It is these qualities that make it the "natural" place for God and for all that is sacred. As soon as the child starts to represent the world according to a scientific model, his world-view becomes a hybrid mixture of scientific and religious representations. The child who is at this hybrid stage finds it more natural, for example, to say that God is "in space" or "in the universe" rather than to admit that God is "in Heaven". The absolute vertical axis is abolished because the child recognises that the high and the low are related to man. God is often seen as a superman somewhere in space who rules over the universe; when the child (11 to 12 years) recognises the anthropomorphic nature of his representation, he tends to identify God with a "force" that spreads over the universe. It is only in a third stage (not reached by all subjects) that the subject—i.e. the adolescent—ceases to mix scientific representations and religious symbolism into a hybrid whole. This stage differs from the previous one in that the subject no longer feels the need to accommodate his religious conception of "Heaven" with a scientific one of the "universe" (or vice versa). He understands that the symbolism of this vertical axis is not at all the same as a scientific representation of space, and that this symbolism can remain a privileged figurative means, rooted in the human condition, for representing transcendency or a liberating experience.

To reach this third stage, the subject must have at least a vague "theory" about scientific knowledge and religious symbolism. The coordination of two belief systems—the big bang theory and the biblical account of creation, to mention but the two examples given above—even presupposes the beginnings of a "meta-theory" about these theories or beliefs. The subject has to think about what he wants to coordinate. This brings us back to the question we raised at the beginning of this chapter, the question left open in the debate between Piaget and Ricoeur: if we define philosophy as the coordination of values, can we consider that it has its own, specific system of thought, i.e. that it is different from scientific knowledge? I would like to suggest a reply that takes into account the genetic approach described above and uses a central element of Piaget's theory.

In Piaget's theory, coordination and equilibration are two inseparable notions; it should therefore be possible to find correspondences between our interpretation of the coordination of values and the Piagetian theory of equilibration as set out in *The equilibration of cognitive structures* (Piaget, 1985). The coordination between different belief systems can, in fact, be considered as a special case of the second major form of equilibration described by Piaget: that between different sub-systems of thought. It is interesting that Piaget found it necessary to add a third form of equilibration that is different from the second but presupposed by it—i.e. the equilibration between sub-systems and a whole that includes them. For Piaget (1985:8), this third form is the progressive equilibrium between differentiation and integration; it is immediately obvious that this description is perfectly adapted to the constitution of modern mind described by Max Weber, and to the role that we attributed to philosophy within this modern mind.

What are the consequences of this correspondence between the coordination of values and theory of equilibration? If it is true that the coordination of values involves the two forms of equilibration mentioned above, then one must presuppose which cognitive system is capable of distinguishing and conceptually integrating the different fields to which our experience relates—i.e. science, morality, aesthetics and possibly religion. We thus arrive at a "Piagetian" argument in favour of Ricoeur's thesis: it is the third form of equilibration—when applied to the coordination of values—which leads us to the conclusion that philosophy has a totalising or inclusive thought of its own.

The next question is, from what level do we find such an inclusive and totalising conceptual system? Philosophical systems come to mind here first, of course, but in the perspective of a genetic approach these are an extreme case. But already children—and even more so adolescents—possess or construct their own conceptual systems, as the example of the 17-year-old schoolboy shows: he develops a whole dualistic system to accommodate the values in which he believes. One should not forget that ordinary language is an extremely rich and suggestive conceptual means, to which we refer constantly. Ordinary language contains classifications—the different classes of beings, the distinction between the animate and inanimate world and the degrees of life, etc.—that we understand spontaneously as a hierarchy of values. It should also be remembed that one can construct a total and circular system with few concepts (at a pinch, a single concept A is enough, because everything that does not belong to A is non-A; see Piaget 1971a:157), which partly explains perhaps the natural tendency of the mind to want to dominate the whole of reality by means of a few concepts—although the danger of this sort of undertaking is obviously that of over-simplification. But do not these few allusions show that the work, the possibilities and the dangers of "natural" philosophy foreshadow the tendencies that one finds in the course of history, but on the level of professional philosophers?

To conclude, I would like to affirm that the definition of philosophy as a coordination of values seems to me relevant, not only as regards our history or modern mind, but also on the psychogenetic level, since it translates one of the main functions—if not *the* main one—of what one could call the natural philosophy of the subject, and especially of the developing subject. The remarks I have made about the links between this natural philosophy and that of professional philosophers have perhaps shown the interest that a genetic approach holds for philosophy and its history. Of course, one needs to know a lot more about the development of philosophical thought, its mechanisms, its advantages and its dangers. And this brings us to the relevance of such a notion of philosophy for education: should it not be one of the major aims of philosophical education to provide the adolescent with the intellectual means he needs for this coordination of values to take place in an increasingly reflected and autonomous way?

REFERENCES

Broughton, J. M. (1981). Genetic logic and the developmental psychology of philosophical concepts. In J. M. Broughton & D. J. Freeman-Moir (Eds.), *The cognitive-developmental psychology of James Mark Baldwin.* Noorwood: Ablex, pp. 219–276.

Cassirer, E. (1922). *Das Erkenntnisproblem in der Philosophie und Wissenschaft der neueren Zeit.* Erster Band. Berlin: Cassirer.

Cassirer, E. (1923–1929). *Philosophie der symbolischen Formen.* Band I-III. Berlin: Cassirer.

Cassirer, E. (1944). *An essay on man: An introduction to a philosophy of human culture.* Newhaven/London: Yale University Press/Oxford University Press.

Fetz, R. L. (1981). Genetische Semiologie? Symboltheorie im Ausgang von Ernst Cassirer und Jean Piaget. *Freiburger Zeitschrift für Philosophie und Theologie, 28,* 434-470.

Fetz, R. L. (1982). Pour une ontologie génétique: Jean Piaget et la philosophie moderne. *Revue Internationale de Philosophie, 36* (142–143), 409–434.

Fetz, R. L. (1985). Die Himmelssymbolik in Menschheitsgeschichte und individueller Entwicklung: Ein Beitrag zu einer genetischen Semiologie. In A. Zweig (Ed.), *Schriften zur Symbolforschung, Band II: Zur Entstehung von Symbolen,* Bern: Lang, pp. 111–150.

Fetz, R. L. & Oser, F. (1986). Weltbildentwicklung, moralisches und religiöses Urteil. In W. Edelstein & G. Nunner-Winkler (Eds.), *Zur Bestimmung der Moral.* Frankfurt: Suhrkamp, pp.443–469.

Fowler, J. W. (1981). *Stages of faith. The psychology of human development and the quest for meaning.* San Francisco: Harper & Row.

Gablik, S. (1976). *Progress in art.* London: Thames & Hudson.

Habermas, J. (1981). *Theorie des kommunikativen Handelns,* Erster Band: *Handlungsrationalität und gesellschaftliche Rationalisierung.* Frankfurt: Suhrkamp.

Habermas, J. (1983). *Moralbewusstsein und kommunikatives Handeln.* Frankfurt: Suhrkamp.

Kohlberg, L. (1971). From is to ought: How to commit the naturalistic fallacy and get away with it in the study of moral development. In T. Mischel (Ed.), *Cognitive development and epistemology* New York: Academic Press, pp. 151–236.

Kohlberg, L. (1984). *Essays on moral development II: The psychology of moral development.* San Francisco: Harper & Row.

Oser, F. & Gmünder, P. (1984). *Der Mensch: Stufen seiner religiösen Entwicklungen: Ein strukturgenetischer Ansatz.* Zürich-Köln: Benziger.

Piaget, J. (1930). *The child's conception of physical causality.* London: Kegan Paul, Trench, Trubner. (First French ed., 1927).

Piaget, J. (1951). *Play, dreams and imitation in childhood.* Melbourne, London: Heinemann. (First French ed., 1945).

Piaget, J. (1971a). *Biology and knowledge: An essay on the relations between organic regulations and cognitive processes.* Chicago: University of Chicago Press. (First French ed., 1967).

Piaget, J. (1971b). *Insights and illusions of philosophy.* New York: World Publishing. (First French ed., 1965).

Piaget, J. (1972). *Epistémologie des sciences de l'homme.* Paris: Gallimard.

Piaget, J. (1985). *The equilibration of cognitive structures: The central problem of development.* Chicago: University of Chicago Press. (First French ed., 1975).

Piaget, J. & Inhelder, B. (1969). *The psychology of the child.* London: Routledge and Kegan Paul. (First French ed.: 1966).

Piaget, J., Ricoeur, P., Fraisse, P., Zazzo, R., Jeanson, F. & Galifret, Y. (1966). Psychologie et philosophie. *Raison présente, 1,* 51–78.

15 Laws of Consciousness as Norms of Mental Development

Eduard Marbach
University of Bern

An attempt is made in this chapter to sketch an answer to the following question: How can one account for the cognitive development of the child as *mental* development? The concept of the mental is explained here in terms of consciousness: a certain mental activity is said to consist of a certain form of consciousness. These more or less complex forms are elaborated by a method based on reflection upon the mental activities themselves, and not by some analogy with something other than these activities. The forms can be seen as making up *laws of consciousness* since the statements concerning them establish theoretically what belongs to the very sense of such and such a form of consciousness. This elaboration of forms or laws of consciousness is, as is well known, the task of a phenomenology of consciousness as conceived by E. Husserl.[1]

The question that has just been raised "hides" the expression of a wish, i.e. that of understanding the cognitive development of the child as mental development. Expressing the wish to reach this goal may be seen as a first, so to speak empty, answer to a question Piaget put to me in 1976. His question was: Why is a phenomenologist interested in genetic psychology?

Piaget liked to emphasise that Leibniz had "grasped better than anyone else the operatory dynamism of intelligence and had been able to reply to Locke that the latter's empiricism could not explain the *ipse intellectus*"

Mrs Angela Cornu-Wells (Geneva) has kindly made numerous grammatical corrections of my text, for which I am very grateful.
[1] 1859–1938.

247

(Piaget, 1971b:57; see also Piaget, 1969:367; Piaget & Inhelder, 1969:28). Leibniz, in turn, referring to Locke's *Essay concerning human understanding* (1690) and more particularly to "the question whether there are ideas and truths born with us", had pointed out that "the question of the origin of our ideas and maxims is *not preliminary* in philosophy, and one has to have made great progress to solve it well. However, I think I am entitled to say that our ideas (even those of the sensible things) come *from our own depths*".[2]

A fuller answer to Piaget's question would have to be placed within the framework that has just been very roughly sketched. For, in my view, the phenomenological analyses of the intentionality of mental activities—i.e. of consciousness—as they are presented in Husserl's work, are part of a concrete elucidation of the *ipse intellectus*. To be sure, in this chapter I can only present a glimpse of the envisaged enterprise. I do, however, directly address the problem of the relationships between Husserlian phenomenology and genetic psychology, particularly Piaget's.

My whole argument revolves around questions related to the notion of consciousness. Like Husserl, I shall use the distinction between phenomenological origin—also called "epistemological origin", [*erkentnistheoretischer Ursprung*]—and psychological origin—or even biological, neurophysiological, etc. origin—with regard to the questions concerning consciousness.[3]

In a comment on Z. Pylyshyn's text "Computation and Cognition", G. A. Miller made the following point:

> I believe that *consciousness is the constitutive problem of psychology*. That is to say, I am as dissatisfied with a psychology that ignores consciousness as I would be with a biology that ignored life or a physics that ignored matter and energy. Since I assume that psychology is a cognitive science, I assume that cognitive science inherits the problem of consciousness."

In his response to the commentaries, Pylyshyn said that Miller, among others, had suggested

> phenomena that may not be capturable within a computational cognitive theory. The case of consciousness is especially clear. In this case we not only lack an approach that seems equipped to clarify the mystery of conscious

---

[2] See Gottfried Wilhelm Leibniz, 1962, "Quelques remarques sur le livre de Mons. Lock intitulé Essay of Understanding", 1695, 3/13 February 1697:6 (translation and emphasis mine).

[3] See, for example, Husserl's January 1904 letter to the psychologist Theodor Lipps, published in Schuhmann, 1977: 146–150 in particular; or Husserl, 1984a:§35 in particular.

experience (certainly neither a functionalist approach like the computational one, nor a biological approach has even succeeded in formulating the problem coherently)—we don't have the faintest idea of what it would be *like* to have such a theory..., so that we might [not] recognize an adequate theory if one were proposed.[4]

Of course, I do not want to suggest that what I present here, and which draws on Husserl's theory is the solution to the problem of consciousness. But it may be a contribution towards such a solution. However, in order not to get lost in the ocean of difficulties, mysteries, etc. linked to the notion of consciousness, let us have the courage to be very elementary. Let us not aim at more than the first few steps of the ABC of consciousness!

First, an outline of what can be done by means of a phenomenological analysis of consciousness is given. This makes it very clear what cannot be done on this basis alone. At this juncture, a normative point of view is brought to bear and the need to turn towards genetic psychology is explained in this light. This step is briefly illustrated by means of an event that has been emphasised in developmental psychology, especially in Piaget's work—namely, the passage from the level of sensorimotor activity to that of representation. My approach will no doubt give rise to a number of objections and I, in the conclusion, anticipate one possible objection. In this, I am inspired by what has been forcefully advanced by Piaget in, for example, his *Insights and illusions of philosophy* (1971b).

Now, it would seem best to start from a concrete example. Indeed, it is one of the main theses of this approach that mental activity itself, and not an analogy of it, has to be considered. Moreover, starting from an example of mental activity has the advantage of giving a more palpable sense to what otherwise is only globally designated by the term "consciousness". Thus an attempt must be made to say something about some type of mental activity. We arrive at a first approximation by verbs in ordinary language. When we talk, we all use expressions such as "I see", "I hear", "I touch" (generally, thus, "I perceive"), "I remember", "I imagine", "I saw a picture", or "I imagine having seen a picture", etc. Verbs are indicative of activities. In German, verbs are called *Tätigkeitsworte*.

For our purposes, it is important to notice that an activity is always taken to be a mental activity. To be sure, the activities are extremely diverse. Here, elements of an analysis of a few very basic activities are used—namely, perceiving, remembering and imagining.

In order to have a common point of reference, take, for example, "remembering an evening at a restaurant with a group of friends". Try to

---

[4] See *The behavioral and brain sciences*, 1980, 3:146 and 166 (emphasis partially mine). See also J. Russell, 1984: 136ff, where I rediscovered Miller's remark.

remember, for instance, next to whom you were sitting, or something like that. This is an example of an activity of the type "remembering something". Now, the main task of the phenomenologist doing reflective analysis is to delimit forms of consciousness. It is not an analysis that directly tackles the content. In this sense, it is irrelevant whether I remember x, or y, or z. Incidentally, I said that the analysis may be based on the example of remembering an event with a group of people. I could just as well have said, remember anything you like. It is crucial to understand that it is not the content as such that is important—it is the activity of referring to a content. In the phenomenological analysis, an attempt is made to specify what the activity consists of. By the same token, it may be added that it is not important what the motive is for remembering something, nor why it is that one may remember it time and again, etc. Husserl's approach is thus a specific one, but, it seems to me, nevertheless relevant to certain psychological problems.

In the following paragraphs, a somewhat formalised notation is used, although it is not one used by logicians. Since we are not dealing with logic, but with phenomenology, an effort should be made to understand the signs used here from the point of view of what is at stake in the reflective analysis of consciousness.[5]

I start from the following thesis or, if you prefer, hypothesis: the function of consciousness, or of intentionality, is to establish reference to an object [Gegenstandsbezug] in one way or another. The question that guides the analysis of our example is, then, simply the following: how do I refer to something that is not present, here and now? The answer that is presented proposes a form of consciousness, i.e. a form of referring to something, that is different from the form corresponding to any other type of mental activity. I said that the content as such is irrelevant, namely in the sense of the particular content of this activity taken individually. However, it should be clear that the type, or kind, of the objective correlate to which the activity under consideration refers does make a difference. Thus, it is relevant to know whether we consider a concrete situation or object or whether we take a state of affairs [Sachverhalt], a mathematical equation, etc. In this chapter, we deal with elementary cases as they are found when reference is made to a spatially and temporally individualised object, situation or event.

Now, in remembering the restaurant scene, henceforth designated by x, I establish a relationship to an x that is not present. In the notation, the

---

[5] To designate the mental activities under consideration, letter-triplets based on ordinary English verbs will be used. Thus, "remembering" will be expressed by REM, "imagining" by IMA, "perceiving" by PER. For some background information concerning the use of the notation, see Marbach, 1984: 213ff., in particular.

point of the intentional relation to x is indicated by means of parentheses as follows: (REM)x. The content, designated by x, is now taken solely as a correlate of the corresponding activity, which, in turn, is designated by the letters inside the parentheses. In the example, "(REM)x" thus indicates that x is solely considered as "something remembered as such". In other words, in the phenomenological notation, the sign x (or y, z, etc), when it appears as "phenomenologically bound" to a pair of parentheses, must be interpreted as representing something distinct from, but at the same time inseparable from the corresponding mental activity. The x is therefore not taken as it is "in and by itself" so to speak. The question we want to answer, when talking of something past, can thus be put as follows: How is the past given to me? It is given to me in a certain form of mental activity. By virtue of a certain activity, I have a relation to the past as such, as past. In this sense, there is no past without my referring to it, or someone else's referring to it. In our example, then, if the "x" designates "the evening at the restaurant", my referring to x is established by virtue of an activity of which I am aware when I remember it.

Let us now be more specific. First of all it is important actually to remember something! If we are not engaged in psychology or phenomenology, and if we are not otherwise theoretically interested, for example, in what is happening in the brain while we remember something, we are directed in our everyday lives towards the x. For example, if I were to express my remembering of the evening on the basis of the actual activity itself and not on the basis of an analysis of this activity, I would talk of the persons with whom I was there, what we discussed. I might also remember that while at the table in the restaurant, I anticipated doing this or that later on, etc. Thus, I am always turned towards the x, y, z, and I am talking about them when I express my remembering. This activity of which I have a non-thematic (or latent) consciousness—i.e. I "know" that I am remembering—is itself performed, but it is not itself turned into a theme. I am aware of remembering, but I do not have a thematic awareness of what remembering as mental activity consists of. To make it explicit, I must stop remembering. I must start reflecting upon the activity itself which must be represented by me, rather than be actually performed by me.

In our concrete example and put into ordinary language, when I reflect I take account of the fact that my referring to x was such that I remembered, for example, next to whom I was sitting at the table. Now, to be sitting somewhere is a perceptual or sensible activity in the sense that, even though I did not specifically pay attention to it, I felt the pressure of the chair and the table, I changed my position, etc. In short, I refer to the situation of sitting next to someone in the past by means of a perception of x. In the notation, this bit of reflective analysis may be written as follows:

(REM [(PER)x])x

that is, I remember x by representing a past perceiving of x. The crucial feature here is that my reference to x is not immediate. On the contrary, it is mediated by another consciousness, which, in turn, is not the one I actually have now. That other consciousness is said to be implied in my reference to the x of the past. Whichever x we take, it can be said that in my referring to x there is a complication in the intentional relation to x that does not occur in the case of perception.

For example, when I perceive something now in this room, I have an awareness of referring to it directly. It could be said that a being-in-contact-with is taking place between the (visually, tactually, etc.) moving body of the perceiving organism and the bodily-present surrounding world. In so talking, I wish to draw attention to the immediacy that strikes one in the case of touching or grasping something. I propose to view perceptual activity in general as an immediate referring to its correlate x, to be written as (PER)x. On the other hand, in the case of remembering, this "being-in-contact-with" is no longer true: it is only represented. If I remember having been there, next to a person, it is only *as if* I were again in contact with the past situation (or it is only as it were, or quasi). In the notation used above, this modification in my awareness is indicated by means of the pair of square brackets.

Another aspect should be mentioned briefly. In an activity of the type "remembering", I would say that I believe that what I am remembering actually took place. In order to indicate this point, the sign ⊢ will be used. It is put in front of the square brackets, which, as was just explained, are used to designate the activity that is represented in my actual remembering. At this stage of our analysis, we thus get:

(REM ⊢ [(PER)x])x

The sign ⊢ thus serves to indicate that in my remembering x, I bestow a character of belief upon the represented activity, which, in our elementary example, consists of a simple perceiving of x. It is important to make this moment of belief explicit: this becomes apparent at once if one contrasts an activity of the type "remembering" with that of imagining. For instance, I imagine that I might have been sitting next to someone else in the restaurant or that, now, I might be going for a walk, etc. In such a case, my referring to x is also mediated by a perception. However, when reflecting on the activity and not simply and straightforwardly imagining the situation, one realises that one had a latent awareness of not believing in the imagined situation. Nor would one deny that the situation had taken place. With Husserl, one could speak of neutrality regarding the situation: I am neutral with respect to what I imagine, I do not take it as being true, nor as being false.[6] In the

---

[6] See, for example, Husserl, 1913, republished in Husserl, 1976:§§109–111.

notation, using the sign − for "neutrality', the form of the activity of imagination could thus be presented in a first approximation as follows:

(IMA − [(PER)x])x

that is, I imagine x by representing a neutralised quasi-perceiving of x. In short, a fundamental difference between two kinds of acts of representation would seem to exist. On the one hand, there are acts involving a position, a belief, that what I remember, or what I represent in another manner, actually was the case, will be the case, etc., thus allowing for the possibility of error. On the other hand, there are acts in which I do not believe, nor deny, but where I merely imagine something or merely think of something as being the case.

I now wish to draw attention to another point that is important when considering the question of the transition from the sensorimotor level to representation. Notice that the x was written twice in the notation of REM x and of IMA x, whereas in the case of perception, (PER)x, it appeared only once. This notation indicates that it is only by virtue of two activities, one of which is not actually performed, that I obtain the *identity* of something. The identity of x, which I remember, is given to me only because I do not refer to x solely from *one* perspective. On the other hand, when remembering, I refer to x, the one (i.e. the same x) that I had perceived in the past. It is for this reason that the x is indicated twice. It does not mean that we are faced with two situations—one that would arise when I actually remember something, and another that took place in the past and that would only be given to me by virtue of a mental representative [*Stellvertreter*] in my remembering. It means rather that I am referring to the past situation itself, although in a manner different from the direct referring that is established in actual perception. In the notation, this modification is indicated by the square brackets, as was explained above. These brackets are crucial. They indicate that the activity expressed in these brackets is not actually performed, but that it is nonetheless contained in the manner of referring to an object that is accomplished by the activity that is actually performed. Husserl speaks here of "intentional implication".[7]

To be sure, intentional implication is very different from logical implication. It is not a matter of consequence or of deductibility. On the contrary, with the intentional implication, what is said to be implied is contained within the activity. For example, if (except, of course, for purposes of reflective analysis) one were to take the expression ⊢[(PER)x] outside the expression (REM)x, one would commit a phenomenological nonsense. Concretely, in phenomenological language, the expression

---

[7] See, for example, Husserl, 1976: §§99ff.; Husserl, 1959:§§44f.; Annex II; Husserl, 1973: Nr.10; Husserl, 1980: Nr.14, Nr.15. See also Marbach, 1984.

⊢[(PER)x] (or, more generally, the expression of any activity said to be intentionally implied) is to be found only when integrated into another expression, which, in turn, designates the activity that is performed and which may be submitted to the reflective analysis.

Thus, in the activities of REM x and IMA x outlined above, there is, so to speak, a minimum of activity that is necessary in order to have something identical as a correlate, namely a certain multiplicity on the side of the mental activity itself by virtue of which I refer to that which is identical (the situation of the restaurant, in our example). By contrast, in perception as I have defined it here, there is not yet identity in the true sense of the term. I will come back to this.

Since my interest is to convey an idea of phenomenology as an attempt to determine *forms* that differ depending on the mental activities submitted to the analysis, I would like to comment briefly on two other aspects pertaining to acts of the type we have been considering. So far, it all looks rather "ethereal"! It was said that I remember an x which is not given now, and I remember it by means of a perception that is not actual—it all sounds rather mysterious. However, it must now be emphasised that it all functions the way it does only because at the same time I am aware of being present here. I do not only establish a reference to something absent, past and the like. Thus, the foundation, basis or ground that I establish in the presentation of the bodily [*leibhaft*] given surroundings should be indicated as well. The triplet PRE may stand for the actual bodily presentation in general. The surroundings, s, appear phenomenologically bound to PRE, as (PRE)s. The whole expression is put in subscript position and topped by a horizontal bar, so as to indicate that the activity of representing x is grounded, or founded in $\overline{(PRE)s}$. Thus, all the while I am remembering, I do not lose touch with the present. Otherwise, I would be dreaming (daydreaming), i.e. I would be in immediate contact with the x. In representing x, however, I am aware of only representing x and that means that, at the same time, I make something present also. This may be summed up in the notation as follows:

$$\overline{(PRE)s}(REM \vdash[(PER)x])x$$

Moreover, I would like to complete the expression by adding i quite to the left of the formula. This will turn out to be very important! As I described very briefly above, there is a sort of identification on the objective side by virtue of a multiplicity of activities. Now, it must be added that, in an activity of this kind, we also need a union point on the subjective side. In the example, there is my activity of remembering, which contains another activity: that of having perceived. At the same time, there is my actual perception of the present surroundings. But these are not fragmented activities: rather, there is a subjective union point, usually called "I". We say: "*I* remember that *I* was there . . .", etc.In the notation, which is meant to mirror what the reflective analysis makes explicit, this centre of the subjective unity will thus be indicated modestly by the little *i*! Thus, we eventually arrive at the following phenomenological form of an elementary kind of remembering:

$$i \frac{}{(\text{PRE})_s} (\text{REM} \vdash [(\text{PER})x])x$$

that is, I, while grounded in the bodily presentation of my surroundings *s*, am remembering *x* by representing a quasi-perceiving of *x* (a perceiving *x* as it were), bestowed with the actuality-character (belief).

A mental activity of this form exhibits, among other properties, a sort of conflict between presence and absence. Indeed, the more I engage in reviving the past, for instance by seeing as it were again the situation of the evening in the restaurant, the more I am turned towards *x*, and the more I lose contact with the present situation *s*, with being here in this room. Conversely, when I look attentively into this room, I cannot at the very same time look as it were at something belonging to the situation that I am representing in my remembering or imagining. This phenomenon is well-known in experimental psychology and has been studied under the title of "modality-specific interference".[8]

These few remarks must suffice here. The notation that I have used should help to suggest that there is a great deal of complexity involved when phenomenological analysis is brought to bear on mental activity. For each sign used in the notation, a descriptive comment based on reflection can be given. In this sense, the notation allows us to draw attention to what phenomenologists call constitutive moments pertaining to such and such a form of consciousness. Phenomenologists believe, then, that such forms of consciousness can be established on the basis of reflection upon the mental activities themselves.

The approach envisaged here has, as is all too apparent, serious limitations. In the present context, especially, such a reflective analysis of a form of consciousness tells us nothing as yet about the question of mental development. Is the form of remembering that has been described above characteristic of the remembering activity of a child at age 2, at age 5, at age 10, or of an adult only, etc.? Well, nothing has been said so far about variations that may occur in the course of cognitive development, and this could not be done on the basis of reflection upon the activity itself of perceiving, remembering, imagining, etc.

On the other hand, we could claim that, with the method we use, we get insight into what remembering (*mutatis mutandis* every mental activity) considered as a mental activity consists of. It has already been shown that

---

[8] For a brief discussion of the experimental work, that of L. R. Brooks in particular, see, for example, Richardson, 1980: 54–59, or Morris and Hampson, 1983: 167–170 in particular.

this knowledge is to be had independently of the particular content of x, and of the motives of the performance of such mental activity. Now it must be emphasised that this understanding of the very form of a mental activity, such as perceiving, remembering, imagining, etc., is also acquired independently of any developmental question. What has been done so far should be viewed as a conceptual analysis, i.e. an attempt to clarify the very sense or meaning of the concept of mental activity under consideration. What we have obtained is an elucidation of its phenomenological (or epistemological) origin as referred to above. This is achieved by having recourse to the consciousness by virtue of which the sense of that which I wish to determine is given to me [*Gegebenheitsbewusstsein*]. Thus, in our example, if I wish to clarify the sense of what it means to establish a reference to something past, I must, as a phenomenologist, have recourse to the consciousness of the past, i.e. to the mental activity that is described by the phrase "remembering something". It is only by going back to the origin in this way that I learn (from its source; *ursprünglich*) what it means to be able to refer to something pertaining to the past as such. I find it, in Leibniz's phrase, "in my own depths", in the "*ipse intellectus*".

Let us now turn to the notion of *norm*, which figures in the title of this chapter. I said at the beginning that an answer would be suggested to the question of how to reach the goal of understanding cognitive development as mental development. As I see things, the proposal to view laws of consciousness as *norms* follows from setting up this goal.

I consider that purely formal logical laws, which govern the genuine thinking of any subject, can be viewed as norms to be respected if, in one's own thinking, one aims at truth. It is true that, when formal logical laws are taken by themselves, they do not appear to be normative. They do not state what *ought* to be the case, but rather what is the case regarding purely formal logical matters. However, it is precisely because these laws of formal logic state on purely conceptual grounds the case in genuinely logical matters, but not with regard to logical problem solving of concrete subjects (say, children at age 4, age 8, etc.), that they can serve as norms. By stating what is logically consistent, compatible or incompatible they can tell us whether concretely given cases of logical reasoning are, or are not, correct (in accordance with the logical laws as norms).[9]

Somewhat analogously, I would like to suggest—and in this I follow Husserl—that phenomenological forms of consciousness, as described above in the example of the mental activity of "remembering something", may be taken to be laws of consciousness. That is to say, they may be

---

[9] Relevant Husserlian texts, e.g. in Husserl, 1900, republished in Husserl, 1975:§§14, 16; Husserl, 1901, republished in Husserl, 1984b: §64; Husserl, 1984a: §§ 9, 10, 39–41; and Annex XIII, 380–387. See also, for example, Piaget, 1973:34–42; Piaget 1967a: 38.

viewed as governing the way of remembering something of any subject who has the ability or competence to establish reference to something past as such. In other words, this amounts to saying that any subject (or organism) that has intentional experiences of, say, perceiving, remembering, imagining etc. as well as combinations thereof would be subordinated to the corresponding phenomenological laws of consciousness. Accordingly, then, it may be proposed that these laws of consciousness may also be considered as *norms*. They are norms that ought to be respected and brought to bear interpretatively, if in one's theorising about cognitive development one aims at genuinely understanding it as mental development—i.e. if one aims at understanding development from the angle of consciousness.

However, it is clear that such forms or laws of consciousness cannot prescribe the factual course of cognitive development beyond the laws of purely phenomenological dependencies among mental activities, such as found in the intentional implications and modifications of consciousness. Such a law of phenomenological dependency may, for example, be seen to hold between the mental activities of perceiving and remembering or imagining. It may be said then that, since both remembering and imagining intentionally imply the mental activity of perceiving in the way in which they establish reference to something remembered or imagined, it is impossible to find a course of development in which there is first remembering and/or imagining, and only later perceiving. But whether, on the basis of perceiving that has to happen to begin with, there in fact subsequently develops representation at all is not a question that can be answered on phenomenological grounds alone. Nor, *if* representation does develop in given cases, is the question of which of remembering or imagining will appear first a purely phenomenological question. In other words, the phenomenologist alone cannot decide whether there will first be a mental activity that bestows the intentionally implied past experience with the character of belief (see above regarding the sign ⊢), thus allowing for errors, or whether, *in fact*, there first develop more or less "free-floating", neutral (see above) evocations of something absent. Quite generally, then, the phenomenological laws of consciousness leave certain connections between mental activities open as possibilities. Or conversely, there are factual connections between the mental activities to be found in the empirical world that are *not* necessarily required to occur on purely conceptual grounds. These connections are open to genuine empirical investigations, whose aim will be to determine connections between the cognitive functions that are subordinated to empirical regularities or laws, such as are found in theories of developmental cognitive psychology, for instance.

Now, I consider it to be a legitimate enterprise for a phenomenologist to be theoretically interested precisely in the factual course of mental development.[10] At this point, then, the phenomenologist obviously needs the help of developmental psychology. He will rely on well-established findings of that discipline, which studies the psychological and even the biological (neurophysiological, etc.) origin of cognition as the matter of fact that it is. However, instead of simply endorsing the theoretical interpretations of the findings given by scientific biology and scientific developmental psychology, the phenomenologist will then, in a normative turn [normativer Wendung], or by way of application [Anwendung], introduce the point of view of the laws of consciousness that are to be established on the basis of reflection upon the mental activities themselves.

Let me very briefly illustrate this point. Sticking to our elementary level of analysis, let us consider the psychological finding of the transition from sensorimotor activity to the level of representation. Piaget's very detailed account of the relevant facts indicates that such a transition takes place during the second year of life of the human baby. From the phenomenological point of view, what strikes me quite particularly is this: When describing the achievement of representation, as opposed to a merely sensorimotor activity that is constructing its here-and-now universe, Piaget tends to use expressions such as "prolongation" and/or "extension", "enlargement", "acceleration" with regard to space and time. For example, he says that, with the advent of representation or thinking [pensée], action is situated in a much larger spatio-temporal context, which confers a new status on action as an instrument of exchange between the subject and objects. Piaget explains that with the progress of representation, the distances between the actions and their object increase, both in time and in space, in the sense that past or future as well as present events, and spatially distant as well as near ones, can be evoked.[11] This description seems to me rather too metaphorical. It suggests a kind of linear development, where reference to an object is established beyond the here-and-now of sensorimotor activity, e.g. to a more or less "distant past".

As a phenomenologist, I would want to argue that, for an observable behaviour to be genuinely at the level of representation of something absent (past, etc.) as such, the organism (e.g., the human baby) would have to be subordinated to those phenomenological laws of consciousness that tell us what it is to establish reference to something represented. Thus, on the basis of what was explained earlier in this chapter, this would mean that, in addition to a continuing presentation of one's surroundings by

---

[10] See Marbach, 1982, where the argument for cooperation between a phenomenological and a genetic epistemology is presented at some length and special attention is given to the problem of empathy [Einfühlung] and the method of "constitutive deconstruction", on which the phenomenologist has to rely.

[11] See, for example, Piaget, 1972:23, or Piaget, 1971a: chapter VII.

means of one's body, a radical modification or break with the sensorimotor way of referring to x would have to occur. In short, the terms "prolongation" etc. would not seem to be appropriate to account for the discretely different phenomenological forms of consciousness, which the phenomenologist is interested in; namely, on the one hand, the form pertaining to the here-and-now universe of a simple (PER)x and, on the other hand, the various forms pertaining to the varieties of universes of representation such as, for example,

$$i_{\overline{(PRE)s}} \; (REM \vdash [(PER)x])x$$

(see p. 255). In a simple perceiving (PER)x at the sensorimotor level, there is immediate being-in-contact with the surroundings through one's looking, touching, smelling, etc. At this level, there is no need to construct an identical x as such to which the organism would refer and, correspondingly, there is no need for the notion of a subjective union-point "I". There is the body of the organism, and the unity of the perceptual activity is actually given by the functioning body. In sharp contrast to this, with the phenomenological forms of representation, we at once get a complexity of constitutive moments. They account for the fact that, from the point of view of consciousness, radically novel achievements as regards the reference to an object come into effect. From the point of view of the reflective analysis, it would seem impossible for them to be "extracted" from the basic level of (PER)x by "prolongation", etc., or even by "differentiation" and "reconstruction". For, to remind you of our example, when I remember the evening at the restaurant I do not perceive this past event at all. I perceive it only, as it were, again; my awareness (consciousness) of x is radically modified, independently of the spatially and temporally greater or lesser distance between the x and me.

In conclusion, let me hint at an objection that may have come into your minds and which was certainly the one Piaget addressed to phenomenology. For example, in *Insights and illusions of philosophy* (1971b), Piaget emphasised the importance of the possibility of verification, which he found missing from phenomenological analysis. He would say that he felt confident when observing a child of age 7 or age 12, because he would be able to observe another one and still another one, and so on, if he did not understand something well enough in a given case. And that with a hundred such observations he could make cross-checks and the necessary controls. Piaget objected that in phenomenological analysis, there is only one subject observing one subject, him/herself, so that verification is virtually excluded (Piaget, 1971b:110ff).

However, in another passage, where Piaget alludes to the current meaning of the word "truth" as that which can be verified, he points out that the method of verification that one chooses is not important, provided that it is accessible to others and that it guarantees that one is not centred on oneself or on the authority of a master, but that what was proposed should be controllable by all those who doubt (Piaget 1971b:79ff).

Well, it is my hope that by stressing the analysis of forms of consciousness as distinctly different manners of referring to something and by using a sort of outward projection in the notation in order to guide reflection upon the mental activities under consideration, I have succeeded in providing a method of analysis that lends itself to verification. The fact remains, however, that in trying to understand cognitive development from the point of view of consciousness, I do not see how one can get around the reflective analysis of "one's own depths": for, consciousness occurs with me, with you, and you, etc.—it is not "out there".

REFERENCES

Husserl, E. (1959). *Erste Philosophie (1923/24), Zweiter Teil: Theorie der phänomenologischen Reduktion* (Husserliana VIII, ed. by R. Boehm). Den Haag: M. Nijhoff.

Husserl, E. (1973). *Zur Phänomenologie der Intersubjektivität, Text aus dem Nachlass, Erster Teil 1905–1920* (Husserliana XIII, ed. by I. Kern). Den Haag: M. Nijhoff.

Husserl, E. (1975). *Logische Untersuchungen, Erster Band: Prolegomena zur reinen Logik* (Husserliana XVIII, ed. by E. Holenstein). Den Haag: M. Nijhoff. (First published 1900 and 1913.)

Husserl, E. (1976). *Ideen zu einer reinen Phänomenologie und phänomenologischen Philosophie, Erstes Buch: Allgemeine Einführung in die reine Phänomenologie, I. Halbband* (Husserliana III/1, new ed. by K. Schuhmann). Den Haag: M. Nijhoff. (First published 1913, 1922 and 1928.)

Husserl, E. (1980). *Phantasie, Bildbewusstsein, Erinnerung: Zur Phänomelogie der anschaulichen Vergegenwärtigungen, Texte aus dem Nachlass (1898–1925)* (Husserliana XXIII, ed. by E. Marbach). Den Haag: M. Nijhoff.

Husserl, E. (1984a). *Einleitung in die Logik und Erkenntnistheorie, Vorlesungen 1906/1907* (Husserliana XXIV, ed. by U. Melle). Den Haag: M. Nijhoff.

Husserl, E. (1984b). *Logische Untersuchungen, Zweiter Band, Zweiter Teil: Untersuchungen zur Phänomenologie und Theorie der Erkenntnis* (Husserliana XIX/2, ed. by U. Panzer). Den Haag: M. Nijhoff. (First published 1901 and 1921.)

Leibniz, G. W. (1962). *Philosophische Schriften, Sechster Band: Nouveaux essais.* Berlin: Akademie-Verlag.

Marbach, E. (1982). Two directions of epistemology: Husserl and Piaget. *Revue Internationale de Philosophie, 36,* 435–469.

Marbach, E. (1984). On using intentionality in empirical phenomenology: The problem of "mental images". *Dialectica, 38,* 209–229.

Miller, G. A. (1980). Computation, consciousness and cognition. *The Behavioural and Brain Sciences, 3*: 146.

Morris, P. E. & Hampson, P. J. (1983). *Imagery and consciousness.* London: Academic Press.

Piaget, J. (1967). *L'épistemologie et ses variétés. In J. Piaget (Ed.). Logique et connaissance scientifique.* Paris: Gallimard.

Piaget, J. (1969). *The mechanisms of perception.* London: Routledge & Kegan Paul. (First French ed. 1961.)

Piaget, J. (1971a). *Biology and knowledge.* Chicago: University of Chicago Press. (First French ed., 1967.)

Piaget, J. (1971b). *Insights and illusions of philosophy.* New York: World Publishing. (First French ed., 1965.)

Piaget, J. (1972). *The principles of genetic epistemology.* London: Routledge & Kegan Paul. (First French ed., 1970).

Piaget, J. (1973). *Introduction à l'épistémologie génétique,* Vol. 1: *La pensée mathématique.* Paris: Presses Universitaires de France. (First published 1950).

Piaget, J. & Inhelder, B. (1969). *The psychology of the child.* London: Routledge & Kegan Paul. (First French ed., 1966.)

Richardson, J. T. E. (1980). *Mental imagery and human memory.* London: Macmillan.

Russell, J. (1984). *Explaining mental life: Some philosophical issues in psychology.* London: Macmillan.

Schuhmann, K. (1977). Ein Brief Husserls an Theodor Lipps. *Tijdschrift voor Filosofie, 39,* 141–150.

CLOSING DEBATE

This is the transcription of the major points of the discussion which closed the course on "Piaget today". The discussions consisted of spontaneous reactions to the contents of the talks and of answers to written questions put by the participants to the speakers. The debate was presided over by Hermine Sinclair.

Susan Carey

I would like to begin by thanking the organisers of this course—especially Bärbel Inhelder who could not be here—and Hermine Sinclair. I think the central problem we are faced with here is "Piaget tomorrow". As an American psychologist, I think that I can describe with dismay the difference between the general levels of interest in Europe and in the United States in the issues that have been discussed this week, which I think are, in a way, more interesting than many issues that are discussed in developmental psychology or cognitive psychology in the United States. And one reason is that Piaget is not the central figure that he once was in American psychology, and the question is why not and where have those issues gone? I think one of the reasons is that the issues are very difficult, and people prefer to work on easier issues. The other reason is a perceived dogmatism in the Unites States—a perception of a dogmatic insistence on some of the particular views that I think are not necessarily central to pursuing the issues. What I would like to propose very briefly here is a

---

Edited by Angela Cornu-Wells.

framework that we might all agree upon. The question is—for us Americans—how do we get the feel of the importance of these issues and the possibility of making progress on them? I think we can all agree that a characterisation of development is going to begin with a characterisation of the initial state and a characterisation of the environment and the mechanisms by which the initial state is transformed. Of course, any empirical question that is worth its salt is also deeply a theoretical question, but there are some fairly straightforward empirical questions about the characterisation of the initial state, namely, what is innate and how structured is what is innate? And there are two really important theoretical issues here. One is how much of what is innate is highly domain-specific-structured? And this is where the issue of stages arises—how much of development is going to be captured by characterising the restructuring of domain-specific structures? And, of course, the last set of issues—these are all descriptive ones—involves the problem of the mechanism of change as well.

Now, there are also a series of theoretical–empirical questions that have arisen in this course which I think have to do with the proper idealisation of our science. The question is, what can you carve out and separate from other things so that you can make progress on them. I think there has been a certain tension in the course, with Broughton and Papert and Aebli arguing that the idealisations of Piaget and other people interested in cognitive development will not work. You cannot separate the logical and the epistemological from the cultural and the social. And I think Rolando García gave an answer to that claim. The point is that we must make some idealisations in order to make progress; you have to carve out some smaller parts of the problem in order to make progress in science and of course it is only the success of the science that tells you whether your idealisation is justified or not. I think that this issue of the proper idealisation will be another way of thinking about some of the controversies that will come up in the general discussion. As I say, I am not trying to make any claims, I am just trying to lay out a space here and a plea that we think of halting the trivialisation of the work that developmental psychologists do.

Barry Richards

I would like to echo Susan Carey's comments of thanks, particularly to Hermine Sinclair and Bärbel Inhelder, and would hope that the following remarks might contribute to the useful debate that has occurred this week.

One thing that has emerged from the lectures is the clear tendency towards fragmentation in developmental psychology. Harry Beilin noted that there are now many different theories rather than a single paradigm, and the speakers have indicated some of the lines of division, if only metaphorically. There are divisions between the hards and the softs, the alienated and the integrated, the totalitarians and the anarchists. There is also tension between those who like large theories and those who prefer small theories. The latter seem more interested in data—they feel that if truth lies in the data, then this is what one ought to be attending to. The former care less about data, supposing that only a theory can illuminate the truth. Though it may be tempting to elaborate these divisions, I suspect that this would only divert our attention from what is urgently needed, namely more integration.

Fragmentation in science is usually thought to be dangerous, if not disastrous, since hypotheses tend to be recognised as insights only from the viewpoint of an integrated and stable theory. When there is no such theory, one finds it difficult to distinguish insight from aberration. One possible "antidote" to the tendency towards fragmentation in developmental psychology might be detected in a concern common to several of the speakers, namely representation. This is central to Piaget's thought and to the thoughts of many who derive their inspiration from him. It is also at the core of cognitive science. But what is the nature of representation, and what is its role in cognitive processing? These questions seem to be of common concern and may provide a useful stimulus towards integrating different theoretical perspectives. Though the integration may be limited in character, it may nevertheless be sufficient to differentiate insight from aberration.

There is one final thing I should like to say. Those who are theoretically motivated might be seen to have two distinguished allies, namely Piaget and Chomsky. Piaget had a comprehensive theory, or at least a theoretical perspective, which both directed his search for data and provided the basis for its interpretation. He appreciated that no data are by themselves significant, i.e. they do not determine their own interpretation. Without a theory, data have no particular "shape". On the primacy of theory, Piaget and Chomsky are clearly in agreement. For Chomsky it is the theory that counts—one may disagree about the details of transformational grammar, and indeed about its coherence, but one cannot deny its fruitfulness as a source of insight into natural language. Piaget's theory has been similarly fruitful for the study of cognitive development. There may be a lesson here—that "grand" theories, despite their deficiencies, provide the appropriate means for seeking insight and advancing science.

Harry Beilin

At this point the law of diminishing returns begins to operate in that I have very little to add to what has been said. I cannot miss the opportunity, however, to express my appreciation to all those who have been working very hard to make this programme a success; and from my point of view it has been an enormous success. Everyone comes to Geneva with a personal history, and in my history Geneva plays an important part, even if this is the first time I have been here on a professional basis. So, I am very grateful for the opportunity I have had to make a contribution to this year's proceedings, and, in the way one says that the best way to learn is to teach, in that sense I have also profited greatly from the experience.

The view I have of the state of the field, I have already pretty well elaborated in my talk, and it parallels in part the words of Susan Carey. There is no question that if one looks at the American scene in developmental psychology, it tends to be chaotic, and the thing that distressed me most over the past few years is the extent to which American psychologists have increasingly rejected not just Piaget's theory itself but what underlies the Piagetian research programme, the assumptions that inform it. The reasons for this shift in ideology are quite profound, and the evidence for it is to be seen in the comparable rejection of Chomskyan theory, the views of Levi-Strauss and of a number of other like-minded structuralists. There is something taking place of a deeper sociological–historical nature that is reflected in this change in orientation. Nevertheless, it is difficult not to despair when one sees the baby thrown out with the bath water—particularly for developmental psychologists, who love babies. There is thus a natural desire to retrieve, or at least retain, much of what is valuable and critical to the Piagetian programme. There is no question in my mind but that the Piagetian tradition will undergo change. I came to the course, in part, to see what is happening at the source with respect to such change. One always looked to Geneva for inspiration, and we were always sensitive to the changes taking place in thinking here. From the experience of the course, however, the picture is not at all made clear. At least to me. What kinds of changes are taking place here, and who is making them? I hope that someone from Geneva will have something to say about what they see as the current status of Piagetian research and theory and where they think it is likely to go.

In any case, I think there will be two groups who will be developing the theory or at least aiding its evolution—those in Geneva, and a number elsewhere around the world. From the representation of people at the course this year, it is very clear that they come from all over. The Piagetian tradition is not simply a Genevan, Swiss, English, European and American phenomenon any longer. It consists of a wide variety of people who have derived inspiration from the ideas embodied in the Piagetian research programme, and they are everywhere. And since there is no question in my mind that the programme will evolve, what I hope to see is an integration between structuralist forms of developmental theory and those that are closer to the functionalist forms we see dominant at the moment.

Again, let me state my appreciation for the opportunity to have expressed my views here this year.

Hermine Sinclair

Thank you. I am going to add one sentence of my own. Someone said something about a defensive and a conservative attitude being at the basis of Piaget's theory. I am quite happy to keep this conservative attitude. We have seen, and Piaget often said and wrote when reporting on experiments with children, that if you reject a theory in all its breadth and all its details too quickly, you will never get anything other than chaos. What we have seen in children is that progress occurs when a theory is pushed to its very limits, and I therefore have no hesitation in avowing that we have not yet understood Piaget's theory enough to push it to its furthest limits. And I think that part of the trouble you referred to in the state of affairs nowadays is that people are ready to reject theories at the first sign of something else interesting appearing or of the theory being subject to certain criticisms, or simply to propose to forget that theory and have something new. As a psychologist, I personally think that the limits of Piaget's theory and our understanding of it have not been reached and that we can push it far further, and that, in fact, we should push it further even within its own boundaries. Now, having made this personal declaration, which I should not have done, I think the next person to talk will be Rolando García.

Rolando García

I am not in a very good position to comment on what happened during the course because due to known telluric reasons I arrived only towards the end. So, at the risk of being out of focus, I will rather refer to certain questions that came to my mind when I saw the title of this course. Is it possible to pinpoint certain contributions that we may consider as having a lasting value, regardless of the fate of specific aspects of Piagetian epistemological theories? I do believe that there is a "before Piaget" and an "after Piaget" in the theory of knowledge. In this connection, it seems to me that the main point is this: no matter how much is accepted or is rejected of Piaget's ideas, there are problems in epistemology that cannot be formulated the same way after Piaget's findings in the psychogenesis of knowledge. Let us consider, for instance, his position against empiricism. Piaget's main contribution started in a period when science was completely dominated by empiricism. It was a period, particularly in the Anglo-Saxon world, when any scientist working in any laboratory or doing any type of work—whatever he said about this work—was consciously or not an empiricist. It was the period of the apogee of logical empiricism and other brands of empiricism. In the 1950s there were many reactions against empiricism, but I think it is fair to say that it was still possible for empiricists to survive with some reconstruction of their theory.

The findings of the Piagetian school went much deeper into the heart of the theory. For the first time, such findings provided an empirical proof of the inadequacy of empiricism as a theory of knowledge. Paradoxically enough, as Piaget often remarked, the empiricists never gave an empirical proof of what they advanced as an explanation of the "source" of knowledge.

The difference between empiricism as a philosophical position and empirical science has not often been made. And, from my point of view, the possibility of having non-empiricist foundations of empirical science without falling back on some form of a-priorism has not been firmly established outside genetic epistemology. This brings me to the next point I want to make. Once empiricism is rejected and you still hold back from returning to a-priorism, the only way open is constructivism. I firmly believe that if you want to have a theory of knowledge that accounts for everything we know about psychogenesis and about the history of science, you must adopt a constructivist approach. In this connection, we may distinguish two aspects of Piaget's contributions. On the one hand, he has established in a conclusive manner the need for a constructivist theory of knowledge; and, on the other, he has provided such a kind of theory. In my view, the first is very well-established, but I am willing to accept that certain aspects of Piaget's theoretical interpretations are not so well-established. Here, however, I very much agree with what Hermine Sinclair just said. I am not in agreement with Popper. I do not believe that the falsification of one consequence of a theory allows us to reject the theory. The history of science has proved that this is not the case. It shows that a theory is overthrown when there is another theory, sufficiently consistent, that is able to explain everything that the previous theory explained, plus something else. It is rather easy to improve on some of Piaget's experiments and to contradict some of his interpretations; it is rather easy to find flaws in the theory. What I claim is that we do not have today an alternative theory with the above-mentioned characteristics, which are required to substitute for Piaget's theory.

Let me now jump to another point where the contribution of Piagetian theory is *today* extremely important. It is a common feature of many epistemological theories to refer to the interaction between subject and object and to consider that the interaction starts with the action of the subject on the object. There are, however, important differences about the interpretation of the role of action in the cognitive processes. In general, action is taken as providing knowledge *directly*. Such is the case in empiricist theories, including most brands of dialectical materialism (but not Marx). I think that one of the main contributions of genetic epistemology was to show that the primary role of action is not to provide knowledge directly, but to provide the means for constructing the instruments through which assimilation of the object in the process of knowledge becomes possible. In this respect, although sometimes they seem to speak the same language, genetic epistemologists and members of the schools of dialectical materialism are saying quite different things.

Another point where, in my view, genetic psychology and epistemoloy have made a lasting contribution, but that I will mention only very briefly, concerns the evolution of the cognitive system. I do believe that there is today sufficient evidence about the fact that all natural systems—open systems—evolve by successive reorganisations. This seems to be an essential aspect of evolution. I believe that Piaget is one of the pioneers in the discovery of evolution as a process that is neither linear nor continuous and that concepts such as stability, instability, dynamic equilibrium (or "equilibration") play a key role in the understanding of such processes. This, by the way, provides solid bases for the genetic structuralism that characterises his theory of knowledge.

The final point I would like to make is about the social contribution or the influence of cultural patterns on the genesis of knowledge. I shall try to give a very brief account of one of the factors that enters into this subject and how I interpret the position of Piaget about it. If we start with the opposition between subject and object, I believe that his position is that when we speak of objects of knowledge, the object is not neutral. It is always socially determined; it is not given in isolation, it belongs to a certain society, with a certain culture, at a certain moment. The subject of knowledge is also socially determined, but the way in which the subject develops the *means to apprehend the object of knowledge* is determined more by the inner mechanisms of psychogenetic construction. I do not believe that there is any truth in the position that Piaget put all the emphasis on one of the sides, that he eliminated or ignored the other. The other is there with all its characteristics. In the same way, I disagree with certain propositions made yesterday in the sense that the scheme of equilibration completely eliminates the social aspect. I think this is wrong. The scheme of equilibration refers to the mechanisms by means of which the subject apprehends the object of knowledge, not to the way in which the object is provided as such. In this sense, Piagetian theory is simply a theory that has to be further elaborated—as has been the fate of all scientific theories that we maintain today. This is to me one of the greatest contributions of Piaget. Epistemology before Piaget was mainly speculative philosophy. Now it is a science. It is a science that you could develop like any science, that will show that many of the former interpretations have to be changed or completed like in any science in any period of history. But the fact that it is a science gives us some hope for the evolution, for the further understanding of this phenomenon we call the cognitive system. And the fact that it is a science is to me Piaget's highest merit.

Jean-Jacques Ducret

I would just like to make a remark about what Rolando García has said. I completely agree with his thesis. I have one reservation, however, which arises perhaps from the evolution of Piaget's work. If we look at Piaget's early work, he raised questions both of a sociological and of a biological nature in epistemology. But the basic question he raised in this first stage was biological, and it remained biological throughout his work. There was a period at the end of the 1920s and beginning of the 1930s when Piaget momentarily put emphasis on the sociological point of view. He attacked the problem of knowledge as a sociologist, and this concords with the view that the object is a socially determined construction. But one should not forget that, deep-down, Piaget remained a biologist. There is a passage in one of his early books, *Judgement and reasoning in the child,* where he concludes: what I have done in these first books is to study knowledge from the sociological point of view; but one should never forget the biological point of view. And I have the impression that the same is true for the last Piaget: that the object of scientific knowledge is a social production. But if one goes back to the source of the constitution of the object—to the origin of intelligence—this has a strong biological component; this does not mean that it is innate but constructed according to the biological constraints of the organism. We therefore have these two factors which constantly influence Piaget's work, but it would be wrong to put Piaget too much on the side of the biologist and that of the individual, just as it would be wrong to look at knowledge only from the sociological standpoint in the sense that science is an eminently sociological affair. Beneath science, there is the world of each individual organised in a certain way during infancy. And when we go back to the baby, we find biology firmly anchored—not in the sense of innatism, but in that of coordinations. I think you would agree on this point.

Hermine Sinclair

We seem to be moving away from psychological-logical structures and epistemological questions. I do not know whether you want to continue in this vein or come back to something more psychological? Among the more psychological questions, there is one from Robert Lawler. He will forgive me if I condense it a bit. It is on structures and description of structures— and no doubt he means cognitive structures. What is the role of these structures in psychogenesis on the one hand and in the history of science on the other? What exactly are cognitive structures? Are they just descriptions without any functional impact? How do structures intervene in behaviour?

Robert Lawler

Let me be explicit about this question. In previous visits to Geneva, I have been asked to indicate some relation between the sort of work I have done and the theories of Piaget, and how the kind of structures I describe in my work relate to Piaget's structures. I have sat here as a student, I have read Piaget off and on, and I have tried to figure this out. I am looking for some help. If anyone here can tell me how the structures that are central to Piagetian theory intervene in behaviour and how they affect psychogenesis, I would like to know. I see it less as a challenge than a request for information.

Susan Carey

I would like to say something about one part of Robert Lawler's question, which was: How do these structures or systems intervene in an explanation of human behaviour? This is where the issue that Barry Richards raised about representation plays a central role. I think that the kinds of cognitive theories that we are working with now, which are very consistent with Piagetian ideas, postulate mental representations of these systems, and computations over those representations that one appeals to in explaining different aspects of behaviour for the different kinds of systems. So, if it is a logical system, you appeal to those representations and the kinds of computations definable by those representations to explain the inferences or judgements people make about what is validity or not, or the way people come to make a proof. The domain of cognitive phenomena to be explained by the positive systems, the way you think they should be represented and the kinds of computations over them, is like any other scientific issue. Part of showing how it explains behaviour is specifying what the domain of behaviours to be explained is. For example, Chomsky's work, a system *par excellence,* attempts to explain why some sentences are in the language and some are not. That is the domain of phenomena this work is meant to explain, mediated by your judgements of them. And an internal mental representation of a theory—which I agree is another example of a structure *par excellence*—is meant to explain all sorts of aspects of behaviour including the hypotheses subjects will actually entertain, and the way subjects (the subjects in our experiments being children) will put evidence, and so on. So these systems are meant to play a very direct role in explaining very specific aspects of behaviour, and the domain of behaviour that is supposed to be explained by each structure is part of its characterisation.

Henri Wermus

I shall try to answer this question, which concerns me also. There are two possible ways in my opinion to get rid of the very difficult concept of structure, and particularly that of cognitive structure. The first approach, which was also mentioned by many people here, is to speak about systems rather than structures. There are, however, big differences between the two. First, elements, parts of a system, which are sub-systems, are also systems. In systems, one has to take account of the interactions between sub-systems. Secondly, the system differs very much from a structure, in the sense of a mathematical structure, in that a system has an evironment, and there is an exchange between the environment and the system, which grows and changes its state. There are several mathematical descriptions, such as transition functions, output functions; these are elaborate mathematical instruments, which are involved, in my opinion, in some efficient way in cognitive science also. A first approach then is the systemic models of cognitive structures. The second approach is to consider structures as theories. This means that one tries to write axioms—I do not say that children have axioms in their heads—to describe or represent a stage (it is better to say stage rather than structure) of competence of a child. At each level of development, a child has some degree of cognitive competence. And that competence depends on the development of his representations, on the sub-systems of his logic, on his memory experience and so on. All these items should be formulated as axioms that describe exactly what the theory means.

Hermine Sinclair

I have another question, which goes in the same direction but is more particularly addressed to Rolando García. The question comes from Henri Schneider. One problem that comes up when one tries to make more precise the analogy between the evolution of open systems in the way Prigogine has described it, on the one hand, and cognitive development, on the other hand, is the problem of the elements. What are the elements that make up the fluctuations that become simplified and therefore the new structure? In physics, we have molecules. But what would cognitive molecules look like? While Rolando García is coming forward, I would like to give you the Piagetian answer: cognitive molecules are schemes, operatory schemes.

Rolando García

The two questions are, indeed, much related. Let me try to say how I look at the problem. First of all, I shall make a small criticism of Piaget. I believe that many times he refers to structures when he means systems, and one thing I find lacking in the theory is the fact that the consideration of a system as such is not clear in Piaget's work. And I believe we have to talk about systems, the elements of systems and the stucture of the system. This differentiation is fundamental because a number of important properties of the system, such as stability, vulnerability, and so on, are properties of the structure and not properties of the elements. It is quite clear that any physical, biological or chemical system becomes unstable when the set of internal relations cannot stand any more. So in order to study the evolution of a system, it is absolutely necessary to differentiate between the elements of the system and the relations among the elements. I agree with Hermine Sinclair that in the cognitive system, the schemes are elements, but the elements are also the facts of the world that have to be understood and explained, and of course the system of relations we put into the actual world is the kind of logic we have elaborated in order to make this relation and interpret it. And the stability of the system is not the stability of the elements themselves, it is the stability of the relations between the elements. This does not mean to say that the relations are independent of the elements: it is true that the kind of relationship between the elements depends on the elements themselves, but these are different levels of explanation, and I believe that another comment that needs to be made when we consider structures and systems is the fact that we have to consider levels of explanation. For instance, in order to understand how a molecule is built in chemistry, you do not need to study the inner structure of the nucleus of each one of the atoms. It is enough to know certain characteristics of the atom (such as the outer electrons) which provide the balance. But in order to explain why there are so many "free" electrons in an atom, we have to go to the inner structure of the atom, which is another level of explanation. So there are structural levels and there are relationships among the levels, and the relationships at one level depend on the inner structure of the elements, but the characteristics, the properties of a structure at a certain level are not directly determined by the elements themselves. This is the way I understand the evolution of open systems.

This poses another problem. It is one of the serious problems we have now. I have been studying this in connection with some physiologists and neurophysiologists in Mexico. How are the structures of different levels causally related? The cause of the changes in a relationship between elements is not a sort of mechanical effect, like the piston in the motor that finally moves the wheels by a set of mechanical connections. What is becoming quite clear to us in the examples we have been able to work out in detail is that Prigogine's ideas may help the understanding of causal relations between structures, i.e. systems with structures one within the other. Let us take, for instance, the motion of the heart: you have the organic level, the cellular level and the molecular level. In order to explain the contractions and dilatations of the heart, you have to analyse the three levels. Now, the molecular level does not act directly, mechanically on the cellular level nor does the cellular level on the organic level. What happens is that the inner structure has pulsations or modifications that act as perturbations in the following levels. When the perturbation exceeds a certain threshold, then the instability of the higher level is released, and what happens depends on the internal dynamics of the higher level and not on anything else. Now all this is at the very beginning. I think that the understanding of systems, structures, causal relations, levels of structuration, levels of explanation, and so on requires much further elaboration. We are at the beginning of an extremely important era for the understanding of the evolution of complex systems, and the cognitive system is one of the most complex we know. I do not know whether I have answered anything or just introduced more confusion.

Hermine Sinclair

Unless someone wants to react to this point, I would like to go towards the socio-genetic influences. We can always come back to systems, concepts, elements, open systems, levels, etc. On the point of sociogenesis and psychogenesis, we have two questions from Robert Maier.

Robert Maier

My first question is addressed to Rolando García. I am not sure that I understand the status of the distinction between social influences determining the direction of development, and mechanisms of development. I do not see where you can find this kind of distinction. Perhaps it is because you have some idea now in mind, but how can you justify such a distinction in the history of science? I would even agree here with Susan Carey's way of seeing things. She also supposes that we see mechanisms in ontogenesis and in the genesis of knowledge, but she finds that finally what we see is a kind of development of modern science in children. It could not have been the same before the Renaissance. Now, if this is true, then what Rolando García said cannot be true. I suggest, but I am not sure, that you are in danger of a kind of idealism when you make this distinction, i.e. projecting ideas as being real. I do not think this is the case, but in the formulation it comes over something like this.

Rolando García

I do not believe that I am being idealistic at all when I take history as empirical material on which to elaborate. For the epistemology of science, history is the empirical material. So, when I say that there are sociological, economical and political factors that provide a certain directionality, I am basing what I am saying on very concrete historical examples. I used as an example the very beginning of the social sciences in three different countries: France, England and Germany. What Comte aimed at in his sociological theory can only be explained through the history of France, for he based what he was looking for on the state of France after the French Revolution and the Napoleonic wars. Moreover, there were a lot of reactionary people around Comte, trying to restore the old order that had been perturbed by the revolution, and the whole direction of sociological research was around this idea of how to restore order. There was no authority, no legitimity, the previous monarchic and religious order had been completely destroyed by the revolution and the ideas that went with it. If you go to England, this sort of preoccupation does not exist in that period, and you do not find people working on this line. On the other hand, you have the industrial revolution, you have a tremendous economic boom in England, which became really the first power in the world at that moment. The result was *The wealth of nations* by Adam Smith. Adam Smith is a product of a certain history within England, and it happened in England—not in Germany. In Germany, an Adam Smith makes no sense. If you go to Germany at that time, the kind of preoccupation was entirely different. So there is a sort of directionality, particularly at that period— which is why I am so interested in it—a sort of directionality to the research, to the preoccupations, to the main ideas, in each one of these countries, which can only be explained through the history of each one of them. Of course, later on, these differences in nationalities are not clear. Science becomes more unified, more uniform, there is a sort of exchange. But we are studying the origins of certain ideas, and at the origin I think this sort of directionality exists. In modern science, the fact that nuclear physics has developed so much is due to a very clear historical and political fact, i.e. the atomic bomb. Its development produced a hypertrophia of all physics, and in many countries—even in underdeveloped countries— physics became equivalent to atomic physics or nuclear physics, which was a complete distortion of what physics should be, taking into account so many other problems that were not taken into consideration. This was historically determined, but it did not determine the *content*—i.e. the inner structure—of the theories that emerged. Now, if Maier calls this "ideal-ism", I will ask him to define idealism for me because I do not understand.

Robert Maier

May I just make a remark. If there were some kind of knowledge system let us say in the last century, a complex whole of social and epistemic aspects, what kind of equilibration would act only on the epistemic aspects and not on the social aspects? How would it make the distinction? If equilibration does not know how to discriminate, then the sociogenesis will be different, and it will have different mechanisms from the ontogenesis. It could only be the same if both are distinguished, and a distinction, in my opinion, involves some idealism, i.e. positing some ideas as in principle separate from this kind of complex whole when they are in fact part of it. That is the problem. For me, the alternative is either that ontogenesis and the development of sociogenesis are not the same, they do not have the same mechanisms, or you are in danger of adopting the kind of position that cannot be defended in a coherent way.

Rolando García

I think there is a very great confusion here of levels of explanation, levels of structures, levels of equilibration. There is, of course, a problem of equilibration at a social level, that provides a certain context for the development of certain ideas that belong to another level. This interplay between different levels of structures and different levels of explanation is one of the key problems in the genetic structuralism we are talking about. So if you confuse the levels, the whole thing becomes chaotic. Now, of course, in order to explain what happened at the social level, you have to follow the mechanics, the dynamics of that level. But that level is related to another level with a different dynamic. Using again the example of the heart as an organ, the fibres of the heart and the molecules, they belong to different levels and each level has a different dynamic. But they are absolutely interrelated, and, as I said, it is not that the protein pushes the fibre. This is wrong. The protein produces a perturbation that releases the mechanism at another level, which then follows with the dynamics of that level. When the latter exceeds a certain threshold, it will influence the mechanisms of the other level and the new level will evolve in accordance with its own inner dynamics. But if you put the three levels together, you will not understand anything because the dynamics are different.

Susan Carey

I never claimed that the mechanisms are the same at the two levels of descriptions, because I do not know what the mechanisms are either. I see my research programme as extremely more modest. The first question I am asking is simply: do we need to appeal to intuitive theories, that is, to conceptual structures that have enough of the properties of not intuitive theories that we might want to call them theories? Do we need to appeal to them to account for cognitive behaviour even of young children? Question two: in the course of the restructuring of knowledge in development, do we have to appeal to the kinds of restructuring described by Rolando García in the restructuring of physics, when conservation of energy was appreciated? Now that kind of restructuring, as Kuhn has very adequately described, appeared in the evolution of theories way before the flowering of science in the sixteenth and seventeenth centuries. The questions arise in describing developments within Greek science and so on. So, the question I am asking—it is an empirical question—is a double one: do we need to appeal to intuitive theories in understanding cognitive behaviour even of young children, and do the same hardest problems of restructuring—the same relations between Theory One and Theory Two that arise in the history of science—arise in the development of children? I think the answer to both these questions is yes. That is the only claim I am making now.

Hermine Sinclair

I think we have a good example of the fact that each one of us has a particular version of some theory. I also think that the foregoing is a good example of a mixture of levels. Everyone has his own level.

Robert Maier

I come back to the question I wanted to ask J. Broughton. I will be very schematic. You said that cognition is related to authority and manipulation. And you try, in a kind of hermeneutic reading of Freud, to remake Hegel. You use for this purpose a different kind of knowledge, founded by hermeneutics, and a kind of Hegelian totalisation. Are you not restricting the knowledge system too much? I think certainly that there are power aspects in it, but that there are also liberating ones. You seem to neglect them and you invent another kind of knowledge, which I mistrust very strongly. This hermeneutic kind of knowledge is very dangerous. I would prefer to extend the knowledge system we have, while recognising the dangers. My second point is that the kind of totalisation you make is either too great, too imperialistic or on the contrary too restrictive—it is anthropocentric. We must involve the biological dimensions which you forget. So my problem is: certainly there are norms related to knowledge, coming out of the constitution of knowledge systems, but I think there is no other way of knowing than the logical–mathematical way. If you understand it only in an authoritarian way, you miss Piaget, and if you totalise it with Hegel, you are getting too anthropocentric.

John Broughton

Let me respond first with regard to "hermeneutics" and then on the topic of "authority".

I think I detect a certain irony in the question! In fact, I have been wondering this week whether there might have been a degree of transatlantic miscommunication going on all along—a discursive difference, perhaps, between the Americans and the Europeans. In general, it seems, "we Americans" tend to miss the subtle irony in your European style of discourse. To be specific, I know from a breakfast conversation with Dr. Maier that he is very much involved in the use of hermeneutic methods in his own work.

A similar comment could, perhaps, have been made to Piaget himself, were he here, and I think he might have enjoyed the irony too. A methodological examination of Piaget's work reveals the interesting fact that the way in which it was conducted did not conform well to his own theory. This has been pointed out by a number of psychologists, starting with Bernie Kaplan and Rob Wozniak, 15 or 20 years ago, and more recently by Howard Gruber. This issue was the topic of some discussion at the Piaget Memorial Conference at Columbia in 1981. To give a specific example, the Piagets' study of infants shows little evidence of the use of formal operational logic or scientific method. Rather, it is a textbook case of the application of interpretive or hermeneutic methods, presupposing a structural orientation, but nonetheless phenomenological in orientation. The re-interpretation of the infant data by Werner van der Voort in Habermas' erstwhile group at the Max Planck Institute in Starnberg provides considerable support for Wozniak's original claim.

As my colleague at Teachers College, Herb Ginsburg, has described so nicely, Piaget's methodological orientation underwent a series of alterations. However, his preferred method, foreshadowed in the methods chapter at the beginning of *The child's conception of the world*, was never one of hypothesis-testing. Admittedly, certain "negations" entered into the reasoning. But the overall method was less a combination of deduction and induction than "abduction", if I may have the gall to re-introduce Peirce's term.

At the risk of repeating myself, let me respond to R. Maier's comment about authoritarianism by trying to clarify our understanding of the nature of authority. I think we make a fundamental error, an authoritarian one perhaps, if we accept the common-sense assumption that authority lies in an oppression of one group by another. Unfortunately, this common assumption has been fortified in the social sciences by equilibration theories. These days, one of their strongholds is cognitive developmental theory.

There is a dubious political metaphor at the core of this equilibrational approach which we could refer to, in the present context, as the perceptual metaphor of the mountaineer: we arrive at an appropriate "view" of something by "rising above" and then "looking down" on it. We are disinclined to try the inverse metaphor: reaching an understanding by "going under" or finding the "roots" of something. When we talk of "reflecting abstraction", for instance, we tend to visualise it as "rising" to a greater level of generality. When the objects of our view are other subjects, of course, our knowledge implies a subordination and stratification of some kind. Some are "overlooked" by others.

Admittedly—and here I can agree with R. Maier—this sense of elevation can be liberating. The leaders of great liberation movements—in the American context, one harks back to Martin Luther King—were people who were able to formulate the issues in terms of uplifting generalities. Certainly, these individuals used "power-full" mechanisms of cognitive abstraction. But, at the same time, they refrained from using equilibration models. The goal of "lifting up" is not the same as that of "looking down". It is not beyond the imaginative capacities of even us, the privileged, to realise that were we members of a minority group struggling for life with more or less limited success; theories of equilibration would not readily spring to mind as a means of representing our efforts. If anything, they would be useful only as a caricature of the oppressive mechanism itself. The production and stabilisation of systems would hardly appear as a means of emancipation to such people. Rather, they would be experienced as engulfing. This is because systems theories, on account of their synthetic power, tend to subsume "lower" levels under the "higher" levels of control that they set up. Apropos of this, let me remark that in our discussion today, supposedly on "sociogenesis", I heard nothing sociological at all. Society and culture were absorbed into more general concepts of equilibration and systems of control.

Dr. Maier accuses me of forgetting the biological dimension. *Au contraire*, I find the biological dimension of organismic thinking exerting its pernicious influence everywhere in mainstream social science discourse, and I regret only its imperialism.

I would suggest an alternative conception of authority that avoids a spatial reification of "above/below" and focuses instead on the symbolically mediated, interpretive nature of power. European thinkers such as that ex-psychologist Foucault suggest that authority may lie in the symbol systems that different social groups share, not in hierarchical relations between those groups. But the shared medium does not serve all equally. Foucault's point is that power works by presupposition. One does not need to impose the authority of one's argument if one has the power to set the terms of argumentation outside of which the formulation of meaning is to be deemed intolerable—to be "looked down on". The confident choice contained in the statement that "there is no other way of knowing" amounts to a *negation* of the other ways and of those who pursue them. Neglect supersedes force: One does not need to coerce those who are systematically overlooked.

To select an example close to home, once we accept the shared language of "norms" and "values", a terminology that has established for itself a certain currency here today, the battle is already lost. The concepts of "norms" and "values" are not neutral entities. Historically, they emerge from a specific political tradition, the discourse of utilitarianism forged for the waxing British empire, and these terms give rise to an ethics of instrumental relativism that was part and parcel of nineteenth-century British foreign policy. Philosophically sophisticated psychologists have objected to an uncritical accommodation to this terminology. For example, in his critique of the obsession with instrumental *utility,* Kohlberg has demonstrated why we need to distinguish "morality" from "values", "principles" from "norms", and inquire into the development of the former rather than the latter.

If we are able to dig under the authority of the cognitive, the equilibrium, the system, rather than always escalating it to another meta-level of reflective abstraction, we stand a chance—I believe the only chance—of avoiding that "totalisation" of which I stand accused!

Robert Maier

You mentioned Foucault, and I think there is here a very strange misunderstanding because Foucault, without knowing it, was one of the greatest Piagetians. He said that truth comes from power systems, and power systems are established by classifications and hierarchies, by Piagetian structures. He analysed very finely and precisely how they were established in hospitals, in schools, in military education, at work. These kinds of Piagetian structures produced truth systems, and these truth systems had dominating effects from the point of view of the oppressed. But you can go in a different way: you can see Foucault as the analyst who showed that the Piagetian categories are historically established. And you can use him to see that there is also a liberating approach in it, and not only this kind of dominating approach. So I would use Foucault as a Piagetian, against this kind of reduction of Piaget.

Hermine Sinclair

Anyone else on the subject of norms?

Eduard Marbach

J.-J. Ducret's question regarding the passage from "phenomenological forms" to "norms" provides the opportunity to add a few remarks on an important link in my argument that I am afraid I have not pointed out explicitly, so I am grateful for the question. We have been exploring the phenomenological form of the mental activity of remembering something. It was explained that such forms may be considered as laws of consciousness. Now, with the move from laws to norms that I am suggesting, more careful attention should be given to the following point: The forms or laws of consciousness that we were discussing were established on the basis of a *descriptive* procedure. They are meant to be statements about that which *lawfully* is the case regarding consciousness, and not merely incidentally in a given example. Thus, the crucial notion of *necessity* is implied here. A fuller presentation of my proposal to view laws of consciousness as norms of mental development should elaborate on this. The procedure of establishing a law (or form) of consciousness—such as $(REM)x$ [see Marbach, Chapter 15, this volume]—would have to be presented as being a procedure of considering variations of the mental activity under study such that the proposed form appears as *invariably* the same throughout the range of possibilities. The form would thus appear to be the necessary (lawful) form in the sense that it would state that which *cannot possibly* be otherwise if the requirement is maintained that it be a case of (say) remembering x, etc. Thus, it would have to be shown more precisely that those laws are not merely inductive generalisations, i.e. empirical laws. Instead, in a way to be compared to the relationship between "pure" and "applied" mathematics, it should be made clear that those laws of consciousness are to be seen as "pure" laws attempting conceptually to define the very forms of *possible* consciousness of this or that kind (and, a fortiori, of empirically occurring cases). If such a procedure of defining the laws of consciousness were accepted, the normative turn that I suggest would seem to be a legitimate one. If, however, such "pure" laws were not within our reach, it would have to be admitted that quite different forms of consciousness, e.g. of remembering x, etc., may actually be occurring in the empirical world. The grounds for proposing to consider the phenomenological forms as norms to be applied to one's interpretation of mental development would then break down.

Harry Beilin

I would like to take the opportunity to react to Hermine Sinclair's response to the question I posed earlier as to current Genevan attitudes towards changes in Piaget's theory—what "Piaget today", in my view, is about—and Roland García's response as well.

They in effect said different things, and in typical Piagetian fashion I will try to integrate them. Mimi [Hermine Sinclair] seems to be saying that at least some Genevans and other Piagetians are taking a conservative stand in extracting from the theory all that it implies—by testing further its implications and connotations and extending these to as many domains as possible. It is, in truth, a very conservative stand: it holds that the theory itself should remain intact and that only its internal structure should be explored and explicated. From García, I have the sense that the theory is seen as a more dynamic phenomenon, that it is in need of modification or elaboration in those aspects of it that later experience has shown were not adequately conceptualised.

I am reminded of Lakatos's views about the nature of science and how theory should respond to disconfirming evidence. In accord with Hermine Sinclair's view, Lakatos says that a theory should not give up its position too easily in the face of competing theory or evidence. It should confront all attempts at replacement and all attempts at rejection, on both empirical and theoretical grounds. At the same time, a theory can become degenerating if it does not respond adequately to cumulating evidence of its inadequacies, and in this instance I see Lakatos in support of García's research strategy. It is my belief that both approaches, Hermine Sinclair's and García's, will be pursued to keep the Piagetian tradition from degenerating; at best retaining its progressive character, and at the least, seeing its potential fully recognized. By following Hermine Sinclair's tactic of understanding the full implications of the theory, as it stands, and with García, seeing the theory undergo change to the extent it is necessary, the Piagetian research tradition will be true to its core assumptions and will fulfill its essential mission.

HERMINE SINCLAIR

This is a very nice integration. It almost sounds like the last word for today. I would just like to say thank you very much to everybody for having been so enthusiastic and for having initiated so many discussions. Let us meet again.

Author Index

Acredolo, L.P. 187
Aebli, H. 6, 217, 218, 220, 224, 226, 229, 264
Afrifa, A. 114
Altman, I. 206
Amsel, E. 114
Anderson, J.R. 49
Andreassen, C. 185, 186, 192
Angell, J.R. 41
Apostel, L. 71
Appel, L.F. 193
Appleyard, D. 203, 204, 205
Aristotle 146–7, 234
Austin, G.A. 52

Bachelard, G. 136
Baillargeon, R. 55, 144, 158, 218
Baldwin, J.M. 41, 42, 56
Baltes, P.B. 53
Bandura, A. 230
Baumrind, D. 117
Baur, M. 113
Beilin, H. 4, 5, 41, 50, 55, 56, 59, 60, 61, 264, 265–67, 281–282
Benjamin, J. 117–118, 120
Bergman, A. 173
Bernstein, B. 115
Beth, E.W. 65, 66, 69, 70, 74, 127
Bisanz, J. 185
Blasi, A. 112n
Block, J. 175
Block, J.H. 175
Block, N. 38
Boden, M. 39–40, 49
Boll, M. 77
Böök, A. 203
Borel, M.-J. 2, 65, 68
Borkowski, J.G. 191
Bourbaki, 3, 109
Bower, T.G.R. 112

Bragonier, P. 120
Brainerd, C.J. 52
Broughton, J.M. 4, 5, 112–118, 238, 264, 277, 278–280
Brown, A.L. 187, 226
Bruner, J.S. 45, 52, 53, 211, 218, 225, 226, 230
Buck-Morss, S. 118n
Buehler, K. 225
Bullock, M. 158

Carey, S. 6, 54, 141, 144, 145, 154, 157, 158–159, 263–264, 266, 271–273, 274, 276–277
Carnap, R. 77
Carnot, S. 131, 133–134, 135, 137, 138–139
Case, R. 56, 141
Cassidy, D.J. 187
Cassirer, E. 239, 241
Cavanaugh, J.C. 189, 191
Cellérier, G. 2, 8, 12, 15, 16
Chandler, M. 113
Chi, M. 142, 161
Chodorow, N. 117
Chomsky, N. 5, 37, 38, 40, 44, 45, 47, 54, 61, 265, 266, 271
Clairaut, A.C. 129
Claparède, E. 59
Clapeyron, E. 134, 137, 138n
Clausius, P. 137, 138n, 139, 140
Cohen, R. 206, 211, 215
Cohen, S.L. 211, 215
Colding, L.A. 129
Cole, M. 53
Coleridge, S.T. 134n
Comte, A. 130, 275
Cooper, R.G. 193
Corman, H.H. 167
Cornoldi, C. 6, 7, 183, 185

Cowan, P. 114
Crider, C. 154

Darwin, C. 17, 27, 41
de Caprona, D. 1
De Beni, R. 185
De Loache, J.S. 187, 188, 197
Dennett, D.C. 38–39, 40
Dewey, J. 41, 42, 59
Dijksterhuis, E.J. 131
Dinnerstein, D. 117
Dixon, R.A. 53
Dörner, D. 224n
Downs, R.M. 203
Ducret, J.J. 66, 270, 281
Duncan, B. 207
Dürer, A. 119

Ebbinghaus, H. 183
Eliot, J. 207
Einstein, A. 9
Escalona, S.K. 6, 165, 167, 170
Euclid, 105

Faraday, M. 131, 135, 137
Fetz, R.L. 7, 233, 238, 242, 243
Fillimore, C.J. 222
Fischer, K.W. 52, 56, 62
Flavell, J.H. 52, 60, 157, 186, 187,
  191, 193, 194, 198, 226
Fodor, J.A. 38n, 39, 50, 54–55
Foucault, M. 279, 280
Fowler, J.W. 238
Fraisse, P. 235
Freud, A. 114
Freud, S. 10, 115, 277
Furth, H.G. 113–114

Gablik, S. 238
Gaerling, T. 203, 211
Galanter, E. 44
Galifret, Y. 235
Galileo 146–147
García, R. 3, 5, 11, 127, 128, 139, 144,
  264, 267–270, 272–274, 275, 276,
  281, 282
Gauss, C.F. 104

Gelman, R. 54, 55, 56, 144, 158, 218
Gentner, D. 222
Gholson, B. 52, 56
Gibson, E.J. 46, 53, 56
Giddens, A. 116
Gilligan, C. 3, 102, 103–104, 108, 112,
  114, 118
Gilliéron, C. 113
Ginsburg, H. 278
Glaser, R. 161
Glick, J. 53
Gmünder, P. 238
Goblot, E. 77
Goethe, J.W. von 134, 136
Golden, R. 113–114
Goodnow, J.J. 52
Gouldner, A.V. 116
Gréco, P. 11, 109
Green, F. 157
Greenfield, P. 218, 225
Grenspan, S.L. 165
Grize, J.-B. 2, 11, 69, 77, 101, 108,
  110, 221
Grove, W.R. 131, 134n, 135
Gruber, H.E. 110, 113, 116, 278
Guntrip, H.H. 115

Habermas, J. 114, 116, 236, 240–242,
  278
Hagen, J.W. 185
Halford, G. 141
Hall, G.S. 41
Halmos, P.R. 79
Hampson, P.J. 255n
Hardy, G.H. 104
Harris, J.E. 199
Hart, R.A. 207
Hasher, L. 188
Haste, H.W. 121
Hauert, C.-A. 55, 64
Hegel, G.W.F. 118, 121, 234, 240, 277
Helmholtz, H. von 131
Herschel, W. 135
Hilbert, D. 77, 109
Hilgard, E.R. 43
Hirn, G.A. 131
Hoeffel, E.C. 112n

Holt, R.R. 114
Holtzmann, K. 131
Honey, M. 113, 114
Hoppe, S. 218
Horn, H.R. 195–196
Hudson, L. 121
Hultsch, D.F. 53
Husserl, E. 247–250, 252, 253, 256

Inhelder, B. 1, 12, 13, 16, 66, 78, 112,
145, 165, 183, 184, 188, 204, 205,
239, 248
Istomina, Z.N. 188–189

Jacob, F. 27, 32
James, W. 41, 42
Jeanson, F. 235
Jones, B. 117
Josselson, R.E. 116n
Joule, J.P. 136–137n, 138–139

Kail, R. 185
Kant, I. 73, 236, 238, 240, 241
Kanter, R.M. 115
Kaplan, B. 116, 118, 278
Kaplan, M.M. 118
Karmiloff-Smith, A. 13
Keil, F.C. 54, 55, 155–157
Keller, E.F. 117, 121
Kelvin, Lord see Thomson
Kershner, J.R. 207
Kessen, W. 51
King, M.L. 279
Kintsch, W. 222
Klahr, D. 50, 51
Kluwe, R.H. 226
Kobsa, A. 72
Koestler, A. 60
Kohlberg, L. 102–103, 104, 108, 112–
113, 114, 116, 237, 238, 241, 280
Kosslyn, S.M. 49, 205, 225
Kreutzer, M.A. 198, 199
Kuhn, T.S. 4, 5, 40n, 67, 130–133n,
135, 136–137, 139, 140, 277

Lacan, J. 115
Ladd, F.C. 203

Lakatos, I. 40n, 282
Lange, G. 188
Laudan, L. 40n
Laurendeau, M. 158
Lawler, R. 270–271
Leadbeater, B. 114
Leibnitz, G.W. 134, 234, 247, 248, 256
Leonard, C. 198
Leontiev, A.A. 60
Leresche, G. 85
Lerner, R.M. 53
Lervig, P. 134n
Levi-Strauss, C. 45, 47, 54, 266
Liben, L.S. 206
Liebig, J. 131
Lindberg, E. 203
Lindsay, P.H. 222
Lipps, Th. 248n
Livingston, R.B. 210, 211
Locke, J. 154, 247, 248
Lockman, J.J. 214
Looft, W.R. 116
Lynch, K. 203, 204

Mahler, M.S. 173
Maier, R. 274, 275, 276, 277, 278, 279,
280
Marbach, E. 7, 247, 250n, 253n, 258n,
281
Marcia, J.E. 114
Marr, D. 39–40
Martin, R. 69
Martini, A. 185
Marx, K. 56, 269
Matalon, B. 69
Maury, L. 84
Mays, W. 127
McCarrel, N. 193
Merleau-Ponty, M. 114
Merz, J.T. 129
Meyer, J.R. 131
Miller, G.A. 43, 44, 248, 249n
Minsky, M. 16, 26
Moely, B.E. 185
Mohr, C.F. 131
Moore, M.K. 112
Morris, P.E. 255n

Mounod, P. 55

Naess, A. 69
Neisser, U. 39n, 53, 64
Nelson, K. 51, 52, 64
Newcombe, N.206
Newton, I. 66, 136, 145, 146
Norman, D.A. 39n, 205, 222

Oersted, C. 135
Ohm, G. 136
Oliver, R.S. 218, 225
Olsen, M.G. 187
Oppenheimer, R. 9
Oser, F. 238, 242, 246
Osgood, C. 44, 121
Overton, W.F. 46

Papert, S. 2–3, 16, 101, 104, 118, 121, 264
Parsons, T. 45
Pascual-Leone, J. 56, 141
Patterson, A.H. 206
Peano, 109
Peirce 42, 278
Peltier, 135
Perlmutter, M. 188, 189, 191
Piaget, J. *see* Subject Index
Piatelli-Palmerini, M. 5
Pick, H.L. 187, 214
Pinard, A. 158
Pine, F. 173
Pinker, S. 205
Pipp, S.L. 52, 56
Popper, K. 4, 268
Pomerantz, J.R. 225
Pribram, K.H. 44, 63
Prigogine 272, 274
Pylyshyn, Z.W. 39n, 225, 248

Rapaport, D. 44, 114
Rawls, J. 241
Rees, E. 161
Reese, H.W. 46
Regnault, 135
Reich, W. 115
Rest, J.R. 218

Richards, B. 3, 87, 88, 90, 95, 264–265, 271
Richardson, J.T.E. 255n
Ricoeur, P. 7, 233, 235, 236, 244, 245
Riesen, M. 218
Ritter, K. 135, 187
Rosch, E.H. 53, 64
Rousseau, J.-J. 220, 229–230, 231
Rumelhart, D.E. 39n, 205, 222
Russell, B. 77
Russell, J. 56, 249n
Ruthemann, U. 226

Salatas Waters, H. 185, 186, 192
Sampson, E.E. 117
Scarry, E. 121
Schadler, M. 204, 207
Schecter, B. 113, 121n
Schelling, F.W.J. von 134, 136
Schiller, F. von 134
Schmid-Schoenbein, C. 218
Schneider, H. 272
Scholnick, E.K. 56
Schumann, K. 248n
Schwartz, S.P. 205
Scribner, S. 53
Seebeck, T. 135
Séguin, M. 131
Seiler, Th.B. 218
Seltman, M. & P. 72, 79
Serrus, Ch. 77
Shapiro, D. 114–115, 120
Shemyakin, F.N. 207
Shepard, R.N. 49
Shohat, L. 113
Shultz, T. 158
Shweder, R.A. 57–58
Siegel, A.W. 203, 204, 205, 206, 207, 208, 210
Siegler, R.S. 52
Simon, H.A. 39n, 48, 51
Sims-Knight, J. 193
Sinclair, H. 263, 264, 267, 270–271, 272, 273, 274, 277, 281, 282
Smirnov, A.A. 192, 193
Smith, A. 130, 275
Smith, C. 143, 145

Smith, G. 205
Smith, J.E. 113
Smythies, J.R. 60
Spelke, E.S. 54, 55
Stanovich, R.E. 185
Staub, F. 226
Stea, D. 203
Steiner, G. 6, 203, 205
Steiner, H.-G. 221
Sternberg, R.G. 54
Strauss, E. 117
Sullivan, H.S. 115
Szeminska, A. 11, 204, 221

Thomson, W. (later Lord Kelvin) 135,
    137, 137n, 138, 138n, 139, 140
Tolman, E.Ch. 44, 224
Tulving, E. 184
Turkle, S. 3, 106, 107

Vinh-Bang, 11, 221
Vonèche, J.J. 4, 113, 116
Voort, W. van der 278
Voyat, G. 114

Weber, M. 7, 236–238, 239, 244
Wallace, D. 96n.
Wartofsky, M.W. 56, 64
Watson, J.B. 42
Weinert, F.E. 226
Weiss, R. 114
Wellman, H.M. 186, 187, 191, 194
Wermus, H. 101, 272
Werner, H. 173
Wertheimer, M. 43, 104, 227
White, R. 114
White, S.H. 203, 205, 206, 207, 208,
    210
Winnicott, D.W. 120
Wiser, M. 145
Wittmann, E. 221
Wohlwill, J.F. 206, 218
Wootten, J. 113
Wozniak, R. 278

Yussen, S.R. 193

Zacks, R.T. 188
Zahaykevich, M.K. 116n, 118n
Zarem, S. 113
Zazzo, R. 235
Zimmerman, B.J. 53

Subject Index

Accessibility 18, 25, 32, 34
Accommodation 19–20
Acculturation 228–231
Action
    role of 268–269
Activity 44, 115
    need for 228
Adaptation 35–36, 42, 43, 51, 115–117
Adolescence 112–113
Aggression 113
Affective development *see* Interaction
Animacy 115
Animism, childhood 158–160, 171
Appearance – reality distinction 157
Application of constancy judgments
218
Argumentation 71
Art 237, 238
Artificial intelligence (AI) 45, 61
Assimilation 19, 29, 31
    and accommodation (Piaget) 9, 227
    generalizing 30
    reciprocal 32
    recognitive 29
    recursive 31
    reproductive 29
Attachment 117–118
Attentional resources 185, 190
Authority 11, 111, 118
    authoritarianism 116n, 118n, 120,
        277, 278–279
Autonomy 114, 117–118, 120, 237,
241, 245
Awareness 191
Axiomatisation 109

Behavior
    difficulties in children 177
    rule described, rule governed, rule
        following 38, 39

Behaviorism 38, 42, 43
    associationism 43, 50, 53
    Hull–Spence theory 43, 44
    S–R psychology 41
    verbal mediation 44
Biological vs sociological (Piaget) 270
Biology, domain of 145, 147–159
British empirism 130, 133
British science 129, 130
British sociology 130

Calculus 66, 68, 71, 72–73, 74
Caloric
    principle of conservation of 136
    theory of 136
Case of arguments in proposition 222
Causal concepts 146, 158, 161–162
Causes of development 142
Central processor 190
Childhood 113
    animism 158–160, 171
Chunking 208
Class inclusion 143
Cognition *see also* Thought
    and social class 175
    biological 113
    cognitive psychology 117, 120
Cognitive development 37–62, 87–88,
116, 120, 165–180, 255ff *see also*
Development, Functionalism,
Interaction
    biological 113
Cognitive era 44–45
Cognitive map 203
Cognitive, masculine authority of 111–122
Cognitive psychology 117, 120
Cognitive repertoire 12
Cognitive science 38, 39
Cognitive structures 270–271 *see also*
Structure

ad hoc elaboration of 218
and behavior 271
and open systems 272–274
and procedures 12
elementary 10–11
elements of 272–273
Cognitive system 126, 127
Cognitive unconscious 10
"Computer culture" 106
Computationalism 38, 39, 45, 48, 50
Computationally-inspired theorists 48
Concept formation 224
Conceptions of biology 146–160
Conceptual change 146–147
Concrete operations 116
Consciousness 117 see also
Intentionality, Mental activity,
Reference
    concepts of 121
    form of 247, 250ff, 255, 256, 260
    latent (non-thematic) 251, 252
    law of 247–260
Conservation
    differential 17–19, 29
    of substance 221–222
Conservation vision of man (Piaget)
228
Construction 217–232
    of new objects 222
    of new action schemes 222–223
    qualitative 222
Constructivism 47, 60
    and a-priorism 268
    and constructibility 28–35
    and empiricism 268
    epistemological 12, 19, 20
    psychological 12, 14, 16, 20, 24, 26,
        28, 33, 35
Contexualism 48, 51, 52–54, 59, 60
    context 42, 44, 47, 48
    ecological psychology 46
    neo-Vygotskyans 53
Continuous vs dis-continuous memory
tasks 186–188, 196
Contradiction and disequilibration 136
Control 13, 17, 24, 30, 34
Conversion processes 132, 134–140

Cooperation 27, 30, 34
Coordination of schemes 9
    of values 233–245
Correspondences 11
Creativity 120
Curiosity 228
Cybernetic model (Piaget's) 116
Cybernetics 44, 53

Death 121–122
Décalages
    horizontal 218, 226
Decentration 133, 173
Declaration-question (discrimination)
196
Defense
    military 121–122
    molluscan 121
    psychodynamic 114, 120–21
Dependence 118
Desequilibration 136
Development see also Cognitive
development
    autonomous 230
    characterisation of 264
    cognitive-developmental theory
        116–117, 120, 122
    concepts of 114, 116–117
    critical developmental psychology
        122
    developmental theory 116
    ego 116n, 118
    faith 116n
    masculine 117–118
    moral 102–103, 113–114, 118
    motives to 227, 230
    of boys 118, 120
    of self see Self
    sciences of 4, 5ff
    social 113
Developmental theory 37
Dialectical materialism 268–269
Dialectics 11
Didactic applications of cognitive
psychology 226
Didactic nature of Piagetian
experiments 220
Distance receptor systems 166–167
Dogmatism in psychology 263

Domain
  -general change 141–145, 160–161
  -specific change 141–142, 145–161,
    264
  specificity 47, 48, 54
Domination 117, 120 *see also* Mastery

Ego 117
  control 174, 175
  development *see* Development
  strength 115
Egocentrism 113, 171
Emergence
  functional 26, 32, 35
Emotional connotation 206
Empiricism 267–268
  and empirical science 268
Energy
  and perpetual motion 132
  conservation of 130–132, 136–140
  conversion of 131, 132, 137, 138
Engine(s)
  and energy conservation 132
  and transfer of heat 133
  efficiency of 133
Epistemological analysis 131
Epistemological obstacle 136, 138
Epistemology 15–19, *see also* Genetic
epistemology
  adolescent 112
  genesis of 112–113
  Piagetian 128
  scientific 9, 269–270
Equilibration, Equilibrium 8, 15–16,
19–21, 23, 115, 218, 226–228, 231,
244–245, 269
  social 276
Everyday life
  cognitive constructions in 220–225
Evolution 117
Expectation 211
Experience patterns
  and impulse control 176–177
  and IQ 178–179
  definition of 117
Experimentalism 44
Explanation

functional 37, 38, 45, 46
structural 46

Falsification of a theory 4, 268
Feedback 213, 215
Feminism 119
  feminist psychology 117–118, 120
Figural metaphor 208
First-degree entailment 90–91
Force(s)
  and energy 139
  and matter 132, 134
  correlation of 135
  conversion of 139
Formal operations 112–113, 116
Formal thought 2
  and morality 104
  and non-formal proofs 104–106
Formalise, Formalisation 2–3, 66, 67,
72–73, 74, 104, 221–225
Formalisms 48, 49, 50, 61
Fragmentation in psychology 3–4, 5–
6, 8, 264–265, 266
Frame of reference 213 *see also*
Reference system
French rationalism 129, 134
French revolution 130, 133
French science 129, 133
French sociology 130
Function
  mathematical 11
  and structure 15–36
Functional
  analysis 21–5
  limitations 28
Functionalism 4, 11, 37, 111, 116–117
  current 38–55
  and structuralism 8ff, 21–28
  historical roots of 41–44
  new 45–55
  philosophical 37–40
  psychological 40–41

Gender 111–112, 121–122
  hierarchy 117–119
Generator 17, 18, 30, 32, 33
Genetic epistemology 5, 10, 60, 61,
112, 117, 120–121, 237, 239

see also Epistemology
stage theory 53, 56, 60
Genetic metaphysics 113
Genetic psychology 128
Genetic semiology 239
German science 129
Gestalt
  psychology 227
  theory 43, 44
Grouping (Piaget) 224
Graphic skeletons 208
Group 10
  IGDR 84
  IHBN 84–5
  INRC 78, 79, 80–4
  of Klein 84, 85
  ISTQ 85
  IXYC 84–5

Habitual activities 209
Heat *see also* Temperature, Caloric
  and electricity and light 135
  and mechanical work 131, 132, 137,
    138
  conservation of 134, 135, 139
  dynamical theory of 138
  measurement of 137
  production of 138
  transfer of 133, 135, 138
Hermeneutics 39, 40, 53, 277–278
Heteronomy 118
Hierarchical integration 205, 208, 213
Historical-critical method 128
Historical roots of new functionalism
  41–44
History of science 145–147, 160–162
  as epistemological laboratory 131
  as memory of science 131
Holistic representation 205, 214
Home (environment) 208, 211–212, 214
Hypotheses in mental development
  229
Hypothesis testing theory 44, 45, 52

Iconic representation 205, 206
Identification 230
Identity 113–114, 116n

Idealisation 264
  logico-mathematical 2–4, 107,
    108
Idealism 274–275
Ideology
  political 116
Illness 113
Imitation 230
Impulse control
  and experience patterns 176–177
  and IQ 174, 179
  and SES 175
  concept formation 173
  emergence of 174
Individualism 117–118
Individuation 115, 117–118, 120
Inductive inference 147–153
Industrialisation 133
Industrial Revolution 130, 133
Inferential power 141
Information processing capacity 141–
  142, 213
Information processing theory 38, 45,
  47, 48, 56
  means-end analysis 56
  procedural knowledge 56
Information theory 44
Injury 120–122
Innate structures 264
Intellectualisation 114
Intentionality 38, 39, 248, 250 *see also*
  Consciousness, Memory, Mental
  activity, Reference
  intentional implication 252, 253f,
    257
  intentional modification 252, 253f,
    257
Interaction cognitive/affective
  development 165
  at 6–8 months 166–171
  at 2–4 years 171–179
  methodological problems 180
Interdisciplinary research 1, 6, 7
Intersubjectivity 118
Intimacy 117–118, 121 *see also* Love
Introspection 191
Invariance 136, 140

Knowledge 225
  net 19, 24, 25, 32, 34
  sociogenesis of 127–140

Landmark knowledge 210–211
  organising function of 207
  selection of 206, 208, 209
Landmark learning 206, 210–211
Landmarks 204ff, 206, 208–209, 212, 213
"Landmarks prints" 210
Language 71–72
Large size environment 203–206, 206–208
Liberalism 117
Life
  concepts of 121n
Limbic neuronal discharge 210
Limbic system 210
Linkage
  constructive 229
Locomotion 206, 210, 211, 213
  subordinate function of 211
Logic 112, 117
  and culture 107
  and morality 3, 104
  and value 101
  classical 89–90
  logicians' 66, 67, 69–70
  natural 2, 65–75
  operatory 63, 71, 77–85
  psychologists' 101
  subjects' 101
  value of and logic of values 101–110
Logical positivism 44, 45
Logical reasoning 87–99
Love 113, 117 see also Intimacy

Macrogenesis 20, 25
Mapping 203
Mastery 114–115, 118 see also
Domination
  master-slave dialectic 118
Maturity 116, 118
Meaning 3, 11, 13, 235–236
Means-end relationship 198
Measurement

and Romantic movement 136
Mechanical work 132–135, 137–138
Memory 6, 17, 18
  and intelligence 183–184
  episodic vs semantic 184
  experiences retrieval 197
  goal 198
  for locations 187–188
  incidental vs intentional 186–189, 192–194
  natural contexts vs. laboratories 188–189
  organisation in see Organisation
  questionnaires see Questionnaires
  -span 142
  strategies 184–189
  tasks vs. systems 184, 192–197
  see also Metamemory
Mental activity 247, 249ff, 255f, 257f see also Consciousness, Intentionality
Mental map 204
Mentalism 44, 45, 48
Meta-cognition 227
Meta-logic 80–84
Metamemory 189–200
  development 195–197
  interviews 191–192, 198–200
Metaphor 113, 115, 121
Metaphysical self 113–114
Microgenesis 20, 25
Misogynism
  in Piaget 120
  origins of 117–118
Modal/non-modal representation of knowledge 225
Models
  of number 109
  subject's 106–108
Modern mind 236–237
Molluscs 111–112, 116, 121
Monitoring 185
Moral development 238, 241
  stages of 102
Moral principles 102–103
Mother-Child relationship see
Sensorimotor intelligence

Motivation 229
  intrinsic 227
Motives to development 230
Motor exploration 207
Motor interpretation of spatial
  learning 212

Narcissism 117
Natural kinds 154–157
Naturphilosophie 132, 134, 135
Neo-nativism 48, 54–55
  a priori constraints 54
Neo-Piagetian theory 55–56
Network 224
Network-like representation 205, 214
Neuropathology 177
Neurosis 115
New connectionism 61
New synthesis 37–64
Newtonian science 129
Newtonian tradition 138
Norm, Normative, Normative fact 2,
7, 67, 68, 70, 281
  of mental development 247–60
"Now-Print!" – process 210
Number 23–26
  construction of 106
  models of 109
  Piaget's concept of 108–110

Object 73–74
  concept 88, 93–95
  permanence 112
Objectivism 117–118, 120
Objectivity 117–119, 120
Observational learning (modelling)
209, 213, 215
Obsession 115–116, 121
Oedipal complex 118
Ontogenesis 128
Ontological vs logical development
238
Ontology 113–114
Operant learning 88, 96–98
Operatory logic 77–85
Operationism 116
Organisation in memory 185

Origin 248
  phenomenological 247, 256
  psychological 248, 250

Paradise lost 173
Paranoia 115
Passivity 115–116
Period of the construction of theories
  "intra-" 138
  "inter-" 138
  "trans-" 138
Personality 114, 116n, 120
  development 165
Perspective 113
  integration 211
Phenomenalism 53
Philosophy 38, 67, 112
  and coordination of values
    233–246
  and science 244–245
Phylogenesis 16, 128
Piaget
  ad hoc constructions 217
  adolescent thinking 112
  and enlightenment 57
  and information-processing theory
    56, 61
  and Leibniz 247–248
  and Ricoeur 234ff, 244
  and Rousseau 219
  assimilation/accommodation 9, 227
  biology 111–112, 121, 270
  Boolean structure 79
  challenge to 55ff, 101–102, 263,
    266, 267
  childhood animism 158
  cognitive development and
    affectivity 165, 171–172
  conservation 160, 221–222
  conservative vision of man 228
  constructivism 268
  cybernetic model 116
  decentering 173
  developmental learning 88
  domain-general characterizations
    141, 145
  empiricism 267ff

epistemology and psychology 15–16, 68–69
equilibration 15–16, 59, 68, 227–231, 244–245, 269
formalisation 221
functionalism 8ff, 47, 59, 111
genetic epistemology 237–238
grouping 224
hierarchy 245
idealisation in 3–4, 68, 264
logic 77–78, 101
mathematical functions 221
meaning 16, 59, 70, 235
mémoire au sens large/au sens strict 184
memory and intelligence 183–184, 190, 197
memory and semiotic function 171–172, 184
memory strategies 188
methodology 200
misogynism in 120
moral development 238
mother–child relationship 172
natural logic 65ff, 69ff
normative facts 2, 67
number 109
ontogenetic and historical development 144
open systems 269
operatory logic 80
phenomenology 247–248, 259–260
philosophy 233ff, 240–241
physical knowledge 60
primacy of theory 265
reasons 68
representation 224–225, 258, 265, 271
role of action 268
scientific reasoning 114
semiotic function 239–240
social factors 269–270
spatial cognition 204, 207
stage theory 142–143
structuralism 8ff, 47
structural model 10, 116
structures and systems 271–273

values 234
see also Cognitive; Consciousness; Construction; Functionalism; Logic; Memory; Sociology; Spatial reasoning; Structures; Theory; Values
Planning 185, 190
Play 9–10
Political structure 129, 130, 134
Pragmatics 11ff
    linguistic 54
Pragmatism 42
Premature infants 173
Problem
    -solving 12ff, 25, 28–30, 32, 35, 226
    universe 25, 31, 34, 36
Procedures 15, 16
    and structures 12
Process 44
Processing models
    parallel 48
    serial 48
Production systems 48, 50
    self modifying 50, 61
Projection 147–150, 152–153
Propositional analysis 222
Psychoanalysis
    affinity to Piaget 165–166
    and structure formation 172
    ego-oriented 44
    ego psychology 6, 165, 172
    Freudian 10, 59
    structural changes and symbolisation 172–173
Psychogenesis 16, 20, 21, 27, 30, 33
Psychology 15–19, 67, 145, 247f
    genetic (developmental) 247, 248, 249, 258ff

Quadruple 81
Questionnaires
    memory 191–192, 198

Rational reconstruction 116
Rationalisation 114, 116–117, 120
Reaction formation 115
Reality 113, 114n, 117
Reason, Rationality 68, 71, 74

Reasoning, logical 87–99
Recall vs recognition 184
"Recognition-in-context" memory 210
Re-equilibration 138
Reference 250, 253, 254, 258ff, 260 see also Intentionality
  immediate (direct) 252, 254, 259
  mediated 252ff, 258, 259
  system 205, 207, 213, 214
Rehearsal 184–185
Reinforcement 213, 215
Relations
  Euclidean 204, 205, 207, 214
  projective 204, 205, 207, 214
  topological 204, 205, 207, 214
Relativism 53, 54
Religion 238
Remembering 250ff, 254, 255, 259 see also Mental activity
Representation 47, 48, 49, 56, 252–253, 254, 257, 259
  analogue 49
  propositional 49
  symbolic 48
  of knowledge 225
Resistance to training 160–161
Restructuring of knowledge 145–162
Reticular formation (system) 210
Reversibility 120, 212
Role-taking 113, 117
Romantic movement 130, 136
Route knowledge 205, 207, 211, 214
  symbolic representation of 212
  temporal integration of 213
Route
  learning 205, 208, 211
  maps 205, 208
Routes 205, 206, 211
Rule systems 52

Safety 120–122
Schema theory 52
Scheme 16, 17, 24
Science, sociology of 127–140
Scripts 52
Selection 17–19

Self 112, 114
  bounded 117
  development of 112–117, 118
  epistemological 112–113
  false 119
  isolation of 114n, 120
  metaphysical 113–114
  omnipotent 115
  Piaget's 114n
  separate 117, 120
  -sufficient 117
Semantic network 224
Semiotic function 171ff, 239
Sensorimotor activity, 249, 253, 258ff
  and maternal characteristics 167–168
  distance vs near receptors 167
  impact of mother's absence 168–170
Sensorimotor schemata 211
Sensory modalities 168, 170, 180
Serial learning process 211
Serial representation 212
Significant others in mental development 230
Simplexe 82–83
Skills 52
Small-scale model 207
Small-size environment 208–215
Social sciences 129, 130
Socialisation, cognitive 228–231
Socio-economic context 130, 134
Socio-economic structure 129
Sociogenesis 128, 130, 136
  of knowledge 127–140
  of science 5, 136, 274–276
Socio-genetic analysis 128
Socio-genetic component 129, 136
Socio-genetic method 128
Sociological component 129, 136
Sociology of science 5, 127–140
Soviet psychology 53, 60
  copy theory 53, 60
Spatial cognition 204, 206, 208
  prefigurations of 208ff
Spatial networks 205
Spatial representation 6, 203–215
  of the home 209, 213

Spatial task demands 213
Sprite Logo 107
Square of oppositions 81
Stability/instability of constancy
judgments in children 218–219
Stages of development 5–6, 141–145,
160–161 *see also* Moral development
and personality 165–166
sequence 116
structures 116
sub-stage 116
theory 113, 144–145
transitional (Piaget) 217, 218
Standard tests of intelligence 173
Strategic attitude 185–186, 189
Strategies
and heuristics 52
in Memory 184–186, 187, 190
Strategy
computational 29–30
epistemic 29–30
Structuralism 37, 41, 44, 45, 47
and functionalism 8ff, 21–28
Structure 20, 21, 24, 26 *see also*
Cognitive structure
algebraic 78, 79, 85
and function 15–36
lattice 78, 79, 80–1, 85
Piaget's structural model 10, 116
Structure d'ensemble 60
Style
psychological 106
hard 107, 265
soft 107, 265
Subject
active 115
agency of 14, 117
-object dualism 113
-object relationship 268–269
social determination of 269
subjectification 118
subjectivity 117–118, 120
Symbolism
symbolic forms 239–240, 243–244
symbolic functioning 10, 171ff
Synthesis structural and functional 25–
28

System of transformations 138

Technology 121
Temperature
and efficiency of engines 133, 134
and transference of heat 133
as measure of heat 137
Text problems 226
Theoretical vs empirical 264–265
Theories of mind
enlightment vs romantic 57, 58
modularity 54
Theory
change 141–162, 277
top-down, bottom-up 47, 48
Thermodynamics 134
Thought
formal 112
see also Formal operations
logico-mathematical 113–114
reflective 112
scientific 114, 117
Topographical schema 207
Transformation and invariance 139,
140

Values 234, 237, 245
coordination of 233–245
of logic and logic of values 101–110
and norms 7, 280
Vantage point 208
Vulnerability 120–121

Weltanschauung 115, 129, 135, 136, 138
Western rationalism 236–237
Whereness of goals 209
Will 120
World view 242–244
paradigm, disciplinary matrix,
research program, research
tradition 40